"[A] PROBING STUDY . . .

Unlike the familiar, granite image of Moses, Kirsch sees a man torn by fits of violence, prone to arguing with God, marked by physical handicaps, reluctant to be a savior."

—*Los Angeles Times*

"Kirsch's book is strengthened by both a close reading of the Torah and his intimate knowledge of rabbinic folklore that grew up around the biblical tale, to help fill in the famous silences in the Bible."

—*Houston Chronicle*

"In *Moses*, Kirsch paints a fascinating picture of the biblical Moses as a complex man subject to mood swings ranging from compassion to rage, from piety to pomposity."

—*The Denver Post*

"Even the most learned will find previously unfamiliar material explained in a clear, intelligent and accessible fashion. . . . There is a tremendous amount of fascinating material for anyone interested in Moses and his family as well as some wonderful insights."

—*Jewish Journal*

Please turn the page for more reviews. . . .

"A RAFT OF INTERESTING CONJECTURES AND FACTS FILL THESE PAGES."
—*The Christian Science Monitor*

"A serious, sometimes brutal anatomy of Moses . . . Kirsch doesn't gloss over the rough stuff. . . . Among the best of the new crop of 'historical search' writers."

—*San Diego Union-Tribune*

"Books treating religious themes and written for a popular audience seem to abound today. Many of these writers, though not biblical scholars, are rigorous in their historical reconstruction and provide readers biblical information that is quite enlightening. This is such a book. . . . [It] brings Moses to life and makes scholarship available to a popular audience."

—*The Bible Today*

"[Kirsch expresses himself with] zeal and showmanship . . . skill and sensitivity. . . . Kirsch is very good at providing the cultural and social background necessary for a close reading of all the tales told of Moses . . . but he's at his very best in showing how the text of the Bible holds together, in one compelling portrait, the many images of Moses that compete for the reader's attention as his life unfolds from birth to death. . . . Kirsch leaves nothing out of his account, and doesn't gloss over any of the passages. . . . He distills valuable insights into the biblical Moses out of sources as varied as the early rabbis through Baruch Spinoza in the seventeenth century to Sigmund Freud and Martin Buber in the twentieth."

—*Toronto Globe & Mail*

From the bestselling author of *The Harlot by the Side of the Road* comes an even more controversial conversation on the topic of Moses. . . . Kirsch brings an intelligent perspective to the Bible as both a work of literature and a sacred text. . . . As fresh and exposing as the unmasked face of Moses himself."

—*The Jewish Transcript*

"[Kirsch] reveals a Moses that will forever banish Charlton Heston's portrayal from the popular consciousness (and not a moment too soon). . . . Kirsch's scholarship and storytelling skill introduce us to a much more interesting and compelling figure than we'd known before."

—*Yoga Journal*

MOSES

Also by Jonathan Kirsch

THE HARLOT BY THE SIDE OF THE ROAD
Forbidden Tales of the Bible

MOSES

A LIFE

Jonathan Kirsch

BALLANTINE BOOKS • NEW YORK

A Ballantine Book
Published by The Ballantine Publishing Group

http://www.randomhouse.com/BB/

Library of Congress Catalog Card Number: 99-90419

ISBN: 0-345-41270-2

Text design by Holly Johnson
Maps by Mapping Specialists, Ltd.
Cover design by Cathy Colbert
Cover photo: Michaelangelo Buonarroti. Moses, from the tomb of Julius II.
San Pietro in Vincoli, Rome, Italy. Courtesy of Scala/Art Resource, NY.

Manufactured in the United States of America

First Hardcover Edition: November 1998
First Trade Paperback Edition: November 1999

10 9 8 7 6 5 4 3 2 1

For Ann, Adam, and Jennifer,
Remember us in Life, O Lord who delighteth in life . . .

And for my mother and stepfather, Dvora and Elmer Heller,
and inscribe us in the Book of Life . . .

And in loving memory of my father, Robert (Reuven) Kirsch;
my grandparents, Rose (Rachel) Nisman and Morris (Moshe) Nisman;
and my father-in-law, Ezra Benjamin,
May their names be recalled for a blessing.

I have set before thee life and death,
the blessing and the curse;
therefore choose life, that thou mayest live.

—MOSES
DEUTERONOMY 30:19

Four hundred years of bondage in Egypt, rendered as meta-
phoric memory, can be spoken in a moment; in a single
sentence. What this sentence is, we know; we have built
every idea of moral civilization on it. It is a sentence that
conceivably sums up at the start every revelation that came
afterward: "The stranger that sojourneth with you shall be
unto you as the home-born among you, and you shall
love him as yourself; because you were strangers in the
land of Egypt."

—CYNTHIA OZICK
MEMORY & METAPHOR

Contents

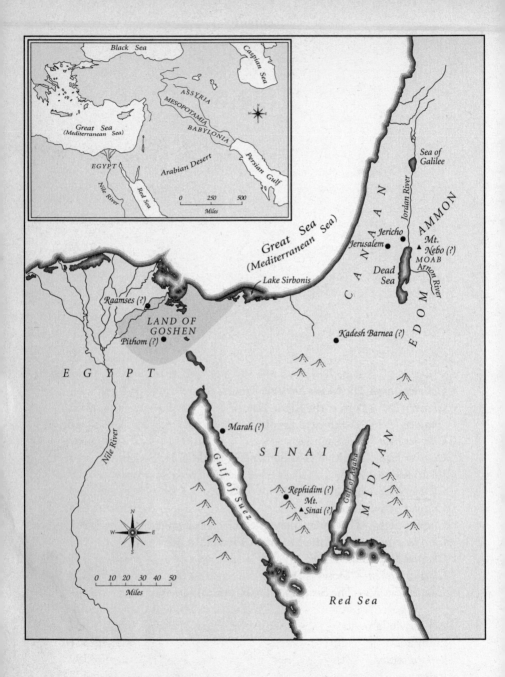

Chapter One

THE MOSES
NO ONE KNOWS

God answered, "While the light of truth is not in thee
Thou hast no power to behold the mystery."
Then Moses prayed, "O God, give me that light. . . ."
　　　　　　　　　　　　—JAMI, *DIVINE JUSTICE*

The Bible is remarkably blunt and plainspoken in telling the life story of Moses. Unlike the sacred writings and court histories of other figures from distant antiquity, which tend to dress up their heroes as saints, kings, and even gods, the Bible portrays Moses with brutal honesty and flesh-and-blood realism. Indeed, the essential impression of Moses that we are given in the Bible—and the real genius of his depiction at the hands of the biblical authors—is that he was born like every other infant, grew to manhood with all the impulses and excesses of which real men and women are capable, lived a life marked with passions that are perfectly human, and came to a tragic end that is no less riddled with ambiguity and contradiction than any other human life.

"There is nothing divine about Moses," observes the eminent Bible scholar Gerhard von Rad,[1] and, as if to remind us of this crucial fact, the Bible refers to him with a simple, sturdy, and straightforward phrase— "the *man* Moses." (Exod. 32:1, 23; Num. 12:3)

Yet much of what we *think* we know about Moses is simply made up, and much of what the Bible does say about him is left out of both sacred and secular art. When they conjured up the visions of Moses that are so deeply familiar to us today, Renaissance artists and Hollywood moguls alike felt at liberty to make him over into a shimmering icon—the ultimate irony for the first iconoclast in recorded history. Even the learned theological commentaries and richly decorated sermons of the clergy tend to leave out the more scandalous incidents of his troubled and tumultuous life. Ironically, some of the most intriguing details to be found in the biblical account of Moses never find their way into art and literature, sermons and Sunday school lessons, and what is invented is often much less interesting than what has been left out. So we are left to wonder: Who, after all, is the *real* Moses?

As we shall discover in the pages that follow, Moses is the most haunted *and* haunting figure in all of the Bible. To be sure, he is often portrayed as strong, sure, and heroic, but he is also timid and tortured with self-doubt at key moments in his life. He is a shepherd, mild and meek, but he is also a ruthless warrior who is capable of blood-shaking acts of violence, a gentle teacher who is also a magician and a wonder-worker, a lawgiver whose code of justice is merciful except when it comes to purging and punishing those who disagree with him, an emancipator who rules his people with unforgiving authority. Whatever he may have looked like—and the Bible never really tells us—the fact is that he hid a disfigured face behind a veil for the last forty years of his long life. He is God's one and only friend, and yet he is doomed to a tragic death by God himself.

But as we shall soon see, the real Moses has been concealed from us, sometimes by subtle manipulation of the ancient text, sometimes by pointed silence and sins of omission, and sometimes by unapologetic censorship or outright lies, first by the priests and scribes who were the original authors and editors of the Bible, then by the preachers and teachers who were the guardians of the sacred text, and finally by the artists and bards who interpreted the Bible in works of art and literature. Devout tradition in both Judaism and Christianity has always felt obliged to portray Moses as unfailingly good and meek, dignified and devout, righteous and heroic—and that is why we do not hear much about the passages of Holy Writ in which Moses is shown to act in timid and even cowardly ways, throw temper tantrums, dabble in magic, carry out purges and inquisitions, conduct wars of extermination, and talk back to God. The real Moses—the Moses no one knows—was someone far richer and stranger than we are customarily allowed to see.

THE REAL MOSES

Two or three thousand years of art, theology, politics, and propaganda have turned Moses from a mortal man into a plaster saint. Among pulpit clergy and Bible critics alike, both Christians and Jews, Moses is hailed as Lawgiver, Liberator, and Leader, the prophet who bestowed upon Western civilization the Ten Commandments and the very idea of "ethical monotheism," the hero who led the Israelites out of slavery in Egypt and delivered them to the portals of the Promised Land. According to Jewish tradition, he is Moshe Rabbenu ("Moses, Our Master"), a phrase that honors his role as "the greatest of all the Jewish teachers."[2] Christian theology regards Jesus as "the new Moses," and the Gospel of Matthew depicts Moses as a ghostly witness to the transfiguration of Jesus atop a sacred mountain (Matt. 17:3). Islam, too, recognizes Moses as among its first and greatest prophets: the Koran characterizes Moses as the one who first predicted the coming of Mohammad, whom Muslims regard as an inheritor of the mantle of prophecy once worn by Moses and Jesus.

"And there arose not a prophet since in Israel like unto Moses," enthused the author of the Book of Deuteronomy, "whom the Lord knew face to face." (Deut. 34:10)*

So Moses tends to loom up as much larger than life. He was "the pattern prophet,"[3] the first and greatest of the seers whose writings make up much of the Bible itself. He was regarded as the role model for earthly kings from David and Solomon to the more recent royals of Western Europe who claimed to rule by divine right. In both Jewish and Christian tradition he was thought to be the precursor of the Messiah, and the key moments in the life of Jesus are presented in the Gospels as a reenactment of the Moses story: Pharaoh's death sentence on the

---

*All quotations from the Bible are from *The Holy Scriptures According to the Masoretic Text* (Philadelphia: Jewish Publication Society, 1961), an English translation from 1917 that closely follows the familiar King James Version, unless otherwise indicated by an abbreviation that identifies another translation. A complete list of Bible translations and the abbreviations used to identify them can be found on page 400. "Adapted from . . ." is used in the endnotes to indicate when I have omitted or rearranged portions of the original text or combined text from more than one translation of the Bible. I have taken the liberty of making minor changes in punctuation, capitalization, and the like, or omitting words and phrases that do not alter the meaning of the quoted material, without indicating these changes in the text.

firstborn of Israel predicts Herod's slaughter of the innocents; the crossing of the Red Sea is understood by some Christian commentators as a symbolic baptism of the children of Israel; and the miracle of manna and quails anticipates the miracle of loaves and fishes.

The exalted and sanctified Moses has been a man for all seasons and every age. Ancient sages identified Moses as the inspiration for and counterpart of a whole pantheon of pagan gods, including the Egyptian scribal god Thoth and the Greek messenger god Hermes. Like these pagan deities, Moses was traditionally credited with the invention of the alphabet and the art of writing.[4] Philo of Alexandria shoehorned Moses into the conventions of Hellenistic philosophy as "the epitome of ideal humanity"[5] and "the best of all lawgivers in all countries."[6]

Fresh interest in Moses as a liberator flared up in the fires of the French Revolution, and the very same man who symbolized kingship to the ancien régime was claimed as a symbol of liberation by the oppressed people who sought to behead their king. African-Americans who were literally enslaved in the Land of the Free enshrined Moses in their folk culture as well as their churches: "Go down, Moses" can be seen as one of the earliest anthems of the civil rights movement in the United States. More recently, Moses has been brought fully into the New Age as "the true Empath," in the words of essayist Ari Z. Zivotofsky, who invites us to regard Moses as a man who is "not only caring and concerned for others, but also . . . willing and ready to act upon those feelings."[7]

Moses was even appropriated by the worst enemies of the Jewish people in what must rank as the single most cynical use of a much abused biblical figure. During World War II, the Nazi bureaucracy that ran the machinery of the Holocaust printed up a supply of currency especially for use by the Jewish inmates of the "model" concentration camp at Terezin, a showplace that was operated for the benefit of inspectors from the International Red Cross, who were never allowed to see Auschwitz or Bergen-Belsen or Dachau. As if to taunt the doomed men, women, and children of Terezin with their own impotence, the image of Moses was imprinted on the concentration camp currency—and the Nazis chose a rendering of Moses that showed him at his most potent and militant.

No matter what political and theological agenda he is made to serve, Moses is usually presented as a purely ideal figure, always humble, mild, and righteous. Truth be told, however, the biblical Moses is seldom humble and never mild, and his conduct cannot always be regarded as righteous. At certain terrifying moments, as the Bible reveals to anyone who is willing to read it with open eyes, Moses rears up as arrogant, bloodthirsty, and cruel.

THE MASK OF MOSES

Among the oddest and most often overlooked moments in the life of Moses is the mysterious disfigurement that results from his close encounter with God on the holy mountain called Sinai. When Moses descended after forty days and nights in the company of God, he discovered that something strange had happened to his face—his own brother, Aaron, and the rest of the Israelites were afraid even to look at him. From that moment on, Moses wore a veil or a mask to conceal his deformity. The eeriness of the incident and the odd ways it has been explained away are emblematic of how and why the image of Moses has been so persistently misunderstood over the centuries.

The Bible does not offer a straightforward explanation of what happened to the face of Moses that made it so fearful. The earliest translation of the Hebrew Bible into Latin renders the obscure text in a manner that suggests Moses sprouted horns. Thus instructed by the Latin Bible, Michelangelo famously rendered Moses as an otherwise heroic figure with a set of slightly diabolical horns on top of his head!* A more accurate translation of the original Hebrew text suggests that Moses had suffered something we might describe as a divine radiation burn—his face literally glowed with celestial radiance. "And the children of Israel saw the face of Moses," the Bible reports, "that the skin of Moses' face sent forth beams." (Exod. 34:35) According to the Bible, the face of Moses was masked from the day he descended Mount Sinai with the Ten Commandments in his arms until the day of his lonely death in

---

*The imperfect work of the early Latin translators and the conventions of Renaissance art inspired the notion in some circles that *all* Jews are horned. My junior high journalism teacher, a Jewish man who served in World War II, recalled that he woke up one night in the barracks to find a fellow draftee, a man from the rural South, kneeling by his bunk and staring at the top of his head. "I've never met a Jew before," the soldier explained, "and I wanted to see your horns."

the wilderness of Moab. Only when Moses engaged in one of his frequent tête-à-têtes with God—and then reported his conversation to the people—did he take off the face-covering.

So Moses was, quite literally, a masked man. Despite the imaginative efforts of Greco-Roman historians, Renaissance artists, and Hollywood movie-makers, we do not know what Moses actually looked like. Artapanus, an author of late antiquity, described Moses as "tall and ruddy, with long white hair, and dignified."[8] A tale preserved by the rabbis in the early Middle Ages imagined that Moses was exactly ten cubits, or approximately fifteen feet, in height.[9] Artists working in medieval Europe often rendered Moses as a lookalike of Jesus, but Michelangelo offered a now iconic vision of Moses that strongly resembles a horned version of the Roman god of the sea, Neptune. Cecil B. DeMille apparently worked from Michelangelo's high-culture model in casting, coiffing, and costuming Charlton Heston as the matinee-idol vision of Moses in *The Ten Commandments*, which has become the definitive image of Moses in late twentieth century popular culture: "I want to see Moses," one delegate to the 1996 Republican national convention told a newspaper reporter to explain why she was attending a cocktail party featuring Heston. But the Bible itself, which chronicles the life and works of Moses at epic length, never describes his features or any aspect of his physical appearance, with or without his mask.

Indeed, the Hebrew Bible rarely gives us a physical description of *any* character in the biblical narrative. Unlike other writings of the ancient world—and especially Greco-Roman civilization—the Bible does not exalt the strength or beauty of the human body. Now and then, someone might earn a bit of grudging praise. "Behold now," Abraham says to Sarah, "I know that thou art a fair woman to look upon." (Gen. 12:11) But according to pious tradition, one's physical appearance is less important than one's godliness (or lack of it), and a physical description is given only when it is crucial to understanding the fate of a particular man or woman.*

The Bible discloses that Moses was "slow of speech," which is usu-

---

*Sarah's beauty, for example, is noted to explain why Abraham passes himself off as her brother rather than her husband when they travel to Egypt. "And it will come to pass," Abraham frets, "when the Egyptians see thee, that they will say: This is his wife; and they will kill me, but thee they will keep alive." And, in fact, the fair Sarah ends up in the harem of Pharaoh! (Gen. 12:12–15).

ally interpreted to signify that he suffered from a stammer—but only because one of the biblical authors sought to make the ironic point that God's spokesman suffered from a speech impediment and required divine assistance to get his message across to Pharaoh. Other than his stutter and his disfigured face, however, the Bible is silent on Moses' physical characteristics. "We do not know whether Moses was tall or short, thin or heavy—an unpardonable omission in the Greek style of writing," one rabbinical scholar has written by way of explanation. "We do not know these things because they are not relevant to Moses' role as an intermediary between God and His people."[10]

Even if his face and overall appearance remain a matter of purest speculation, the Bible allows us to see and understand the inner nature of this man Moses with a degree of honesty and intensity that is sometimes unsettling. The Bible shows us Moses in his moments of fear and doubt, his black spells, his childlike tantrums and dangerous fits of rage, and his long, difficult, and sometimes even dysfunctional relationship with God, whom he was perfectly willing to hector, cajole, and threaten when the spirit moved him to do so. And yet, paradoxically, the passages of the Bible where Moses is revealed with the greatest intimacy are precisely those that are most often skipped over by the hagiographers who want us to see Moses as an icon—and an icon, no matter how gilded and glittering, is always smaller than life.

Of course, storytellers have always felt at liberty to borrow Moses from the Bible and recast him as the one-dimensional figure of both high art and pop culture that has become so familiar to us. And yet even as they seek to glorify Moses, even as they dress him up as a demigod or a matinee idol, the storytellers leave out the most intriguing and provocative facts of his life. In that sense, Moses remains a masked man even when the veil is stripped away from his face.

THE SORCERER AND THE
SCORCERER'S APPRENTICE

For example, the Bible does not always depict Moses as a well-behaved monotheist who toted the tablets of the Ten Commandments wherever he went. Sometimes he shows up in the guise of a sorcerer with as many tricks up his sleeve as a lounge-act magician in Las Vegas. Armed with the so-called rod of God—a shepherd's wooden staff, but we might as well call it a magic wand—Moses worked all kinds of sideshow legerde-main to impress both Pharaoh and the ever dubious Israelites. First he announced the divine commandment against making graven images, then he fashioned a bronze snake that he used to cure snakebite. And he was equipped with the mysterious Urim and Thummim, a tool of divination that may have consisted of a pair of inscribed gemstones used to consult God for answers to yes-or-no questions, not unlike a Magic 8 Ball at a children's birthday party.

Some of his tricks, of course, are famous. Moses engaged in a contest of dueling magicians in the court of Pharaoh by casting his staff to the ground and turning it into a snake. The Bible, which sometimes allows us to glimpse a livelier sense of humor than do the sermonizers who came later, renders the encounter as a kind of burlesque: when Pha-raoh's magicians matched Moses by turning *their* staffs into snakes, too, Moses' snake promptly devoured the other snakes as if to make the point that all magicians may be created equal, but some are more equal than others.

Other works of magic were not so playful. Moses used the rod of God to call down upon Egypt the Ten Plagues—boils, vermin, plague, pestilence, and so on. The sufferings of the Egyptians built to a blood-thirsty crescendo when God himself struck down the firstborn children of Egypt, rich and poor, guilty and innocent. And the Bible describes a magic-soaked ritual that Moses used to protect the Israelites when God ranged across Egypt in search of the firstborn—the blood of a slaugh-tered lamb was smeared above the doorways of the slave dwellings to catch the attention of a deity who was so intent on killing that he might not have noticed if he alighted on one of his Chosen People. Compared to the pristine and even prissy preachments of the Ten Commandments, the blood ritual strikes us as raw and primitive.

So the Bible preserves the fingerprints of a faith that seems pro-foundly at odds with all three religions that regard Moses as the Law-giver. And a still deeper mystery can be discerned just beneath the surface of the biblical text: Who, after all, taught Moses the tricks of the sorcerer's trade? According to a few intriguing clues buried in the Bible, Moses was tutored in the ways of magic by his father-in-law, an enig-matic figure named Jethro, who is plainly described as a pagan priest but who played a decisive role in the enlightenment of Moses and the des-tiny of the Israelites. It was Jethro, not Moses, who offered the very first sacrifice to Yahweh. According to a slightly revisionist reading of the

Bible, Jethro was a sorcerer and Moses was his apprentice—an apprentice who eventually replaced his master.

The revelation of the One God by Moses has been praised as a great leap forward in the history of religion, a moment when the faith of ancient Israel was purged of the superstitious claptrap that had always burdened the rest of humanity. Moses introduced Yahweh as a god of justice and mercy, a god for whom right conduct was more important than rituals of worship, a god who seemed to disdain idol worship and all the trappings of magic that go with it. Yet Moses himself was a magic-user. "Moses the sorcerer, the healer, the dispenser of oracles, the Faustian magician," one Bible scholar points out, "is a different figure from the man who summarized the essence of piety and morality in a few lapidary sentences of the Decalogue."[11]

"HAVE YE SAVED ALL THE WOMEN ALIVE?"

Moses appeared as a humble shepherd in the biblical scene where he first encountered God, and the Bible praises his mildness and modesty: "Now the man Moses was very meek, above all the men that were upon the face of the earth." (Num. 12:3) Yet the mild-mannered Moses was already a man-killer—he had murdered an Egyptian taskmaster in cold blood—and he would kill again with much greater ruthlessness and in vastly greater numbers.

The carnage that set the Exodus into motion predicted the scale and scope of the violence that was to come. "And it came to pass at midnight, that the Lord smote all the first-born in the land of Egypt," we are told in the Bible, "from the first-born of Pharaoh that sat on his throne unto the first-born of the captive that was in the dungeon." (Exod. 12:29) Guilt or innocence does not figure in the fate of Egypt, nor does the Bible own up to the irony at work here—the death of the firstborn is necessary only because "the Lord hardened Pharaoh's heart" (Exod. 11:10) in the first place!

Moses himself conducted a series of bloody purges, each one more ruthless than the one before, within the encampment of the unruly Israelites in order to rid himself of the doubters and dissenters who seemed to proliferate among them. The apostates who dared to worship the golden calf were put to death—"Put ye every man his sword upon his thigh," Moses told his priestly praetorian guard, "and slay every man his brother, and every man his companion, and every man his neighbor" (Exod. 32:27)—but not before Moses ground the idol into powder and literally forced the stuff down the throats of the Israelites. Three thousand died on that day, we are told; but worse was yet to come. Surely it was the warrior instinct in Moses, and not his humility, that inspired the frank admiration of Napoléon Bonaparte, who regarded him as "the one man of mark in all Biblical history, not excluding Jesus!"[12]

When the Israelites later succumbed to the temptations of pagan gods and goddesses and the sacred harlots who worshipped them, God sent a plague that killed twenty-four thousand of his Chosen People— and Moses, in order to appease God and bring an end to the plague, decreed the death of every man who "commit[ed] harlotry with the daughters of Moab." (Num. 25:5) Then Moses sent the army of Israel on a punitive campaign against the Midianites, whose women had apparently joined their Moabite sisters in seducing the men of Israel; the fact that his wife and father-in-law were Midianites, too, did not deter him. The Israelites succeeded in slaughtering every male among the Midianites, and the women and children were brought back to the encampment as captives. But Moses was stirred to yet another rage at the very sight of them.

"Have ye saved all the women alive?" Moses complained to the captains of his army—and then a coldblooded command fell from the lips of the True Empath. "Now therefore kill every male among the little ones, and kill every woman that hath known man by lying with him." (Num. 31:15, 17)

So the emancipator is also the exterminator, although the bloodthirsty and ruthless nature of Moses is almost never spoken out loud. If the purges and massacres are mentioned at all in sermons and Sunday school lessons, they are explained away as the harsh but just punishment that God decrees for sinners and seducers. The awkward fact that the victims include wholly innocent men, women, and children is rarely mentioned at all. "The war against the Midianites presents peculiar difficulties," hems and haws J. H. Hertz, the late chief rabbi of Great Britain, in his otherwise authoritative commentary on the Bible. "We are no longer acquainted with the circumstances that justified the ruthlessness with which it was waged, and therefore we cannot satisfactorily meet the various objections that have been raised in that connection."[13]

To contemporary Bible readers, Moses may appear to be less sympathetic than some of the victims of his stern authority. Among the several insurrections that Moses put down, for example, is the one led by a man named Korah who dared to challenge his authority over the nation of Israel. If the Israelites were a "nation of priests," as Moses himself proclaimed and Korah now reminded him, why did they need Moses and Aaron—or *any* priest, for that matter—to act as a go-between with God?

"Every member of the community is holy and the Lord is among them all," taunted Korah, who voiced the very sentiments that would inspire freethinkers across the ages in the struggle for religious freedom. "Why do you set yourselves up above the assembly of the Lord?" (Num. 16:3 NEB) For his impudence, Korah and his cohorts were punished with a severity and a showiness that were intended to deter other dissenters. "And the earth opened her mouth," we read in the Bible, "and swallowed them up." (Num. 16:32)

Moses, then, is not always presented in the Bible as the emancipator of enslaved men and women, nor does he always symbolize the blessings of liberty. At certain moments in the biblical narrative, Moses comes across as an autocrat and an authoritarian, a stern and punitive high priest, a man who was ruthless and single-minded in enforcing the truth as he alone was given the light to see the truth.

THE MAN GOD BEFRIENDED, THE MAN HE SOUGHT TO KILL

Above all, what makes the life of Moses so strange and unsettling, what sets him apart from every other man and woman who ever lived, and what contemporary clergy find so awkward and embarrassing, is his profoundly intimate but also deeply troubled relationship with God. If Moses was the man God befriended, as we shall discover, he was also the man God sought to kill.

Moses is the only man in the Hebrew Bible to encounter God "face to face." (Deut. 34:10) No man may see God and live, we are told, but Moses was permitted to gaze upon God in all his glory. God vowed that he would appear to ordinary mortals only in dreams and visions and "dark speeches" (Num. 12:8), but Moses and God spent countless hours in direct conversation, sometimes on the sacred mountain but more often in the cozy confines of a tent set aside for their private use. "With him do I speak mouth to mouth," God said of Moses, "face to face, as a man speaketh unto his friend." (Exod. 33:11)

God and Moses were on intimate terms with each other, but their intimacy often resembled that of a cranky old couple in a bad marriage. Moses displayed a shocking tendency to kvetch to God about the burdens of leading the Israelites out of slavery. "Wherefore have I not found favour in thy sight, that thou layest the burden of all this people upon me?" demanded Moses, sounding more like Woody Allen than Charlton Heston. "And if thou deal thus with me, kill me, I pray thee." (Num. 11:11, 15 KJV) And God was forever threatening to break forth in violence against his Chosen People. "Now therefore let me alone," God fumed to Moses in a typical outburst, "that my wrath may wax hot against them." (Exod. 32:10 KJV)*

In fact, the tension between God and Moses could spin wildly out of control and turn suddenly dangerous and even life-threatening. The single most bizarre passage in all of the Bible—and the one most often censored by fussy Bible teachers—reveals how God actually stalked Moses and sought to kill him at the very moment when God had just selected him for the crucial mission of liberating the Israelites from slavery in Egypt. God expended much time and effort in convincing the reluctant Moses to take the job, and then, just when Moses gave in to God's demands and set out for Egypt, God showed up at the encampment where Moses and his family were bunked down for the night and tried to murder him. Only an eerie blood ritual performed by Moses' wife, Zipporah, managed to turn away the divine assault at the last moment and save his life.

But God's homicidal rage welled up again many years later. Moses spent the last forty years of his life doing exactly what God asked him to do, and he succeeded magnificently in his task: the Israelites were ultimately transformed from a ragged band of ill-tempered and ill-disciplined slaves into an army and a nation, and they were ready to invade and conquer the land that had been promised to them by God. And then, almost in a fit of pique, God decided that Moses would not join the rest of the Israelites in crossing the Jordan River into the land of Canaan after all. Instead, Moses would be permitted one fleeting glance into the Promised Land from atop Pisgah on the far side of the Jordan River—and then he would die. To explain and justify God's harsh decree, the Bible offers an obscure and trivial incident of

*Personal pronouns referring to the Deity are capitalized in some, but not all, translations of the Bible. Quotations follow the usage of the source translation.

disobedience that had taken place long before: Moses, we are told in the Bible, was punished because he *struck* a rock in the wilderness of Sinai in order to draw water for the Israelites instead of *speaking* to the rock as God would have preferred. But the punishment does not fit the crime, and the long, arduous, and faithful ordeal of Moses seems to count for nothing at all.

A bittersweet tale has attached itself to the death of Moses in the rabbinical legend and lore that have grown up around the Bible. The Bible reports that Moses pleaded with God to allow him to cross into Canaan before his death, but the rabbinical storytellers elaborated upon the biblical text by imagining that Moses recites no less than fifteen hundred urgent and eloquent prayers. As it turned out in both Holy Writ and rabbinical storytelling, God was unmoved by his pleas. Indeed, one tale told in the rabbinical literature imagines that God kills Moses with a single divine kiss—just as God breathed life into Adam at the moment of Creation, he draws out the last breath of life from Moses with his own lips.

According to the Bible, God himself insisted on bearing off the body of Moses to a secret burial place, "and no man knoweth of his sepulchre until this day." (Deut. 34:7) A certain tenderness can be seen in the gesture, as if God were honoring Moses in one final intimate act. But even so there is a barb in the final encounter between God and Moses—since God alone knew where Moses was buried, the Israelites were unable to visit his grave, honor his memory, and venerate the mighty deeds of the man who liberated them and bestowed upon them faith, law, nationhood, and a homeland. The heartbreak of his fate is underscored by the manner of his death and burial: Moses failed in the very task to which he devoted his life only because God, who set him to the task, decided to snatch the prize away from him at the last moment.

So the life of Moses came to a tragic end, one that is not often mentioned in sermons or Sunday school lessons because it offers such a bleak and dispiriting message about the futility of human endeavor and the unpredictability of divine will. Surely it was the same sense of despair that turned the thoughts of the Reverend Martin Luther King Jr. to the death of Moses on the very last night of *his* life. The stirring words of the sermon he delivered in a steamy Memphis church on that night in 1968 are well remembered and often quoted, although his specific and pointed allusions to the sorrowful fate of Moses may be lost on those who are not familiar with the Bible.

"Like anybody, I would like to live a long life . . . [b]ut I'm not concerned about that now," King said only hours before he was shot down. "I just want to do God's will. And He's allowed me to go up to the mountain. And I've looked over. And I've seen the promised land." And then he spoke out loud the ominous message that his Bible-reading audience, mindful of the story of Moses, surely already knew: "I may not get there with you."[14]

THE SEARCH FOR THE HISTORICAL MOSES

Somewhere beneath all the magic and miracles, the battles and bloodletting, the troubled and ultimately tragic encounter between God and Moses—somewhere behind the mask that conceals the real face of Moses—we hope to find the mortal man whose life is celebrated so grandly and yet so enigmatically in the pages of the Bible. Did a flesh-and-blood human being called Moses ever really exist? Where and when did he live and die? Did he do the remarkable things that are described in the Bible? And if so, did he leave any trace in the archaeological record that corroborates the biographical details that we find only in the pages of Holy Writ?

For those who regard the Bible as the Received Word of God, these are impudent and impious questions with one obvious answer: Moses was born exactly when and where the Bible tells us; he lived and died exactly as the Bible tells us; he did all the marvelous things that the Bible reports. Indeed, according to devout tradition, the first five books of the Bible, the so-called Five Books of Moses (or "Torah" in Jewish usage) are actually works of history and autobiography authored by Moses himself: "From the mouth of God to the hand of Moses," as the Sabbath liturgy of Judaism proclaims every time the Torah is read in a synagogue. True believers point to a single line in the Book of Deuteronomy as scriptural evidence of Mosaic authorship: "And Moses wrote this law [torah], and delivered it unto the priests and the elders of Israel." (Deut. 31:9)[15]

Starting in late antiquity, however, and continuing with ever greater fervor over the centuries and millennia, some awkward questions have been asked about the "historicity" of the Bible in general and Moses in particular. "Is it really true," Voltaire wondered out loud in his *Philosophical Dictionary* some two hundred and fifty years ago, "that there was a Moses?"[16] Critical scrutiny of the Bible has reached a fever pitch over the last one hundred years or so, and today it is no longer taken for granted that Moses wrote the Five Books of Moses—or, for that matter, that Moses ever existed at all.

Voltaire was neither the first nor the only open-eyed reader of the Bible to notice the evidence that suggests Moses did not write—and could not have written—the books that are traditionally attributed to him. The Bible, for example, speaks of Moses in the third person, an odd way for a man to write of himself. Moses is described as the most humble man who ever lived, which strikes us as something a truly humble man would hardly boast about. Moses is credited with knowledge of people and events that would have been unknown to anyone living at the time of the Exodus, and yet, at the same time, he appears to have made mistakes about people and events that he ought to have known and seen for himself. The sacred mountain where God bestowed the Ten Commandments upon Moses is sometimes called Sinai and sometimes called Horeb, and his father-in-law is identified as Reuel in one passage, Jethro in another, and Hobab in a third! And Deuteronomy, the last of the five biblical books attributed to Moses, presents itself as an autobiographical work that describes the death of its own purported author.

"It is as clear as the sun at noon that Moses did not write the Five Books of Moses," wrote the seventeenth-century philosopher Spinoza,[17] whose candor was rewarded with excommunication by the Jewish community and the burning of his books by order of the pope.

The apparent flaws in the biblical text have convinced Bible critics and scholars that Holy Scripture was actually the handiwork of "ancient literary artisans"[18] who lived and labored at various times and places over the millennia. None of these sources, who are nowadays regarded as the real authors of the Bible, is believed to have been a contemporary of Moses, and each one seems to have held a slightly different opinion of who Moses was and what he did. "Not one word of these stories," insists Bible scholar Elias Auerbach, "goes back to Moses himself."[19] The image of Moses that emerges from the Bible itself is a mosaic of odd biographical fragments, and we cannot know with certainty which of these pieces of a life are authentic.

WHO WROTE THE BIBLE?

The biblical author whose work is generally regarded as the most ancient and perhaps the most authentic is known as the Yahwist because he (or she)* generally called God by his personal name, Yahweh. The depiction of Moses in the threads of biblical narrative attributed to the Yahwist tends to be understated and down-to-earth. "He was no worker of miracles, no founder of a religion, and no military leader," writes Gerhard von Rad about the treatment of Moses by the Yahwist. "He was an inspired shepherd whom Jahweh used to make his will known to men."[20]

By contrast, the biblical author known as the Elohist—a source who preferred to use "Elohim," the Hebrew word for "god," instead of God's personal name—regarded Moses as a much more exalted and potent figure. The Elohist was probably a priest from the northern kingdom of ancient Israel, perhaps one who claimed to descend from Moses himself, and his contribution to the Bible sought to justify the authority of the priesthood by praising its purported founder and draping him in the mantle of a miracle-worker.

Still more priestly propaganda is found in yet another biblical source, the Priestly source, who is responsible for those lengthy and often tedious chronologies, genealogies, and codes of law that pop up in (and slow down) the otherwise suspenseful storytelling of the Bible.

The last book of the Five Books of Moses, Deuteronomy, is generally credited to still another source, the Deuteronomist, a theological propagandist who may have lived during the reign of the reformer-king Josiah and whose work has been characterized as a "pious fraud" that was concocted to validate Josiah's purge of the priesthood and centralization of worship in Jerusalem.**

All of these threads of authorship are interwoven in the first five books of the Hebrew Bible, and sometimes traces of several different authors can be teased out of a single passage, even a single sentence. The

---

*A compelling argument can be made that several portions of the Hebrew Bible were written by women, and the biblical source known as the Yahwist, or "J," is described by literary critic Harold Bloom in *The Book of J* as "a *Gevurah* ('great lady') of post-Solomonic court circles, herself of Davidic blood, who began writing her great work in the later years of Solomon, in close rapport and exchanging influences with her good friend the Court Historian, who wrote most of what we now call 2 Samuel."

**The biblical author known as the Yahwist is often identified by the letter code "J" because "Yahweh" is spelled with a *J* in German, the language of so many pioneering Bible scholars of the last century or so. Similarly, the Elohist is "E," the Priestly source is "P," the Deuteronomist is "D." The editors (or "redactors") who assembled the various threads of biblical narrative into the work we know as the Bible are collectively known as the Redactor, or "R."

work of collecting and combining these various sources is attributed to still another biblical source, the so-called Redactor, a term that refers to a school of priests and scribes who compiled, edited, and perhaps even censored and rewrote the work of the biblical authors who came before them.* The fractured quality of the biblical sources makes the figure of Moses all the more enigmatic, since the Yahwist is sometimes envisioning a very different man than the one the Elohist has in mind.

SOURCES AND WITNESSES

Much of what we think we know about Moses appears nowhere in the Bible. None of the various sources had much to say about the infancy, childhood, or adolescence of Moses, and a careful reading of the biblical text reveals a gap of forty years in his life story that remains a complete mystery. But, like nature, the human mind abhors a vacuum, and the life story of Moses has been richly and sometimes wildly embellished in the folklore of the Jewish people, the tales told by the rabbis and sages, the dreamy histories of ancient chroniclers, and the confabulations of ancient Bible translators and commentators. Thanks to what one Bible scholar calls "the novelistic love of embellishment, a characteristic which is attributed to ballad singers of all ages,"[21] a whole literature of fable and fairy tale has grown up around the otherwise plain and sometimes paradoxical figure of Moses as we find him in Holy Writ.

The biography of Moses starts with the Bible, of course, where his life story is played out in fits and starts throughout Exodus, Numbers, Leviticus, and Deuteronomy. Moses is seldom mentioned in the later books of the Hebrew Bible, and the New Testament reprises only a few

---

*My summary of the theories of Bible authorship is highly simplified. Over the years, Bible scholars have purported to detect a great many other sources within the biblical text, and they continue to debate the age, gender, and authenticity of each source. Conventional scholarship agrees, however, that the Bible was written (or at least written down) by many different authors at many different times and places and for many different theological and political purposes. At some late stage in its composition, the work of these various authors was combined by a group of editors to create the single book we call the Bible. Thus, the sources generally identified as D, P, and R were probably not individuals but rather groups of like-minded authors and editors whose work may have spanned several generations.

of the key events in his life in order to establish Moses as the precursor of Christ. But the Bible is not the only source of storytelling about Moses in the literature of ancient Israel and later tradition.

Imaginative priests and scribes began to elaborate upon the life story of Moses even before the sacred writings of the Israelites were canonized in the form that we call the Bible. The earliest translations of the Bible into Aramaic, a sister-language of Hebrew that was the common tongue of Palestine by the time Jesus of Nazareth was born, include scenes and dialogue about Moses and other biblical figures that appear nowhere in the original Hebrew text. And the Septuagint, the first Greek translation of the Bible, includes a whole library of books that were excluded from the Hebrew Bible but came to be appended to the Christian Bible as the Apocrypha in Protestant usage and the Deuterocanon in Catholic usage. These sources (or "witnesses" as they are sometimes called in Bible scholarship) offer some startling glosses on the life of Moses.

By far the richest source of storytelling about Moses, however, is a vast collection of legend and lore that first began to appear in antiquity and continued to accumulate over the centuries. Some of these stories about Moses and other Bible favorites are parables and morality tales whose authors pressed Moses into service as a convenient role model. Some are wild conjectures that are meant to fill in the gaps and resolve the contradictions of the biblical text. Some are fairy tales in which familiar biblical characters are shown to work magic and perform miracles, embark on exotic adventures around the world and into the heavens, and perform feats of strength and heroism.

"Both folk imagination and scholar's wit coaxed and forced from its pages a multitude of tales and a host of fancies unforeseen and unsuspected by the writers of the Bible," wrote one contemporary Jewish scholar about the storytelling that has grown up around the Bible. "Devout centuries wove endless fantasies around the characters and occurrences depicted in the holy Writ."[22]

Many of the tales about Moses that flowered in the storytelling traditions of Judaism, known generally as *haggadah*, found their way into two important works of rabbinical literature: the Talmud, a vast compendium of Jewish law and lore; and the Midrash, a series of commentaries in which biblical texts were explained, elaborated upon, and applied to contemporary moral and ethical issues. The rabbinical writings preserved in the Talmud and the Midrash are thought to embody the "oral" law and tradition of Judaism dating back into distant antiquity, but both works began to take written form in the early centuries of the Common Era and continued to grow as successive generations of rabbis and sages added their own commentaries.*

Another source of Jewish myth and legend are the writings of ancient Jewish chroniclers and commentators—including Flavius Josephus, Philo of Alexandria, and an anonymous source known only as Pseudo-Philo because his work was once mistakenly attributed to Philo—who retold and explained the sacred history of Israel for a mostly pagan readership in the Roman Empire and the Hellenistic world. These Jewish authors, who embraced the ideals of Greek culture and philosophy known as Hellenism, influenced how the Hebrew Bible was understood by other cultures and faiths, including earliest Christianity. Indeed, some scholars characterize their work as "Hellenistic Jewish midrash" and trace their influence into the text of the New Testament itself.[23]

Philo of Alexandria, also known as Philo Judaeus, was the scion of a prominent Jewish family who lived and worked in the early first century C.E. in the city of Alexandria, an outpost of Hellenism in Egypt and the site of the largest Jewish expatriate community outside of Palestine. So distinguished was Philo that he was selected to lead a delegation of Jewish emissaries to the court of the emperor Caligula in Rome to protest the mistreatment of Jews in Alexandria. And, like his near-contemporaries in the Hellenistic world, Philo was something of an apologist and a propagandist who felt at liberty to leave out the awkward and inconvenient details of Holy Writ while adding a few flourishes of his own that were meant to appeal to the sensibilities of his readership.

Flavius Josephus was born as Joseph ben Matthias in 37 C.E.,** shortly after the supposed date of the death of Jesus of Nazareth, and he was raised and educated in the loftiest circles of the Jewish aristocracy of Palestine under Roman occupation. At age twenty-nine, Josephus was

---

*Generally, when I identify "the rabbis" or "the sages" as the source of extrabiblical stories about Moses, I am referring to the rabbinical commentators whose work is preserved in the Talmud or the Midrash. Most of these stories are drawn from two important collections of Talmudic and Midrashic storytelling, Louis Ginzberg's definitive seven-volume anthology, *Legends of the Jews*, and Angelo S. Rappoport's three-volume anthology, *Ancient Israel*. Specific citations to Talmudic and Midrashic sources can be found in the works that are referenced in the endnotes to each chapter.

**C.E. (Common Era) is equivalent to A.D. (*Anno Domini*, or year of Our Lord) and B.C.E. (before the Common Era) is equivalent to B.C. (before Christ). The terms are used in Jewish sources and some scholarship in order to avoid the theological implications of B.C. and A.D., and I have used them here for the same reason.

recruited to serve as a general in an ill-fated war of liberation against Rome, but he promptly defected to the enemy and was rewarded with Roman citizenship, an imperial pension, and an apartment in the palace of the emperor, where he spent the rest of his life writing memoirs and histories.

Moses figures prominently in the work of both men, including Philo's *De Vita Mosis* (*The Life of Moses*), a biography of Moses; and the masterwork of Josephus, *Antiquitates Judaicae* (*Jewish Antiquities*), a grand account of biblical and postbiblical Jewish history. Moses is mentioned, although rather less prominently, in the *Biblical Antiquities*, a "rewritten Bible" once thought to be the work of Philo of Alexandria but now attributed to Pseudo-Philo. All of the extrabiblical sources—storytellers, rabbinical sages, and ancient chroniclers—enhanced the biblical account of Moses with incidents and ideals that owe little or sometimes nothing at all to what we find in the Scriptures.

Some Bible scholars are willing to entertain the notion that the extrabiblical sources preserve long-lost historical traditions and perhaps even a few nuggets of historical fact that did not make it into the Bible. Josephus, as Sigmund Freud discerned, "seems to know other traditions than the Biblical one,"[24] and one of his later translators credited him with access to "much completer copies of the Pentateuch, or other authentic records now lost, about the birth and actions of Moses, than either our Hebrew, Samaritan, or Greek Bibles afford us, which enabled him to be so large and particular about him."[25] And Philo explicitly claimed to know more than the Bible says. "[I] shall proceed to narrate the events which befell [Moses]," wrote Philo by way of introduction to *De Vita Mosis*, "having learnt them both from those sacred scriptures which he has left as marvelous memorials of his wisdom, and having also heard many things from the elders of my nation. . . ."[26]

Of course, it is more likely that the stories that appear in the extrabiblical sources were simply made up or borrowed from the myth and legend of other cultures by priests and rabbis, teachers and preachers, bards and troubadours. We might say of Moses, as one scholar writes of Homer, that "he was given suitable lives, not a true one."[27] But the legend and lore have so permeated the life story of Moses that much of what we think we know about him does not come from the Bible at all.

INVENTING MOSES

Questions about the authorship and historical reliability of the Bible are even more unsettling precisely because no ancient source *except* the Bible mentions Moses or the vast saga of the Exodus. The ancient Egyptians, who were compulsive chroniclers of their own rich history, somehow failed to notice the presence *or* the absence of a couple of million Israelite slaves, the afflictions of the Ten Plagues, the plague that took the life of every firstborn child on a single night, or the miraculous events at the Red Sea. Indeed, no archaeological evidence of any kind, no contemporaneous writings from anywhere in the ancient Near East, nothing at all outside the Bible makes even a passing mention of Moses or the events of the Exodus.

So we have to wonder whether Moses, as some scholars have argued, is merely a character in a grand historical novel, the invention of storytellers who fashioned a national epic to unify the many tribes that formed the nation of Israel. Perhaps, as other scholars have argued, Moses was a symbolic figure conjured up by the priestly caste of late antiquity as way of explaining and justifying their own authority in the religious bureaucracy of ancient Israel. According to one influential school of Bible scholarship, we ought to speak of "the Mosaic office" rather than a man named Moses.[28]

All but the true believers among contemporary Bible critics are willing to concede that the "historicity" of Moses remains open to question. "[E]very scholar who has tried to make his way through the mass of traditions," writes Bible scholar Geo Widengren, "knows that the endeavour to sift the evidence in order to find some tangible historical facts leaves us with a most unpleasant feeling of uncertainty."[29]

Since we lack any reliable evidence one way or the other, the search for the historical Moses has remained a speculative and sometimes slightly desperate enterprise. "No historian can regard the Biblical account of Moses and the Exodus," insisted Sigmund Freud, "as other than a pious myth."[30] But scholars continue to expend great effort and ingenuity in trying to prove that the Bible preserves a kernel of history and not merely an elaborate fairytale.

Archaeologists will hold up an intriguing papyrus document from ancient Egypt—for example, the official dispatch of a border guard who reported that Semitic nomads were crossing into Egypt in search of pasturage during a time of famine—and they will see in these few lines an echo of the arrival of the patriarch Jacob and his tribe. A tomb painting of a gang of slaves at work under the whips of Egyptian overseers in ancient Egypt has been hailed as an example of what life must have been like for the enslaved Israelites. A scrap of ancient papyrus that preserves an account of the uprising and escape of a gang of conscripted workers is seen as a slave rebellion that echoes the events of the Exodus. A couple of daring scholars even argued that some exceedingly obscure rock inscriptions found in the Sinai preserve "contemporary testimonies" about Moses, although their efforts "are discarded nowadays as imaginative failures."[31]

But not one of these intriguing clues amounts to conclusive proof that a man named Moses really lived or that the events of the Exodus ever took place. Indeed, as we shall see, an open-eyed reading of the Bible suggests that what took place in the ancient Near East may have been something startlingly different than what is depicted in the Bible. And even the rare Bible commentator who comes to the subject with the faith of a true believer is forced to concede that we are still waiting for an answer, whether from science and scholarship or divine revelation, about what really happened.

"Critics have descended upon the Mosaic documents with sharp scalpels and have dissected them, seemingly without mercy. Few other Biblical authors have had their writings more viciously torn apart," writes fundamentalist Bible commentator Paul F. Bork. As for the apparent flaws and contradictions in the biblical text, Bork declares himself untroubled: "As for why Moses wrote as he did, we may have to wait for an answer either through archaeological evidence or until he himself will tell us in the new earth."[32]

About the best argument that conventional scholarship can summon up for the historicity of Moses is that the saga of the Exodus is too unlikely—and Moses himself is ultimately too compelling—to have been merely a figment of some ancient storyteller's imagination. Why, it is argued, would the chroniclers of ancient Israel make up something as ignoble as four hundred years of servitude in a foreign land unless it were a fact of their history? And if it was, then history itself proves that the Israelites managed to make their way out of Egypt and into the land of Canaan. So the circular argument ends with a bemused shrug: Moses or someone very like him must have existed if only because it is hard to imagine the history of Israel without him.

"Though we know nothing of his career, save what the Bible tells us, the details of which we have no means of testing, there can be no doubt that he was, as the Bible portrays him, the great founder of Israel's faith," insists Bible scholar John Bright. "And a faith as unique as Israel's demands a founder as surely as does Christianity—or Islam, for that matter."[33]

After all, *someone* must have served as the charismatic leader around whom the tribes of ancient Israel rallied, or so goes the argument for the historicity of Moses. Someone must have introduced the deity known as Yahweh to "a rude mass of slaves and Bedouins,"[34] as one scholar puts it, and taught them that Yahweh was not merely one god among many but the one and only God. Someone turned these restless and demanding men and women into a people and then a nation. Above all, someone proposed that God is a single all-powerful deity whose universal law demands right conduct and not merely right belief. "To deny that role to Moses," Bright concludes, "would force us to posit another person of the same name."[35] Or, to express the same remarkable notion in slightly different words, if Moses had not actually existed, it would have been necessary for the ancient Israelites to invent him. And perhaps they did.

THE MISSING MAN

The ancient Israelites are famously described in the Bible as a stubborn and unruly people who are quick to whine and complain about their ordeal under the leadership of Moses—"stiff-necked" is the phrase used by the translators of the King James Version. The making and worship of the golden calf by the Israelites in the wilderness of Sinai, for example, was an act of defiance toward Moses rather than God; the Israelites seemed to believe that the idol would take the place of Moses and lead them onward to the Promised Land. The patience of God *and* Moses was sorely tried by the bad attitude of the Israelites, and God threatened more than once to exterminate his Chosen People and start all over again with the offspring of Moses! So pronounced was the restiveness and unruliness of the Israelites—"And the people were as murmurers, speaking evil in the ears of the Lord" (Num. 11:1)—that Bible scholarship recognizes and studies something called "the murmuring tradition" in Holy Writ.

The murmuring of disgruntled former slaves may echo an "anti-Moses tradition" that is thought to have played a crucial role in the politics of ancient Israel. The Bible preserves faint traces of the bitter rivalry for power among various priestly factions, some of whom claimed descent from Moses and others who descended from Aaron, the first high priest of Israel. The various factions contended for power by currying favor with one or another pretender to the throne, and the rivalry among them may explain why one of the biblical authors thought to depict Aaron and Miriam, the brother and sister of Moses, stirring up dissension and even open rebellion against Moses.

"Hath the Lord indeed spoken only with Moses?" they complained. "Hath He not spoken also with us?"(Num. 12:2)

The fact is that Moses has not always been regarded as a sanctified figure. A faint anti-Moses tradition can still be detected in the pages of Holy Writ, and he attracted even less-flattering attention from historians and propagandists in the Hellenistic world, who condemned him as "an impostor and prating mountebank" and depicted him as a leper with running sores.[36] A still more ancient source, an Egyptian chronicler of the third century B.C.E. named Manetho, characterized Moses as a renegade Egyptian priest who made himself king over a colony of lepers and conspired with the conquerors of Egypt, the feared and hated Hyksos, to set the Israelites against the Egyptians.[37]

Some fifteen centuries later, Sigmund Freud came to much the same conclusion, arguing in *Moses and Monotheism* that Moses was an Egyptian, not an Israelite, who made himself the leader of a slave rebellion in order to promote an early form of monotheism that had been briefly adopted and then rejected by the ancient Egyptians. Freud went even further in his remaking of Moses by arguing that the Israelites turned against their Egyptian master and replaced him with a second man whom they also dubbed Moses; the first Moses was murdered in the wilderness by the Israelites, Freud argued, and the second Moses was a Midianite whom they recruited to take his place. To hear Freud tell it, then, there were actually two men named Moses, and neither of them was an Israelite at all![38]

Perhaps even more surprising is a subtle but persistent tendency within both Christian and Jewish tradition to downplay the figure of Moses. The Gospels make it clear that Jesus of Nazareth offered a new covenant to replace the one given to Moses at Sinai, and so Moses is essentially written out of Christian theology. "Moses is dead," wrote Martin Luther, and by this he meant that Moses was wholly superseded by Jesus.[39] But Jewish tradition, which continues to embrace Moses as "Our Teacher," is arguably even harsher on Moses. Mindful of the human impulse to elevate a charismatic man to the status of a god, the ancient rabbis were sparing in their praise of Moses, and the man who is described in the Bible as the greatest prophet in history came to be regarded with a certain ambivalence in both theology and ritual. "Judaism is not 'Mosaism,' " we are cautioned by the rabbinical authorities. "God, not Moses, gives His Torah to His people Israel."[40] In one final bit of irony, the traditional version of the Haggadah, a book of prayer and ritual that is used in the celebration of the Passover seder, does not mention the name of Moses at all.

Moses is the missing man of the Bible in another sense. According to a strict reading of the Bible, there is a forty-year gap in the life of Moses: he seems to drop off the biblical radar screen between his flight from Egypt and his arrival in Midian. To explain what happened to Moses during the missing years, the rabbis concocted a fabulous tale of his adventures in Africa—Moses makes his way from Egypt to Ethiopia, reinvents himself as a mercenary, covers himself with glory on the field of battle, acquires an African wife, and eventually raises himself to the royal rank. Only then, at the age of eighty, does he abdicate the throne of Abyssinia and head off to Midian and his rendezvous with destiny as described in the Bible itself.

Then Moses literally disappears from the landscape of biblical history once and for all. As reported in the last few lines of Deuteronomy, God carried off his body to a secret burial place, and only rarely is he mentioned again in the Bible. Among the prophets whose writings are preserved in the Hebrew Bible, Moses is barely invoked at all,[41] and the prophet Hosea could not even bring himself to use the name of Moses when he alluded to the saga of liberation: "And by a prophet the Lord brought Israel up out of Egypt." (Hos. 12:14) Among the 150 psalms in the Book of Psalms, the name of Moses appears only eight times. By the time we reach the Book of Kings, the Bible describes how the last relic of Moses still in the possession of the Israelites—a bronze snake that he fashioned to cure snakebite—was removed from the Temple at Jerusalem and destroyed.

Still, the figure of Moses has always been so compelling—and the biblical account of Moses so baffling—that scribes and storytellers have felt at liberty to wildly embellish the spare text that we find in the Bible itself. The pious sages who created the anthologies of rabbinical literature known as the Talmud and the Midrash preserved a whole literature of Moses that ranged from simple aphorisms and parables to ornate fairy tales and folktales, some of which may derive from a long-lost historical memory and much of which is plainly the work of imagination. Ancient chroniclers of Jewish history retold his life story in a way that was intended to win the hearts and minds of the Hellenistic world. The New Testament presents Moses as a witness to the transfiguration of Jesus, and the Koran hails him as the herald of the coming of Mohammad. Propagandists of the ancient world turned Moses into a target for the very earliest stirrings of what we would now recognize as anti-Semitism. As a result of these accretions and distortions, the man we recognize as Moses is not quite the same man who is described in the pages of the Bible. To discern the real Moses, we will need to excavate the layers of elaboration under which the figure of Moses has been buried, dust off the oldest relics of his life and work, and hold them up to the light.

HORSE AND CHARIOT

Contemporary Bible scholarship seems to take special delight in demystifying the miracle stories in the Holy Scriptures. The Bible reports that Moses turned the water of the Nile into blood, but Greta Hort, a Bible scholar with an ecological bent, argues that all of the Ten Plagues can be explained as a chain reaction of natural disasters that began with the pollution of the Nile River by "blood-red flagellates from the high mountain lakes at the sources of the blue Nile."[42] According to the twentieth-century scholar and philosopher Martin Buber, the manna that was miraculously provided to the Israelites in the wilderness of Sinai was actually "a secretion of a cochineal insect, tasting like crystallized honey, which covers the tamarisk bushes at the time of the apricot harvest."[43] And the parting of the waters of the Red Sea—a miracle so beguiling that it is re-created every fifteen minutes on the Universal Studio tour—has been explained away as the result of unseasonal winds, or a tidal wave following a volcanic eruption, or maybe a ridge just beneath the surface of the water on which the Israelites made their way.

Even the most jaded Bible critics, however, are willing to concede that some fragments in the Five Books of Moses come down to us from distant antiquity and preserve at least some faint echo of what ordinary men and women knew and believed about the world in which they lived. Perhaps the best example is the so-called Song of Miriam, two sparse lines in the Book of Exodus that describe in a curiously oblique way what Bible scholarship calls "the event at the sea."

> Sing unto Yahweh for He is highly exalted:
> The horse and its chariot has He thrown into the sea.
> (Exod. 15:21)

Conventional wisdom once held that the Song of Miriam as preserved in the biblical text is only a fragment of a longer hymn that has been lost to us. But Martin Buber insists that the Song of Miriam is intact and complete—the Bible offers us a chant of victory in its entirety. The song consisted of a call-and-response in which one woman sang out the first line and a circle of women sang out the second line as they danced around her. The event that is celebrated in the song was the miraculous victory of the fleeing Israelites over their Egyptian pursuers at the Red Sea; the woman who presided over the victory celebration was the prophetess Miriam; and the dancers were the newly liberated slave women who had escaped into the wilderness at last.

For various technical reasons, the Song of Miriam strikes many Bible scholars as especially ancient and authentic. Similar call-and-response chants and circle dances have been observed in other cultures in the Near East and elsewhere around the world even in our own time. The sheer brevity of the Song of Miriam is seen as evidence of its antiquity: "Shorter is older" is one of the hoary aphorisms of Bible scholarship.[44] But the spare two lines of text in Exodus are compelling, too, because they summon up a scene so vivid that we can readily see it in our mind's eye.

Somewhere in the barren wastes of the Sinai, we are invited to imagine, a small band of Israelites is sheltering in a clearing surrounded by outcroppings of jagged gray rock. They are mostly women and children who were sent ahead into the wilderness while the menfolk formed up into ranks to engage the soldiers whom the Pharaoh of Egypt had sent in pursuit of the fleeing Israelites. The women pitched their tents, kindled their night fires, fixed a hasty meal of flat bread and porridge, then gathered around the fires in little clusters of two or three, whispering urgently but quietly to each other about what might have happened when the war chariots of Pharaoh, the most powerful armed force in the ancient world, finally overtook the fugitive slaves.

Now a lone figure makes his way over the verge of the rocks and scrambles down to the encampment, breathless and bruised. His clothes are bloodspattered, his leather sandals ragged and torn. The messenger brings word from the battlefield: The army of Pharaoh has been destroyed! The Israelites have been spared! Even now they are making their way across the desert to join up with the women and children, and Pharaoh himself is dead along with his defeated army!

The Song of Miriam says very little about how the battle was actually won. No mention at all is made of the famous details that we find in other passages of the Bible, the miraculous parting of the waters to allow the Israelites to pass or the closing of the waters over the pursuing Egyptians. All we know from Miriam's victory chant is that God cast a nameless enemy into the sea. But the very notion that a band of fugitive slaves might survive an encounter with Pharaoh's army was miraculous enough.

So it was that the Israelites saw a miracle in the battle report that reached them in the desert. And so we might imagine how the good news was received by the Israelites who camped in the Sinai on that glorious night. The women who listen to the messenger and his remarkable news are moved to celebrate the miraculous victory in a ritual so ancient that we do not know where or when it began. One by one, the women gather around the crone who is regarded as priestess and prophetess, taking up the drums and cymbals and tambourines that they carried out of Egypt and moving in a slow, solemn circle around her as she sings out.

"Sing unto Yahweh," intones the old woman named Miriam, "for he is highly exalted."

"The horse and its chariot," respond the dancing women, "has he thrown into the sea."

And so went the victory celebration, the call and the response, many women circling around one woman, long into the night and down through history, until the scene finally reached the pages of Holy Writ and earned a place among the many other accounts of what happened to the Israelites in Egypt and the wilderness of Sinai.

Moses is nowhere mentioned in the Song of Miriam, even though Miriam herself is characterized by some (but not all) of the biblical authors as his sister. Some scholars argue that Miriam is real but Moses is made up. Others suggest that both of them existed but were not really brother and sister—Miriam, they argue, was a priestess and prophetess in her own right who contended with Moses for spiritual leadership among the Israelites. But the Song of Miriam allows no role at all for the man called Moses.

So it is that Moses turns up missing in the Song of Miriam as he does again and again in the Bible itself.

Let us go in search of him now.

Chapter Two

BORN AT
THE RIGHT TIME

Down among the reeds and rushes, a baby boy was born. . . .
—PAUL SIMON, "BORN AT THE RIGHT TIME"

The man we know as Moses was born amid the shrieks of mothers and the bawling of their babies, or so the Bible suggests; but these sounds were not the familiar birth-song of labor and delivery. Up and down the lanes of the slave quarters where his mother and father dwelled, women cried out in terror and their babies picked up the cry as the death squads of the Egyptian king made their way from house to house in search of the male offspring of the Israelite slaves.

"Every son that is born ye shall cast into the river," Pharaoh had decreed, "and every daughter ye shall save alive." (Exod. 1:22)

The slaughter of slave babies was roughly equivalent to the culling of a herd. The Israelites were beasts of burden in ancient Egypt, and they possessed neither the weapons nor the will to fight back. Yet the Israelite slaves were not too taxed by their hard labor or their hard life simply to go to sleep when they took to their beds at night—no, the Israelites proved themselves to be remarkably active in bed, and alarmingly fertile, too.

"And the children of Israel were fruitful," the Bible attests, "and the land was filled with them." (Exod. 1:7)

A purely strategic concern was at work in history's first recorded ef-

fort at genocide. Would the multitude of slaves someday rise up and topple Pharaoh from the throne of Egypt? Would they make an alliance
with the enemies of Egypt and serve as a fifth column in support of an
invading army? Egypt had experienced precisely such treachery sometime in the second millennium B.C.E., when the land was conquered by
a mysterious horde known to us as the Hyksos, a Semitic people who
drove their chariots into Egypt from the land of Canaan and beyond,
deposed the rightful pharaoh, then ruled as overlords for more than a
century before being driven out—the very word Hyksos, sometimes
translated as "Shepherd Kings," actually means "rulers of foreign lands."[1]
For the Egyptians, who regarded all outsiders with both fear and contempt, the memory of the Hyksos invasion may have stoked anxieties
over the Israelites who teemed along the banks of the Nile in the land
of Goshen. Starting with the seventy souls who had accompanied the
Israelite patriarch Jacob into Egypt, according to the biblical account,
the people of Israel had grown to number in the hundreds of thousands
and perhaps even millions.[2]

"Behold, the people of the children of Israel are too many and too
mighty for us," Pharaoh mused to his counselors in private reaches of
the royal palace. "Come, let us deal wisely with them." (Exod. 1:9–10)

WHOSE WORD WILL STAND?

Pharaoh's notion of wisdom was simple and brutal—he would thin out
the herd, so to speak, by killing off as many Israelites as possible. At
first, he contented himself with conscripting the Israelites and working them to death. The slave battalions were marched out to work sites
around Goshen, and their taskmasters were ordered to lay on the whip
and put the hordes to the hardest of labor. The slave bosses, never gentle or generous toward conscripted laborers, foreign born or native born,
bestirred themselves to even greater exertion to satisfy the orders from
the palace.

"They made their lives bitter with heavy work at mortar and brick,
and with all kinds of labor in the field," is how the Bible records the ordeal. "All the work they exacted of them with ruthlessness." (Exod.
1:14)[3]

The spare biblical account is richly embellished in the legend and lore preserved by the rabbis of late antiquity and the early Middle Ages in anthologies such as the Talmud and the Midrash. As if to explain how the Israelites, so great in number, were subjugated so easily, the rabbis suggested that the Israelites were enslaved by trickery. According to one such tale, the men of Israel are recruited on the promise that they will be paid for their work, and they are handed a shekel for each brick, at least at first.[4] Pharaoh himself hangs a brick-press around his neck and joins the Israelites at the building sites as a gentle reproach to any Israelite who refuses to work: "Does thou mean to make us believe thou art more delicate than Pharaoh?" the taskmasters would taunt. But then the wages are withdrawn, and the Israelites find themselves working as slaves. "By means of such artifices and wily words the Egyptians succeeded in overmastering the Israelites," the rabbis imagined, "and once they had them in their power, they treated them with undisguised brutality."[5]

We do not really know whether such stories have any faint connection with historical reality, nor do we know whether the Pharaoh of the Oppression, as he is called in biblical commentary, corresponds to one of the flesh-and-blood pharaohs whose reigns are recorded in the annals of ancient Egypt and whose mummies reside under glass in museums all over the world. The pharaoh who enslaved the Israelites was dubbed Meror, "the Bitter One," in the folklore of the Jewish people,[6] but the favorite candidate among scholars and theologians is the celebrated Ramses II, who reigned from circa 1279–1213* B.C.E. Intriguingly, a document from ancient Egypt known as the Leiden Papyrus preserves an official report on efforts to supply corn for a gang of workers who were quarrying stones for a gateway that was being erected in honor of "Ramses, the beloved of Amon." These workers are described by a

---

*The dating of Moses and the Exodus is highly problematic. According to the chronology established by a literal reading of the Bible (1 Kings 6:1), the Exodus took place in 1446 B.C.E., a couple of centuries before the reign of Ramses II. The *Encyclopedia Judaica* confidently places Moses "in the first half of the 13th century B.C.E.," which supports Ramses II as the pharaoh of Exodus. However, a stela attributed to Merneptah, son and successor of Ramses, suggests that the Israelites were already established in Canaan by 1200 B.C.E., when their defeat by Egyptian arms was recorded: "Israel is laid waste, his seed is not" is the first mention of the Israelites in any ancient source outside the Bible. For reasons we shall explore in greater detail, Moses cannot be fixed with certainty in any specific historical period.

hieroglyphic script that has been interpreted to refer to the Hebrews*, at least by some scholars, and thus raises the tantalizing notion that the sight of Israelite slaves at work on a building in honor of Ramses II is a recorded fact.[7]

The corvée, an ancient practice of raising vast armies of labor by conscription, had long been used by the pharaohs to build palaces and pyramids up and down the Nile, and the Bible reports that the battalions of Israelite slave laborers were put to work at building granaries in the royal treasure-cities of Pithom and Ramses. But the real motive of Pharaoh in enslaving the Israelites was population control rather than public works. As if the latter-day taskmasters of Nazi Germany had heeded the lesson of the biblical text, the very same technique was one of the methods of mass murder used to kill more than six million Jewish men, women, and children during the Holocaust. "I was assigned to work outside digging ditches . . . in the freezing cold and rain, wearing only the thin striped dresses issued to us," recalled a Jewish dressmaker named Sally Sander who was pressed into service as a slave laborer, and her testimony evokes the plight of the Israelites in ancient Egypt. "The ditches weren't to be used for any particular purpose. The Nazis were merely trying to work us to death, and many did die of sickness, cold, exhaustion and starvation."[8]

Four thousand years or so earlier, the Egyptians had been equally brutal—and just as effective—in the use of hard labor as a method of mass murder, or so attested Philo of Alexandria, the ancient Jewish chronicler. "And so they died, one after another, as if smitten by a pestilential destruction," he wrote, "and then their taskmasters threw their bodies away unburied beyond the borders of the land, not suffering their kinsmen or their friends to sprinkle even a little dust on their corpses, nor to weep over those who had thus miserably perished."[9]

Still other ancient commentators offered a few imagined details that were intended to suggest Pharaoh's genocidal motives. In one Talmudic account, the Egyptians force the enslaved Israelites to make their

---

*"The Hebrews" is a term sometimes used in the Bible to identify the Israelites, but it generally appears only when the Israelites are presented as sojourners in the land of Egypt. Some scholars argue that the Hebrews and the so-called Habiru who are mentioned in ancient Egyptian documents are, in fact, one and the same. But the identity of the Habiru, and their relationship to the Israelites, remains an enduring mystery of biblical scholarship, a mystery that we will have occasion to revisit in chapter seven.

beds on the ground near the building sites where they labor, on the pretext that marching back and forth between home and work is a waste of time that prevents the labor battalions from making enough bricks to satisfy their daily quota. But the underlying rationale is more sinister; the Egyptians seek to keep the Israelite men apart from their wives in order to prevent the making of yet more Israelite babies. God himself recognizes the ulterior motive, the ancient rabbis imagined, and vows to frustrate the plan of Pharaoh.

"Unto their father Abraham I gave the promise, that I would make his children to be as numerous as the stars in the heavens, and you contrive plans to prevent them from multiplying," God is depicted as saying to Pharaoh in the Midrash. "We shall see whose word will stand, Mine or yours."[10]

"IF IT BE A SON, THEN YE SHALL KILL HIM"

Since the rigors of slave labor were apparently not enough to depress the birthrate of the all-too-fruitful Israelites, Pharaoh resolved to take a more direct approach: the population of slaves would be reduced by the simple expedient of slaying the firstborn male offspring of every Israelite family. And Pharaoh hit upon what seemed to be a clever stratagem for the slaughter: he recruited the midwives who attended the birth of slave babies and he pressed them into service as executioners.

"When ye do the office of a midwife to the Hebrew women," went Pharaoh's instructions to the midwives of Egypt, "ye shall look upon the birthstool: if it be a son, then ye shall kill him; but if it be a daughter, then she shall live." (Exod. 1:16)

The idea of murdering babies and even whole tribes was hardly a novel one; infanticide was a familiar practice in the ancient world, and mass murder was both a method and a goal of warfare. But the women who were so skilled in seeing to the birth of babies turned out to be disappointing baby-killers. Whether out of faintheartedness or, as the Bible suggests, fear of divine punishment, the midwives defied the orders of their monarch and simply refused to kill off the newborn sons of the Israelite slaves: "But the midwives feared God, and did not as the king of Egypt commanded them, but saved the men-children alive." (Exod. 1:17) When Pharaoh learned that his plan had failed and the Israelites continued to multiply, he summoned two of the midwives, one named Shiphrah and the other named Puah, to the palace to find out why.

"Why have you done this thing?" demanded Pharaoh, half-choked with rage over the fact that he had been openly defied by a clutch of common midwives, "and saved the men-children alive?" (Exod. 1:18)

Shiphrah and Puah knew that their own lives were at stake. The monarch of ancient Egypt was regarded as an incarnation of the god Horus, child of the sibling lovers Osiris and Isis, or so taught the priests who tended to such matters, and even if the worldlier folk could not quite take it seriously, the monarch had been raised to regard himself in precisely that way. But the midwives must have found it difficult to look upon a man, no matter how high and mighty, and see a god; they had attended too many births to forget that Pharaoh, no less than the scrawniest slave baby, started out as a bawling infant tied to his mother by a cord of flesh and blood.

So the midwives dared to make excuses to their king. The Hebrew women were more like cows than human beings—once they went into labor, they dropped their babies so quickly that mother and child were done and gone by the time the midwives got word of the imminent birth and showed up at one of their hovels. Sorry to say, the midwives simply arrived too late to strangle the baby boys as Pharaoh had commanded. "Because the Hebrew women are not as the Egyptian women," the midwives explained, "for they are lively, and are delivered ere the midwives come unto them." (Exod. 1:19)

Shiphrah and Puah have long fascinated scholars and theologians. The uncertain phrasing of the original text does not make it clear whether they were Israelites or Egyptians, although the Masoretic Text regards them as Hebrews[11] and a tale preserved in the rabbinical texts insisted that Shiphrah is actually Jochebed, the mother of Moses, and Puah is his sister, Miriam. According to the rabbis, when the righteous midwives were rewarded for their heroism—"So God made the midwives prosper," the Bible reports, "and gave the midwives homes and families of their own, because they feared him" (Exod. 1:20–21 NEB)— what is meant is that Jochebed was given the privilege of bearing Moses, and Miriam was destined to marry Caleb, a hero of the Exodus, "and from Miriam's union with Caleb sprang the royal house of David."[12]

Other sources suggested that the midwives were Egyptian women who had converted to the faith of ancient Israel, and imagined that Pharaoh resorted to every manner of guile in motivating the midwives to murder the slave babies, first by "gentle words and promises" and then by "making even amorous proposals to the younger one, which, however, she indignantly rejected."[13] Still later, the early church fathers expended much effort in explaining how these two valiant women could be seen as righteous even though they lied to their king—the lies they told, after all, served a higher purpose of preserving human life— and the tale of the God-fearing midwives "became the classic passage for all later medieval discussions of lying."[14]

To Pharaoh, who surely knew little of the ways of women, and still less about the mystery of childbirth, the excuse offered by the two midwives for their dereliction of duty must have sounded plausible enough. The Bible describes the fecundity of Israelite women with a Hebrew word (*chayot*) that is translated in the King James Version as "lively." (Exod. 1:19) But the word actually means "animal-like,"[15] and it must have seemed to Pharaoh that the Israelites were reproducing like vermin. Indeed, Pharaoh embraced what one Bible scholar calls "a common racist notion, according to which the Other is closer to Nature"[16]—after all, it was hard for him to look upon the masses of the Israelites and see them as anything but animals ready for the slaughter.

POGROM

Now Pharaoh turned from the midwives to the populace at large to carry out the mass murder of babies. "And Pharaoh charged all his people," the Bible reports, "saying, 'Every son that is born ye shall cast into the river.' " (Exod. 1:22) Both ancient tradition and contemporary pop culture encourage us to imagine a squad of professional executioners at work: the baby-killers are described as "bailiffs"[17] or "emissaries"[18] or "inspectors"[19] in the rabbinical literature, and they are depicted as soldiery in both Renaissance art and Hollywood movies. But the biblical account confirms that the slaughter of the innocents was, in fact, the first recorded pogrom in history, a state-sponsored orgy of bloodletting in which every good Egyptian, soldier and civilian alike, was invited to participate as a civic duty. According to one tale, the Egyptians manage to murder ten thousand babies, and another storyteller puts the number at six hundred thousand.[20]

"The people," it is adjudged in the Talmud, "were guilty along with Pharaoh."[21]

In fact, the rabbis credited the Egyptians with a certain blood-curdling creativity in their genocidal work. According to one tale, a daily quota of bricks is imposed on each slave by the taskmaster, and the result of each day's work is counted up at sunset. "If even one brick was short, then the youngest child of the Hebrew labourer who had not made up his toll of bricks was seized and built into the wall in the place of bricks," the story goes. "[T]he ruthless overseers penetrated into his house and snatched away his beloved child from the arms of the weeping and desperate mother. Alive the child was built into the walls."[22]

According to one poignant tale in the Midrash, the death squads who are sent into the slave quarters adopt a clever but cruel ploy: the more resourceful baby-killers bring along an Egyptian mother and her child. When they enter an Israelite home, the captain of the guard gives the Egyptian babe-in-arms a hard pinch to make it cry out in pain. The bawling of the Egyptian baby would prompt any hidden Israelite baby to start crying, too. The soldiers easily find their way to the concealed child—betrayed by its own tears—and carry out their mission, silencing its cry once and for all.[23]

THE FAT OF THE LAND

A terrible irony is at work in the slaughter of the innocents at the command of Pharaoh as depicted in the Bible. According to the Book of Genesis, Egypt was a fairy-tale kingdom where magical and even miraculous things happened, a sanctuary where food and shelter might be found in times of famine, a welcoming place where a man might be elevated to the pinnacle of privilege and power if only he caught the attention of the pharaoh—"a champaign country blessed with rich soil," as one ancient chronicler put it.[24] Indeed, the biblical saga of Israel in Egypt reaches a glorious crescendo in the closing pages of Genesis, where Joseph is raised from lowly slave and prisoner to the high office of viceroy, second only to Pharaoh himself, and he beckons his father, Jacob, and his eleven brothers to join him in the land of Egypt. Thus did the whole of Jacob's clan make the momentous trek down to Egypt, and the Israelites came to dwell in the land of a much kinder and gentler pharaoh than the one we will soon come to know in the Book of Exodus.

The land of the pharaohs figures decisively in the history of Israel as reported throughout the Bible. Egypt was a superpower of the ancient world, and the royal capital was to the biblical authors of the first millennium B.C.E. what Athens and Rome, Paris and London, New York and Tokyo would be in the centuries that followed—a center of arts and letters, commerce and industry; a repository of vast wealth. By contrast, the city of Jerusalem was a backwater, and the priests and scribes who lived and worked there seemed to regard Egypt with the kind of awe and anxiety that provincials have always felt toward the metropolis.

The very first encounter between the Israelites and an Egyptian pharaoh, for example, dates back to the wanderings of the patriarch Abraham, who made his way to Egypt in search of food to sustain his family during one of the long and deadly famines that were commonplace in the ancient world. According to a remarkable tale told in Genesis, a tale in which Abraham passed off his wife, Sarah, as his sister and she ended up in the royal harem, Abraham was not only saved from starvation but came away from Egypt "rich in cattle, in silver, and in gold" under circumstances that cast the pharaoh of Egypt in a rather flattering light (Gen. 12:18–19, 13:2). Indeed, Abraham's experience in Egypt encourages us to see the mighty pharaoh as a gentle and generous monarch, perhaps even more goodly than the patriarch himself.

Abraham's good fortune in Egypt is an augury of much greater glory that will be bestowed by yet another pharaoh on Abraham's fortunate great-grandson, Joseph, several generations later. Joseph, the favorite son of the patriarch Jacob, was sold to a passing caravan of Midianite slave-traders by his jealous and treacherous brothers. When the caravan reached Egypt, Joseph was sold off to a captain of the guard in the royal palace and ended up in a dungeon after he was falsely accused of making sexual advances toward his master's wife. But the Bible makes it clear that Joseph was destined to prosper in Egypt despite every effort by his adversaries to betray him or kill him off. Thanks to his gift for the interpretation of dreams, far surpassing "all the magicians of Egypt, and all the wise men" (Exod. 41:8), Joseph soothed Pharaoh's nightmares and famously predicted seven years of plenty and seven years of famine. So the young man who was sold into slavery and ended up in a dungeon was raised to glory in the land of Egypt: Joseph was favored by his God, his father, and his king, and he is presented by the biblical author as a royal personage in his own right.

And Pharaoh said unto Joseph: "See, I have set thee over all the land of Egypt." And Pharaoh took off his signet ring from his hand, and put it upon Joseph's hand, and arrayed him vestures of fine linen and put a gold chain about his neck. (Gen. 41:41)

The food stores at Joseph's disposal in Egypt attracted the hungry and homeless from across the ancient world, and among them were Joseph's now repentant brothers. "Go, get you unto the land of Canaan," Joseph told his brothers after revealing his identity to them, "and take your father and your households, and come unto me; and I will give you the good of the land of Egypt, and ye shall eat the fat of the land." (Exod. 45:18) Thus did the people of Israel arrive in Egypt at a moment of glory and abundance, Jacob and his sons and their families, precisely seventy men, women, and children. The whole enterprise was blessed — one might even say it was orchestrated—by God himself, who spoke to Jacob "in the visions of the night" as the party traveled toward Egypt.

"Fear not to go down into Egypt, for I will there make of thee a great nation," God said to Jacob. "I will go down with thee into Egypt, and I will also surely bring thee up again." (Gen. 46:3–4)

"A WANDERING ARAMEAN WAS MY FATHER"

Egypt was the furnace in which the twelve tribes of Israel, each named after one of the sons (or grandsons) of Jacob, were forged into a single people and a single nation—a saga that is celebrated at length and in detail in the Bible. Abraham was a restless wanderer who decamped from the ancient city of Ur, and his sons and grandsons were tent nomads who followed their herds of goats and flocks of sheep from one pasturage to the next in the primal rhythm of nomadic life. But the wanderings of the Israelites ended when they arrived in Egypt.

"Every shepherd is an abomination unto the Egyptians," Joseph warned his father and brothers before presenting them to Pharaoh (Gen. 46:34), giving expression to the fear and loathing that the farmer has always felt toward the herdsman. But the monarch granted the blood relatives of his favored viceroy "a possession in the land of Egypt, in the best of the land," a region that the Bible calls the land of Goshen (Gen. 47:11).

"Lo, here is seed for you," Joseph instructed his brothers and their households, "and ye shall sow the land." (Gen. 47:23)

We do not know whether a place called Goshen actually existed in ancient Egypt or where the land of Goshen might have been located—the Egyptian archaeological record knows no such place, although the physical description of Goshen in the Bible seems to suggest a location in the delta where the Nile flows into the Mediterranean, a broad stretch of flatlands that receive the deposits of rich soil from upriver. Some biblical scholars speculate that the pharaoh who elevated Joseph to high rank and invited the Israelites to establish themselves in the land of Goshen was, in fact, one of the so-called Shepherd Kings—the Hyksos invaders. Joseph, too, is utterly absent from the historical record of ancient Egypt, which otherwise noted everything from the price of bread to the regnal years of every pharaoh who sat on the throne for two millennia.

Here in Goshen, the Bible confirms, the Israelites finally gave up the ways of the nomad and settled themselves on the land, living in houses rather than tents, tilling the soil rather than following the flocks. "The tradition of the pyramid faces that of the campfire," explains Martin Buber[25]—and the pyramid prevails. Indeed, what is described in the Bible is nothing less than the first step in what Jacob Bronowski calls "the ascent of man," the transformation of humankind from ragged and restless tribal hordes to settled urban civilizations, and the very same momentous step was repeated throughout the world of distant antiquity as the first cities and states began to appear.

"A wandering Aramean was my father," goes the credo of the ancient Israelites as recorded in the Book of Deuteronomy, "and he went down into Egypt, and sojourned there, few in number; and he became there a nation, great, mighty, and populous." (Deut. 26:5)

The sojourn of Israel in Egypt lasted some 430 years (Exod. 12:40). Jacob grew old and died, and then Joseph and his brothers too. The Israelites remembered and revered their forefathers: Jacob's remains were carried back to Canaan for a traditional burial in the land that God had promised but not yet delivered to his Chosen People. Joseph's body was embalmed in the fashion of the Egyptians, and his mummy was stored in a coffin against the day when the Israelites would return to the Promised Land. That day was far off, as it turned out, but meanwhile the Israelites prospered and proliferated in Egypt: "And the children of Israel were fruitful, and they teemed, and they multiplied, and they became vast in exceeding abundance, so that the land was filled with them." (Exod. 1:7)

According to the Bible, the population of Israelites in Egypt included six hundred thousand men who were capable of bearing arms (Exod. 12:37). If the biblical head count of draft-age men is accurate, contemporary scholarship calculates that the number of women, children, and elderly would have brought the total population of Israelites to 2.5 million—"a fantastic number," Elias Auerbach concedes, and one that suggests the Israelites did not require God *or* Moses in order to throw off the shackles of slavery. "With such a figure the Israelites would not have been obliged to emigrate from Egypt," he observes. "They could have conquered it without much trouble and subjected their oppressors."[26]

Indeed, the ancient rabbis seemed to understand that the biblical census figures were probably an exaggeration, but they gamely argued that the astounding population growth of the Israelites was the result of an uncanny and even miraculous birthrate among the Chosen People. "Leading a moral and virtuous life, the Hebrews were thriving exceedingly in Goshen," the rabbis insisted, and the women gave birth to six babies at once, sometimes twelve, sometimes even more.[27] "Some say sixty at each birth," the rabbis wrote, and then admonished their readers: "[A]nd don't wonder at it, for the scorpion, a swarming creature, spawns sixty at once."[28]

Yet there is something dark and dangerous in the biblical account of how the Israelites first came to Egypt, a faint undersong that sets the scene for the birth of Moses and predicts the ordeal that the Israelites will be compelled to endure in order to win their liberty. God, who had acted so insistently to send the Israelites into the land of Pharaoh and to bestow his blessings upon them in Egypt, now fell silent, and the favoring light that seemed to shine on the Israelites seemed to dim and then die out.

The ancient sages insisted that every act of human passion, no matter how impulsive, and every twist of fate, no matter how unlikely, is authored by God even if the Bible does not say so. The fall from grace in Egypt, they believed, did not mean that God had lost interest in his creatures or that his love had turned to anger. Quite the opposite was true. "God had so ordained that the love of the Egyptians for the children of Israel should be changed into hatred," the rabbis taught, "so that they should turn to the Lord."[29] The same notion is embraced by contemporary theologians in order to charge the matter-of-fact account that we find in the Bible with exalted meanings. "God's history is not transcendental heavenly history," writes one Bible scholar. "It stoops to earth and appoints men with their deeds and words as signs."[30]

All we know with certainty from the Bible, however, is that no more will be heard from or about God during the long years of exile in Egypt. God seemed to forget about the Israelites, and they did not seem to pay much attention to *him* during that sojourn. At last, at a moment when Joseph's coffin has been gathering dust in some forgotten crypt for four centuries, the Bible reports an ominous but fateful event. "There arose in Egypt," the biblical author announces in a phrase that rings with peril, "a pharaoh who knew not Joseph." (Exod. 1:8)

The long slumber of God was over, and the terrible ordeal that would turn a nation of slaves into the Chosen People was about to begin in earnest.

"A GOODLY CHILD"

The birth notice of Moses in the Bible is simple and spare. An Israelite man, who is first identified in the biblical text only as "a man of the house of Levi," was wed to an Israelite woman, "a daughter of Levi," and the couple fulfilled the very first commandment of the God of Israel— "Be fruitful and multiply" (Gen. 1:28)—even as the newborn baby boys of Israel were being put to death all around them.

> And the woman conceived, and bore a son; and when she saw
> him that he was a goodly child, she hid him three months.
> (Exod. 2:2)

These crucial figures are not named in the Bible when we first encounter them, and their ordeal during the three months of concealment is left entirely to our imagination. Other babies were being seized and drowned, but the terse biblical text reports that the "goodly child" was successfully concealed for the first three months of life. Nevertheless the Levite couple surely lived in fear of the day when one of the death squads that ranged through the slave quarters of the Israelites would hear the cry of their newborn son, pound on the door of their hovel, and wrench the baby from the arms of his mother, just as they had done up and down the lanes and alleys of Goshen.

But the woman was determined that her son would not suffer the sorry fate of so many other innocent babes-in-arms. Drawing on resources of courage and ingenuity that make her seem truly heroic, she took it upon herself to defy the will of Pharaoh and deny the baby-killers at least one victim.

> And when she could no longer hide him, she took for him an ark of bulrushes, and daubed it with slime and with pitch; and she put the child therein, and laid it in the flags by the river's brink. (Exod. 2:3)

A tale preserved in the Talmud credits the child's mother with a poignant and bittersweet thought: "Perhaps I shall not live to see my son under the marriage canopy," she thinks to herself as she fashions a canopy to cover the little ark, but at least she will shelter him under one right now.[31] And the Bible reports that the older sister of the nameless infant maintained a vigil over the ark as it floated away: "And his sister stood afar off, to witness what would be done to him." (Exod. 2:4) But the effort at rescue was a desperate act, and neither of these intrepid women knew whether the little ark would stay upright and afloat in the Nile, or where the baby would end up if it did, or whether he would survive at all.

Still, the Bible offers a subtle signal that predicts the success of their daring ploy. Like the ark itself, the baby would be picked up and carried along by the current of a freshening stream of sacred history. The Hebrew term used by the biblical author to describe the frail little boat of woven reeds in which the baby was sheltered is *teba*, a word that appears elsewhere in the Bible only once, and then to describe the mighty vessel in which Noah and a precious remnant of human and animal life sought refuge from the flood that destroyed the rest of life on earth.[32] Something momentous was at stake, we are meant to understand: the survival of an enslaved people and the destiny of humankind would depend on the ark that now floated in the shallows of the Nile and the goodly child who was sheltered inside.

"WOE UNTO THIS PREGNANCY!"

Not until much later in the biblical narrative do we learn that the father of the goodly child is Amram and the mother is Jochebed (Exod. 6:20), or that Moses has an older brother named Aaron and an older sister named Miriam (Exod. 6:20, Num. 26:59). In fact, a close reading of the Bible reveals a great many awkwardnesses and contradictions in the family history of Moses. Amram appears to have been married to his own aunt—a clear violation of the law against incest that is found in the Book of Leviticus (Lev. 20:19). Jochebed is described as the daughter of Levi, one of the twelve sons of Jacob, who lived many generations earlier according to the chronology in the Book of Exodus. The Bible suggests that Moses was the firstborn and only child of Amram and Jochebed, then abruptly introduces the watchful big sister who followed Moses in his little boat of reeds, and later seems to indicate that Miriam was born *after* Moses (Num. 26:59).

Much effort has been required—and much has been expended—by both theologians and scholars in explaining away these oddities. The incestuous marriage between Amram and Jochebed is seen as another example of the "inbreeding characteristic" that we find among the patriarchs[33]—a reference to the fact that both Abraham and Isaac passed off their wives as their sisters (Gen. 20:12, 26:7). Amram might well have been old enough to marry his father's sister, Jochebed, if Amram's father had been born early in the marriage of his parents and Jochebed had been born late. Rabbinical tradition tried to resolve the chronological problems in the Bible by calculating the age of Jochebed as 126 on the day of her marriage to Amram, and contemporary scholarship argues that the "chronological implausibility" of the biblical text can be explained if we regard one troublesome passage, where the sojourn of Israel in Egypt is said to have lasted 430 years (Exod. 12:40), as a pious overstatement rather than literal truth.[34] As for the nameless young woman who played such a crucial role in the birth story of Moses by surveilling the baby as he floated down the Nile, perhaps it was not Miriam at all—or so suggested a medieval commentator who was struggling to make sense of the biblical text. A modern Bible critic points out that Miriam may have been mentioned after Moses in the genealogical passages of the Bible not because of her birth order but rather because she was female.[35]

New and surprising details about Moses were offered by the rabbis and sages who embroidered the spare account that we find in the opening passages of Exodus even as they attempted to explain away the difficulties in the text. Jochebed's name, the rabbis explained, meant "divine splendor" and referred to "the celestial light that radiated from her countenance." Her first two children, born during the bitter oppression of the Israelites, were given names that reflected the general misery of the Israelites: "Miriam," we are told, means "bitterness," and "Aaron" means "Woe unto this pregnancy!"[36] The rabbis imagined that Amram divorces Jochebed after the birth of Miriam and Aaron, acting out of despair over Pharaoh's decree and anxious to avoid the birth of a doomed son.

Another tale shows Amram as the president of the Sanhedrin,[37] a council of elders that did not come into existence until many centuries later in the land of Israel, and has him ordering *all* of the Israelites to divorce their wives. But Miriam scolds her father for his rash order. "Your decree is harsher than Pharaoh's!" she is made to say. "Pharaoh's struck at the boys only, while yours strikes at boys and girls alike."[38] Yet another tale told by the ancients credits young Miriam with the power of prophecy. "[T]he spirit of God came upon [her] by night," according to the author known as Pseudo-Philo, and delivered an augury to Miriam in a dream. "[B]ehold a man in a linen garment stood and said to me: Go and tell thy parents: behold, that which shall be born of you shall be cast into the water . . . and by him will I do signs, and I will save my people."[39] Amram and Jochebed remarry in a ceremony that celebrates life even under the threat of death: Aaron and Miriam dance around the wedding canopy, the rabbis imagined, while angels from on high cry out, "Let the mother of children be joyful!"[40]

The most compelling explanation for the flaws and omissions in the biblical text, however, is less fantastic and yet somehow even more unsettling than the rabbinical literature suggests. Some scholars argue that all of the unlikely details of the family history of Moses were written into the Bible by authors and editors who came along at a relatively late date in its composition and sought to flesh out the meager account of the birth of Moses in the early verses of Exodus.[41] In fact, some of the same Bible scholars who wonder aloud whether Moses ever really existed are willing to argue that both Miriam and Aaron were real people, prophets in their own right, who were given an imaginary blood relationship with Moses by biblical propagandists who sought to elevate and glorify them by linking them to the Bible's greatest prophet.

THE PROMISED CHILD

Implausibilities in the biblical account of the early life of Moses were far less troubling to some ancient readers of the Bible than the humble circumstances of his birth and the mundane manner of his rescue. What passed for biography in the court histories and sacred texts of the ancient world more often resembled an ornate song of praise, full of omens and auguries, richly imagined scenes of both splendor and struggle, and miraculous displays of divine will. And so, even though the biblical authors contented themselves with the brief notice that we find in the opening lines of Exodus, the sages and storytellers who came later insisted on dressing up Moses in what they fancied to be more suitable garb.

Thus, for example, the mother of Moses divines the miraculous qualities of the child she carries in her womb from the fact that she suffers no pain in labor or in delivery—or so the sages imagined. She carries him for only six months, and yet, at birth, Moses promptly stands up on his own two feet, strolls about the house, chats with his dumbfounded parents, and, as befits a child of such preternatural maturity, declines his mother's breast. At the very moment of his birth, as if to eliminate any question of his celestial origins and stellar destiny, "the whole house was filled with radiance equal to the splendor of the sun and the moon."[42] At the age of four months, prophecy comes out of the mouth of the babe. "In days to come, I shall receive the Torah from the flaming torch," the precious (and precocious) child was imagined to announce to his mother and father.[43]

God, too, was given a role in the myth and legend of ancient tradition that owes nothing at all to Holy Writ. "[T]he child out of dread of whose nativity the Egyptians have doomed the Israelites to destruction shall be this child of thine," God announces to Amram in one of the tales. "His memory shall be celebrated while the world lasts, and not only among the Hebrews, but among strangers also."[44]

Of course, the birth of a child who is destined for glory or doom (or both) is common enough in legend and lore around the world and in every age. Thanks to Sigmund Freud, the ancient Greek myth of Oedipus is the single most familiar example of "the promised child who is exposed and rescued."[45] Similar stories can be found in the writings of the Greek historian Herodotus about Cyrus II, the Persian monarch who conquered Babylon in the sixth century B.C.E.,[46] and in the myths about the legendary founders of Rome, Romulus and Remus. Indeed, the life of Moses can be seen as a kind of Cinderella story that embodies "the favorite storyteller's motif of 'the success of the unpromising.' "[47] Perhaps, as Martin Buber speculates, the Bible simply and unabashedly "fills gaps in the transmitted biography [of Moses] by carefully drawing on the treasury of legendary motifs common to early humanity."[48] The biblical authors, in other words, may have borrowed freely from the myth and legend of several civilizations other than their own in order to flesh out the life of Moses.

The birth story of Moses in the Book of Exodus is so strongly reminiscent of another tale from the ancient Near East, for example, that some scholars believe that one of the biblical authors merely cut and pasted the story from a Mesopotamian text that describes the birth of an Akkadian monarch named Sargon, who reigned in the third millennium B.C.E.

> Sargon, the mighty king, king of Agade, am I.
> My mother was a changeling, my father I knew not. . . .
> My changeling mother conceived me, in secret she bore me.
> She set me in a basket of rushes, with bitumen she sealed my lid.
> She cast me into the river which rose not [over] me.
> The river bore me up and carried me to Akki, the drawer of
> water. . . .
> Akki, the drawer of water, [took me] as his son [and] reared me.[49]

So Sargon was drawn from the Euphrates, just as Moses would later be drawn from the Nile, and he came under the protection of the Babylonian goddess of love and fertility known as Ishtar, a powerful deity who may prefigure the flesh-and-blood women who come to the rescue of Moses. But Sargon differs from Moses in important ways. His is essentially a rags-to-riches tale of distant antiquity. The word translated as "changeling" may, in fact, refer to a high priestess of ancient Mesopotamia whose traditional vow of chastity meant that Sargon must have been conceived in a forbidden tryst with the king. Thus the infant was set adrift because of his illegitimate birth,[50] and only when Sargon caught the eye of Ishtar was he raised to high rank in spite of the low station of his adoptive father. What's entirely missing in the story of Sargon is the terrible peril that stalked the infant Moses, who was condemned to die by the decree of Pharaoh and who was set adrift in the river in a desperate effort by his mother to evade that death sentence.

Some scholars claim to glimpse beneath the surface of the biblical life story of Moses a subtext that more closely resembles the myth of Oedipus, who was exposed to the elements and left to die because his father, the king, sought to foil the prophecy that young Oedipus would one day replace him on the throne. The Bible, of course, makes no such suggestion—Pharaoh decreed that *all* of the baby boys born to the Israelites were to be murdered, and his only stated concern was that the Israelites had grown too numerous, a rationale for mass murder that is known among Bible scholars as "the 'genocide' tradition."[51]

But something else may be hidden beneath the text of the Bible. After all, why would Pharaoh seek to rob himself of a ready supply of slave labor? "Ordinarily a ruling nation, particularly in the Ancient Near East, would not think of destroying its labor supply," observes Bible scholar Brevard Childs, "but would look favorably on its increase." What's more, even if it were state policy to exterminate the Israelites rather than enslave and exploit them as a kind of natural resource, "one does not reduce the number of a people by destroying the males, but rather the females." So we are left to conclude either that the biblical account, as Childs puts it, "is not bothered by lack of rigorous logic,"[52] or that something crucial has been left out of the Bible as it comes down to us.

Some scholars argue that the genocide tradition in the birth story of Moses conceals an older version of the tale in which the future liberator of the Israelites is the real and only target of the death sentence pronounced by Pharaoh. Intriguingly, the slaughter of the innocents is mentioned nowhere else in all of the Hebrew Bible except in an oblique reference in the Psalms: "He turned their heart to hate His people. . . ." (Ps. 105:25)[53] Perhaps, then, the Bible once included a now suppressed tradition which held that it was not *all* baby boys that Pharaoh sought to kill, but rather one baby boy in particular—a baby whom Pharaoh feared because he had been warned by his seers that the child was destined to dethrone him.

Such speculation can be found in a rich array of ancient writings, including the Midrash, the early Aramaic translations of the Hebrew Bible, the writings of Josephus, and even some Greek texts in which the

Bible stories were retold as quaint curiosities for a pagan readership.[54] Most intriguing of all, the same theme appears in the New Testament, where many of the crucial events in the life of Jesus hark back to the life of Moses. When Herod learned of the birth of Jesus of Nazareth from the three wise men from the East—"Where is he who has been born king of the Jews?"—he ordered the death of all male children in Bethlehem under the age of two in a desperate effort to kill the promised child. Jesus was spared only because an angel urged Joseph to flee with his family to Egypt until Herod himself was dead, thus fulfilling a biblical prophecy that specifically evokes the memory of Moses. "Out of Egypt have I called my son," goes the Gospel of Matthew (Matt. 2:15 RSV) in a pointed allusion to a verse from Hosea: "And by a prophet the Lord brought Israel up out of Egypt." (Hos. 12:14)

The received text of the Hebrew Bible offers no such explanation for the slaughter of the innocents by Pharaoh, but one Bible scholar argues that the Oedipal theme may have been embraced in the earliest traditions of ancient Israel and then expunged from the Bible by the biblical editors collectively known as the Redactor, who came along several centuries later and cleaned up the text of the Bible.[55] A story preserved in the rabbinical literature may be a remnant of the original version of the birth story of Moses, a version in which Pharaoh is warned that a nameless child who will be born among the Israelites is destined to topple him from the throne and lead the Israelites out of Egypt.

In that account, Pharaoh wakes up from a shattering nightmare in which the elders and nobles of Egypt were weighed against "a sucking lamb"[56] on the scales of justice, and the frail suckling outweighed them. Troubled and confused by the nightmare, Pharaoh summons the wise men of his court to decipher these strange images. According to the confabulations of the ancient storytellers, who were fond of compressing and conflating the characters of the Bible in odd and surreal ways, the wise men in Pharaoh's court include three figures whom we recognize from other times and places in Holy Writ: "the great magician" Balaam, the pagan prophet whose talking ass will famously outwit him in the Book of Numbers; Reuel, the Midianite priest who will become the father-in-law of Moses in the Book of Exodus; and Job, the faithful servant of God whose righteousness will be sorely tested by Satan in the Book of Job. Balaam interprets Pharaoh's dream to mean that "a son will be born unto Israel, who will destroy the whole of our land and all of its inhabitants." So Balaam counsels Pharaoh to eliminate the as-yet-unborn liberator of the Israelites by ordering the death by drowning of *all* of the sons of Israel.[57]

"[B]y water thou mayest hope to exterminate the Hebrews and wipe them out from the face of the earth," warns Balaam. "If, therefore, it please the King, let him hearken unto my advice and decree that all the male children born unto the Hebrews be cast into the river."[58]

Pharaoh follows Balaam's advice, but his plan is foiled. On the very day that Moses is rescued from the Nile, the astrologers of Pharaoh's court report that they have confirmed the death of the promised child: "Long live the King! We bring thee glad tidings, for we have read in the stars that the boy destined to redeem Israel and to bring calamity upon Egypt has met his fate in water. No longer needst thou fear him, O great King." And so the slaughter of the innocents, which is never mentioned again in the Bible after the birth of Moses, comes to an abrupt end.

To explain why the astrologers were mistaken, the rabbis imagined that they had been "misled by a vague vision, for they had read in the stars that Moses was to die one day on account of water." The vision of the astrologers is accurate but their timing is off; the death of Moses will be linked with water in an odd and oblique way, as we shall see, but not until the distant future: "Water was, indeed, the doom of Moses, but that did not mean that he would perish in the waters of the Nile."[59] Pharaoh, however, is relieved by the assurances of his court astrologers and calls off the carnage, and so "the new-born babes of Israel were saved from drowning."[60] Not only is Moses spared on that momentous day, but also some six hundred thousand other male infants who were "begotten in the same night with him, and thrown into the water on the same day, [and] miraculously rescued with him."[61]

Of course, the birth and rescue of Moses are described in the Bible without these trappings of mystery or miracle. Moses was just another bawling slave baby whom Pharaoh sought to kill out of purely genocidal motives. The baby was spared from Pharaoh's decree because a pair of midwives evaded the order to murder babies and then because his mother refused to deliver him to the death squads. He survived on the waters of the Nile in his precarious little boat because an intrepid older sister watched over him as he floated away. And he was plucked from the river by a privileged young woman who did not care that the baby was the offspring of the despised Israelite slaves. Centuries of pious commentary have urged us to see the hand of God in these events, but the Bible credits a succession of otherwise unremarkable women with the rescue of the man who would go on to change the world.

THE PRINCESS AT HER BATH

When the ark finally came to rest among the reeds, the curious construction of slime, pitch, and bulrushes caught the eye of a woman who happened to be bathing in the Nile on that morning. As it turned out, she was the daughter of the very man who had issued the death sentence that had prompted the desperate little voyage.

> And the daughter of Pharaoh came down to bathe in the river; and her maidens walked along by the river-side; and she saw the ark among the flags, and sent her handmaid to fetch it. And she opened it, and saw it, even the child; and behold a boy that wept. (Exod. 2:5–6)

Here was yet another moment of acute peril for baby Moses. Would the daughter of Pharaoh dutifully carry out her father's order by tipping the ark over and letting the infant drown? Would she push the ark of reeds back into the current and let it float away to its own uncertain fate? Surely nothing in her upbringing in the court of Pharaoh and her station in life as a royal princess suggested otherwise, but the young woman reacted to the curious sight not with hate or indifference but with a mothering impulse.

"And she had compassion on him," the Bible reports, "and said: 'This is one of the Hebrews' children.'" (Exod. 2:6)

The words were overheard by the watchful girl who had been following her baby brother down the river, and now she presented herself to the Egyptian princess and her retinue with a bold proposal.

"Shall I go and call thee a nurse of the Hebrew women," she said, "that she may nurse the child for thee?"

"Go," said the daughter of Pharaoh (Exod. 2:7–8).

So the girl fetched her mother back to the riverside, and a deal was struck between the slave woman and the Egyptian princess, the birth mother and the adoptive mother of the goodly child.

And Pharaoh's daughter said unto her: "Take this child away, and nurse it for me, and I will give thee thy wages." And the woman took the child and nursed it. And the child grew, and she brought him unto Pharaoh's daughter, and he became her son. (Exod. 2:9)

To judge from the original text of the Bible, God played no discernible role in any of these matter-of-fact dealings among the women who collaborated in the rescue of Moses. Purely human impulses are at work—a mother's terror at the prospect of her baby's death, an older sister's concern for the safety of her baby brother, a childless woman's compassion for the cries of an abandoned infant—and purely human ingenuity provides the means by which the child is spared. Indeed, all three of them are presented as hardheaded women who solve problems in the here and now by practical means rather than prayer or magic. Nothing even faintly miraculous happens to Moses in the biblical account of his infancy, and it is only because of these three strong and competent women that Moses is returned to his mother's breast and, quite literally, the bosom of his people, at least for a while.

GODDESSES AND RESCUERS

So it was not God himself who saw to the survival of the goodly child on whom so much depended. "God seems to be taking such an enormous risk to let everything ride on two helpless midwives [and] a frail ark," observes Brevard Childs,[62] and yet *all* of the women around Moses—so compassionate and courageous, so bold and resourceful—are sufficient to the task.

More recently, the women who watched over Moses have been recast as protofeminist heroines. "Women (and mothers in particular)—despite, or rather because of, their powerlessness—may have an important role in teaching the weak and threatened young sons how to trick hostile oppressors," argues feminist Bible critic Ilana Pardes, "how to submit to paternal will and at the same time usurp the father's position."[63] And Pardes makes an even more startling proposition. The women who come to the rescue of Moses are "strikingly close to representations of guardian goddesses in polytheistic texts," she argues, and they may function as the Hebrew equivalents of other "goddess-rescuers" who can be found in abundance in the myths of the ancient world, ranging from the goddess Ishtar, who was imagined to marry each of the reigning kings of Babylon; to Athena, protectress of Odysseus; and Venus, patroness of Aeneas.[64]

"With the rise of monotheism, goddesses are dethroned," writes Pardes. "God is one and as such He is male. Yet female guardianship does not vanish. It is transferred to the human realm and perceived as the role of female characters, of mothers in particular."[65]

The last of the women who came to the rescue of the infant Moses turned out to be the unlikeliest of guardians: she was not only a pagan, not only an Egyptian, but the daughter of the man who had ordered the slaughter of babies. These ironies prompted the ancient rabbis to concoct an elaborate fantasy around the simple encounter described in the Bible—and, notably, to fashion a role for God in the birth and salvation of Moses that is markedly greater than the one attributed to him in the Bible.

God sends a plague of scorching heat down on the Egyptians, the rabbis imagined, in order to drive Pharaoh's daughter to the river to cool off. The basket bobs in the water some sixty ells (225 feet) from the shore, but her arm grows suddenly elastic and allows her to reach across the distance and pluck the basket out of the Nile. The plague of heat that drove her to the cooling waters has raised "leprosy and smarting boils" on her skin, but she is miraculously cured at the very moment she touches the infant—the first of a series of dermatological miracles that will mark the life of Moses.

The princess realizes that the baby whom she rescues from the Nile must be one of the thousands of Israelite newborns who had been doomed to death by her father,[66] and the Bible encourages us to imagine that dead and dying babies floating downstream from the slave quarters must have been a common sight during those terrible days. Tradition proposes that she is familiar with the distinctive weaving style of the Israelites and so she recognizes the swaddling as an Israelite blanket, or that she identifies the infant as an Israelite because he is circumcised—"the boy bore the sign of the Abrahamic covenant," as one storyteller rather delicately put it[67]—although the Bible never reports the circumcision of Moses and, in fact, the practice was no less common among the Egyptians than among the Israelites.

When Pharaoh's daughter retrieved the bawling baby from the boat of reeds, according to the Bible, "she was filled with pity for it." (Exod.

2:6 NEB) The rabbis, however, spun out a more elaborate version of the tale: the princess recalls her father's order to the people of Egypt and is about to cast the slave baby back into the water in compliance with that decree when the angel Gabriel gives the child an invisible blow in order to set him to pitiable tears. "[A] feeling of motherly tenderness stirred in the bosom of the childless princess," and she suddenly "felt as if she were looking upon the radiance of Divine Glory."[68]

Indeed, the rabbis insisted that Pharaoh's daughter is a pagan with a heart of gold, and they fancied that she has fled to the cooling waters of the Nile from her father's court in order to "cleanse herself as well of the impurity of the idol worship that prevailed there." By contrast, her attendants are loyal to the Pharaoh and try to persuade her to leave the Israelite baby to his fate: "Dost thou desire to transgress thy father's edict?" So God sends the angel Gabriel to silence their protests by burying them alive in the bowels of the earth.[69] To honor the Egyptian princess for her compassion, God dubs her Batya (or, in some versions, Bithia), a name that is understood to mean "daughter of God." At the end of her days, she is rewarded by God for her fidelity and courage. "Bithia never tasted death," the rabbis imagined, "being one of those who entered Paradise alive."[70]

The pious storytellers were moved to give God a more prominent role in the early life of Moses than what is actually reported in the Bible, but unless we persuade ourselves that God's hand is at work in the birth story of Moses, the biblical account forces us to ponder some troubling questions. Why would a mother cast her son into the waters of the Nile, even in the comfort of his little reed boat, thus placing the helpless infant at risk of drowning or worse? Was she resigned to his death? Philo did not even mention the boat of reeds in his retelling of the tale, and stated only that the mother and father of Moses "exposed their child on the banks of the river, and departed groaning and lamenting, pitying themselves for the necessity which had fallen upon them, and calling themselves the slayers and murderers of their child."[71] The parents of Moses, Philo seemed to suggest, simply condemned their child to death by exposure to the elements out of desperation and resignation.

Despite the fact that the ancients commonly resorted to the exposure of unwanted children as a means of population control, neither theologians nor scholars can bring themselves to entertain the notion that the parents of Moses were simply trying to kill him. "Hebrew parents do not willingly expose their children," Childs points out.[72] The explanation that has been embraced by both Jewish and Christian apologists over the centuries is that the parents of Moses were placing their faith and trust in God even though nothing had been heard from or about him for nearly four centuries. "It is better to expose the child and entrust its fate to Providence, than let our secret be discovered and the boy seized and put to death," Amram says of the decision to cast Moses adrift in the Nile in one rabbinical tale. "The ways of the Lord are many, and He, in His mercy, will protect the child and fulfill the prophecy concerning him."[73]

But the Bible describes the world into which Moses was born as a cold and dangerous place where babies are not always protected by divine providence, a strikingly modern landscape that resembles the death camp at Auschwitz, the killing fields of Cambodia, the body-littered villages of Bosnia, Rwanda, and Algeria. "The grim reality is that even when redemption finally comes, it is accompanied, not by the heroic martyrdom of the brave partisan, but by the senseless murder of children," writes Brevard Childs. "The salvation promised by God is not greeted by a waiting world, but opposed with the hysterical fanaticism which borders on madness."[74] Only the courage and compassion of the women around Moses preserved him from the deadly effects of that madness.

"BECAUSE I DREW HIM OUT OF THE WATER"

The Egyptian princess who came upon the curious sight of a baby in a basket on the waters of the Nile was a pampered and privileged young woman, the daughter of a king who was regarded as a god, a highborn woman who was surrounded, day and night, by a small army of courtiers who attended to her every need and her every whim. One would have thought she would shun a bawling baby who required such urgent attention and tender care, a baby under a sentence of death issued by her own father—and yet her heart was filled with not just compassion but high ambition for the boy-child. Then and there, the princess resolved to spare the infant's life, to keep him and raise him as a child of her own, to shelter the condemned slave baby within the court of Pharaoh. The nameless foundling, she vowed, would become a prince of Egypt.

We do not know what the "goodly child" was called by his own father and mother before he was rescued from the Nile and renamed by the daughter of Pharaoh, but surely his Israelite parents called him *something*. One story told in the Midrash insists that Amram names his son Tobia, which means "God is good,"[75] but rabbinical legend and lore provide us with plenty of other possibilities. In these accounts he is known by his father as Heber (meaning "reunited") and by his mother as Jekuthiel ("because I set my hope upon God, and He gave him back to me"). His sister calls him Jered ("because she had 'descended' to the stream to ascertain his fate"), and his brother calls him Abi Zanoah ("because his father, who had 'cast off' his mother, had taken her back"). His grandfather dubs him Abi Gedor ("because the Heavenly Father had 'built up' the breach in Israel when He rescued him"), and his nurse refers to him as Abi Soco ("because he had been kept concealed in a 'tent' for three months"). And the people of Israel call him Shemaiah ben Nathanel, "because in his day he would 'hear' the sighs of the people, and deliver them from their oppressors, and through him would He 'give' them His own law."[76]

The name bestowed upon the slave baby by the Egyptian princess comes down to us as "Moses" in English translations that derive from an early Greek version of the Bible. But the original Hebrew text gives the name as *Mosheh*, which resembles the word-fragment (*mose*) used in the language of ancient Egypt to name a child who was born on the anniversary of a particular god; the name of the pharaoh Thutmose, for example, means "The god Thoth is born" and refers to the deity in the Egyptian pantheon who was imagined to serve as a celestial scribe.[77] Some say that "Moses" is a "bilingual pun" that faintly echoes the Hebrew word *masheh*, which means "to draw out." And that is precisely the meaning ascribed to the name by the biblical author.[78]

"And she called his name Moses," the Bible reports (Exod. 2:10), "and said: 'Because I drew him out of the water.' "

Chapter Three

A PRINCE OF EGYPT

And the child unlucky in his little State,
Some hearth where freedom is excluded,
A hive whose honey is fear and worry,
Feels calmer now and somehow assured of escape. . . .
   —W. H. AUDEN, "IN MEMORY OF
   SIGMUND FREUD"

The daughter of Pharaoh readily accepted the Israelite girl's offer of a wet-nurse from the same tribe as the foundling child himself. Clearly the princess did not try to fool herself into believing that she had come across an abandoned baby of Egyptian blood. "Why, it is a little Hebrew boy," she said as soon as she laid eyes on Moses (Exod. 2:6 NEB). Once she heard the helpful suggestion of the young woman who appeared by the river so suddenly and so conveniently—"Shall I go and call thee a nurse of the Hebrew women?"—the princess did not hesitate to take advantage of the offer. "Go," said Pharaoh's daughter, and the young girl promptly fetched back the mother of the foundling to serve as a wet-nurse (Exod. 2:7–8).

Pharaoh's daughter accepts the services of a Hebrew wet-nurse because the slave baby refuses to suckle from the breast of the Egyptian woman recruited for the same duty, or so says a tale from the rabbinical literature that was told for weighty politico-theological reasons. God prompts Moses to reject the breast of an Egyptian in favor of an Israelite precisely because he has already decided that the slave baby will be called upon to play a crucial role in the destiny of the Israelites. "The Lord had so ordained it that none of the women of Egypt could boast afterwards of having been the nurse of the Elect of the Eternal,"[1] goes the old rabbinical tale. "Nor was the mouth destined to speak with God to draw nourishment from the unclean body of an Egyptian woman."[2]

In fact, the bargain struck by the princess and the slave girl conforms to the common practice of the ancient Near East. Archaeologists have retrieved boilerplate contracts from distant antiquity in which the legal rights of professional wet-nurses were set forth in detail, and in at least one recorded case, the baby was turned over to the wet-nurse when the birth mother failed to pay the agreed-upon wages![3] And so, when the slave girl returned with a careworn woman dressed in the distinctive garb of an Israelite, the princess was curt and businesslike toward the sole applicant for the job of nursing her adoptive son. "And Pharaoh's daughter said unto her: 'Take this child away, and nurse it for me, and I will give thee thy wages.' And the woman took the child, and nursed it." (Exod. 2:9)

PRINCELING

So Moses was suddenly returned to the slave quarters where he had been born, now as the adoptive grandson of the king of Egypt, perhaps even a future pharaoh himself. No longer at risk from Pharaoh's decree of death by drowning, he was entitled to all the privileges and prerogatives of a princeling of royal blood. Tradition suggests that Moses spent two years in the custody of his birth family (although the Bible nowhere discloses that the daughter of Pharaoh realized that the Hebrew wet-nurse was actually the foundling's mother), and then he was reclaimed by his adoptive mother.

"When the child was old enough," the Bible reports, "she brought him to Pharaoh's daughter, who adopted him and called him Moses." (Exod. 2:10 NEB)

Here, as elsewhere, the Bible raises many more questions than it answers. Not until Moses was returned to Pharaoh's daughter by his mother was he given the name by which he is known in the Bible and down through history. So what did Jochebed call him? The ancient rabbis, as we have already seen, bestowed a great many names on the child—his mother calls him Jekuthiel, his father calls him Heber, his sister calls him Jered, and so on[4]—but the Bible itself is utterly silent on the question, and nowhere are we told that his own mother and father ever knew him as Moses.

One of the paradoxes of the biblical text is that the name bestowed upon Moses is a pun—but, as we have seen, it is a pun in the Hebrew language, the tongue of his birth parents, and not in the ancient Egyptian language, the tongue of his adoptive mother and grandfather. The Bible tells us that Pharaoh's daughter called the child Mosheh—a Hebrew word that was rendered as "Moses" in the first Greek translation of the Bible and later in various English translations—and that she chose the name "because I drew him out of the water." (Exod: 2:10) Thus, the biblical author credits the daughter of Pharaoh with knowledge of the language spoken by the enslaved Israelites and suggests that "Mosheh" derives from the Hebrew word *masheh*, which means "to draw out."

In their retelling of the tale, Philo and Josephus ignored the biblical explanation of the naming of Moses and instead suggested that his name was derived from an Egyptian word for water (*mos*), "from what had happened when he was put into the river."[5] They came a bit closer to the truth of the matter by identifying his name as Egyptian, but all of these explanations were wrong. The name chosen by Pharaoh's daughter for her Israelite son is a common Egyptian name—or at least a fragment of one—and it identified the child who carried the name with one of the gods in the Egyptian pantheon. As we shall see, the authentic Egyptian origin of the name of Moses is seen by some scholars as evidence that Moses was a man of flesh and blood who was born and raised in Egypt just as the Bible suggests.

THE WONDROUS CHILD

The intelligentsia of ancient Rome, which embraced the ideals of Hellenistic culture and conveyed them throughout the classical world, simply could not understand a saga in which the apparent hero was not exactly heroic. So the Jewish sages and scholars who explained the stories of the Hebrew Bible to a readership throughout the Roman Empire were reluctant to admit that the Bible depicts the newborn Moses as a mewling infant born to a couple of Israelite slaves. The best examples of the Hellenistic makeover of Moses are the works of Philo of Alexandria and Flavius Josephus; these authors dressed up Moses in the mantle of a classical Greek hero to make him more palatable to their ancient readers, and in so doing, they changed forever how we perceive the figure of Moses.

Both Philo and Josephus understood that the flawed and troubled mortal who is depicted in the Bible would not impress a reader accustomed to the deities and heroes of Greek and Roman mythology, and so they insisted on presenting Moses as "the greatest and most perfect man that ever lived," as Philo put it.[6] Like other Bible commentators of late antiquity and the early Middle Ages, Philo and Josephus felt at liberty to tamper with Holy Writ, leaving out the awkward or off-putting incidents, tinkering and tampering with the text to suit their rhetorical purposes, and adding a great many colorful and tantalizing details that appear nowhere in the Bible. Indeed, it is likely that both Philo and Josephus were drawing upon the same rich tradition of biblical exegesis that can be found in abundance in the major anthologies of rabbinical commentary, the Talmud and the Midrash.

The Bible does not tell us, for example, what Moses actually looked like. But the Hellenistic tradition dictated that a hero ought to be blessed with perfection of both body and mind. So Josephus, when describing the birth of Moses, insisted that "the wondrous child" embodied the ideal qualities that the pagan readers of the ancient world expected to find in one destined to greatness.

"And as for his beauty, there was nobody so unpolite as, when they saw Moses, they were not greatly surprised at the beauty of his countenance," Josephus gushed. "[N]ay, it happened frequently, that those that met him as he was carried along the road, were obliged to turn again upon seeing the child . . . and stood a great while to look on him; for the beauty of the child was so remarkable and natural . . . that it detained the spectators, and made them stay longer to look upon him."[7]

Indeed, Moses was seen by the ancient storytellers as the answer to the prayers of suffering humanity in general and one suffering woman in particular. Pharaoh's daughter, dubbed Thermutis by Josephus and Bithia (or Batya) in the rabbinical literature, is presented as a childless woman who longs for a son of her own, and the sight of baby Moses bobbing on the waters of the Nile is interpreted by Bithia as a divine response to her yearnful prayers. Still, Pharaoh's daughter recognizes that her father might not feel quite so benign toward a Hebrew foundling, and so, according to Philo, she feigns a pregnancy, resorting to "all sorts of contrivances to increase the apparent bulk of her belly, so that he might be looked upon as her own genuine child," and when Moses is returned to her by his real mother, she sends word to her father that she has given birth to a son.[8]

As it turns out, the princess need not have worried, at least according to another tale told by the sages, because Pharaoh himself falls under the same thrall that Moses exerts on all who behold him. Although his adoptive mother keeps him hidden from Pharaoh's eyes at first, by the time Moses is three years old she can no longer resist the temptation to show off her foster son. "My royal Father! Before thy assembled court I confess that this child of such wondrous beauty and noble mind is not my own son," she says as she reveals the true origin of the foundling and boldly places the child in the arms of Pharaoh. "Through the bounty of the River Nile I have received him as a precious gift, and I have adopted him as my son, so that he may one day inherit thy throne and kingdom."[9]

Here we come to yet another moment of terrible peril for young Moses. By her frank confession, the princess gives reason enough for Pharaoh to conclude that the foundling is one of the Hebrew babies whom he ordered to be drowned in the Nile. But Pharaoh does not respond to his daughter's confession by summoning the palace guard and ordering the death of his adoptive grandson. Rather, Pharaoh falls under the same spell that seems to affect everyone who lays eyes on young Moses. "Attracted by the magnetic beauty of Moses," the tale goes on, "he took the child, kissed and hugged it, keeping it close to his breast."[10]

The Bible reveals nothing at all about the experiences of Moses as a child or an adolescent in the court of Pharaoh—one moment we see him as a suckling, a slave baby at risk of his life, the next moment as a fully grown man, a prince of Egypt. But a powerful irony can be detected in the legend and lore offered by the ancients to fill in the blanks of the biblical narrative. Moses, the doomed child of despised slaves, is suddenly the adoptive grandson and heir apparent of Pharaoh. The oracle that condemned so many Israelite babies to death seemed to be fulfilling itself: Moses, it now appeared, would someday seat himself on the throne and wear the beehive crown of the king of Egypt.

"WHAT SHALL BE DONE TO THIS EVIL CHILD?"

Tradition imagines a fateful day in the royal court of Egypt when young Moses betrays his own destiny to his adoptive grandfather with nearly fatal consequences. The tale first appeared in the writings of Josephus, then found its way into the Midrash, and eventually earned a cherished place in countless sermons and Sunday school lessons—but this charming fairy tale appears nowhere in the Bible.

Pharaoh's daughter is dandling the toddler on her lap as she sits between her father and mother at the high table where the royal court has assembled. Around them sit the princes of the realm and the royal counselors, including the wizard Balaam and his two sons, and Pharaoh wears the bejeweled crown of gold that symbolizes his might and power. The crown catches the eye of young Moses, and to the shock of the gathered courtiers, no less than of the princess and Pharaoh himself, the child playfully seizes the crown and places it on his own head in mimicry of his grandfather. Then he clumsily knocks the crown off his head and giggles with delight as the pretty thing falls to the floor and rolls away. According to an even more elaborate version of the tale, Moses hops down from his mother's lap, scurries to the fallen crown, and tramples it underfoot, all to the horror of Pharaoh and the royal court.

"Great was the dismay of the King and his counsellors," goes the tale. "Such an action on the part of the child could only augur evil to the King and the safety of the realm."[11]

Balaam sees in the playful young Moses the very child who had been identified in a dream of Pharaoh's as the dread enemy of Egypt, and he regards the child's impudent gesture as a willful act of defiance and scorn. "Remember, O king, that this child is one of the Hebrew race, and, endowed with more wisdom and cunning than other children of his age, he has acted with deliberation and purposely," Balaam warns Pharaoh. "The day will come, O King, when this evil child will tear the crown from thy head and enslave thy people."

Balaam hastens to offer the same suggestion he had given once before: "My advice, therefore, is to slay him at once and thus save Egypt from perdition."[12] But Pharaoh, perhaps mindful of the passion of his beloved daughter for young Moses, is not quite ready to take off the head of his adoptive grandchild. Rather, he resorts to the dillydallying that we will later come to see as a common characteristic of the Egyptian monarchs. He summons all of the noblemen of Egypt to his court, all of the wizards and wise men, and puts a question to them. "What is your opinion, O my counsellors," Pharaoh asks, "and what shall be done to this evil child who has taken the royal crown from our head and trampled it underfoot?"[13]

From the very first caucus, Pharaoh's counselors agree with Balaam that the child ought to be put to death, and they debate among themselves only as to the proper means of execution. Some argue for the quick and merciful stroke of a sword across the child's neck; others insist on a slow death by fire. Before the matter can be decided, however, God intervenes by placing among the noisy crowd of princes and soothsayers an emissary of his own who poses as one of Pharaoh's faithful courtiers. Some versions of the story cast the Midianite priest named Jethro, future father-in-law of Moses, in the role of heavenly rescuer, but the job was more commonly assigned by traditional storytellers to the archangel Gabriel, who is said to have taken "the shape and form of an old man and mingled with the counsellors of Pharaoh."[14]

"Do not listen, O King, to the advice of thy counsellors to slay the child," says the mysterious old man to Pharaoh. "It will be innocent blood that thou wilt shed, for this child is still young and . . . knows not what he is doing."[15]

The old man comes up with a remarkable proposal of his own. To determine whether young Moses acted with ill will and evil intent in snatching the crown from Pharaoh's head, the emissary suggests an ingenious test. Bring two bowls and place them before the child, he proposes, one filled with lustrous gold and sparkling jewels, the other filled with red-hot coals. The child's guilt or innocence would be determined by whether he reaches for the bowl of treasure or the bowl of fire.

"We shall then see whether the child is wiser than befits his age," the old man explains. "If he stretches out his hand and takes the gold and precious stones, then he is certainly endowed with wisdom and understanding beyond his years—he must have acted with design [and] therefore deserves death. But if he grasps the live coals, then his action therefore was only the result of a childish fancy and he is innocent."[16]

The test appeals to Pharaoh, and Balaam sees no point in protesting. At Pharaoh's command, the two bowls are prepared and brought forth and placed on the cold stone floor where young Moses now sits in curious silence. The child's eye falls on the bowls and their sparkling contents. And, sure enough, Moses makes his choice—he leans forward and reaches out with one plump hand as the others watch in tense silence.

Gabriel watches, too, and he sees that young Moses is reaching for the bowl of jewels. If the child grasps one of the gemstones, he will be put to death. So the spectral essence of the angel leaves the body of the old man, as the tale goes, and flashes across the room to the place where Moses sits. Silently and invisibly, Gabriel takes the hand of Moses in his own astral hand, guiding it away from the jewels and instead placing it over the bowl of coals. The child's fingers close around one large chunk of coal that burns red hot. Moses drops the coal, cries out in pain, and brings his burned fingers to his mouth to soothe the scorched flesh. But a few glowing embers cling to the hand of Moses, and so Moses burns his lips and tongue when he thrusts his fingers into his mouth.

"For all of his life, he became slow of speech and of a slow tongue," the rabbis paused to explain, referring to the infirmity of Moses that is disclosed in the Bible.

Still, the wound serves its purpose for now: Moses is proven to be innocent, and his life is spared once again. From that day, the storytellers assure us, young Moses is safe from Pharaoh: "God Himself turned the king's mind to grace."[17]

But the counselors of the king are less impressed by the ambiguous results of the test of the two bowls, and they continue to regard the child with suspicion. His adoptive mother, who understands all too well how a jealous courtier might work his will in subtle ways, resolves to distance herself and Moses from the palace and its crowd of schemers. She shelters him in her own quarters, according to tradition, and attends to the task of preparing him to one day occupy her father's throne.

SACRED CHARACTERS AND
SECRET KNOWLEDGE

The tutelage of young Moses in the court of Pharaoh is not described in the Hebrew Bible, but a single line from the New Testament offers the intriguing suggestion that he was initiated into the arcane and exotic mysteries of ancient Egypt, a notion that subtly but powerfully transforms our idea of Moses from a simple and pious figure into something of a magus.

Moses was learned in all the wisdom of the Egyptians, and was mighty in words and in deeds. (Acts 7:22 KJV)

The same intriguing notion appears in the writings of Philo and Josephus, who may have been contemporaries of Jesus of Nazareth, and in the rabbinical legend and lore that began to accumulate during their lifetimes. "Bithia spared no costs to have her foster-son educated as befitted a royal prince," goes one account. "His masters instructed him in the vast learning and wisdom of the Egyptians, so that the boy soon surpassed all his masters in learning and knowledge."[18]

Tutors are summoned from across Egypt and its neighboring lands and even distant Greece, according to Philo, although he insisted that the Greeks agree to travel to Egypt only because they are lured by "the temptation of large presents."[19] Elsewhere in the ancient world, rumors of the gifted child who has been born into the family of Pharaoh prompt scholars and scientists to make their way to Egypt on their own initiative and freely offer their services. Thus is Moses initiated into not only the arcana of ancient Egypt—"the philosophy which is contained in symbols," as Philo put it, "which they exhibit in those sacred characters [called] hieroglyphics"—but also in arithmetic and geometry, art and music, Assyrian literature and Chaldean astronomy, "and the whole science of rhythm and harmony and metre."[20] Moses masters the language of each of the seventy nations that were thought to compose the ancient world. Ironically, the boy's chief tutors were imagined by the rabbis to have been Jannes and Jambres, sons of the bloodthirsty Balaam.

Moses is a preternaturally gifted student who "acquired knowledge so easily that it seemed as if he were only recalling to his mind instruction which he had already learned before."[21] His heart and mind seem to spontaneously reject all notions of evil, and he disciplines himself to lead a life of purity and simplicity amid the opulence of the royal palace: "The luxurious life at the court of Egypt offered the young foster-son of the princess many temptations, but Moses persistently refused to be lured by pleasures and sin," goes a tale in the Midrash. "Upon his brow he wore the royal diadem, but his heart was full of noble and pure sentiments, and great thoughts filled his mind."[22]

Here, again, is the pure and pristine Moses who was offered to the Greco-Roman world as a godly man and perhaps even a god himself. "He conquered all the passions to which idle youth, reared in opulence and luxury, will easily fall prey," goes one tale, "so that all his friends . . . readily believed that the soul of the young Hebrew was not human, but divine, and that even his body was composed of divine elements." According to the Hellenistic version of the life of Moses, which found its lushest expression in the writings of Philo and Josephus, "Moses never lived or acted like other mortals, for he excelled all men in noble and elevated sentiments."[23]

Philo, for example, showed Moses as a near-ascetic who eats sparingly of the rich, exotic, and abundant footstuffs offered to Pharaoh and his family at the royal banquet table—"For he never provided his stomach with any luxuries beyond those necessary tributes which nature has appointed to be paid to it"—and, "as to the pleasures of the organs below the stomach," he stoically ignores any spasm of sexual yearning that he might experience, "except as far as the object of having legitimate children was concerned." As a young man, Moses does not allow "his youthful passions to roam at large without restraint," Philo assured his readers, despite the fact that life in the royal palace offers him "ten thousand incentives" for indulging in pleasures of the flesh. Moses is "a practiser of abstinence and self-denial," Philo concluded, and he feeds the appetites of his heart and soul but never his body, "being above all men inclined to ridicule a life of effeminacy and luxury."[24]

Still, even some of the most adoring texts seem to hold out the possibility that Moses experienced the lusts and longings of an ordinary man. Even Philo suggested that Prince Moses, so strong and so handsome, finds it necessary to suppress his own carnal appetites "by force," as if to acknowledge that Moses is not only a flesh-and-blood creature but a hot-blooded one.[25] A certain subtle dissidence can be read between the lines of the otherwise pious texts, a faint notion that something less than divine might be found in the innermost nature of Moses. The very notion that Moses was adept in the arcane mysteries of the ancient world suggests he was a magic-worker rather than a strict monotheist. Not a few propagandists throughout the Roman Empire, as we shall see, openly attacked Moses as a traitor, a charlatan, and a leper-king.

A certain revisionism toward Moses can be detected in the Bible itself, the traces of an anti-Moses tradition that insinuated itself into Holy Writ. The biblical authors were willing to depict Moses as a man with unfortunate and sometimes even catastrophic flaws and failings, a neurotic and a depressive, a wounded healer and a weary prophet. God displayed a punitive and even murderous rage toward Moses on more than one occasion and, as we shall see, judged him to be unworthy of his most cherished ambition in life. For the moment, however, the countertradition only hints at the moral flaws of young Moses when we are told that "he constantly strove to conquer all of his passions and evil inclinations and to lead a life of virtue and purity."[26] Only much later in the life of Moses will we find him openly accused of treachery by the unruly Israelites and, still later, by God himself.

MOSES AND MONOTHEISM

Some eighteen centuries after Josephus and Philo, another Jewish author came along to reinterpret the life of Moses and make him over in a new and startling image. Sigmund Freud, the celebrated founder of psychoanalysis, was also a fan of Moses and something of an amateur Bible critic. He indulged both of his passions in a curious intellectual enterprise titled *Moses and Monotheism*, a work that scandalized Bible scholars of his era no less than his theories of human sexuality outraged his fellow practitioners of medicine and psychology.

Freud pointed out that the prince abandoned by his kingly father and raised by paupers is a common theme in fable and folklore around the world. Thanks to Freud himself, the most familiar of all these stories is the ancient Greek myth of Oedipus, who is exposed to the elements and left to die by order of his father, the king of Thebes, and is then rescued by a peasant who delivers the infant to the foster family that raises him. Elements of the same birth saga can be found in other myths and legends, including those of Amphion, Cyrus, Gilgamesh, Heracles, Karna, Romulus, Paris, Perseus, Telephos, and Zethos, according to a list compiled by Freud himself.[27]

Yet as Freud himself delighted in pointing out, the biblical account of Moses differs from the myth of Oedipus and other foundling princes in one crucial detail: Moses is a mirror image of Oedipus, a pauper raised as a prince. Rather than being born into a noble family and then raised in "a humble and degraded one," as was Oedipus, Moses is born into a slave family and raised in the palace of Pharaoh.[28] And Freud, who was apparently unsettled by the notion that such an exalted man might have started out in life as a slave, fashioned a startling and intentionally provocative argument to explain the reversal of roles in the birth story of Moses. "The man Moses, the liberator and lawgiver of the Jewish people," Freud proposed, "was not a Jew,* but an Egyptian."[29]

Freud argued that the Bible embodies a crude rewrite of the life story of Moses by the Israelites who adopted him as their political leader: " 'National motives' had transformed the myth into the form now known by us."[30] The real Moses was a highborn Egyptian, he insisted, "perhaps indeed a member of the royal house," who was converted to monotheism during the reign of the pharaoh Akhenaton, an authentic revolutionary who abolished the worship of the traditional gods and goddesses in the fourteenth century B.C.E. and decreed that all of Egypt must worship the sun-god Aton as the one and only god. Akhenaton and his queen, Nefertiti, established a pristine new capital in the splendid isolation of a place called El-Amarna in order to purify the spiritual practices of Egypt, but they managed to alienate and infuriate the traditional priesthood with their religious innovations. After their deaths, the pharaoh and his queen were condemned by their successors, their new capital was abandoned to the desert sands, their statues and monuments were defaced, and the old gods were restored.

According to Freud, Moses survived the purge that followed the death of Akhenaton and Nefertiti. The renegade Egyptian prince did not give up his own secret ambition—to gather his own followers, establish himself as their king, and teach them a revolutionary new faith that recognized only a single all-powerful god. But Moses would not make the same mistake as Akhenaton. "The dreamer [Akhenaton] had estranged himself from his people," Freud wrote. "Moses . . . conceived the plan of founding a new empire, of finding a new people, to whom he could give the religion that Egypt disdained." When Moses considered the available resources for nation building in ancient Egypt, he settled on the enslaved people of Israel—a leaderless mob of unruly Semites living in appalling misery who might welcome the attentions of a well-

---

*The description of Moses as a "Jew" is inaccurate and anachronistic. Moses is described as a member of the tribe of Levi—one of the twelve tribes of ancient Israel—and so he is properly identified as a Levite or an Israelite. "Jew" is a term derived from the tribe of Judah and refers to the descendants of the tribe who survived the invasions, conquests, and dispersions that resulted in the destruction of ten of the twelve tribes. Freud apparently described Moses as a Jew because he recognized that Moses is embraced by the Jewish people as its greatest prophet and teacher.

meaning Egyptian aristocrat like himself. "These he chose to be his new people," Freud asserted. "A historic decision!"[31]

The audacious proposal that Moses was born an Egyptian prince and not an Israelite slave—and that his single greatest innovation, the idea of ethical monotheism, was borrowed from a pagan king—is hardly the most startling argument in *Moses and Monotheism*. The founder of psychoanalysis accused the Israelites of committing an outrage of mythic proportions against Moses, and he claimed to have found the evidence of their crime in the pages of the Bible. As we shall come to see, Freud proposed that there were *two* men named Moses in the history of ancient Israel, and one of them was murdered to make way for the other. Not surprisingly, none of Freud's arguments met with much enthusiasm from Bible scholars when he first proposed them, and they are now dismissed as the eccentricities of a dabbler. "That a scholar of so much importance in his own field as Sigmund Freud could permit himself to issue so unscientific a work, based on groundless hypotheses, is regrettable," sniffs Martin Buber, a towering moral philosopher of the mid-twentieth century and, not incidentally, an accomplished Bible scholar and translator in his own right.[32]

Freud's impulse to debunk the Bible and rewrite the life story of Moses might best be understood in psychoanalytic terms. Moses was (and is) a commanding figure in Judaeo-Christian tradition, and Freud's effort to topple him from his pedestal rings with the Oedipal urge that Freud himself studied and celebrated. And the perverse scenario offered by Freud, which can be read as a calculated insult to the most cherished belief in Jewish tradition, reveals something unsettling about his discomfort with his own identity—Freud was a Jewish physician who sought to attract adherents who were not Jewish in the belief that psychoanalysis would be dismissed as a "Jewish science" if the movement were identified with Jewish practitioners. "I almost say that only [Carl Jung's] appearance has saved psychoanalysis from the danger of becoming a Jewish national concern," he wrote of Jung, "a Christian and the son of a pastor," whom he anointed as his "crown prince" in the years before their famous falling-out, rather like Moses naming Joshua as his successor on the threshold of the Promised Land.[33]

Freud was hardly the first or only commentator to suggest that Moses lifted his revolutionary notions of God from the ancient Egyptians or that he was an Egyptian himself.[34] In fact, Freud was echoing a

notion that can be found in the writings of some of the earliest propagandists in the long and sorry history of anti-Semitism—the Egyptian
chronicler Manetho, who insisted that Moses was a renegade Egyptian priest and the self-appointed king over a leper colony, characterized
the exalted struggle for liberation that we know as the Exodus as a matter of eliminating a threat to public health in ancient Egypt: "[W]hen
the Egyptians had been exposed to the scab and to a skin infection, and
had been warned by an oracle, they expelled [Moses] together with the
sick people beyond the confines of Egypt lest the disease should spread
to a greater number of people."[35]

The same ancient libel against Moses found its way into the work of
other polemicists in the Hellenistic world, and both Philo and Josephus
attested to his origins as an authentic Israelite in a conscious effort to
repudiate the slanderous attacks on a revered figure in Judaism. To the
extent that Moses was raised and tutored in the ways of ancient Egypt,
they implied, the experience was a seduction and a corruption—and it
would take the ordeal of forty years in the wilderness of Sinai to purge
Moses and the Israelites of the evil influences of their former slave-
masters.

IMPURE AND WICKED WAYS

The author of Genesis hardly notices the faith of ancient Egypt or the
ritual practices of its kings, all of whom are depicted as good-hearted
and generous of spirit. But the pharaohs whom we encounter in the
Book of Exodus are meant to be seen as villains, and none quite so villainous as the one who sought to kill Moses and then ended up as his
foster grandfather. As limned by the author of Exodus and the storytellers who elaborated upon the biblical text, the pharaohs were vain
and heartless idolators, befuddled by crude superstition and a childish
reverence for idols of mute stone, so focused on life after death that they
were blind to human suffering on earth.[36] To hear the ancients tell it,
the whole of Egypt was tainted with "the impurity and wicked ways
practised by the King and his suite."[37]

At first glance, the fearful picture that we find in biblical sources appears to be confirmed by the vast accumulation of funerary objects that
have been excavated from the sands of Egypt and placed on display in
museums all over the world—richly embellished mummy cases and sar-

cophagi of polished black basalt, linen-wrapped corpses of the kings who were buried in them, and highly ornamented canopic jars in which were placed the royal viscera, the intestines in a jar decorated with the dog-headed Hapi, the liver and gallbladder in a jar capped with the hawk-headed Kebhsnaup. Long before the Bible was written, the Book of the Dead was a revered text in ancient Egypt, and a papyrus copy was placed in even the humblest tomb. The impression we are given by these relics is that every day of life was lived in solemn anticipation of death.

"It is from these that we are enabled to form an opinion of the character of the Egyptians," wrote Sir J. Gardner Wilkinson, a nineteenth-century Egyptologist. "They have been pronounced serious, gloomy people, saddened by the habit of abstruse speculation. . . ."[38]

But the archaeological record suggests that ancient Egypt was hardly the seething pit of darkness that is depicted in biblical legend and lore. Quite in contrast to the stern-faced pharaohs and their consorts carved in austere black basalt, the ancient Egyptians delighted in arts and crafts rendered in bright and even gaudy colors, and flowers were especially cherished. Buried along with the dead kings, for example, were some of the cheerful artifacts of daily life—a child's doll, a toy mouse, a pair of colorful clay balls, a board game called Snake. The scenes painted on the tombs reveal that Egypt gloried in its own vigor and vitality: the land of the pharaohs was an affluent, bustling, and cosmopolitan place, a thriving center of international commerce and diplomacy that attracted caravaners and emissaries from all over the ancient world, a bountiful land whose abundant produce made it a place of refuge during times of famine just as the Bible suggests.

Even the cult of death emphasized the crucial importance of right living. The theology of ancient Egypt imagined that a dead man or woman would be weighed on the scales of justice at the threshold of the netherworld—a scene that is frequently depicted in the Book of the Dead and other ancient sources. On one side of the scales is the heart of the deceased, which was understood to contain all of his deeds, good and bad; on the other side is a feather that symbolized the goddess of truth and justice, Maat. If the heart outweighed the feather, the deceased would be promptly dispatched by the crocodile Ammit, who was the Devourer of the Dead. If the feather outweighed the heart, the deceased would be welcomed into the heavenly precincts of the Field of Reeds by the god of the netherworld, Osiris.

"Justice is the great gift of God," goes an aphorism from a book of wisdom that comes down to us from ancient Egypt. "[H]e gives it to him whom he chooses."[39]

Still, the biblical account of the life of Moses persists in presenting Egypt as a place of unrelieved darkness and despair. "The Hebrew Moses of the Bible has kept an image of Egypt alive in the Western tradition that was thoroughly antithetic to Western ideals," writes contemporary Egyptologist Jan Assmann, "the image of Egypt as the land of despotism, hubris, sorcery, brute-worship, and idolatry."[40] One of the cherished assumptions of historians and theologians alike is the idea that Moses worked a revolution in the history of human faith when he rejected the funerary cult that so fascinated the ancient Egyptians. "[I]n spite of the omnipresent mystery of death," writes Gerhard von Rad, "Israel . . . deprived the dead and the grave of every sacral quality." As we shall see, Moses would promulgate a code of law that regarded contact with corpses as a corruption and a theology that had nothing at all to say about an afterlife. "This was a great achievement!" enthuses von Rad, "an achievement that it is wholly reasonable to attribute to Moses himself."[41] If Moses mastered "all the wisdom of the Egyptians," as the New Testament reports, he was so thoroughly repelled by what he had learned that he insisted on purging himself and his people of any trace of their death-obsessed ways.

WHAT THE DRAGOMAN SAID

The best evidence that Moses is a historical figure, according to the arguments of pious scholarship,* is found in the way the archaeological leavings of ancient Egypt are reflected in the Hebrew Bible. The arrival of Abraham and his clan in Egypt during a time of famine and the same journey undertaken by Jacob and his sons are echoed in reports of border crossings by Semitic tribes that can be found in ancient archives. A nobleman might entrust his household to a factotum just

---

*By "pious" (or "devout") scholarship, I mean the work of Bible scholars who embrace the teachings of their religion (whether Judaism, Christianity, or Islam) and thus treat the Bible as Holy Writ, as opposed to secular scholars who regard the Bible as a work of human authorship that is appropriately studied from a literary, historical, anthropological, or other academic approach. Some scholars, of course, would say they use both approaches at the same time.

as Potiphar did when he purchased Joseph from a band of slave-traders. Just as Joseph's dream of seven cows was understood to mean seven years, the hieroglyph for "cow" was used in some Egyptian inscriptions to indicate "year." The pharaohs routinely delegated the governance of Egypt to men who held the same royal office to which Pharaoh later elevated Joseph, and the badges of high office that symbolized Joseph's authority, a signet ring and a golden chain, can be spotted in tomb paintings. Among the high-ranked courtiers of ancient Egypt were men from Asia Minor and beyond, and one source speaks of "the foreign rule of a Syrian." Even the span of life attributed to Joseph, 110 years, appears to reflect the numerological traditions of ancient Egypt.[42]

Some scholars point to the Egyptian names and titles that appear in the Bible as evidence of its accuracy and authenticity. The kings of ancient Egypt are called by their proper title, *pharaoh,* a term that derives from the Egyptian word for "great house" (*per-ao*) and refers to the palace where the kings lived and reigned. Several prominent Israelites who will figure importantly in the life of Moses, including Miriam, Phinehas, and Hur, are thought to bear Egyptian names; Phinehas "was a very common Egyptian name in that period," writes the venerable Bible scholar W. F. Albright, "meaning 'the Negro' or 'the Nubian,' presumably given to a man because of mixed blood or swarthy complexion."[43]

Perhaps the most intriguing clue to the real origins of Moses is the name bestowed upon him by his adoptive mother: "And she called his name Moses [Mosheh], and said: 'Because I drew him out of the water.' " (Exod. 2:10) As we have already noted, the word-fragment *mose* is a common suffix in the names of ancient Egyptian kings. Curiously, the biblical author seems unaware of the Egyptian origin of the name and struggles to explain it by looking for a root meaning in the Hebrew language, as if to make the rather bizarre suggestion that the daughter of Pharaoh knew the tongue of the Israelite slaves and chose a Hebrew name for her adopted son. Or perhaps the biblical author knew full well that Moses carried an Egyptian name and sought to explain the name in terms that his original readers would understand. In either case, some credulous scholars concluded that the Egyptian origin of the name of Moses proves that the Egyptian setting of his life story is authentic.

Indeed, there was a time when it was argued that the biblical text and the archaeological record were sources of equal historical reliability—and each one supported the other. "[T]he frequent mention of the Egyptians in the Bible connects them with the Hebrew records," wrote an

Egyptologist in the mid-nineteenth century, "of which many satisfactory illustrations occur in the sculptures of Pharaonic times."[44] But the supposed touches of authenticity in the biblical text may be nothing more than an effort by the biblical author to dress up his biography of Moses by drawing on a limited and imperfect knowledge of ancient Egypt. For example, it is unlikely that the daughter of Pharaoh would leave the comforts of the palace and bathe in the waters of the Nile, which was even then a muddy and malodorous place where one might encounter crocodiles or worse; the aristocratic and affluent men and women of ancient Egypt preferred "the pleasure to be found in a well-tended garden, a pool, an arbour and the discreet attention of servants."[45] Nor is it likely that Pharaoh would have established his court in such close proximity to the slave quarters of the Israelites in the land of Goshen—after all, Goshen is believed to refer to a region near the delta of the Nile River, while perhaps 90 percent of all the archaeological evidence of ancient Eygpt comes from the distant region of Upper Egypt.[46]

Even the supposed linkages between the biblical text and the archaeological record raise more questions than they answer. For example, the name of the Syrian who served as chancellor to a queen of Egypt is found in a papyrus that dates from around 1200 B.C.E., centuries after the supposed life of Joseph. The investiture of Joseph with a ring, a robe, and a chain of gold corresponds more closely to the court rituals of Assyria in the eighth century B.C.E., and the practice may not have reached Egypt until a century or so later. The use of a cow to symbolize a unit of time is found no earlier than the reign of the Ptolemies, the successors to Alexander the Great, who brought Greek culture to Egypt at a time when the Bible was largely complete. Even the camels that supposedly carried Joseph to Egypt in a caravan of Midianites—or were they Ishmaelites?—are a gross anachronism in the biblical narrative, since camels were not domesticated and used as beasts of burden until centuries after the events depicted in the Bible. The tomb paintings of ancient Egypt that depict the arrival of caravans from Canaan show donkeys, not camels.[47]

Above all, the doubters wonder how the court historians of ancient Egypt, who were obsessive chroniclers of both the grand and the mundane, managed to overlook such crucial biblical events as the viziership of Joseph, the enslavement and attempted extermination of the Israelites, the mass exodus of the slave nation, the plagues that devastated Egypt and cost the lives of its firstborn, and the defeat of Pharaoh and his armies at the Red Sea. The ancient Egyptians preserved everything from fishhooks to toilet seats—but nowhere in the archaeological record are the events of the Exodus or the existence of a man called Moses ever mentioned.

By way of rebuttal to these skeptics, the argument has been made that the historical record keeping of ancient Egypt, which seems so rich and so abundant, is really quite spotty. "What is proudly advertised as Egyptian history," wrote Sir Alan Gardiner, an influential Egyptologist, "is merely a collection of rags and tatters."[48] The period of conquest and occupation by the Hyksos is a two hundred year blank in the otherwise rich historical record of ancient Egypt.[49] Even when they resumed their work, the chroniclers of ancient Egypt, who were court propagandists and not academic historians, were inclined to omit the more embarrassing moments in the otherwise glorious history of Egypt. For example, a battle between the armies of Ramses II against a Hittite army in the thirteenth century B.C.E. is recorded in temple carvings throughout Egypt as a glorious victory—a bit of propaganda-in-stone that "hoodwinked" countless generations of historians starting with Herodotus—and it was not until the discovery and translation of a Hittite account of the same battle that scholars were forced to conclude that the glorious victory was "probably no better than a shaky draw," if not a marginal victory by the Hittites.[50] So we are asked to believe that the scribes of ancient Egypt were instructed to leave out the events of the Exodus because they reflected so poorly on the prowess of Pharaoh and the power of Egypt.

But there is quite another explanation for the utter absence of archaeological evidence for the existence of Moses. The apparent richness of authentic detail in the biblical account, the revisionists have proposed, can be regarded as an artful but thin cover-up, the handiwork of a resourceful storyteller who knew just enough about the culture of Egypt to dress up his tale with a bit of local color. "It is all the sort of vague general knowledge," writes T. Eric Peet, an early twentieth century British archaeologist, "that any ancient tourist spending a few weeks in Egypt at almost any date after about 1600 B.C. might have acquired from his dragoman."*[51]

Indeed, an intriguing clue in the biblical text suggests the saga of

---

*"Dragoman" is a term used in the Near East to describe an interpreter, especially one who translates the Arabic, Turkish, or Persian languages.

Moses and the Exodus may have originated at a far more recent time and in a much different place than what we are given to understand by a couple of millennia of pious scholarship. The clue is to be found in one of the most familiar details of the biblical account: the Egyptians, we are told by the biblical author, pressed the Israelite slaves into making bricks out of mud and straw.

The biblical account of the oppression of the Israelites appears to be corroborated in one often-reproduced tomb painting from ancient Egypt in which the making of mud bricks by a gang of slaves is depicted in explicit detail. The ancient muralist depicted the drawing of water from a pool, the kneading of clay with short hoes, the casting of bricks in wooden molds laid out to dry in the sun, and the finished bricks being carried off to some construction site, all under the watchful eye of taskmasters armed with rods or whips. "These scenes illumine the story of how the Hebrews made 'bricks without straw' during their oppression in Egypt," insists Bible historian Bernhard W. Anderson.[52]

Now it is perfectly true that mud bricks were commonly used in Egypt for humble constructions such as private houses and even for some of the earliest and most primitive pyramids—indeed, the modern word "adobe" is derived from the Egyptian language. But the fact remains that the monumental architecture of the pharaohs, the pyramids and obelisks and statuary that were already emblematic of ancient Egypt during the lifetime of the ancient historian Herodotus, were fashioned out of stone, not bricks. As we shall come to see, the notion that an army of slaves was put to work making crude bricks out of mud and straw in a country that gloried in constructions of quarried and dressed stone is a clue to the real authorship of the Bible and the authenticity of the man we call Moses.

The oldest fragments of the Bible may have been written down as early as 1000 B.C.E., but the Bible in its current form probably began to take shape during the long period of exile in Babylon during the sixth century B.C.E. When the Israelites first arrived in Babylon, they were reduced to raw grief—"By the rivers of Babylon, / There we sat down, yea, we wept, / When we remembered Zion" (Ps. 137:1)—but when they were finally permitted to return to the land of Israel, they carried "the torah of Moses," a set of sacred writings that probably consisted of "the full Torah—the Five Books of Moses—as we know it."[53] So it is possible that some scenes that supposedly describe the experience of the Israelites in bondage in ancient Egypt were, in fact, inspired by the much more recent experience of exile in Babylon, a place where stone was scarce and where, as a result, a humbler material was used to build the ziggurats and palaces for which it was so celebrated. As Will Durant observes, "there was no end to the making of bricks in Babylon."[54]

IN COLD BLOOD

The Bible is utterly silent on what happened to Moses from the day he was rescued from the Nile until the bloody encounter that prompted him to flee the court of Pharaoh once and for all. All we know from the biblical account is that baby Moses was plucked from the Nile by Pharaoh's daughter, farmed out to his birth mother for nursing and rearing, and then returned to his adoptive mother. The Bible picks up the story on the day when Moses, a grown man and a prince of Egypt, wandered out of the palace and came upon a scene that opened his eyes to the fate of his fellow Israelites.

> And it came to pass in those days, when Moses was grown up, that he went out unto his brethren, and looked on their burdens; and he saw an Egyptian smiting a Hebrew, one of his brethren. (Exod. 2:11)

Now it is perfectly true that a man of leisure in ancient Egypt might amuse himself by doing exactly what is depicted in the Bible. "It had, in fact, become a convention that a man of high position should find entertainment in watching others work," writes one Egyptologist, "particularly when the work was on the land."[55] But nothing in the Bible has prepared us for the man Moses had become or the way he responded to the sight of an Egyptian beating an Israelite. Moses "smote" the taskmaster, and the plain meaning of the biblical text is that he intended to kill the man and succeeded in doing so. Here is the first moment in the Bible where Moses betrays a characteristic that we will encounter again and again in the remarkable story of his life—Moses was a moody and brooding man given to sudden outbursts of anger that would sometimes find expression in a decisive act of physical violence.

At first glimpse, the killing seems justifiable and even praiseworthy. Moses rescued a fellow Israelite from a beating or worse and inflicted a kind of rough justice on a nameless functionary who symbolized the worst excesses of the Egyptian monarchy. But Moses displayed a less heroic characteristic in the moment before his encounter with the taskmaster: the Bible makes it clear that Moses acted with icy calculation before actually delivering a death blow to the taskmaster.

> He looked this way and that, and, seeing there was no one about, he struck the Egyptian down and hid his body in the sand. (Exod. 2:12 NEB)

MOSES THE MEEK

Rabbinical tradition simply could not acknowledge that the Lawgiver was capable of such cold-blooded brutality, and so the rabbis set themselves the task of acquitting him of the questionable conduct that is reported in the Holy Scriptures. Thus began a long and continuing tradition of emasculating the real Moses and turning one of the Bible's most potent and powerful men into something of a wimp.

The rabbis depicted Moses as a kind and compassionate man whose peaceful nature inclines him to words of consolation and gestures of comfort. Because he is allowed to visit his birth mother throughout his childhood, Moses grows up with an intimate knowledge of his origins as an Israelite. On his visits to Goshen, Moses strips himself of his princely garb and sets to work alongside the slaves. "My dear brethren, bear your present hard lot, but be of good cheer and lose not your courage," he encourages them in bland platitudes. "Better times will soon follow."

Troubled by the cruelty of the taskmasters, Moses reallocates the burden of work, taking the loads of brick and mortar from the backs of old men and women and giving them to the young and strong, "thus making each labour and toil according to his strength, which was already a step towards lightening the sufferings of the slaves." He manages to persuade Pharaoh to give the Israelites a day of rest each week, craftily arguing that an exhausted slave was a poor worker. "Such a forced labour, O King, is not profitable to thee," Moses urges, proposing that the seventh day of the week be set aside as a day of rest, "for on this day, consecrated to the planet Saturn, work is anyhow not crowned with success."[56] The taskmasters and even Pharaoh himself stupidly assume that Moses, the crown prince, is making these efforts to improve the speed and efficiency of the work, but his real motive is to spare his fellow Israelites at least a bit of suffering.[57]

"The bond which attached the young prince to his own family and people was stronger than the golden chains and necklace he wore as prince of Egypt," the old story goes. " 'Alas,' he cried bitterly, 'I had rather die than witness the affliction of my brethren.' "[58]

Even so, the rabbis insisted, Moses is so gentle and mild that his tender feelings for his adoptive family linger long after he realizes how cruelly they are exploiting the Israelites. Moses is slow in coming to hate the oppressors, the rabbis wrote, because he is "too noble to forget his benefactors, or to diminish the love and gratitude he owed them." Only the weight of their many outrages against the enslaved Israelites "compelled [him] to declare war on Pharaoh," and even then, "he was yet deeply attached to Pharaoh, and especially to his foster-mother Bithia, whose love he never forgot."[59]

The rabbinical spin doctors were especially anxious to pretty up the picture of how Moses behaved at the moment of his deadly attack on the Egyptian taskmaster. The Bible plainly states that Moses looked around before striking the taskmaster in order to make sure that there were no witnesses. Yet the Talmud argues that his real motive is to see if anyone else might intervene to protect the slave and thus spare Moses the unpleasant task of spilling the blood of another human being. When he sees that no one else is willing and able to do what is necessary, Moses acts courageously to carry out what he sees as his solemn moral duty.[60]

Then the sages brought their version of the incident to a bloodless climax by invoking the miraculous if deadly power of God. To strengthen his resolve, Moses pauses to address an urgent prayer to God before raising his hand against the Egyptian, and the pious gesture spares Moses the necessity of delivering the blow: "Scarcely had the Ineffable Name left his lips and the sound reached the ears of the Egyptian, when the latter fell down to the ground and died, even before the hand of Moses touched him."[61]

The bland Moses who appears in these tales embodies a mostly praiseworthy quality that permeates the rabbinical literature—a deep revulsion toward physical violence and a pious tendency to look to heaven for salvation and vindication when faced with oppression on earth. By the time these tales were first set down in the Talmud and other rabbinical works, a remnant of the Jewish people was living under Roman occupation in Palestine and the rest of them were condemned to exile elsewhere in the world. An insurrection against Roman occupation in the second century C.E. ended in a bloody and humiliating defeat, and the experience taught them that resistance leads to catastrophe. Their strategy of survival was to go along and get along with the powers that be—a coping mechanism that would serve the Jewish people in exile for a couple of thousand years—and so they seemed to find the militant Moses who is actually depicted in the Bible to be awkward and inconvenient.

BASTINADO

As if to exonerate Moses and explain away his brutal attack, legend and lore emphasized the cruelty of the Egyptians. "[S]ome of the overseers were very savage and furious men," railed Philo, "being, as to their cruelty, not at all different from poisonous serpents or carnivorous beasts— wild beasts in human form—being clothed with the form of a human body so as to give an appearance of gentleness . . . but in reality being harder than iron."[62] The man whom Moses killed is depicted in one elaborate yarn as a vile and repulsive malefactor who fully deserves his fate.

The Israelite slaves, the rabbis imagined, are directed in their labors by overseers chosen from their own ranks, and the Hebrew overseers report to Egyptian taskmasters—ten slaves to each Hebrew overseer, and ten overseers to each Egyptian. One of the Hebrew overseers is married to a young woman "beautiful of face and figure and faultless in body,"[63] a talkative creature who chats up her husband's taskmaster when he calls at their house with a new work order. "The beautiful Israelitish woman enkindled a mad passion in his breast," the rabbis suggested, adopting the age-old stance of blaming the victim and casting the woman in the primal biblical role of seductress, and the victim of her wiles "sought and found a cunning way of satisfying his lustful desire" by means of a cruel but clever ruse.[64]

The Egyptian taskmaster orders the Hebrew overseer to rouse his gang of slaves before dawn the next morning and march them out to the work site. The Egyptian waits and watches. When he sees that the overseer has dutifully obeyed his order, the Egyptian slips into the man's house, crawls into bed next to the man's wife, and begins to caress her body. Thinking that the demanding hands belong to her husband, the woman yields to him in the silence and darkness.

At daybreak, the light of the rising sun reveals the identity of the man in her bed and the crime that has been committed—the woman weeps in shame and anger, but the Egyptian only laughs at her tears and saunters out with a smirk on his face. At the work site, the Egyptian treats her husband with even greater contempt and cruelty, perhaps because he knows he has acted wrongly and wants to intimidate the man into keeping his mouth shut (as the rabbis proposed), or perhaps because he knows that the woman and her husband are powerless to complain or to punish him. "[M]ore than one bastinado"—the blow of a cudgel—is inflicted upon the wronged man by the man who wronged him, goes the old rabbinical tale, and it is one such blow that Moses witnesses with his own eyes.[65]

The rabbis identified the man whose wife is tricked into adultery as Dathan, an Israelite who is mentioned in the Bible in an entirely different context, and they imagined that an illegitimate son is born to the wife as a result of the seduction. Dathan, as we shall come to see, will later play a crucial if treacherous role in the biblical account of the life of Moses. For now, it falls to Moses to vindicate the cuckolded husband and the defiled wife, and the rabbis proposed that it is Dathan whom Moses avenges on that fateful day when he strikes down the villainous taskmaster.

"Moses, whom the holy spirit had acquainted with the injury done the Hebrew officer by the Egyptian taskmaster, cried out to [the Egyptian]," goes the old tale, "saying: 'Not enough that thou hast dishonored this man's wife, thou aimest to kill him, too?' "[66]

Not content with making out the taskmaster to be thoroughly contemptible and deserving of death—not only a cruel slave-driver but a sexual predator, too—the apologists went even further and conjured up a wordy discourse between a reluctant Moses and God. Moses is filled with "pity and compassion" for the Israelite man and his wife, but his sympathies are not limited to his own brethren, and so he appeals to God for moral instruction before striking the oppressor.

"Lord of the Universe, I am about to kill this man, and yet what right have I to take his life?" the rabbis had Moses say. "He is a criminal just now who deserves severe punishment, but how do I know whether he will not repent one day and atone for his wicked ways by just and pious deeds? Have I read the future to know that this man will not bring forth children who will walk in the ways of the Lord, be merciful and just?"[67]

God answers the prayerful inquiry of Moses with the kind of flash-and-dazzle that we will not encounter in the Bible itself until much later. "[A]nd lo! the heavenly heights were suddenly revealed to Moses, the heavens opened before him, and his eyes witnessed the mysteries of the world below and of the worlds above. He saw the ministering angels surrounding the Throne of Glory and the heavenly court was sitting in judgment over man."[68]

Now the voice of God himself is heard. "Thy scruples, O Moses, just as they are and inspired by noble sentiments, are out of place in this case," God gently scolds. "Know that this Egyptian who has committed adultery and manslaughter many a time and was on the point of slaying the man against whom he has sinned, will never repent, but persist in his evil ways." Then God issues the death sentence: "This man has deserved death, and thou, Moses, hast been called hither to execute the decree of Providence."[69]

So Moses acts only to do God's bidding. "Moses slew, thinking the deed a pious action," Philo hastened to explain. "[I]ndeed, it was a pious action to destroy one who only lived for the destruction of others."[70] Even then Moses does not stain his own hands with the blood of his victim—he merely utters the name of God, and the villain falls dead at his feet. "Not with his hand but with a word of his mouth," goes the old tale, "did Moses kill the Egyptian criminal."[71]

The Bible says otherwise. The real Moses was not quite the conflict-avoider that the rabbis wishfully imagined him to be; rather, Moses was perfectly willing and able to take a man's life with his own two hands. Modern scholarship encourages us to regard the killing as an act of justifiable homicide. "For the Hebrew, for his own people," writes George Coats, "the act should be seen as heroic defense, a risk of his own life for the sake of protecting his brother."[72] Yet we cannot avoid the fact that Moses was cool and cautious enough to take a look around and make sure there were no witnesses before doing the deadly deed. "Moses is anxious that his act be done in secrecy," insists Brevard Childs. "The sequence indicates that the slaying was not initiated in a burst of passion or following a vain attempt to dissuade the oppressor."[73]

The image of Moses that we find in the rabbinical literature, rather than what is actually written about him in the Bible, is what prompted one contemporary Bible critic to call him "the true Empath."[74] But it is also true that Moses comes across as a man whose passivity is almost crippling: he cannot act decisively and effectively, and he is reduced to endless debates with himself and God. Indeed, sometimes it seems that Moses cannot act at all unless God issues a specific command. But, as we shall see, the biblical Moses was not quite such a pacifist, not quite so shy and self-effacing. In fact, the slaying of the taskmaster is our very first glimpse—but not our last—of a Moses who was a willing and even an enthusiastic killer.

"SURELY THE THING IS KNOWN"

Even if he did not pause to consider the implications of his act before raising his hand against the Egyptian, surely Moses realized now that he had placed at risk all that had been bestowed upon him: the affection of his adoptive family, the wealth and privilege of his princely rank, the prospect of ascending to the throne of Egypt. Did Moses look upon the corpse of the dead man and suffer a moment of pain and doubt? Was he rendered breathless with terror and unaccustomed physical exertion as he dragged the corpse across the sand and hastily scraped out a shallow grave? Did his features betray his guilt when he returned to the palace, dusty and sweaty and perhaps even bloodstained?

The Bible does not disclose what Moses thought as he lay down one last time in the palace of the king of Egypt. But it gives us a rich and troubling irony: Moses was not hailed as a hero by his fellow Israelites for his daring act of defiance. Rather, he suddenly faced the threat of betrayal and condemnation by the very people whom he had just championed.

Moses ventured out of the palace on the day after the incident and promptly came upon two Israelites locked in struggle. Still attired as an Egyptian prince, but filled with a newly awakened sense of solidarity with the slave nation into which he was born—and perhaps a sense of his own might now that he had drawn blood with his own hands—Moses tried to break up the fight by scolding the bully.

> And he went out the second day, and, behold, two men of the Hebrews were striving together, and he said to him that did the wrong: "Wherefore smitest thou thy fellow?" (Exod. 2:13)

But his high-minded effort at peacemaking among the Israelites was rewarded with a bitter reproach.

"Who made thee a ruler and a judge over us?" said the man whom Moses had sought to pacify. "Thinkest thou to kill me, as thou didst kill the Egyptian?" (Exod. 2:14)[75]

These words filled Moses with sudden apprehension. "And Moses feared," the Bible reports, "and said: 'Surely the thing is known.'" (Exod. 2:14) He must have reasoned that if these two Israelites knew of his crime, then Pharaoh would soon find out, too. And in fact the Bible suggests that a report of what Moses had done to the taskmaster was carried to the palace, and Pharaoh was moved to both rage and resolve.

"Now when Pharaoh heard this thing," the Bible states, "he sought to slay Moses." (Exod. 2:15)

Just as Moses revealed something important about himself when he struck down the Egyptian taskmaster, the "saucy impudence of the betrayer," as one scholar characterizes the words of the Israelite,[76] was an early warning of the defiance that Moses would encounter when he was finally elevated to leadership of the unruly slaves. History and tradition may regard Moses as a commanding figure, but the Israelites themselves were capable of treating him with open contempt. Here, Moses comes across as almost ludicrous, a dilettante whose single impulsive act of courage was not enough to impress a man who had lived his whole life as a slave. Rather, the Israelite accuser understood that even though Moses wore the garb of a prince and lived under the same roof as Pharaoh, he had placed himself in jeopardy, and the slave felt at liberty to reproach his own accuser.

The two men whose fight Moses tries to break up, according to a tale told by the ancient rabbis, are none other than Dathan, the man whose wife was so cruelly exploited by the taskmaster, and his crony Abiram; both will figure prominently in the biblical account of a rebellion that Moses will later put down in the wilderness of Sinai. The storytellers made Dathan and Abiram into a couple of ne'er-do-wells from the tribe of Reuben, which was already "notorious for their effrontery and contentiousness,"[77] and it is suggested that the two of them feign a fight with each other in an effort to attract the attention of Moses and then draw him into a confrontation. Once Moses is provoked into reproaching the two of them, Dathan and Abiram taunt Moses with their knowledge of his attack on the taskmaster—and then betray Moses directly to Pharaoh.

"Moses dishonoreth thy royal mantle and thy crown," Dathan and Abiram tell the mighty Pharaoh, who remains loyal to the man he has thought to be his own grandson and rebukes the accusers: "Much good may it do him!" So the two traitors grow even bolder: "He helps thine enemies, Pharaoh." Pharaoh is still unmoved, and again he replies: "Much good may it do him!" Finally, they reveal the darkest secret of all: "He is not the son of thy daughter." At last, the traitors have found a way to turn Pharaoh's heart against Moses. "A royal command was issued for the arrest of Moses," goes the old tale, "and he was condemned to death by the sword."[78]

The tale goes on to present Moses bound in fetters and led in a solemn procession to the scaffold where he is to be hung like a hobbled bull and then slaughtered before the smirking courtiers and the hooting crowd. Even as the executioner is sharpening the blade of his sword, a few anxious angels are pleading with God to spare Moses from Pharaoh's last and final decree. "Be assured, my angels," God tells them, "that no harm will be done unto him who is to redeem my people from bondage."

God resorts to a showy display of divine legerdemain to save the life of Moses, according to the old tale, turning the muscle and sinew of his neck into solid ivory, and so the executioner's sword thuds harmlessly against its target every time he delivers what is intended to be a death blow—ten times the sword strikes Moses, and ten times it slips off. Then God summons the angel Gabriel, his celestial jack-of-all-trades, for a big finish to the improvised magic show. Gabriel manifests himself on the scaffold in the human form of the executioner, and the executioner is miraculously transformed into the figure of Moses. "Gabriel, seizing the sword destined to slay Moses, beheaded the executioner," the rabbinical fairy tale concludes, "whilst Moses escaped."[79]

Even as he runs from the courtyard where the scaffold has been erected, according to yet another tale, Moses is pursued by the palace guard, but God intervenes to spare Moses from the deadly intentions of Pharaoh yet again by suddenly striking the soldiers blind. At the same moment, an angel descends from the heavens, sweeps Moses off the ground, and carries him through the skies to a far-distant place some forty days' journey from Egypt, "so that he was safe from pursuit and out of reach of the wrath of Pharaoh."[80]

The Bible tells a starkly different story. Nothing at all is said about the betrayal of Moses, his arrest by Pharaoh, or his miraculous escape—

all of the fairy-tale derring-do is found only in the rabbinical literature. The biblical author allows us to understand that Moses could not and did not go back to the palace where he had lived in comfort and security for most of his life. His rash attack on the Egyptian taskmaster turned him from a prince of Egypt into a fugitive from justice, and he realized that the only safe refuge was somewhere far beyond the reach of mighty Pharaoh. "Moses must flee for his life like every other political fugitive," one contemporary Bible scholar points out, and so Moses set out for the only place in the ancient Near East where he might escape the law of Egypt—the crags and caves of the remote wilderness where a wanted man could hide out from the law.[81]

"Moses fled from the face of Pharaoh," the Bible tells us, "and dwelt in the land of Midian." (Exod. 2:15) Yet again Moses experienced one of the sudden and shocking upheavals that had characterized his whole life—he had been born into a family of slaves, then condemned to death by drowning, then set adrift on the Nile, then rescued from the waters of the Nile by the daughter of the man who sought to kill him, then restored briefly to his birth mother for a couple of years of nurturance, then whisked back to the palace, all before the age of two. And now he suddenly forfeited all of the power and promise that had been bestowed upon him, and he was forced to flee from the deadly rage of his royal benefactor.

The prince of Egypt was now a wanted man. Moses fled across the Red Sea and the wilderness of Sinai until he reached the distant land of Midian. He sought only a safe refuge where the mighty king and his minions would not be able to find him. But Midian, as it turned out, was not merely a hiding place. Rather, the wilderness was the starting point of a long journey that would bring Moses to new and even stranger places. On the run from Pharaoh, Moses finally stumbled across his own destiny.

THE FUGITIVE

No man becomes a prophet who was not first a shepherd.
—MOHAMMAD

The Bible does not disclose the age of Moses on the day he struck down the Egyptian taskmaster and fled from Egypt—one tale puts him at a still-youthful twenty-seven, and the more conventional tradition suggests that he was forty. But we know that Moses was nearly eighty years old when he first set out on the momentous trek that we know as the Exodus. So a bit of quick calculation reveals a probable gap of forty years (or more) in the middle of his life that somehow escaped the attention of the biblical author.

We can imagine that Moses spent some of those years alone in the wilderness before arriving in Midian, and one tradition in the Midrash imagines him as a kind of hermit-philosopher: "Moses preferred solitary places where, undisturbed, he could meditate over the ways of God and the laws of nature, and where the spirit of the Lord of the Universe often came over him."[1] The notion of Moses as an anchorite, alone and at large in the wilderness, has appealed to theologians who see the desert as the birthplace of religions: Jesus and Mohammad, too, spent time in the deserts of the Near East. "*Le Désert est monothéiste,*" wrote the French philosopher Ernest Renan. "Renan's aphorism implies that blank horizons and a dazzling sky will clear the mind of its distractions," explains

Bruce Chatwin in *The Songlines*, "and allow it to concentrate on the Godhead."*[2]

Self-exile in an empty desert is an appealing way to explain the missing years of Moses for those who prefer to see him as a pristine figure, a man wholly given to perfecting his better nature. "Having a teacher within himself," wrote Philo, Moses devoted himself to "the continual study of the doctrines of philosophy, which he easily and thoroughly comprehended in his soul."[3] When at last Moses bestirs himself and walks out of the wilderness after forty years of lonely contemplation, Philo seems to suggest, he is purged of ordinary human longings and failings, filled with noble aspirations, and ready to answer the call of God.

But there is a second mystery in the biblical text that makes the missing years of Moses even more tantalizing. The Bible, as we shall shortly see, tells us that Moses sought the protection of "the priest of Midian" and promptly married one of the priest's seven daughters as soon as he arrived in Midian: "And Moses was content to dwell with the man, and he gave Moses Zipporah his daughter." (Exod. 2:16,21) But a deeply enigmatic passage that appears much later in the biblical narrative suggests that Moses was married to a *Cushite* instead of or in addition to a *Midianite*. (Num. 12:1) "Cush" is the term used in the Bible to identify the country in northeastern Africa now called Ethiopia, and so we are left to wonder: Exactly when, where, and how did Moses happen to meet and marry an Ethiopian woman?

The rabbis supplied an explanation for both mysteries, the missing years of Moses *and* the Cushite woman who supposedly married him. Indeed, many of the stories that found their way into the rabbinical literature were the result of earnest but wildly imaginative efforts to fill in the blanks and explain away the contradictions that appear in the text of the Bible itself. No other figure in the Bible has attracted such a rich and strange accretion of legend and lore, and none of the extrabiblical stories told about Moses are quite so startling as the ones that describe the missing years between Egypt and Midian. Moses

---

*"But life in the desert is not like that!" Chatwin goes on to say in *The Songlines*. "To survive at all, the desert traveler ... must forever be naming, sifting, comparing a thousand different 'signs'—the tracks of a dung beetle or the ripple of a dune—to tell him where he is; where the others are; where rain has fallen; where the next meal is coming from. . . ."

is presented as a dashing figure, a man of action and adventure, and yet, at the same time, a messenger called by God and a man of destiny.

To hear the ancients tell it, Moses is not merely lolling about in the desert and thinking great thoughts during those forty missing years. Instead, the fugitive prince of Egypt reinvents himself as a mercenary, then a general, and finally a king before arriving in the wilderness of Midian and making himself over into a humble shepherd.

SOLDIER OF FORTUNE

At a time when Moses is still living in complacent luxury in the palace of Pharaoh, the ancient storytellers suggested, a war is raging between the kingdom of Ethiopia and the rebellious tributary nations to the east. The courageous king of Ethiopia, a man named Kikanos, rides at the head of his army to subdue and punish the insurgents, and he leaves the royal capital of Saba under the care of two trusted generals, Jannes and Jambres, the sons of the villainous sorcerer Balaam. Their father literally bewitches the people of Saba into acclaiming him as king in place of the crusading Kikanos. Once enthroned, Balaam orders his sons to fortify the royal city against the day when the true king returns from the battlefield and seeks to reclaim his crown.

The fortifications that Balaam erects around Saba seem impregnable. On two sides of the city, the walls are raised to new and formidable heights. On the third side are canals that swirl with dangerous currents from the Nile and Astopus Rivers. To defend the fourth side, Balaam relies on his own "magic arts" and causes the approaches to the city to be infested with deadly snakes and scorpions that will strike at the heels of any creature, man or beast, that dares to enter the no-man's-land. "Thus none could depart," the story goes, "and none could enter."[4]

Balaam's plan works precisely as he intends. Kikanos returns in victory from his war against the rebels in distant lands only to find that the gates to his royal city are barred by Balaam's sons and his palace is occupied by Balaam. Now Kikanos is forced to mount an assault on his own city, but every effort to retake Saba ends in failure. When he directs his loyal troops to attack the high walls of the fortress, they are cut down from above by the archers and spear-throwers whom Balaam has enchanted into serving him. When the army of Kikanos tries to cross the moat, the horses on which his cavalry officers ride are drowned and the rafts that carry his infantry are swamped. And when the king tries in desperation to lead his men across the open ground that is so diabolically littered with snakes and scorpions, the venomous creatures repel the attack. At last the king despairs of taking the fortress by main force and resigns himself to besieging his own royal capital. Kikanos is the irresistible force, Balaam is the immovable object, and so the siege drags on without victory or defeat year after year.

Meanwhile, back in Egypt, Moses comes to blows with the Egyptian taskmaster and then runs for his life. And so it is that Kikanos, in the ninth year of his long siege of Saba, looks up one day and beholds a remarkable sight: a solitary man in the garb of a prince of Egypt wanders into his camp from the desert wastes. According to the ancient chroniclers, Kikanos is no less enthralled by Moses than were Pharaoh's daughter and then Pharaoh, and Moses finds himself being recruited as a soldier of fortune in service to a foreign potentate. Yet again, Moses is spared the necessity of any effort to save himself.

"[Moses] exercised an attraction upon all that saw him, for he was slender like a palm-tree, his countenance shone as the morning sun, and his strength was equal to a lion's," the old tale goes. "So deep was the king's affection for him that he appointed him to be commander-in-chief of his forces."[5]

But Kikanos does not live to see whether Moses will succeed where he has failed in the siege of Saba. The good king falls ill, lies abed for seven days, and then succumbs to his illness; the royal corpse is embalmed and then buried in sight of the gates of his as-yet-unconquered city. The besieging army, grief-stricken and panicky, frets that the insurgents to the east may rise up again and move against them now that the king is dead. So they turn to their newly appointed commander-in-chief and acclaim him as their king in place of the fallen Kikanos. "They hastened and stripped off each man his upper garment, and cast them all in a heap upon the ground, making a high place, on top of which they set Moses," the story goes. "Then they blew with trumpets, and called out before him: 'Long live the king! Long live the king!' "[6]

Seized with new hope and fervor, the nobles of the land issue a proclamation to the people: every man must contribute something precious as a coronation gift. The grateful Ethiopians line up outside the camp to offer treasure from their households, "this one a gold nose ring, that one a coin, and onyx stones, bdellium, pearls, gold, and silver in great abundance." At last, they bestow upon Moses the ultimate symbol of kingship: Adoniah, the widow of Kikanos, will be the queen and consort of King Moses.[7]

On the seventh day of Moses' reign as king of Ethiopia, having dutifully provided the newly minted monarch with suitable wealth and agreeable companionship, the officers and men of the royal army gather around Moses and pointedly demand to know how *he* proposes to conquer the besieged city of Saba. And Moses is quick to answer with a strange decree. He orders every man to go into the forest and fetch back a young stork, to raise the fledgling and teach it to fly; then, when Moses gives the word, each man will starve his stork for three days and bring it to the encampment of the royal army. The storks will be issued to the soldiers on the eve of battle, and with sword in one hand and stork in the other, the soldiers will mount up and ride against the besieged city on the approach where the snakes and scorpions lay in wait. Then the hungry birds will be released to descend on the snakes and scorpions, thus clearing the path to the city. The curious plan works perfectly. "[T]he birds swooped down and devoured all the reptiles and destroyed them," the story goes. "After the serpents were removed in this way, the men fought against the city, subdued it, and killed all its inhabitants, but of the people besieging it there died not one."[8]

King Moses reigns over a land that is now blessed with peace and prosperity. "He conducted the government in justice, righteousness, and integrity, and his people loved and feared him."[9] Only one of his subjects is aggrieved, and it turns out to be Adoniah, the widow of Kikanos and the woman given to Moses as his queen. Adoniah's complaint is poignant: not once during their long marriage has Moses slept with her. Moses shuns the marriage bed and avoids even a glimpse of Adoniah's alluring face or body, the rabbis suggested, because he "feared the stern God of his fathers" and heeded "the word of Abraham regarding Isaac, and Isaac regarding Jacob: 'Thou shalt not take a wife from the daughters of Canaan, nor ally thyself by marriage with any of the children of Ham.' "[10] And so the unhappy queen begins to agitate against Moses within the royal court.

"What is this thing which you, the people of Ethiopia, have done these many days?" Adoniah complains bitterly. "Surely you know that during the forty years this man hath reigned over you, he hath not approached me, nor hath he worshipped the gods of Ethiopia. Now, therefore, let this man reign over you no more, for he is not of our flesh."[11]

Adoniah even offers a pretender to the throne as a rival to King Moses. "Behold," she announces one day, "my son is grown up, let him reign over you. It is better for you to serve the son of your lord than a stranger, a slave of the king of Egypt."[12]

Moses is quick to see that his queen has succeeded in inciting enough ill will to spark a civil war in his once peaceable kingdom: the officer corps remains loyal, but the rabble seems to favor the son of Kikanos and Adoniah, a young man named Monarchos. Still, the rabbis brought the fanciful tale to a bland and rather anticlimactic conclusion. The people of Ethiopia, mindful of their oath of loyalty to Moses, refuse to rise up against him. Moses refuses to keep his crown against their will, abdicates in favor of the rightful heir, and leaves the throne just as abruptly as he first assumed it. "Willingly did the son of Amram yield to the wishes of the people," the rabbis concluded, "and without regret he left the country and the men of Ethiopia, who dismissed him with great honour and rich presents."[13]

Flavius Josephus turned the tale on its head in his biography of Moses, in which Moses besieges Saba as a general of the armies of Pharaoh after repelling an invasion of Egypt by the king of Ethiopia. The daughter of the Ethiopian monarch spies Moses from the ramparts of the royal city, falls in love with him, and agrees to deliver the besieged city to Moses in exchange for his promise to marry her. Moses shows not the slightest shyness in taking full advantage of her generosity: "[W]hen Moses had cut off the Ethiopians, he gave thanks to God, and consummated his marriage," wrote Josephus, "and led the Egyptians back to their own land."[14] Only upon his return to Egypt does Moses fall afoul of a conspiracy of "sacred scribes," and he is forced to flee into the wilderness to escape them—Josephus did not bother to mention the biblical account of the slain taskmaster.[15]

All of these legends and tall tales, so pious and yet so farfetched, were designed to converge with the biblical text and put Moses back on the road in search of a place of refuge and a rendezvous with destiny. King Moses is now sixty-seven years old, according to the ancient storytellers who concocted this unlikely saga, but he is still vigorous enough to make his way across the wilderness to the land of Midian, and he is content to take up the rigorous life of a shepherd: "[I]t was the time appointed by God in the days of old to bring Israel forth from the affliction of the children of Ham."[16]

THE MYSTERY OF MIDIAN

Here the Bible picks up the story of Moses again. When last seen in the biblical narrative, he had slain the Egyptian taskmaster, and suddenly we find him in a distant land, where he sought and found refuge.

> Moses fled from the face of Pharaoh and dwelt in the land of Midian. (Exod. 2:15)

Since the geographical descriptions in the Bible are often vague and sometimes obviously made up, Midian cannot be sited with precision on the modern map of the Middle East. Scholars agree that it was probably found somewhere in the southern stretches of Transjordan, a rugged landscape along the eastern bank of the Jordan River and the Gulf of Aqaba in what is today southern Jordan and northwestern Saudi Arabia. The Bible depicts the Midianites as a tribe of camel nomads, wandering the wilderness in search of pasturage for their sheep and goats, and they have long been imagined to resemble the Bedouins who ranged through the same terrain in more recent times. Ancient Greek and Roman historians equated Midian with Arabia, and Philo used the term "Arabs" to refer to the people whom the Bible calls Midianites.

Like Moses and the people of Israel, the Midianites were thought to be the distant descendants of Abraham; the founder of their nation was a man named Midian, said to have been one of six sons born to Abraham's secondary wife Keturah (Gen. 25:3). Of Abraham's many sons by his many wives and concubines, only Isaac was privileged to receive the blessing of God, and so the Midianites were vaguely understood to be distant cousins of the Israelites who were excluded from Abraham's covenant with God and who contented themselves with the worship of false gods and goddesses. At one point in the Bible, they are shown to worship Baal-Peor, a local deity that was sacred to the people of nearby Moab, but the particulars of their paganism are mostly ignored in the Bible except when Moses, scolding the Israelites for one of their many lapses of faith, condemns the Midianites for "their wiles wherewith they have beguiled you in the matter of Peor." (Num. 25:18)

Later, the Bible suggests that the Midianites were somehow linked to the Kenites (Judg. 1:16, 4:11), a tribe supposedly descended directly from Cain, the son of Adam and the slayer of Abel. "Kenite" is commonly understood in Bible scholarship to mean "smith," and the Kenites are believed to have been wandering coppersmiths; other scholars suggest that they were troubadours, "somewhat like modern gypsies."[17] The fuzzy description of the Midianites in the Bible prompts Martin Buber to shrug off the whole scholarly debate about their history and identity and to conclude that Midian "seems to have been a loose association of tribes with varying origins."[18]

The Midianites ranged out at will from their homeland, or so the Bible suggests, showing up in the deserts of Canaan and the Sinai to pasture their flocks and journeying between Egypt and the outer reaches of the Arabian peninsula to trade in gold, spices, and slaves (Isa. 60:6). It was a Midianite merchant caravan that came upon Joseph and his brothers in Canaan; the camels were loaded with a cargo of gum tragacanth, balm, and myrrh for the marketplaces of Egypt, but the enterprising traders quickly agreed to buy the young man from his brothers for twenty pieces of silver and later resold him upon their arrival in Egypt.* Eventually, the Midianites will come to be portrayed in the Bible as a bitter enemy of Israel: the womenfolk were seen as temptresses who seduced the Israelites into sacred harlotry and other "abominations" during the long trek through the Sinai, and the menfolk as marauders who ravaged the standing crops and peaceful settlements of the Israelites after the conquest of the Promised Land.

The account of the Midianites that we find in the Bible describes a primal scene in the story of civilization: the confrontation between the nomad and the farmer, always an edgy encounter and sometimes a bloody one. Settled peoples, whose land-bound labors produce the surplus of food and goods that is the starting point of civilization, have always been considered an easy target for plunder by nomadic peoples, whose only wealth is what they can pick up and carry away. That is why the sudden appearance of a mounted stranger is an emblem of terror and even apocalypse in the iconography of the Bible: "And I looked, and behold a pale horse, and his name that sat on him was Death, and Hell followed him." (Rev. 6:8) The scene of destruction that we find in the

---

*The Bible refers to slave-traders who carried off Joseph first as Ishmaelites (Gen. 37:25, 27), a term that refers to the tribe descended from another one of Abraham's sons, Ishmael, and then as Midianites (Gen. 37:28). One explanation for the inconsistency is that the passage embodies the work of two distinct authors: the Elohist, who understood the caravaners to be Midianites, and the Yahwist, who knew them as Ishmaelites. Another explanation is that the Midianites may have merged into the Ishmaelites by the time the Bible was completed, and so the terms were regarded as interchangeable.

Book of Joshua, which describes a raid by the Midianites on the land of Israel after it had been conquered and settled by the Israelites, might apply to any number of nomadic hordes throughout history, Tatars and Huns and Mongols no less than Midianites:

> For they came up with their cattle and their tents, and they came in as locusts for multitude; both they and their camels were without number; and they came into the land to destroy it. (Josh. 6:5)

Ironically, the Israelites were themselves a nomadic people until Jacob and his sons arrived in Egypt, where Joseph warned his brethren that the pastoral nomad was thought to be "an abomination" (Gen. 46:34), and they took up their old ways when they followed Moses out of Egypt and wandered through the wilderness. As they marched toward the land of Canaan, the Israelites were regarded as a conquering horde. "Now will this multitude lick up all that is round about us," cried the Moabites at the very sight of the Israelites, "as the ox licketh up the grass of the field." (Num. 22:4) Only much later, when the memories of the wilderness had become a sacred myth, did the biblical sources come to characterize the Midianites as a plague of locusts.

Indeed, the biblical depiction of the Midianites as intruders and destroyers may be a remnant of ancient propaganda aimed at one of the traditional enemies of the Israelites. Although Bible scholarship once regarded the Midianites as "the oldest camel nomads known to us,"[19] more recent studies suggest that the Midian was actually a "a complex and highly sophisticated society" rather than a band of proto-Bedouins, a "cosmopolitan civilization" with political and cultural linkages that ranged "from Anatolia to Egypt."[20] At some point in biblical antiquity, Midian may have reigned over considerable portions of Canaan and the Transjordan, and the Midianites who roamed through ancient Israel may have been imperial tax collectors rather than marauders.

The land and people of Midian were destined to play a crucial and intimate role in the life of Moses and the fate of Israel. Midian is the place where the long slumber of God comes to an abrupt end, the place where Moses will be made over yet again, the place where the saga of Israel, mired for so long in the mud and muck of the brick fields of Egypt, leaps upward and forward with astounding suddenness and force.

MOSES AT THE WELL

"Moses fled from the face of Pharaoh, and dwelt in the land of Midian," is how the Bible describes the arrival of Moses in that fateful place, "and he sat down by a well." (Exod. 2:15)

Josephus imagined that Moses arrives at noon—the sun is overhead, he is hot and tired from the long trek, his lips are parched and cracked. But the Bible confirms that Moses paused before drinking, distracted from his urgent thirst by the remarkable scene that he came upon, an encounter that was beguiling at first but soon turned ugly.

"Now the priest of Midian had seven daughters," the Bible continues, "and they came and drew water and filled the troughs to water their father's flock." (Exod. 2:16)

The sight of so many women at work around the well must have been enchanting and perhaps a bit provocative even to a man who had just completed an exhausting journey across the wilderness. Rarely did the sexes in the ancient Near East enjoy the opportunity to mingle in a relaxed setting, and a well was one of the few gathering places, especially in the open countryside, where a man might encounter a woman who was not a blood relation. So a visit to a well afforded a rare opportunity to banter and flirt. "The Arabs are great breeders of cattle," Philo felt obliged to explain, identifying the ancient Midianites with the Arabic people whom they were thought to resemble, "and they all feed their flocks together, not merely men, but also women, and youths, and maidens with them."[21]

Indeed, a fateful encounter between a man and a woman at a well is frequently shown in the Bible: Abraham's servant came upon Rebekah, the future bride of Isaac, at a well in the land of Aram (Gen. 24:10 ff.), and it was at a well, too, that Jacob was first smitten with a lifelong passion for Rachel (Gen. 29:10–11). A chance meeting at a well is an example of what Bible scholars called a type-scene, a stock scene that follows certain strict conventions and includes certain settings and events—a man arrives from a distant land, he encounters a woman at a well, water is drawn and then shared (but sometimes only after overcoming some obstacle), and a bond of love is ultimately formed between the man and woman. "[T]he contemporary audiences of these tales," suggests Bible scholar Robert Alter, "took particular pleasure in seeing how in each instance the convention could be, through the narrator's art, both faithfully followed and renewed for the specific needs of the hero under consideration."[22]

Sometimes the thread that links one stock scene with another in the biblical text is made explicit in the rabbinical lore, where scenes and characters from throughout the Bible are conflated in fantastic ways. The rabbis suggested that the well where Moses first encountered the daughters of Jethro was the very same well where Jacob had met Rachel, although one incident took place in Midian and the other in far-off Aram several centuries earlier. To the rabbis, it is a cosmic well that exists in a kind of Hebraic dreamtime—"the same well that God created at the beginning of the world, the opening of which He made in the twilight of the first Sabbath eve."[23]

The Bible tells us that the charming scene of seven sisters at the well was shattered by the arrival of a gang of shepherds. Unwilling to wait their turn at the well for fear that there would not be enough water for their flock, they chased away the women and allowed their own sheep to drink the water that had been drawn and poured into the troughs by the women. "And the shepherds came and drove them away," the biblical author writes (Exod. 2:17), suggesting only that the brutes were selfish and lazy. The rabbis, however, turned the tale into an atrocity story—the brutal and bloodthirsty shepherds, the story goes, attempt to sexually molest the young women and then cast them into the well to drown!

Surely Moses saw other casual acts of avarice and brutality on his long journey from Egypt through a mostly unpopulated and wholly unpoliced wilderness where a solitary traveler was always at risk of being set upon by robbers and worse. "[B]ecause the public roads were watched," imagined Josephus, "he took his flight through the deserts, and where his enemies could not suspect he would travel; and though he was destitute of food, he went on. . . ."[24] But Moses had already killed once in the service of fair play, and we know him to be a man with a quick temper, a strong arm, and a stern sense of right and wrong. So he was unwilling or unable to sit back and watch the shepherds torment the seven young women. "Moses stood up," goes the biblical account, "and helped them, and watered their flock." (Exod. 2:18)

The Bible does not specify exactly how Moses helped the young women, but the scene suggests that he championed them and drove the shepherds away. Nothing less ought to be expected of a man who had already slain an oppressive slave-driver and would shortly come to lead a slave uprising against Pharaoh. The sages, however, were no more comfortable with a militant Moses at the well than they were with the manslayer who confronted the taskmaster back in Egypt, and so they concocted a scene in which Moses appears as a speechifying moralist rather than a man of action. He delivers an oration so ornate and so full of pious bluster that any real bully would have laughed out loud. "Are you not afraid to have such cowardly arms and hands? You are long-haired people, female flesh, and not men," says Moses to the shepherds in Philo's version of the tale. "I swear, by the celestial eye of justice, which sees what is done even in the most solitary places, that you shall not take [the water] from them."[25] And, sure enough, piety and pomposity alone are enough to intimidate the brutish shepherds. "Being alarmed at his words, since while he was speaking he appeared inspired," Philo concluded, "and fearing lest he might be uttering divine oracles and predictions, they obeyed and became submissive."[26]

Here the ancient storytellers are still hard at work making over Moses into the good-hearted and God-fearing soul enshrined in the rabbinical literature. Remarkably enough, after subduing the shepherds and fishing the seven young women out of the well, Moses proceeds to water *both* flocks of sheep, first the flock under the care of the abused women and then the flock that belongs to their abusers, "though the latter did not deserve his good offices," as the rabbis conceded.[27] The gesture of kindness does not cost Moses much effort. "[H]e only had to draw a bucketful," the rabbis imagined, "and the water flowed so copiously that it sufficed for all the herds."[28]

Indeed, the rabbinical literature abounds with stories of a kinder, gentler Moses than the one who inhabits the Bible. The Midrash suggests that his sojourn in Midian is an exile imposed on Moses by God himself for having slain the taskmaster back in Egypt—and exile in a designated "city of refuge" is precisely the penalty that is prescribed in the Book of Numbers for one who accidentally murders another.[29] (Num. 35:11–12) That the rabbis of late antiquity and the Middle Ages preferred a mild-mannered shepherd to a ruthless man of war reveals something important about the experience of the Jewish people in exile and the strategy for survival that they embraced until very late in the history of the Diaspora.

STRANGER IN A STRANGE LAND

The Bible pauses in its shorthand account of the early life of Moses to offer details of the unlikely courtship and marriage that began with the incident at the well. The daughters of "the priest of Midian" hastened back to their house, the biblical author reports, and their father was taken aback to see them. "How is it that ye are come so soon to-day?" asked Jethro,* presumably surprised at their early return because they were frequently delayed in watering the flock by the gang of shepherds (Exod. 2:18).

"An Egyptian delivered us out of the hand of the shepherds," the daughters replied, "and moreover he drew water for us and watered the flock." (Exod. 2:19)

So it is clear that Moses was still readily recognizable as an Egyptian, perhaps by his clothing or manner of speech. He may have addressed them in the Egyptian language or with an Egyptian accent— after all, the Bible suggests that Moses spoke both the Egyptian language of the court and the Hebrew language of the slave quarters, and he may have known a smattering of the Midianite language.

The rabbis understood these few words of biblical text to suggest that Moses *told* the young women at the well that he was an Egyptian, and one tale depicts Moses as actively concealing the fact that he was born into the slave nation of Israel. "For this God punished him by causing him to die outside of the Promised Land," the rabbis insisted.[30] But there is another tale that shows Moses bantering with the young women and even bragging a bit about himself: "Your thanks are due to the Egyptian I killed, on account of whom I had to flee from Egypt," Moses tells them. "Had it not been for him, I should not be here now."[31]

The Midianite priest was intrigued enough by the story his daughters told to send for the stranger who had rescued them at the well and who, not least of all, had done him the favor of watering his flock. "And where is he? why is it that ye have left the man?" Jethro gently scolded his daughters. "Call him, that he may eat bread." (Exod. 2:20)

The first encounter between Moses and his future father-in-law comes to a quick fairy-tale ending: "And Moses was content to dwell with the man; and he gave Moses Zipporah his daughter." (Exod. 2:21)

---

*We will have occasion to sort out the many names of the priest of Midian (see chapter eight), but let us call him Jethro for now.

Moses promptly went to work in the family business: "Now Moses was keeping the flock of Jethro his father-in-law." (Exod. 3:1) And soon enough, Zipporah was pregnant: "And she bore a son, and he called his name Gershom." (Exod. 2:22)

So began a relationship that was to play a decisive role in the life of Moses. Philo explained the instant and mutual attachment between Moses and his father-in-law in the same glowing terms that characterize all of his writing about Moses. "And [Jethro] was at once greatly struck by his appearance, and soon afterwards he learnt to admire his wisdom, for great natures are very easily discovered," he wrote, "and so he gave him the most beautiful of his daughters to be his wife."[32] Indeed, the bond between Moses and the priest of Midian is especially intimate. "So he made him his son," wrote Josephus, "and appointed him to be the guardian . . . over his cattle; for, of old, all the wealth of the barbarians was in those cattle."[33]

But the safety and serenity of his sojourn in the household of Jethro were short-lived. Moses himself seemed to understand that he did not really belong in the land of Midian, and the name that he chose for his firstborn son, Gershom, was his way of announcing his sense of alienation: "Gershom" derives from the Hebrew word for "stranger" (*ger*), and Moses chose the name, as the Bible so memorably reports, because "I have been a stranger in a strange land." (Exod. 2:22)

The Hebrew word *ger* can be given a narrow technical definition that approximates the modern phrase "resident alien,"[34] but the word rings with much deeper and darker meanings as it is used in the Bible. The *ger* is the stranger, the outsider, the Other, a beguiling but menacing figure of temptation and corruption. The life of Moses can be seen as one long struggle against the stranger: sometimes the stranger is a seducer who lures the Israelites into the worship of pagan gods and goddesses, and, quite literally, the bed of sin; sometimes an enemy in battle; sometimes an innocent bystander who happens to live on a parcel of land that has been promised to the Israelites by God. Indeed, the Book of Exodus includes openly genocidal orders issued by God to Moses and the Israelites to exterminate the strangers who stood between the Chosen People and the Promised Land.

For now, however, Moses saw *himself* as a stranger, first in the land of Egypt and then in the land of Midian. Thanks to the generosity of the priest whose daughters he had come upon at the well, Moses found a safe refuge from Pharaoh, along with a wife, a family, a livelihood; but still he felt alienated and estranged at some intimate place in his heart and soul. That brooding sense of otherness, the loneliness that seethed within him, created in Moses a yearning for intimacy that was first expressed in his bond with Jethro, and later in his difficult and sometimes plainly dysfunctional relationship with the people of Israel, and, finally and fatefully, in his tense and troubled relationship with God himself.

THE SAPPHIRE WAND

The father-in-law of Moses, first identified only as the nameless "priest of Midian," is a mysterious figure who is sometimes called Reuel (Exod. 2:18), sometimes Jethro (Exod. 3:1), sometimes Hobab (Judg. 4:11). From the moment of his first appearance in the Bible, he played a decisive role in the life of Moses, bestowing upon him a wife, teaching him the ways of the wilderness, tutoring him in the rituals of worship and the rules of government—only God enjoyed a more intimate and influential relationship with Moses.

Folklore and rabbinical tradition found the figure of Jethro—a pagan priest who was mentor to the founder of ethical monotheism—to be both intriguing and troubling. But some modern scholars have suggested that the strong bond between Moses and Jethro as depicted in the Bible is good evidence that the biblical account of Moses in Midian is not mere myth and legend. "[T]he connections between Moses and the Midianites are manifold, detailed and remarkable," writes Bible scholar George E. Mendenhall, "and can hardly be explained on any basis other than historical fact"—although Mendenhall insists that the influential figure of Jethro was probably "promoted" from a keeper of herds to a high priest at some point in the composition of the Bible to make him worthy to serve as the mentor of Moses.[35]

One thread of extrabiblical storytelling protrayed Jethro as a pagan with a heart of gold who realizes the folly of his ways and abandons the worship of idols. Shortly before meeting his future son-in-law, "his priesthood became repugnant to him," and Jethro resorts to a ruse to give up his priestly function without exposing himself to condemnation as a heretic among his own people. "I have grown too old for the duties of the office," Jethro tells his people as he turns over the paraphernalia of pagan worship to them. "Choose, therefore, whomever you would choose in my place." The Midianites are not fooled, however, and they declare Jethro to be an apostate and an outcast. "None might venture to do him the slightest service," the story goes. "Not even would the shepherds pasture his flocks, and there was nothing for him to do but impose this work upon his seven daughters."[36] And the brutality displayed to his daughters by the shepherds at the well is offered as yet another example of how the Midianites torment their former high priest.

Quite a different vision of Jethro can be found elsewhere in the ancient legend and lore, where he is depicted as a distinctly Merlin-like figure who is determined to kill off Moses by means of black magic. The story is told, for example, that Zipporah falls deeply in love with Moses but despairs of making a marriage with him because of the black arts practiced by her father. "My father has a tree in his garden with which he tests every man that expresses a desire to marry one of his daughters," Zipporah explains to Moses, "and as soon as the suitor touches the tree, he is devoured by it."[37]

The tree started out as a kind of magic wand, the rabbis explained, a rod of pure sapphire that God created "in the twilight of the first Sabbath eve" and bestowed upon Adam when the unfortunate man was driven out of the Garden of Eden. The sapphire rod is magically inscribed with the secret name of God that would someday be revealed to Moses and the ten plagues that would someday afflict the Egyptians, and it is passed from generation to generation, from Adam to Enoch, from Enoch to Noah, from Noah to Shem, and later Abraham, then Isaac, "and finally Jacob, who brought it with him to Egypt, and gave it to his son Joseph."

When Joseph dies, the mansion that he occupied as viceroy of Egypt is pillaged, and the sapphire rod ends up in the palace of Pharaoh, where Jethro is serving as one of the king's sacred scribes. Jethro covets the marvelous relic of Creation, filches it from Pharaoh, and escapes with his treasure to far-off Midian. One day, Jethro sticks the rod in the ground, but when he tries to pull it out again, he discovers that the rod has miraculously rooted itself and sprouted branches and leaves. And whenever Jethro demands that one of the young men who court his daughters try to pull the tree out of the ground, the poor fellow is destroyed.[38] Since word of Zipporah's enchanting beauty has spread far and wide, "the strong chiefs of Midian, the sons of Keni and all the mighty men of Ethiopia . . . came and tried to uproot the staff, but without avail."[39]

Then Moses arrives in Midian, and when Jethro puts him to the test, he extracts the tree from the ground with ease. In one cheerful version of the tale, Jethro rejoices at the feat of his future son-in-law. "[Perhaps] he is one of the descendants of Abraham," Jethro figures, "from whom issueth blessing for the whole world." But, again, there is a darker version of the story: Jethro is alarmed at the sudden appearance of a man who bests the devouring tree, and the canny sorcerer recognizes Moses "as the prophet in Israel concerning whom all the wise men of Egypt had foretold that he would destroy their land and its inhabitants." Frightened at what Moses is capable of doing—and fearful, too, of offending either Pharaoh, who detests Moses, or the Ethiopians, who favor him—Jethro seizes him and casts him into a deep pit on his land where Moses would simply starve to death.[40]

Now it is Zipporah who acts boldly to save the life of Moses, thus becoming the latest in a series of sheltering and rescuing women on whom Moses has depended for his survival. She plays on her father's loneliness and frailty, suggesting that the other six daughters should be sent into the far-off hills to tend the flocks while Zipporah herself remains at home and takes care of Jethro. The old man accepts Zipporah's suggestion, and so she is able to slip away now and then to the pit where Moses languishes "and provide [him] with all sort of dainties."[41] For seven years she nourishes him on the sly, and then she confronts her father.

"I recollect that once upon a time thou didst cast into yonder pit a man that had fetched thy rod from the garden for thee, and thou didst commit a great trespass thereby," Zipporah boldly challenges the old man. "If it seemeth well to thee, uncover the pit and look into it. If the man is dead, throw his corpse away, lest it fill the house with stench. But should he be alive, then thou oughtest to be convinced that he is one of those who are wholly pious, else he had died of hunger."[42]

Jethro is curious enough to follow his daughter's instructions, and he calls out to Moses by name as he approaches the pit where, seven years before, he had left the man to die. "Here am I," answers Moses, using the very word (*hineni*) that the Bible author attributes to every man who answers a divine call. The old pagan draws up his prisoner out of the pit, kisses him tenderly, and utters a confession of his newfound faith in Moses and his God. "[B]lessed be God, who guarded thee for seven years in the pit," the Midianite was imagined to recite in a kind of spontaneous catechism. "I acknowledge that He slayeth and reviveth, that thou art one of the wholly pious, that through thee God will destroy Egypt in time to come, lead His people out of the land, and drown Pharaoh and his whole army in the sea."[43]

The stories that attached themselves to the figure of Jethro betray a certain anxiety over the role assigned to the priest of Midian in the Bible. Some pious readers of the Bible may have found it unseemly that Moses fell under the influence of a man who was, after all, a stranger and a pagan. As if to temper the enthusiasm of Bible-readers for Jethro, the rabbinical storytellers insisted on casting him in the role of a sorcerer who seeks the death of Moses. But the biblical author was wholly untroubled by the fact that Jethro was a Midianite and a pagan priest; later in the biblical account, Moses will be shown to display markedly greater affection for his father-in-law than his wife and their two sons, and, still later, Jethro will be given a curiously prominent role in the very first sacrifice to the God of Abraham, Isaac, and Jacob. Arguably, as we shall see, it is a role even greater than the one played by Moses himself, which raises the intriguing but unsettling notion that he may have borrowed some of what we regard as the essential teachings of the Judeo-Christian tradition from the priest of Midian.

THE GOOD SHEPHERD

The man who had been raised a prince of Egypt turned out to possess a gift for the humble work of sheepherding. The biblical author is engaged in a certain irony: The patriarchs were restless nomads who followed their herds and flocks throughout the ancient Near East before Jacob and his twelve sons ended up in Egypt. Joseph encouraged his brethren to give up their wandering ways, but the sojourn of the Israelites as a settled people in Egypt turned out to be a catastrophe that estranged them from God and threatened their very existence. Now Moses was being given an opportunity to embrace the original and authentic identity of his people by shedding the garb of an Egyptian prince and taking up the shepherd's staff. Here is the first intimation of an idea that will take on exalted meanings throughout the Bible: the good shepherd as a metaphor for a king, a prophet, and a redeemer.

The image of Moses as a herder of sheep was celebrated by priests and scribes, sermonizers and storytellers, across many generations and several religions. The notion of god or king as a shepherd and the people as his flock can be found not only in the towering figures of Judeo-Christian tradition—Moses, David, and Jesus—but throughout the pagan faiths of the ancient Near East.[44] "[T]hat man alone can be a perfect king who is well skilled in the art of the shepherd," wrote Philo, "for the business of a shepherd is a preparation for the office of a king to any one who is destined to preside over that most manageable of all flocks, mankind."[45]

The real work of a shepherd is arduous, dirty, and lonely. The flock must be fed and watered every day, and so every day is an urgent search for a new meadow and a new spring. Curious and sometimes unruly animals must be kept from straying too far from the flock. Jackals, hawks, and other predators must be kept at bay with nothing more than a shepherd's hooked staff. Above all, the shepherd is alone in his work—the flock relies wholly on the shepherd, and the shepherd relies on no one but God. Even a matter-of-fact job description of a shepherd's work, however, fairly rings with larger and grander meanings, both spiritual and political, and the Bible makes the most of them.

"Woe to the worthless shepherd that leaveth the flock!" railed the prophet Zechariah in reprimand to the kings of Israel who were the distant successors of Moses, thus suggesting that a worthy monarch, like a good shepherd, must not neglect his duty to those who rely on him (Zech. 11:17). Moses himself will later beseech God to appoint a worthy man to take his place, so that "the congregation of the Lord be not as sheep which have no shepherd." (Num. 27:27) The biblical author means us to see the long and uneventful years of tending the flocks of Jethro as ideal tutelage for the momentous calling that Moses would shortly experience on a lonely mountaintop in the wilderness.

Now the fact is that a real-life shepherd must possess a certain toughness and even ruthlessness. He must be prepared to drive off or kill a predator that threatens the flock; he must be able to abandon a sick or injured animal to its fate rather than endanger the flock by pausing to care for it. But the rabbis insisted on celebrating the mildness and mercy that Moses supposedly displays in his work as a shepherd. "Moses showed loving care, letting younger animals graze first and the most vigorous ones last," they imagined. According to one explanation for the forty-year gap in the biblical narrative, Moses spends the entire period in service to Jethro—and, the rabbis insisted, not once during those forty years is a single sheep in his care attacked by a wild beast. Mindful of the age-old conflict between herdsmen and farmers, the rabbis carefully noted that Moses is vigilant in keeping his flocks and herds from grazing on "private estates," thus imagining the anachronism of "No Trespassing" signs in the wilderness of Midian. Moses was "the most skillful herdsman of his time," wrote Philo in yet another superlative, and he "saw his flocks increase with great joy and guileless good faith."[46]

Perhaps the single most enduring story told about Moses in the rabbinical literature depicts him in pursuit of a single young stray, a lamb in one version and a kid in another, that stubbornly evades the shepherd's crook until, at last, the animal reaches a distant stream and pauses to drink. As Moses catches up with the beast, he does not show the slightest anger or impatience. "Poor kid, I knew not that you were thirsty, and were running after water!" goes the story, which was first told in the Midrash and has often been repeated over the centuries since then. " 'Thou art weary,' said Moses to the kid, and he carried it back to the herd on his shoulder." God witnesses the act of care and kindness, and notes these qualities in the man who would become his greatest prophet. "Thou hast compassion with a flock belonging to a man of flesh and blood!" declares God. "As thou livest, thou shalt pasture Israel, My flock."[47]

No sensible shepherd, of course, would have left the flock alone and at risk while patiently stalking a single frail stray. But the whole point of telling the tale was to make over Moses into a celestial shepherd whose flock is all of humankind, to drape him in precisely the same mantle that would be worn by the Redeemer, a Messiah yet to come in Jewish tradition and Jesus of Nazareth in Christian tradition. Moses' long years of service as a shepherd eventually acquired a profoundly mystical aura, and countless stories were told of encounters between Moses and God, Moses and angels, Moses and demons, all focusing on his goodheartedness toward the poor dumb beasts under his care, and his faithfulness toward God.

One day, according to one of the stories told by the sages, a pure white dove alights upon Moses while he is tending the flock and desperately seeks his protection from a pursuing hawk. Moses hides the frail bird under his cloak, and then, moments later, the hawk swoops down and begs pitiably in a human voice for a morsel to eat. Moses promptly agrees to feed the hawk, but the thought never occurs to him to offer the dove that he is sheltering. Rather, Moses sates the hunger of the hawk with a bloody hunk of his own flesh.

"[T]he future redeemer of Israel cut from his holy limbs a piece of flesh, equivalent in weight to that of the dove, and gave it to the hawk, saying: 'Here is thy nourishment,' " goes the tale. At that moment, both the dove and the hawk reveal themselves to be angels in disguise: the dove is the angel Gabriel, and the hawk is the angel Michael. "We have only come to test thee," they announce, "and to make manifest thy generosity, noble mind, and magnanimity."[48]

Here is the highest expression of Moses as the Good Shepherd, one who literally offers his own body and blood in defense of his flock. The tale originated in the Jewish tradition and yet seems to anticipate the Christian sacrament of communion. Indeed, the New Testament explicitly presents Moses as the precursor and role model of Jesus and evokes his example to validate Jesus as the authentic Messiah. To see the biblical Moses as a Christ-like figure, however, forces us to extract him from the context of the Hebrew Scriptures and make him into someone far more elevated than the flesh-and-blood Moses who was known to the authors of the Bible. The man whom we actually encounter in the Bible would not have recognized himself in the shimmering icon of the Good Shepherd that was fashioned by the teachers and preachers who came along much later.

THE MOUNTAIN OF GOD

Moses spends thirteen years as a shepherd in service to his father-in-law, according to the rabbinical tale that delays his arrival in Midian long enough for Moses to distinguish himself on the field of battle and then on the throne of Ethiopia. Or, if we disregard the fanciful account of his adventures in Ethiopia and cleave to the biblical text, Moses tended Jethro's flocks for some forty years. He was a husband and a father of two sons, a settled and resigned man who seemed to take pleasure in the companionship of his father-in-law, as well as the solitude of the days and nights spent in search of pasturage.

Moses may have still been tending the flocks as he approached the age of eighty, according to the unlikely chronology of the Bible, and he seemed ready to end his long life with a whimper rather than a bang. And how different the moral of the story would have been if Moses had died a shepherd in Midian! The life of Moses would have been understood as a sentimental morality tale—a foundling is spared from certain death by the kindness of humble people, he is raised to the heights of wealth and privilege by a royal princess, then he forfeits his apparent good fortune when he strikes out against injustice, but finally he discovers that the only authentic satisfactions are those to be found in work, friends, and family.

But the story of Moses did not end there, and the cherished rabbinical traditions do not capture the complex, dynamic, and passionate man that he will shortly reveal himself to be. Unbeknownst to Moses, a shepherd at large with his flock in the wilderness of Midian, an eerie, dangerous, and momentous encounter is awaiting him at the peak of some nameless mountain. His life, the destiny of his people, and the history of the world will be transformed by what he finds there.

Chapter Five

THE MAN GOD BEFRIENDED, THE MAN HE SOUGHT TO KILL

*According to the Talmud, a voice from heaven
should be ignored if it is not on the side of justice.*
—ISAAC BASHEVIS SINGER, *A YOUNG
MAN IN SEARCH OF LOVE*

"And it came to pass in the course of those many days that the king of Egypt died," the Bible reports, "and the children of Israel sighed by reason of the bondage, and they cried, and their cry came up unto God."

When the sounds of suffering finally reached the ear of God, he was reminded of his old and long-ignored promise to Abraham that the Israelites would one day live in freedom and prosperity in the land of Canaan:

"And God heard their groaning, and God remembered His covenant." (Exod. 2:23)

Characteristically, the rabbinical storytellers supplied gruesome but wholly imaginary details about the death of Pharaoh that are mentioned nowhere in the Bible—God curses Pharaoh with leprosy as a punishment for his cruelty to the Israelites, and the suffering king is told by his trusted privy counselor, Balaam, that the only way to cure himself is to bathe every day in the blood of a freshly slaughtered Israelite child. The carnage goes on for ten years with no relief for the suffering king—indeed, the rotting leprosy only turns into excruciating boils—and Pharaoh's affliction worsens when God finally causes his chariot to overturn in a freak accident and the king's horse sits on his disfigured face. Even then, Pharaoh lingers for three years, "and his flesh emitted a stench like a carcass cast into the field in summer time in the heat of the sun." Indeed, Pharaoh's body is so putrefied with disease and ravaged by injury that it could not be embalmed "as was usual with kings," and his body is hastily buried in a simple grave.

"Thus the Lord requited him with evil for the evil he had done in his days to Israel," the rabbis wrote, "and he died in terror and shame after having reigned ninety-four years."[1]

No news of the death of Pharaoh, however, had yet reached Moses in far-off Midian, where he now lived with his wife and two sons and tended the flocks of his father-in-law. One day is very much like another for a shepherd, and Moses, like nomadic herdsmen in all lands and all ages, must have marked the passage of time by subtle observation and calculation—the height of the sun in the sky at midday, the distance traveled between sunrise and sunset, the sound and speed of the water that rushed through a wadi after a cloudburst and then disappeared into the rocky soil. The primal rhythms of life stretch out endlessly into the future for a pastoral nomad; each day, each season, each year is measured out in precisely the same way, day after day, until the day of his death. Nothing in his circumstances—and nothing revealed in the Bible so far—suggested any other future for Moses.

And then one day something extraordinary happened to Moses, and nothing was ever the same again.

"HERE AM I"

On that day, Moses led his flock "to the farthest end of the wilderness," as the Bible reports, where he came upon "the mountain of God, unto Horeb." (Exod. 3:1) The text appears to suggest that Moses was merely searching out a fresh supply of fodder for his flock. Flavius Josephus, however, insisted that the locals feared and shunned the place despite its superior pasturage "because of the opinion men had that God dwelt there, the shepherds not daring to ascend up to it."[2] Perhaps out of boldness and curiosity, or maybe only because of his stubborn single-mindedness, Moses led his flock to Horeb—and there he saw a remarkable sight.

And the angel of the Lord appeared unto him in a flame of
fire out of the midst of a bush; and he looked, and, behold,
the bush burned with fire, and the bush was not consumed.
(Exod. 3:2)

Moses struggled to comprehend what his eyes beheld so plainly in
the bright sunlight of a desert afternoon, to explain the impossibility
that presented itself to him.

"I will turn aside now," Moses said to himself, "and see this great
sight, why the bush is not burnt." (Exod. 3:3)

From somewhere inside the burning bush, the Bible seems to suggest, God himself was watching Moses, and now he was ready to get
down to business.

"Moses," called a disembodied voice once, then a second time.
"Moses."

"Here am I," Moses answered. (Exod. 3:4)

Here is the moment that is anticipated from the beginning of the
Book of Exodus, perhaps even from the moment of Creation as described in Genesis. The word that is used by Moses in response to the
voice in the burning bush—*"Hineni!"*—has already been uttered by
Abraham when God called upon him to sacrifice his son Isaac (Gen.
22:1), and it will be spoken again when God summons young Samuel to
prophesy to Israel (1 Samuel 3:4). "Here am I" is the formulaic response
of every mortal who is called to some sacral act by God. But here and
now, as spoken by Moses, the phrase rings with both wonder and terror:
Moses is fully awake and alert to the divine revelation that will put an
end to his quiet life as a shepherd in Midian and put him on the road to
a grand and terrible fate.

MOSES SPEAKS!

Suddenly, if rather subtly, the Bible gives a voice to the man who, until
now, has been a mute and indistinct figure. Now he is shown to engage
in a long, leisurely, and almost matter-of-fact exchange with the deity
who is manifested in the burning bush, the first of many such tête-à-
têtes between God and Moses.

"Do not come any closer," God cautioned Moses from within

the burning bush, and then he instructed his newly snared acolyte in the protocol of parlaying with the Creator: "Take off your shoes—the ground where you stand is holy." (Exod. 3:5)

Moses complied with God's strange demand in meek silence.

"I am the God of your father," said the voice. "I am the God of Abraham, the God of Isaac, and the God of Jacob." (Exod. 3:5–6)

Moses must have realized that he had somehow stumbled into the presence of the ancient and aloof deity of Israel. The Bible confirms that God had been willing to appear to his creatures in human form—chatting with Adam and Eve during an evening stroll in the Garden of Eden (Gen. 3:8), showing up at the tent of Abraham to cadge a meal (Gen 18:8), engaging in a good-natured wrestling match with Jacob (Gen. 32:25, 31). But the voice of God had fallen silent long ago and his face had remained hidden during the long enslavement of the Israelites in Egypt. So fearful was Moses at the sound of the voice from the burning bush, the Bible reports, that he buried his face in the folds of his cloak like a child who hopes that he can make the bogeyman go away by closing his eyes (Exod. 3:6).

Did the thought occur to God that he had gone a bit too far with the flash-and-dazzle of the burning bush? After all, how could he conduct a businesslike conversation with a man who hid his face in his cloak? In any event, the Bible reports that God suddenly launched into a rather grandiose account of himself even without being asked, as if he hoped to calm Moses down and lure him into uncovering his face.

"I have surely seen the affliction of My people that are in Egypt," God said to Moses, "and have heard their cry by reason of their taskmasters; for I know their pains; and I am come down to deliver them out of the hand of the Egyptians, and to bring them up out of that land unto a good land and large, unto a land flowing with milk and honey—"

God now introduced a bit of the ethno-geography of the ancient Near East to his audience of one.

"—unto the place of the Canaanite, and the Hittite, and the Amorite, and the Perizzite, and the Hivite, and the Jebusite."

God continued: "And now, behold, the cry of the children of Israel is come unto Me; moreover I have seen the oppression wherewith the Egyptians oppress them." (Exod. 3:7–10)

And what does all of it have to do with *me*? Moses may have been thinking to himself as God now came to the reason for calling on him.

"Come now therefore," God said to Moses, "and I will send *thee* unto Pharaoh, that thou mayest bring forth My people the children of Israel out of Egypt." (Exod. 3:10)[3]

THE RELUCTANT HERO

Yet Moses did not act like a man in awe of God. When he finally understood that God was recruiting *him* for a task that must have struck him as not only incredible but downright impossible, Moses spoke up boldly— and suggested that God ought to send someone else to do the job.

"Who am I," he blurted out to God with a sudden audacity that may have surprised both of them, "that I should go unto Pharaoh, and that I should bring forth the children of Israel out of Egypt?" (Exod. 3:11)

God did not display even a hint of anger or impatience toward the impudent mortal who questioned his divine plan. Rather, God sought to reassure the reluctant hero with sweet and comforting words.

"Certainly I will be with thee," God said, "and here is what will prove that it was I who sent you: When you have brought the people out of Egypt, you shall all worship God here on this mountain." (Exod. 3:12)[4]

Moses, however, was not yet assured that the companionship of his newfound friend would be enough to prevail over Pharaoh. Indeed, the thought evidently occurred to Moses that the Israelites back in Egypt would regard him as something of a crank if he showed up one day, announced that God had sent him, and ordered everyone to pack up and leave. So the next question that Moses put to God was a clever and calculating one, an effort to test the bona fides of the voice that characterized itself as divine.

"Behold, when I come unto the children of Israel, and shall say unto them: The God of your fathers hath sent me unto you," Moses parried, "and they shall say to me: What is His name?—what shall I say?" (Exod. 3:13)

"I Am That I Am," God replied. "Thus shalt thou say unto the children of Israel: 'I Am' hath sent me unto you. Yahweh, the God of your fathers, the God of Abraham, the God of Isaac, and the God of Jacob, hath sent me to you—this is My name for ever, and this is My memorial unto all generations." (Exod. 3:14)[5]

THE WONDROUS NAMES OF GOD

The revelation of the name of God in Exodus 3:14 is a deeply enigmatic moment that has prompted centuries of conjecture among theologians. God is known in the Bible by a great many names, titles, and honorifics: Elohim, which literally means "gods" but is rendered in English by Bible translators simply as "God"; El Shaddai ("God Almighty")[6] and El Elyon ("God Most High") and El Olam ("Everlasting God"), all of which echo the names of deities in the pantheon of the dreaded and despised Canaanites;[7] and many more besides, including "Lord" (Adonai), "Mighty One," "Fear of Isaac," "God of Hosts," and so on. But Yahweh is God's personal name, his secret name, and the words God uttered in response to Moses' question—*"Ehyeh asher ehyeh"* ("I Am That I Am," or "I Will Be What I Will Be")—are an elaborate bit of wordplay on "Yahweh."*

The game begins with the so-called Tetragrammaton, a word that is spelled in Hebrew with four letters that correspond to the English-language consonants *YHWH*. Since the Hebrew alphabet does not include vowels, we still do not know with certainty how those four letters were pronounced. "Jehovah" was once thought to be the proper phonetic spelling of YHWH, and the word still appears in some Bible translations. Today, "Yahweh" is accepted by most scholars as the spelling that best approximates how the Tetragrammaton was pronounced.

Of course, by long and sacred tradition in Judaism, the name of God is not supposed to be pronounced at all, and the word itself is treated with great ingenuity in Jewish usage to avoid the sin of speaking it aloud: the four Hebrew letters that spell out the name of God (*yod, hay, va'v, hay*) are sometimes replaced in Jewish prayer books and other religious works by the letter *yod* repeated twice and pronounced "Adonai," which is actually the Hebrew word for "Lord." Under certain circumstances, a pious Jew will refer to the deity simply as "HaShem," which

---

*Starting with the King James Version of 1611, the customary practice of English-language Bible translators has been to render *Yahweh*, the personal name of God, as "The Lord," and *Elohim*, the Hebrew word for "god" (or, more likely, "gods"), as "God." When quoting directly from the JPS, which follows the practice of the King James Version, I have occasionally taken the liberty of replacing "The Lord" with *Yahweh*, the word that actually appears in the original Hebrew text of the Bible. The NEB departs from traditional usage by translating *Yahweh* as "Jehovah," an old (and erroneous) phonetic rendering of *Yahweh*.

means literally "The Name." Until the destruction of the Temple at Jerusalem, the name of God was permitted to be uttered only by the high priest, and only in the Holy of Holies, the innermost sanctum of the Temple, and only once each year, on Yom Kippur, the Day of Atonement. By the first century C.E., Josephus was explaining to his readers that God had revealed his name to Moses so that "when he offered sacrifice he might invoke him by such his name in his obligations." But Josephus refused to repeat the holy name, "concerning which it is not lawful for me to say any more."[8]

Much effort and imagination have been invested in decoding those four letters and revealing the secret meaning that is suspected to be hidden away in the name of God. "[A]s a name could not be just empty sound," explains Martin Noth, "a new name necessarily also represented a new revelation."[9] By torturing the imagined roots of the word in ancient Hebrew and Arabic, scholars have proposed that "Yahweh" means "the Eternal One," "the Blowing One," "the Destroyer," "the Thunderer," "the One Who Succors," "the One Who Roars"—but "not a single one is really convincing," as Elias Auerbach writes.[10]

The explanation offered to Moses by God himself—"I Am That I Am"—conceals much more than it reveals. The Hebrew phrase that appears in the original Bible text ("Ehyeh asher ehyeh") begins and ends with a word (ehyeh) in which the syllables of "Yahweh" are inverted—a bit of wordplay that would have been recognized and appreciated by the original readership of the Bible. "I Am That I Am" can also be understood as a rejection of the "technical magic" by which gods and goddesses were customarily worshipped in Egypt and elsewhere in the ancient world. "I do not need to be conjured for I am always with you," explains Martin Buber, "but it is impossible to conjure me."[11] And Brevard Childs concedes that the sentence appears to be "a senseless tautology," but he finds sense in its very senselessness, "as if to say, I am who I am, a self-contained incomprehensible being."[12]

But the phrase by which God replied to the query of Moses atop Horeb can be seen as the "refusal of an answer," as Childs puts it,[13] and that may have been God's point in uttering a kind of divine mumbo jumbo in the first place. "[T]he deeper and more beautiful the philosophical explanation is, the less helpful . . . it is in discovering the intended meaning," writes Elias Auerbach in his biography of Moses, suggesting that the wry banter between God and Moses around the burning bush amounted to "a game of hide-and-seek with the sacred name."[14]

Still, the game was believed to hold out a powerful and desirable prize for anyone who grasped the real name of God. Rather like the fairy tale about Rumpelstiltskin, the malevolent imp whose magical power could be defeated only by guessing his name, the Bible assumes that knowledge of the name of God bestows power upon those who know it. Jacob wrestled with an angel (or was it God himself?) and then refused to release his defeated opponent until he revealed his name (Gen. 32:25–32)—an incident that embodies "the age-old magical conception that knowledge of the right name confers on man some magic power, above all, power over the deity," as Auerbach explains. "That is why the deity is always evasive and does not give its name, nor will it hand this power over to man."[15]

The biblical source who described the scene on Horeb assumed that the real name of God was unknown to the Israelites, but another source has already told us in Genesis 4:26 that the name Yahweh was known to humankind shortly after the Creation.[16] Although the Book of Exodus does not explain when or why the Israelites forgot the name of their deity, it is clear that God has held himself aloof from his Chosen People throughout their long ordeal in Egypt. "God is *deus absconditus*"—a concealed god—as one Bible commentator wrote,[17] echoing the words of Pascal. Only now was God deigning to reveal himself and his name to the children of Israel. Yet the very fact that Moses wanted to know the name of God seems to suggest that it was already a kind of password that he could use to persuade the skeptical Israelites of the truth of his message.

A tale in the Midrash embraced precisely such an understanding of the meaning and use of the name of God. The Tetragrammaton has long been forgotten by the Israelites at large but is still known and preserved as a precious secret by the elders of Israel during their captivity in Egypt. From generation to generation, the elders pass down the proper name of God precisely so that it be can used someday to test anyone who claims to be an emissary of the deity otherwise known by his formal title, Elohim. If Moses is able to invoke the personal name of God when put to the test by elders of Israel, "they would know and be able to confirm his divine commission."[18] That was the point of the encounter on Horeb: God armed his prophet with the secret knowledge of his name, and sent him on his way.

CREDENTIALS

After disclosing his secret name to Moses, God abruptly resumed his lecture—and, like many lecturers, he repeated himself.

"Go and gather the elders of Israel together, and say unto them: 'Yahweh, the God of your fathers, the God of Abraham, of Isaac, and of Jacob, hath appeared unto me, saying: I have surely remembered you, and seen that which is done to you in Egypt,' " God told Moses. "And I have said: I will bring you out of the affliction of Egypt unto the land of the Canaanite." (Exod. 3:16–17)[19]

Next, God seemed to anticipate a rather obvious flaw in his scheme—what if Pharaoh balked at liberating several hundred thousand slaves just because Moses said so? So God came up with a clever ruse by which Moses would be able to trick Pharaoh into letting the Israelites go. "And thou shalt come unto the king of Egypt, and ye shall say unto him: Yahweh, the God of the Hebrews, hath met with us," God instructed. "And now let us go, we pray thee, three days' journey into the wilderness, that we may sacrifice to Yahweh our God." (Exod. 3:18)[20]

If all went according to plan, Pharaoh would be duped into believing that the Israelites would dutifully trek back to Egypt after three days at liberty in the wilderness. Once on the march with Pharaoh's blessings, of course, the Israelites would *keep* marching all the way to the Promised Land! But apparently not even God took the idea quite seriously, because he promptly conceded to Moses that the scheme would not work and proposed another plan that depended on terror and brute force rather than guile and deception.

"And I know that the king of Egypt will not give you leave to go, except by a mighty hand," God continued. "And I will put forth My hand and smite Egypt with all My wonders—and after that, he will let you go." (Exod. 3:19–20)[21]

Lest the Israelites begin to fret about how they would provide for themselves after their liberation, God described an even more unlikely scenario to Moses: the Egyptians who managed to survive the "mighty hand" of God would cheerfully allow themselves to be relieved of their wealth by their former slaves.

"And I will give this people favour in the sight of the Egyptians," God concluded. "And it shall come to pass that, when ye go, ye shall not go empty-handed; but every woman shall ask of her neighbour for jewelry of silver and jewelry of gold, and fine clothing, too—ye shall put them upon your sons, and upon your daughters, and ye shall plunder the Egyptians." (Exod. 3:21–22)[22]

So God's grand plan was now on the table in all of its elaborate and sometimes unlikely detail. Moses would return to Egypt as God's emissary, and God would go with him. To prove his divine credentials, Moses would reveal the name of God to the elders of the enslaved Israelites. Moses would try to trick Pharaoh into giving the slaves three days off to march into the wilderness, but Pharaoh would recognize the ruse and refuse to let them go. Then God would come down hard on the Egyptians, and Pharaoh would change his mind. On their way out, the Israelites would enrich themselves with the spoils freely bestowed upon them by their former slave masters.

Now it was up to Moses—and Moses said no.

SIGNS AND WONDERS

No one can accuse Moses of being a yes-man to the Almighty. Like Abraham before him, and Job after him, Moses was willing to challenge God, debate with him, even hector him. Indeed, the Bible allows us to see Moses as the ultimate naysayer and faultfinder, a man who could see all the flaws in God's plan. Now, at the very outset of their first encounter, Moses began to pepper Yahweh with awkward questions and bold objections. To each of his questions, however, God had a ready answer.

"But, behold, they will not believe me, or hearken unto my voice," said Moses of the Israelites, whose contrariness he already knew, "for they will say: The Lord hath not appeared unto thee." (Exod. 4:1)

God seemed to ignore the complaint and abruptly changed the subject, calling Moses' attention to the shepherd's staff that he still clutched.

"What is that in thy hand?" asked God.

"A staff," answered Moses.

"Cast it on the ground," God commanded.

Moses complied, and the wooden staff instantly and miraculously turned into a serpent, whereupon the Bible reports that Moses abruptly turned and ran (Exod. 4:3).

God called out to the fleeing Moses—"Put forth thy hand and seize the snake by its tail!"—and Moses complied. As soon as his fingers closed around the writhing tail, the serpent turned back into a staff, and Moses found himself holding nothing more than the ordinary shepherd's crook that he had started with (Exod. 4:2–5).[23]

The snake trick was one that Moses could use to dazzle any doubters back in Egypt, as God now pointed out, "that they may believe that the Lord, the God of their fathers hath appeared unto thee." (Exod. 4:5) But God had yet more tricks up his sleeve.

"Put now thy hand into the fold of thy cloak," God told Moses, who again complied. When Moses withdrew his hand from his cloak, he saw that the hand was suddenly disfigured with leprosy and white as snow. "Put thy hand back again," God instructed, and when Moses repeated the process, he saw that his hand was healed and healthy once again (Exod. 4:6–7).[24]

God seemed to understand that the Israelites might not be persuaded by even these signs of divine authority, and so he revealed a third sign that Moses might invoke if the first two were not effective.

"Now, it shall come to pass," God told Moses, "if they will not believe thee and do not hearken to the first sign, then they will hearken to the second sign. And if they will not believe either of the two signs, and will not hearken to thy voice, then thou shalt take the water of the Nile, and pour the water upon the dry ground, and the water shall become blood." (Exod. 4:8–9)[25]

If Moses was impressed by the display of divine legerdemain, he gave no sign of it. Rather, he came up with yet another objection.

"Oh Lord, I am not a man of words, not before and not now," Moses said, "for I am slow of speech and of a slow tongue." (Exod. 4:10)

His protest seemed to take God by surprise—and it surprises the Bible reader too. Nothing mentioned in the Bible so far in the life story of Moses suggests that he suffered from a speech impediment or a lack of eloquence, and Moses has been perfectly at ease in bantering with God until now.* As if suspecting that Moses was merely groping for an excuse not to go to Egypt, God began to display a certain testiness. After

---

*As we have already seen, the rabbinical storytellers imagined that Moses was "slow of speech" due to the childhood injury that he suffered when the angel Gabriel prompted him to pick up a burning coal instead of a sparkling jewel (see chapter three).

all, Moses did not seem to grasp that the he was dealing with the Almighty and not merely some gullible slave master who could be sweet-talked with a few words of whiny self-abasement!

"Who hath made a man's mouth? or who maketh a man dumb or deaf, or seeing, or blind? Is it not I the Lord?" God asked. But it was strictly a rhetorical question, and he did not wait for an answer. "Now therefore go," God said curtly to Moses, "and I will be with thy mouth, and teach thee what thou shalt speak." (Exod. 4:11)

"O my Lord, send, I pray thee, by the hand of him whom thou wilt send," said Moses (Exod. 4:12 KJV).

The meaning of his words is rather obscure, but his lack of enthusiasm for the long trek to Egypt is clear enough.* What he really meant to say was, "O my Lord, I pray thee, please send somebody else," as one Bible scholar has explained the "visceral and desperate" words of Moses.[26]

God did not fail to note the defiant subtext, and "the anger of the Lord was kindled against Moses." (Exod. 4:13) God would make one final accommodation to convince the balky Moses to take the job, but he was plainly not happy about it.

"Is there not Aaron thy brother the Levite?" said God, perhaps engaging in a bit of sarcasm of his own. "I know that he can speak well." (Exod. 4:14)

Moses fell silent, and so God resigned himself to the necessity of sending *two* men on the mission to Pharaoh, Moses *and* his brother. Just as Moses was to be the mouthpiece for God, Aaron would be the mouthpiece for Moses.

"And thou shalt speak unto him, and put the words in his mouth," God instructed Moses. "He will do all the speaking to the people for you, he will be the mouthpiece, and you will be the god he speaks for." (Exod. 4:16)[27]

Finally, God brought the long encounter, at first so startling and then so edgy and unsettling for both of them, to an abrupt end. "And thou shalt take in thy hand this rod," God reminded Moses, pointing out the shepherd's staff that would now serve him as a magic wand, "and with it you will work the signs." (Exod. 4:17)[28]

---

*The NEB translates the same verse in a manner that suggests the intended meaning of the original text: "But Moses still protested, 'No, Lord, send whom thou wilt.'"

Then, as suddenly as the encounter between God and Moses had begun, it was over. Without a single word more or the slightest ceremony of leave-taking, God was gone and Moses was on his way to Egypt.

FIVE HUNDRED PARASANGS

Significantly, God is given a voice but no shape or form in the biblical account of the theophany on Mount Horeb. The men and women who contributed the oldest strands of narrative to the biblical tapestry understood God to be a distinctly camera-shy deity, and the first of the Ten Commandments would forbid the making of his image. So the first encounter between God and Moses in the Bible is left intentionally vague. Indeed, the biblical account of what happened when Moses found himself in conversation with God—an experience that we might imagine to be awe-inspiring and blood-shaking—is striking only in its restraint and understatement.

That God chose to manifest himself in something so ordinary as a bush—"a familiar sight in the pasturelands,"[29] as one Bible scholar observes—seems a humble gesture for the King of the Universe. The flames that Moses saw might have a mundane explanation, too; perhaps it was an ordinary scrub fire or a certain variety of flora so laden with incendiary chemicals that it sometimes bursts into flames.[30] Even the fact that the bush appeared to burn without being consumed can be explained by reference to a rare but hardly miraculous phenomenon. "The favourite explanation of the exegete has been a manifestation similar to St. Elmo's fire," writes the venerable Martin Noth, "and in fact we must imagine something of this sort."[31]

Slightly more exotic is the "angel" who materialized in the burning bush—"And the angel of the Lord appeared unto him in a flame of fire out of the midst of the bush" (Exod. 3:2)—but the appearance of the angel is not described in the Bible, which means we are to understand it as some fuzzy manifestation of God himself rather than as one of the winged cherubs of Renaissance art. "[A] certain very beautiful form, not resembling any visible thing," is how Philo described the figure in the burning bush, "a most Godlike image, emitting a light more brilliant than fire, which any one might have imagined to be the image of the living God." Still, the ancient Jewish chronicler was pious enough to refrain from openly suggesting that what Moses saw in the burning bush *was* God. "[L]et it be called an angel," demurred Philo.[32]*

In fact, Philo insisted on reading the whole incident on Horeb as metaphorical rather than literal. "For the burning bush was a symbol of the oppressed people, and the burning fire was a symbol of the oppressors," he explained, "and the circumstance of the burning bush not being consumed was an emblem of the fact that the people thus oppressed would not be destroyed by those who were attacking them." Philo concluded: "All these circumstances are an allegory."[33]

More recent Bible scholarship suggests that the miracle of the burning bush does not conceal "a hidden and mysterious truth." Rather, it may have been yet more wordplay. "It may be that we do not need to look further than the fact that the Hebrew word for 'bush' (*sene*) points in concealed fashion to Sinai," wrote Gerhard von Rad, "the name of the mountain at which the great revelation of God is to be given."[34]

The tellers of pious fairy tales, however, were not content with the baffling ambiguities of the original text, and no other biblical scene is depicted in the rabbinical literature with quite so febrile an imagination. In order to glorify God and his celestial realm, the rabbis and sages of late antiquity and the early Middle Ages borrowed various images of heaven and hell from Christian, Zoroastrian, and other extrabiblical sources, or simply allowed their own imaginations to run wild. They sent Moses on adventures worthy of a Münchausen, and they far exceeded the Bible itself in magic and miracle. Still, they betrayed a certain nagging anxiety about Moses, and the rabbinical literature allows us to glimpse his darker side, too.

As we have already seen, a certain anti-Moses tradition can be detected in the Bible itself, and the sages were sometimes torn between celebrating the perfect faith of a meek and modest Moses and allowing us to see him as a carping and even cowardly man. Here is what may be the best-kept secret about Moses: Both the biblical authors and the pious commentators were reluctant to praise Moses so extravagantly that he might come to be regarded as godlike or even a god in his own right,

---

*Some Bible scholars suspect that the original version of the incident at the burning bush featured God and Moses only and did not include an angel at all. The argument has been made that angels were routinely written into biblical scenes where God is shown to encounter a mere mortal by priestly censors who wanted to discourage ordinary men and women from entertaining the daring notion that they might come face to face with God without the assistance of an angelic (or priestly) go-between.

and so they presented him with flaws and failings that mark him as a mere mortal.

Moses cannot be bothered to go to the mountain of God, according to one rabbinical tale, and so the mountain is forced to come to him: "Mount Horeb began to move at his approach, coming to meet him, and only stood still when Moses placed his foot on it."[35] Even then, Moses turns away from the "wonderful sight" of the burning bush atop Horeb since he is "little inclined to be interrupted in his work for which he received wages."[36] He scolds God for burdening him with the task of liberation when, as Moses points out, God's promise to Jacob was that God himself would "surely bring thee up again out of Egypt."[37] He points out that God dispatched angels to rescue Hagar and Lot, too—why then doesn't God send a few angels to carry out the task that he is now imposing on Moses alone, especially in light of the vastly greater number of souls he is required to lead to safety?[38] He complains about the difficulty of feeding the multitudes in the wilderness: "Whence shall I procure dainties for those who have borne babies, whence sweetmeats for the pregnant, and whence tidbits for the little ones?"[39] And he shows himself to be arrogant and cowardly at the same time: "Why should I risk the safety of my person," Moses asks God in one tale, "seeing that I know not whether Israel possesses merits making them worthy of redemption?"[40] Moses finally consents to go to Egypt, but only on certain conditions: God must grant him "whatever he desires," including a miraculous cure of his speech impediment, and must "invest [him] with the power of chastising Pharaoh with brute force."[41]

God is patient and forbearing in these tales, at least at first, and he spends seven days in argument with Moses. "He resorted to persuasion," the rabbis explained, "that the heathen might not say that He abused His power as the Ruler of the world, forcing men to do His service against their will."[42] Even God does not enjoy an infinite supply of patience, however, and Moses manages to exasperate him with his crabbing and cadging. "Whence cometh now this effrontery of thine, that thou addressest Me as a servant his master?" God finally rages back at Moses. "Thou speakest too many words by far."[43]

God proceeds to unburden himself of his own grievances against Moses. He accuses Moses of tricking him into revealing his "Ineffable Name" with no real intention of undertaking the mission to Egypt. He callously rejects the plea of Moses for a miraculous cure of his speech impediment. "I might change thee into a new man, and heal thee of imperfect speech," God taunts, "but because thou hast uttered such words, I refrain from curing thee."[44] Indeed, God threatens Moses with the rod of God that was intended to smite the Egyptians. "Thou deservest to be castigated with it," God declares to Moses. "As thou followest the example of the slanderous serpent, so shalt thou be punished with leprosy, wherewith the serpent was punished."[45]

Still, the anti-Moses tradition that can be discerned in the rabbinical literature is overshadowed by flights of fancy in which the humble shepherd is exalted beyond recognition. Precisely because Moses is modest enough to hide his face, the rabbis imagined, God favors him with a grand tour of heaven and hell. His guide is Metatron, "Angel of the Face," and he is escorted from the peak of Horeb to the upper reaches of heaven by some thirty thousand secondary angels. When Moses balks at the privilege—"I am but flesh and blood, and I cannot look upon the countenance of an angel"—Metatron magically transforms his body into "torches of fire" and his eyes into flaming chariot wheels—an image that mimics the visions of Ezekiel (Ezek. 1:15 ff.) and the Merkabah (or "chariot") mysticism that was based on Ezekiel's strange visions.[46]

What Moses sees during his celestial excursion—and, in fact, the excursion itself and the very notion of heaven and hell—would have been wholly unrecognizable to the biblical authors who penned the words that we find in the Five Books of Moses, where heaven and hell are hardly mentioned at all. According to the rabbinical storytellers, Moses visits each of the "seven heavens," where he sees sights that seem to have been borrowed from some overheated apocalyptic tract—and probably were. Moses beholds an angel with seventy thousand heads, "so tall it would take a human being five hundred years to climb to his height," and each head sings the praises of the Lord.[47] He glimpses a heavenly temple with "the pillars thereof made of red fire, the staves of green fire, the threshold of white fire, the gates of carbuncles, and the pinnacles of rubies."[48] By the time he reaches the seventh heaven, he bumps into the Angels of Anger and Wrath, each five hundred parasangs* high and each "forged out of chains of black fire and red fire," a sight that so frightens Moses that Metatron feels moved to em-

---

*A parasang, a unit of measurement used in ancient Persia, is thought to equal approximately four miles or six kilometers.

brace and console him. " 'Moses, Moses, thou favorite of God, fear not, and be not terrified,' " says the angel—"and Moses became calm."[49]

Then the angel Gabriel takes over and conducts Moses on a tour of hell. Moses sees men and women hanging by their eyes, ears, hands, tongues, hair, and breasts, "all on chains of fire." The ones who hang by their eyes are men who had "looked lustfully upon the wives of their neighbors," for example, and the ones who hang by their hair and breasts are women who "uncovered them in the presence of young men, so that they conceived desire unto them, and fell into sin."[50] Other sinners are suffering the stings of two thousand scorpions, each of which has "seventy thousand heads, each head seventy thousand mouths, each mouth seventy thousand stings, and each sting seventy thousand pouches of poison and venom," which the sinners are forced to drink down, "although the anguish was so racking that their eyes melted in their sockets." Gabriel explains that these are the sinners "who delivered their fellow-Israelites into the hands of the Gentiles, who denied the Torah of Moses, and who maintained that God is not the Creator of the world."[51]

The sight of heaven and hell—and the myriad choiring angels that praise Moses everywhere he goes on his grand tour—seems to restore his confidence in himself. Indeed, according to one of the rabbinical tales, Moses once again displays the sheer chutzpah that was so much in evidence back at the burning bush on Mount Horeb. "I will not leave the heavens unless Thou grantest me a gift," he demands of God, who defers to the man Moses: "I will give thee the Torah, and men shall call it the Law of Moses."[52]

FINGERPRINTS

The account of the incident atop Horeb is presented as a seamless narrative in the Bible, but the fingerprints of several different authors can be detected in the biblical text. Each of these nameless men (and possibly women) wrote at a different time, in a different place, and for a different political or theological purpose, starting as early as the tenth century B.C.E., and continuing for several centuries. Only much later, perhaps as late as the fifth or fourth century B.C.E., did the priests and scribes known collectively as "R," or the Redactor, come along to compile and edit the various texts, stitch them together, tweak them in some places, and censor them in other places, thus bringing the Bible to completion in the form that has come down to us.

Yet the text of the Hebrew is full of flaws and contradictions that can be seen as clues to the multiple authorship of the Bible. Why is the father-in-law of Moses called Reuel in one passage, Jethro in another, and Hobab in a third unless he was known to three different biblical authors by three different names? The mountain on which Moses encountered God in the burning bush is called Horeb in one passage—but the same mountain will later be called Sinai when Moses ascended to parley with God and came back down with the Ten Commandments. Although the Bible plainly states that God revealed his name to Moses on Mount Horeb in the land of Midian, the very same encounter will be described in a later passage as taking place in Egypt. And, as we have seen, God is known by a great many different names throughout the Bible, including Yahweh in some places and Elohim in others.

Bible scholars have relied on these clues to tease out the threads of narrative that can be attributed to various authors or sources. The author who uses the term Elohim to identify the deity is known as the Elohist, or "E"—and he is thought to be the source of the scene in which God revealed that his real name is Yahweh during a chatty tête-à-tête with Moses on Mount Horeb. Another biblical author has *always* called God by that name from the beginning of the Bible, and, for that reason, he (or she) is known as the Yahwist, or "J"—and the portion of the biblical text attributed to J does not depict a scene in which God reveals his name to be Yahweh because, as far as J is concerned, God's name has been known to humankind since the days of Adam. Yet another important source of Bible authorship, a school of priestly writers whose work is known collectively as "P" (for *Priesterschrift*, or "priestly writing"), is not represented at all in Exodus 4, although P gives us a second and separate scene in Exodus 6 in which God discloses his name to Moses— and according to P, the moment of God's self-revelation comes only after Moses has already arrived in Egypt.

These and other flaws in the biblical text suggest that the Bible was composed by combining and conflating a great many layers of storytelling from a great many sources. For example, it is the Elohist who knows the father-in-law of Moses as "Jethro" (or sometimes "Jether"); the Yahwist calls him "Reuel," and yet another biblical source seems to think his name was "Hobab." Similarly, it is the Elohist who uses the name Horeb to identify the holy mountain on which God revealed himself to Moses, while the Yahwist knows the holy mountain as Sinai. What's more, the place name Horeb is added to the text of Exodus 3:1 "in such a lame way," as Martin Noth puts it, that the so-called mountain of God in Midian may have been nameless at some early point in the traditions of ancient Israel. Indeed, we cannot know with certainty whether Horeb, Sinai, and the "mountain of God" are one and the same place.[53]

Still, it is possible to discern a good deal about these biblical authors in what they do and do not say about Moses. The Elohist regards Moses as a wonder-worker and seeks to elevate and exalt him by investing him with miraculous powers. For that reason, among others, E may have been a member of a priestly dynasty in the northern kingdom of Israel that claimed to have descended from Moses. By contrast, the Yahwist, who depicts Moses as nothing more than "an inspired shepherd,"[54] may have been a highborn man or woman living and working in the court circles of the southern kingdom of Judah. Thus, for example, the Elohist turns the shepherd's staff that Moses carried into a kind of magic wand, but the Yahwist never even mentions the so-called rod of God.[55]

Each of the biblical sources appears to have known a slightly different set of stories about Moses, and each one sought to put his own or her own moral, political, and theological spin on those stories. "E is more congregational, democratic, prophetic, and ethical in tendency," writes Bible scholar Murray Lee Newman Jr. "J is more priestly, cultic, authoritarian, and dynastic in tendency."[56] Someone among the biblical sources preserved the less-flattering depictions of Moses—the remnants of the anti-Moses tradition—perhaps because he belonged to the priestly caste that claimed descent from Aaron rather than Moses. Somewhere beneath these overlapping layers of storytelling may be detected the faint traces of a flesh-and-blood man named Moses, but he can only be glimpsed through the cracks in the biblical text.

ON THE ROAD

The trek back to Egypt would be arduous and dangerous, the reception by his fellow Israelites would be uncertain at best, and the confrontation with Pharaoh would present Moses with the greatest risk of all, but Moses apparently decided that if he had to go, he would not go alone— he wanted to bring along his wife, Zipporah, and their young sons too. Moses, more deferential to his father-in-law than he had been toward

Yahweh, petitioned the priest of Midian for permission to depart from Midian before setting out on a journey from which he and his family might never return.

"Let me go, I pray thee, and return unto my brethren that are in Egypt," Moses begged his father-in-law, "and see whether they be yet alive."

"Go in peace," said Jethro (Exod. 4:18).

According to a tale in the Midrash, Moses feels obliged to seek leave of his father-in-law because he had promised long ago that he would never depart from Midian without Jethro's permission. When Jethro objects to his plan to take his wife and young sons along—why take more souls *into* Egypt, Jethro scolds Moses, when the whole point of the journey is to take the Israelites *out?*—Moses offers a pious answer. "Should my wife and sons remain in Midian," he retorts, "and not hear the voice of God on Mount Sinai?" Thus persuaded by the earnest words of his son-in-law, Jethro gives his blessing.[57]

The deference that Moses displayed toward Jethro may reflect the rigid protocol that governed the dealings between a man and his father-in-law in the ancient Near East, but it also says something important about the politics of the relationship between Moses and Jethro in particular. Moses, after all, was a fugitive from the court of Pharaoh who had sought the protection of a tribal priest in a distant backwater, but the land of Midian still lay within the sphere of influence of Egypt. Jethro may have enjoyed a certain degree of power and privilege in his locality simply because the armies and emissaries of Pharaoh rarely bothered to show up there, but surely Jethro was mindful of the fact that they might appear at any time without warning. Perhaps that is why Moses, contrary to the tale told by the rabbis, decided *not* to reveal to Jethro the strange encounter on the holy mountain that had inspired his mission to Egypt, or his real purpose in going there. Jethro might not have been so quick to bless the enterprise if he had known that Moses was going to the land of Pharaoh as an agent provocateur and the self-appointed leader of a slave rebellion.

Moses presumably prepared himself for the long journey to Egypt by loading up a string of asses with supplies of food, water, clothing, weapons, tools, and a tent, all the customary provisions that an experienced nomad would bring along on a trek through the wilderness. Then he set his wife and his young sons on a mount of their own, and they all rode out of Jethro's compound in the direction of far-off Egypt. The Bible carefully notes that Moses took along the shepherd's staff that would serve as the symbol of the divine authority that had been bestowed upon him at Horeb. The rabbis charged the scene with even greater eminence by dreamily imagining that the ass on which Moses rides is the very same beast "that had once borne Abraham when he rode to Mount Moriah [to sacrifice his son, Isaac] and upon which the Messiah will one day ride when he appears at the end of days."[58]

Moses, however, apparently had a more urgent and practical problem on his mind—he was a manslayer who had escaped from Egypt and was now boldly returning to the scene of the crime. As if God understood his anxieties, God thought to whisper reassurances into his ear as Moses traveled across the empty desert landscape.

"Go, return to Egypt, for all the men are dead that sought thy life," God said to Moses as he trekked toward the land of the pharaohs, thus revealing for the first time that Moses' adoptive grandfather had passed away and a new king sat on the throne of Egypt. And then God went over the divine scenario yet again: "When thou goest back into Egypt, see that thou do before Pharaoh all the wonders which I have put in thy hand." (Exod. 4: 19–21)

But God was not entirely upbeat in his last-minute briefing of Moses. Indeed, God had an unsettling habit of revealing to Moses exactly how things could and would go terribly wrong—and then, astoundingly, he would take credit for making it all turn out that way!

"But I will harden his heart," God said of Pharaoh, "and he will not let the people go." (Exod. 4:21)

Lest the fainthearted Moses turn his donkey train around then and there, God hastened to reveal the rest of his plan. The magic tricks that Moses was empowered to perform with the rod of God—turning a staff into a snake and water into blood—were feeble when compared to the terrible fate that God had already decreed for Pharaoh:

And thou shalt say unto Pharaoh: Thus saith the Lord: Israel is My son, My first-born. And I have said unto thee: Let My son go, that he may serve Me; and thou hast refused to let him go. Behold, I will slay thy son, thy first-born. (Exod. 4:22–23)

So Moses rode on, perhaps comforted by the knowledge that God intended to back up his promises with blood, but not suspecting who the first target of God's bloodthirstiness would turn out to be.

THE MAN GOD SOUGHT TO KILL

At this moment in the biblical life story of Moses, we come upon what is arguably the single most bizarre and baffling passage in all of the Hebrew Bible. After centuries of silence, God had finally bestirred himself in the heavens and resolved to do something about the suffering of his Chosen People. He decided that Moses was the only man for the job of liberating the Israelites from slavery under Pharaoh, and he expended a good deal of time, effort, and breath in persuading the reluctant Moses to do what was asked of him—God wheedled and cajoled Moses, answered every objection and every argument that Moses could think of, demonstrated all the marvelous signs and wonders that Moses would be allowed to use to prove his credentials and carry out his mission. At long last, Moses agreed to go, promptly settled his affairs in Midian, and set out on the road to Egypt.

And then God decided to kill him.

Moses may have been God's chosen one, the man to whom God revealed his secret name and the physical manifestation of his "glory," the man whom God knew "face to face," the man with whom he would speak "mouth to mouth, as a friend speaketh to a friend" (Exod. 33:11; Num. 12:8)—and yet Moses was also the man whom God stalked and sought to kill.

God's night attack on Moses is described in a mere seventy words in English translation, and even fewer words are allotted to the tale in the biblical Hebrew of the original text. Yet these few words have baffled readers and commentators over several millennia, and the exertions of theologians and scholars who have tried to explain the attack (or explain it away) have produced some of the most outlandish conjecture in the vast literature of Bible commentary.

"And it came to pass on the way at the lodging-place," goes the opening line of Exodus 4:24–26, "that the Lord met him, and sought to kill him."

That God might *want* to kill Moses is a profound theological mystery, but a still more troubling problem is found in the fact that the omnipotent deity *failed* to kill him—and he failed because an intrepid woman, the daughter of a pagan priest, improvised a ritual of blood magic that succeeded in staving off the attack.

> Then Zipporah took a flint, and cut off the foreskin of her son, and cast it at his feet; and she said: "Surely a bridegroom of

blood art thou to me." So He let him alone. Then she said: "A bridegroom of blood in regard of the circumcision." (Exod. 4:24–26)

The biblical author who tells the tale of the night attack was apparently troubled enough by what is depicted to make a conscious effort to blur the details. The use of third-person pronouns in the original text— "he" and "his" and "him"—makes it nearly impossible to know with certainty who is doing what to whom. Similarly, the Hebrew word that is used to describe what Zipporah touched with the bloody foreskin— *reglayim*, which means "legs" or "feet"—is often used in the Bible as a euphemism for the sexual organ, and so we do not know whether it is someone's *legs* or *genitals* that were daubed with the bloody foreskin; nor do we know the dramatis personae whose foreskin and "legs" were involved.

"Just where the 'blood(y) husband' was dabbed with the son's prepuce we can only surmise," cracks the high-spirited Bible scholar Marvin Pope, "but the best guess seems the area where foreskins are located."[59]

Moses was the intended victim of God's homicidal attack, according to the scholarly consensus of several centuries, and his son Gershom was the one whom Zipporah hastily circumcised to provide a foreskin for the curious blood ritual that she performed. But there are dissenters who argue that God actually intended to kill the child rather than Moses, and there is even some debate over whether the child at risk was Gershom, the firstborn son of Moses and Zipporah, or Eliezer, their second-born son.

Conventional wisdom and pious tradition suggest that the whole incident was prompted by the failure of Moses to circumcise his son as he should have. God had long ago announced to Abraham that every male among the Israelites was to undergo circumcision as a symbol of the covenant between God and his Chosen People. "And the uncircumcised male who is not circumcised in the flesh of his foreskin," God commanded, "shall be cut off from his people." (Gen. 17:12, 14) So it is argued that God sought to kill Moses because Moses had neglected to circumcise Gershom.

Somehow Zipporah, the daughter of a Midianite priest, intuited at the moment of the attack that God was aggrieved about someone's uncircumcised genitalia and resolved to do something about it herself. In fact, the Talmud preserves an especially bizarre tradition that Zipporah is alerted to the need to perform a circumcision by an angel who descends from heaven and swallows the whole of Moses' body *except* his uncircumcised sexual organ, thus calling Zipporah's attention to the problem at hand in a particularly memorable way![60] Zipporah hastily remedies the situation by carrying out an emergency circumcision, and then "cast[ing the foreskin] at his feet" to call God's attention to the fact that she has belatedly complied with the ancient commandment. As the Bible confirms, God broke off the attack and the family went on its way once the circumcision was carried out and the bloody foreskin was cast at his "feet."

Of course, there are other ways of making sense of the face-off between God and Moses at the lodging place. Perhaps it was Moses whose uncircumcised sexual organ so agitated God—after all, nowhere in the Bible is it written that *Moses* was circumcised. Most of the ancient sages simply refused to believe that an uncircumcised man would be recruited by God as Liberator and Lawgiver for the Chosen People, and so they came up with a number of ingenious ways to explain the awkward omission in the biblical text: perhaps Moses is circumcised while still in the care of his birth family; or he is circumcised as a prince of Egypt, where circumcision was a routine practice; or he emerges from the womb miraculously circumcised. But others are willing to entertain the daring notion that Moses is not yet circumcised, and God seeks to kill him for precisely that reason[61]—and, if so, Zipporah may perform an emergency circumcision on her son as a surrogate for her husband, whose health can not be endangered at that crucial moment by a circumcision under such stressful and unsanitary conditions![62]

Still other sages simply ignored the whole messy issue of circumcision and proposed that God is moved to homicidal rage by the lack of enthusiasm that Moses continues to display for his mission of liberation, as evidenced by the fact that he delays his departure from Midian, travels at a leisurely pace toward Egypt, and insists on shlepping his wife and young sons along with him. A liberator, the rabbis seemed to suggest, should be made of sterner stuff. "For his lack of faith," goes one rabbinical tale, "Moses was punished while he was on the road to Egypt."[63]

So off-putting is the "irrational, almost demonic atmosphere"[64] of the night attack on Moses, as one scholar writes, that self-appointed Bible censors over the centuries have chosen to clean up the biblical text or simply leave the attack out altogether. The readers of Josephus and Philo, for example, find no mention at all of the inconvenient fact that God tries to kill Moses. The Septuagint identifies the attacker as an angel rather than God himself.[65] An early translation of the Bible into Aramaic, known as a Targum, places the blame squarely on Jethro for the fact that his grandson is not properly circumcised. "The husband wanted to circumcise," Zipporah says in a bit of dialogue that appears nowhere in the biblical text, "but the father-in-law would not permit him."[66] Rashi, a revered Jewish commentator of the eleventh century C.E., insisted that the whole incident is merely a metaphorical account of a physical illness that Moses suffers by reason of his failure to properly circumcise his son. And one tale told in the Midrash goes so far as to cast Satan in place of God as the attempted murderer of Moses.

According to the Midrashic version, the priest of Midian and his Israelite son-in-law make a deal about how the children of the mixed marriage of Moses and Zipporah are to be reared. Half of the children will be circumcised at birth, according to the Israelite custom, and half will be circumcised only at puberty or in preparation for marriage, according to the Midianite custom. Thus Gershom, the firstborn, is circumcised, and Eliezer, the second-born, is not, and it is Eliezer whose uncircumcised genitals are the source of all the trouble at the lodging place.

"On the road to Egypt, Satan appeared to him in the guise of a serpent and swallowed up his body down to his feet," the rabbis imagined. Zipporah, who understands why Satan is devouring her husband, reaches for a sharp flintstone, circumcises their son, and daubs the feet of Moses with the bloody foreskin. "Immediately a heavenly voice called out: 'Spew him out,' and the serpent obeyed."[67]

All of these efforts at cleaning up the biblical account of God's attempt to kill Moses reflect the same poignant impulse—to show that God is a just, merciful, and compassionate deity who is simply not capable of such bloodthirsty conduct toward Moses, and to suggest that someone else must have carried out the night attack. But the impulse is hardly based on the evidence to be found in the Bible itself: God has killed before, and he will kill again. Indeed, Moses will be called upon by God to conduct bloody purges, mass murder, and wars of extermination—and Moses himself will not escape the murderous rage of Yahweh in the end.

Still, the urgent compulsion to exonerate God in the attempted murder of Moses has prompted some truly bizarre speculation about the origin and meaning of the Bridegroom of Blood, as the passage is known among scholars. "We are peering into the deep recesses of a primordial, absolutely mythological religion, which is far older than the time of Moses," writes Elias Auerbach. "Only incidentally and accidentally is Moses, who in this story plays a passive role, connected with it."[68] At the heart of the mystery is the startling idea that the god we know as Yahweh may have started out as someone or something else, a deity or possibly even a demon who was borrowed by the Bible author from some long-lost pagan tradition and inserted into Holy Writ in the strange and misshapen form of the Bridegroom of Blood.

What is most often overlooked in orthodox tradition, however, is the simple fact that God was confronted and, in a sense, defeated by a woman (and a non-Israelite woman at that). Moses must have been grateful that Zipporah was made of sterner stuff than Abraham: the patriarch meekly complied with God's bluff demand to sacrifice his son, but Zipporah took it upon herself to fight back when Yahweh himself sought to take her husband's life. She is obliquely honored for her pluck in the Midrash, where it is told how God seeks to console Zipporah when she laments the fact that she had not been present when the Israelites joined Moses and Miriam in songs of praise to God after the miracle of the Red Sea.

"As Zipporah has been grieved on this account," God is made to say, "she shall be rewarded and her soul will one day be in Deborah, the prophetess, who will sing a song of salvation and redemption."[69]

The point of the tale was not lost on pious readers of the Bible who knew that Deborah, like Zipporah, was a courageous and dynamic woman who took it upon herself to lead the army of Israel into battle against a dreaded Canaanite captain named Sisera when the Israelite commander, Barak, proved too timid to do it by himself. "I will surely go with thee, notwithstanding the journey that thou takest shall not be for thy honour," Deborah taunted Barak in the Song of Deborah, one of the oldest passages of the Hebrew Bible, "for the Lord will give Sisera over into the hand of a woman." (Judges 4:9)

THE MIDIANITE HYPOTHESIS

The world in which Moses lived was marked by an open-minded and all-embracing attitude toward the gods and goddesses worshipped by strangers, a willingness to mix and match deities and rituals that is known as syncretism. The Egyptian goddess Isis was worshipped in various forms throughout the ancient Near East,* and the Semitic goddesses Anat and Astarte were enshrined in temples erected by Ramses II, the favorite candidate for the pharaoh in whose reign the events of the Exodus took place.[70] Moses himself was surely not only familiar but perhaps even comfortable with the gods and goddesses worshipped by his adoptive mother and grandfather in Egypt and his wife and in-laws in Midian.

At the same time, some gods and goddesses in the ancient world were regarded as highly specialized deities who watched over a particular tribe or a specific patch of earth. For example, when the Bible refers to Yahweh as "God of Abraham," "God of Isaac," and "God of Jacob," the biblical author may be harking back to the primitive notion that each man enjoyed the protection of a god of his own, a deity who took special interest in his clan or tribe. So, too, did the Midianites venerate their own gods, and some scholars have proposed the daring notion that Moses, the self-proclaimed "stranger in a strange land," borrowed one of the gods of Midian and made it his own. Some of the oldest and most authentic evidence, they suggest, is buried away beneath the surface of the biblical passage that describes the night attack on Moses.

According to the so-called Midianite Hypothesis,** the deity whom Moses encountered on a remote mountaintop in Midian—and the deity who stalked and sought to kill him at the lodging place on the way out of Midian—may have been one or more strictly local gods into whose jurisdiction Moses had wandered. The god that he ultimately embraced as his own, the god who came to be worshipped by the Israelites as Yahweh at some later point in their ancient history, was originally a tribal deity of Midian—or so argue the proponents of the Midianite Hypothesis.

---

*Isis was known in ancient Israel, and one contemporary Bible scholar argues that the Bridegroom of Blood is a Hebraized version of the Isis myth in which Zipporah is made to play the role of the "rescuer-goddess" Isis and Moses the role of her brother and consort, Osiris. The many layers of meaning in Exodus 4:24–26 are explored in chapter nine of my previous book, *The Harlot by the Side of the Road: Forbidden Tales of the Bible* (New York: Ballantine Books, 1997).

**Because the in-laws of Moses are characterized as Kenites rather than Midianites elsewhere in the Bible (Judg. 1:16, 4:11) the theory is also sometimes called the Kenite Hypothesis. See chapter ten.

The evidence in support of the Midianite Hypothesis is sparse but intriguing. For example, the Bible depicts God as insisting that Moses remove his sandals during their first encounter atop Horeb because "the ground where you stand is holy." (Exod. 3:5) Some scholars argue that the biblical text preserves a primitive belief that Yahweh was originally a local deity whose power was confined to a specific bit of turf in the wilderness of Midian. Even the fact that God commanded Moses to approach him with bare feet may be a remnant of the pagan practice of worshipping the deity in a purely natural state—the priests of ancient Sumeria, for example, "served their gods naked."[71] And perhaps most unsettling of all is the fact that Jethro, not Moses, is credited by the biblical author with making the first sacrifice to Yahweh in the wilderness of Sinai. "And Jethro, Moses' father-in-law, took a burnt-offering and sacrifices for God." (Exod. 18:12)

"If Jethro was a priest who offered sacrifices to Yahweh, presumably he was a priest of Yahweh," writes Murray Lee Newman Jr., neatly summing up the Midianite Hypothesis. "And if Moses first learned the name of Yahweh in this period, he probably learned it from Jethro."[72]

Needless to say, the Midianite Hypothesis is deeply offensive to some pious scholars who do not take kindly to the notion that God started out as some primitive tribal deity in the desert wilderness of Midian. "There are not the faintest indications that any god of the name [Yahweh] was ever honoured in that district," snaps Martin Buber. "For this reason the hypothesis has not unjustly been described as 'an explanation of *ignotum ab ignoto*' "[73]—an explanation that relies on the unknown to describe the unknown. Still, the Midianite Hypothesis is mild stuff indeed when compared to the reading of the Bridegroom of Blood offered by the turn-of-the-century Protestant theologian Hugo Gressmann, an otherwise sober and respectable fellow who managed to scandalize the sedate world of Bible scholarship by suggesting that the deity who sought to kill Moses was actually a sex-addled demon believed by the nomadic tribes of the ancient Near East to be entitled to deflower a virgin bride on her wedding night.

THE BLOOD OF A VIRGIN BRIDE

The Midianites among whom Moses settled, Gressmann proposed, imagined that their tribal god enjoyed a divine droit du seigneur which obliged a woman to submit herself to the deity before sleeping with her husband. One of Gressmann's colleagues added a lurid twist of his own. "[I]t was customary among the ancient Semites for maidens to offer their virginity to the first passing stranger who to them seemed to be the embodiment of the god," suggested A. J. Reinach, "and [the god] thus received his due of the virginal blood."[74]

The night attack on Moses, Gressmann argued, must have actually taken place on his wedding night. The deity sought to kill Moses to prevent him from sleeping with Zipporah before he availed himself of his divine right to her virginal blood. Ever alert and resourceful—and apparently well schooled in what was expected of a Midianite bride by her tribal god!—Zipporah contrived an elaborate ruse to trick the deity into believing that he had already deflowered her: Zipporah hastily circumcised her husband with the sharp edge of a flint, and she used his foreskin to smear blood on the sexual organ (the "legs") of the attacker.

"[God's genitals] became smeared with blood, quite as if he had just had intercourse with her, and his organ had thereby become covered with her virginal blood," went the hot-blooded conjecture of Professor Gressmann. "And when the gullible deity perceived this, he believed that he had received his due, and so he withdrew and left Moses in peace."[75]

Gressmann thus offered an explanation for one of the most impenetrable mysteries of the bloody incident at the lodging place: the enigmatic words that Zipporah used to address Moses after she succeeded in foiling God's attack and sparing his life. Circumcision of marriageable young men and especially bridegrooms, Gressmann suggested, evolved among the nomadic tribes of the ancient Near East as a ritual substitute for the offering of the bride's virginity to the deity: "Surely a bridegroom of blood art thou to me" was supposedly a magical incantation addressed to God by every bride by way of her newly circumcised groom on their wedding night.

Such scandalous conjecture about "the god or demon or whoever conceals himself behind the letters JHWH," as one skeptical Bible scholar sums up Gressmann's theory, has been dismissed as "phantastic, not to say ridiculous" by more cautious scholars. Indeed, the whole scenario proposed by Gressmann strikes some readers as disgusting and others as merely imbecilic. "He must be a very silly god who can be cheated so easily," writes contemporary Bible scholar Hans Kosmala. "Some logicality must be ascribed even to demons."[76]

But the Bridegroom of Blood is a reminder that both God *and* Moses are depicted in the Bible as being quite capable of random and impulsive acts of violence. Freud called the deity who stalked and sought to kill Moses "an uncanny, bloodthirsty demon who walks by night and shuns the light of day."[77] And the Midrash preserves a curious variant of the night attack in which Moses, too, is shown to answer violence with violence at the lodging place: a couple of angels named Af and Hemah are sent by God to kill Moses, and he exacts his own bloody revenge on them after Zipporah frees him from their murderous embrace by performing the blood ritual of circumcision. "When Moses was released by the angels, he attacked them, and he slew Hemah," imagined the rabbinical storyteller, "whose host of angels, however, held their own before the assailant."[78]

The very notion that Moses would attack and kill an angel from on high must have horrified the sages who preferred him in the guise of a humble shepherd. Even the biblical author, who was willing to show Moses as a man capable of bloodshed, insists that "the man Moses was very meek, above all the men that were upon the face of the earth." (Num. 12:3) But the Bridegroom of Blood, so eerie and so blood-soaked, is a perfectly appropriate counterpart to a deity who turns himself into a nightstalker. And we shall encounter both of them again.

Chapter Six

SIGNS
AND WONDERS

But this rough magic
I here abjure; and when I have required
Some heavenly music—which even now I do—
To work mine end upon their senses, that
This airy charm is for, I'll break my staff. . . .
—SHAKESPEARE, *THE TEMPEST*

A s Moses made his way through the wilderness with his intrepid
wife and his newly circumcised son, another slave with a strange
destiny was privileged to hear the voice of God. Back in Egypt, Aaron
was called upon by God to join his younger brother in the momentous
struggle for liberation that was about to begin in earnest.

"Go into the wilderness," God commanded Aaron, "to meet
Moses." (Exod. 4:27)

Aaron is not mentioned at all in the biblical account of the birth
and rescue of Moses. His name appears in the Bible for the first time in
God's encounter with Moses on Mount Horeb. "Is there not Aaron thy
brother the Levite?" God pointed out to Moses when he complained
that he was not up to the job of divine spokesperson (Exod. 4:14). But
there is something suspicious about the way Aaron conveniently shows
up to assist his younger brother at various awkward but crucial moments
in the biblical saga. Scholars tend to agree that the passages about
Aaron and his exploits represent "a secondary intrusion into the Moses
narrative,"[1] a self-serving and somewhat clumsy effort at rewriting history by a priestly caste of ancient Israel that claimed to trace its ancestry
back to Aaron rather than Moses. "Aaron has been inserted into each
of the old Moses stories as opportunity offered," writes Martin Noth,
"while Moses has been pushed to one side."[2]

Indeed, the reunion between the long-separated brothers is almost *too* warm and fuzzy. Aaron dutifully hiked out to "the mountain of God," kissed his long-absent brother, and listened with perfect credulity as Moses told him "all the words of the Lord wherewith He had sent him, and all the signs wherewith He had charged him." (Exod. 4:28) Then the two of them trekked back to Egypt together, presented themselves to the elders of the enslaved Israelites, and announced the daring plan for a slave rebellion. Just as God had ordained on Horeb, it was Aaron, not Moses, who actually addressed the elders, "spoke all the words which the Lord had spoken unto Moses, and did the signs in the sight of the people." (Exod. 4:30)

Although Moses was eighty years old when he arrived in Egypt from Midian, and Aaron was three years older (Exod. 7:7), a tradition in the rabbinical literature ruled out any sibling rivalry between them. "Aaron was rejoiced that God had chosen his younger brother to be the redeemer of Israel," goes one cheery tale, "and Moses was rejoiced that his older brother had been divinely appointed the high priest in Israel."[3] The relations between Aaron and Moses would not always be so friendly, and another rabbinical tale anticipated the friction that would later explode into open insurrection by Aaron against his brother's authority. When they meet on the mountain of God, the rabbis wrote, Aaron scolds his younger brother for bringing along his family. They will only distract Moses from his mission, Aaron complains, and he expresses the same sentiment that was attributed to Jethro in another rabbinical tale. "Our sorrow is already great enough, on account of those who are in Egypt," Aaron says to Moses. "[W]hy dost thou bring more to the land?" According to the rabbis, if not the Bible itself, Moses defers to his brother by promptly dispatching Zipporah and his children back to his father-in-law's house in Midian. And then the two brothers trek on.[4]*

---

*Thus the rabbinical tale offered a neat if implausible solution to one of the inconsistencies of the biblical text. Exodus 4:20 states that Moses brought his family to Egypt, but when Jethro later joined Moses and the Israelites in the wilderness of Sinai, as reported in Exodus 18:5, Zipporah and her two sons were traveling with Jethro from Midian. The rabbis resolved the contradiction by suggesting that Moses heeded his brother's words at their first encounter, journeyed all the way back to Midian, left his family behind in the care of his father-in-law, and then set out again for Egypt!

"I HAVE SURELY VISITED YOU"

To prove themselves to the elders of the Israelites, the Bible suggests, Aaron and Moses put on a display of the legerdemain that God had rehearsed with Moses back on Horeb, turning a shepherd's staff into a snake and back into a staff again, disfiguring flesh with leprosy and then restoring it to health. (Exod. 4:3, 6) But rabbinical tradition held that Moses inadvertently authenticates himself by speaking a secret phrase known only to the elders. The patriarch Jacob had known the words by which the messenger of God would identify himself in generations to come, and he revealed the secret to his son, Joseph, who confided the password to his brother, Asher, who told his daughter, Serah—and Serah, remarkably enough, is still alive when Moses and Aaron present themselves to the Israelites.

"He that will come and proclaim the redemption with the words of God, 'I have surely visited you, and see that which is done to you in Egypt,'" Serah reveals to the elders, "he is the true redeemer." Such were the very words that Moses spoke to the elders, and so "she knew that he was the promised redeemer, and all the people believed in him."[5]

After centuries of enslavement, generation after generation of oppression, and, above all, the long and confounding silence of God, the Bible confirms, the elders and the people of Israel were quick to embrace Moses and Aaron. Indeed, the scene would be repeated over and over throughout Jewish history as self-proclaimed prophets and redeemers, a few earnest ones and many more who were charlatans, presented themselves to the distant descendants of the Israelites in other lands where they endured years of suffering and waited patiently for redemption, wondering why God had fallen silent yet again. Now, however, the faith of the Israelites in Moses was justified.

"And the people believed, and when they heard that the Lord had remembered the children of Israel, and that He had seen their affliction, then they bowed their heads and worshipped." (Exod. 4:31)

So Moses and Aaron set out from the slave quarters where they had so easily won over the Israelites and headed toward the palace of Pharaoh. According to one rabbinical tale, the elders accompany Moses and Aaron on the way to their first encounter with the king of Egypt—but the old men, long accustomed to subservience, grow ever more fearful as they draw nearer to the palace, and so they begin to slip away unnoticed, one by one, until Moses and Aaron find themselves alone at the gates.[6] The two of them encounter some sixty thousand men-at-arms who guard the four hundred doors of the palace, according to another tale, but Moses and Aaron are invisibly conveyed into the presence of Pharaoh by the angel Gabriel.[7]

The splendors that Moses and Aaron behold in the palace of Pharaoh are not described in the Bible, but the storytellers have embroidered the plain text with dreamlike scenes of oriental pomp and ceremony. The grounds are guarded by a pair of ferocious lions who begin to gambol around Moses and Aaron "like dogs round their masters, and followed them wherever they went."[8] They come upon seventy scribes who labor in seventy languages over the vast correspondence required to reign over an empire. Indeed, Moses and Aaron happen to arrive on Pharaoh's birthday, and they find themselves among a gathering of kings from all over the world, each one bearing a golden crown for mighty Pharaoh. But the kings tremble in awe and fall to their knees when the two humble Israelites enter the throne room. "Moses and Aaron resembled the ministering angels," the rabbis wrote, "their stature was like that of the cedars of Lebanon, the pupils of their eyes were like the spheres of the morning star, their beards were like palm branches, and the radiance of their countenances was like the splendour of the sun."[9]

Surely the two of them had been emboldened by their worshipful welcome among the people of Israel and encouraged by the fact that, so far, their mission had gone just as God said it would. And perhaps they were in such high spirits that they did not give much thought to what God had said about what would happen next. If so, Moses and Aaron were about to learn a bitter lesson in the harshness of tyrants and the perversity of God.

"I CREATED MYSELF, AND ALSO THE RIVER NILE"

On that day, Moses presented himself at the palace—a rough-hewn wooden staff in his hand, the dust of Midian on his feet—and demanded to see the king of Egypt. Even without the supposed intervention of the angel Gabriel, the notion that such an audacious request ever reached the ears of Pharaoh was something of a miracle in itself, and the fact that he actually consented to receive Moses and Aaron was even more unlikely. Still, the Bible confirms that Pharaoh granted them an audience, and they spared no breath on matters of protocol.

"Thus saith Yahweh, the God of Israel," Moses and Aaron demanded as soon as they had been ushered into the throne room, " 'Let My people go, so that they may hold a feast unto Me in the wilderness.' " (Exod. 5:1)[10]

"Who is the Lord, that I should hearken unto His voice to let Israel go?" Pharaoh replied. "I know not the Lord, and moreover I will not let Israel go." (Exod. 5:2)

Surely Pharaoh was not surprised that the Israelites believed themselves to be under the tutelage of their own tribal god rather than the pantheon of Egypt. As we have already seen, Pharaoh was comfortable with the proliferation of strange gods and goddesses among the many clans, tribes, and peoples who lived under his imperial rule. Indeed, a few of the more enticing Semitic deities had been embraced by the Egyptians themselves. Still, the Bible suggests that Yahweh was unknown to Pharaoh, and the rabbis told a story in which Pharaoh sends his wise men into the royal library to see what they can find about the obscure deity whose authority Moses has invoked.

"I have not found the name of the Lord in the Book of the Angels," says Pharaoh to Moses and Aaron in a tale from the Jerusalem Targum, an early Aramaic translation of the Hebrew Bible.[11] A more elaborate version of the same story imagined a lively discourse between Pharaoh and the two slaves who stood before him. "Tell me, is He young or old? How many cities hath He captured? How many nations hath He subdued? How long is it since He ascended His throne?"

"He was before the world was created, and He will be till the end of days," says Moses in reply. "The strength and power of the Lord fill the whole world. He created thee and breathed into thee the spirit of life."[12]

"Ye lie, when ye say that your God created me," Pharaoh parries, "for I am the master of the Universe and I created myself, and also the River Nile."[13]

The audience was going badly, and Moses must have realized that Pharaoh was not going to be quite so easy to impress as the Israelites had been. So the Bible suggests that Moses abruptly changed his approach—and, significantly, the biblical text attributes the dialogue to Moses *and* Aaron, as if Aaron had belatedly been written into the scene and given some dialogue to speak aloud in unison with Moses.

"The God of the Hebrews hath met with us," the two said to

Pharaoh. "Let us go, we pray thee, three days' journey into the wilderness, and sacrifice unto Yahweh our God; lest He should fall upon us with pestilence, or with the sword." (Exod. 5:3)

Here Moses revealed a sly and slippery persona more suitable to a bazaar merchant than a prophet and liberator. No longer was Moses demanding that Pharaoh let the people go; now he was begging. No longer was he invoking the power of God; rather, he was fearful of God's power. Indeed, Moses was playing for sympathy by casting himself and his people in the role of victims, not of Pharaoh but rather of Yahweh. He claimed to fear that the divine afflictions of sword and pestilence would fall on the Israelites, not the Egyptians—or so he told Pharaoh.

Above all, Moses resorted to a ploy that would characterize all of his dealings with Pharaoh in the days ahead. He did not call for the liberation of the enslaved Israelites at all. Rather, he asked only for three days off. Once the Israelites had offered the sacrifices that their cranky god demanded, Moses seemed to suggest, they would cheerfully march back to their slave quarters in the land of Goshen and resume their labor under the whips of the Egyptian taskmasters!

Pharaoh was not fooled by the ruse, nor was he touched by the play for sympathy. If the audacious slave was crafty, the king of Egypt was craftier. In fact, the display of weakness by Moses and Aaron only seemed to spark the rage of Pharaoh.

"Wherefore do ye, Moses and Aaron, cause the people to break loose from their work?" Pharaoh railed. "Behold, the people of the land are now many, and will ye make them rest from their work? Get you unto your burdens!" (Exod. 5:4–5)

Pharaoh then used a ploy of his own to make sure that the Israelites would neither trust nor obey these two rabble-rousers who plainly intended to raise a rebellion against him. On the day of their visit, he issued a new order to the taskmasters.

"Ye shall no more give the people straw to make bricks as before—let them go and gather straw for themselves. But the quota of bricks that they are required to make each day shall not be diminished," decreed Pharaoh, and lest the cause of his order be misunderstood, he added a blunt explanation: "For they are idle; therefore they cry: 'Let us go and sacrifice to our God.' So let heavier work be laid upon the men, and let them not regard lying words." (Exod. 5:7–9)[14]

MUD BUT NO STRAW

So the only achievement of Moses and Aaron in their first encounter with Pharaoh was to make the lives of their fellow Israelites even harder. "Thus saith Pharaoh: I will not give you straw," the taskmasters gleefully announced. "Go yourselves, get you straw where you can find it; for nought of your work shall be diminished." (Exod. 5:11)

Mud and straw were the raw materials of brick making in ancient Egypt, and bricks fashioned of mud without a straw binder would crumble and fall apart. "So the people were scattered abroad throughout the land," the Bible tells us, "to gather stubble for straw." Since the urgent search for straw reduced the hours available for brick making, the burden of the slaves was doubled. "Fulfill your work, your daily task, as when there was straw," the taskmasters urged, perhaps with a cruel grin, and the slaves who failed to meet the quota suffered the lash: "Why have ye not fulfilled your appointed task in making brick today as yesterday?" (Exod. 5:12–14)[15]

The Israelites were aggrieved by the new regimen, of course, but they did not bother to ask Moses to intercede on their behalf. Instead, the Israelite chiefs of the slave gangs, who had briefly been eclipsed by the showy newcomer with his bag of tricks, now reasserted themselves and took their grievances directly to Pharaoh. "Why does thou deal thus with your servants?" they complained indignantly, blaming the Egyptian taskmasters for the new burdens that had been laid upon them. "There is no straw given unto thy servants, and yet they say to us: Make brick! And, behold, thy servants are beaten, but the fault is in thine own people." (Exod. 5:15–16)[16]

So the benighted slaves apparently held only their slave-drivers and not Pharaoh responsible for their harsh new regimen. Indeed, like slaves and serfs throughout history, they seemed to suffer from the pathetic delusion that the paramount ruler was a decent and compassionate man who would intercede and lift the burden from their backs. For his own part, Pharaoh wanted to make sure the Israelites understood exactly who was to blame for their latest woes—Moses. But he was too artful to speak aloud his condemnation, and so he referred to the demands of Moses without mentioning him by name.

"Ye are lazy, ye are lazy, and therefore you say: Let us go and sacrifice to Yahweh," Pharaoh replied with cool sarcasm, echoing the words that Moses had spoken on their behalf. "Go now, and work; for no straw shall be given to thee, and yet shall ye deliver the quota of bricks." (Exod. 5:17–18)[17]

Pharaoh's ploy worked just as he had planned. Having slumped out of the throne room full of despair over the mischief that Pharaoh was working at the expense of the slaving Israelites, the delegation encountered Moses and Aaron outside the palace, and now they aimed their grievances at the target that Pharaoh had intended.

"Yahweh look upon you—and judge!" the Israelites cried out to their would-be liberators. "Because you have made us stink in the nostrils of Pharaoh and his people! You have put a sword in their hands to slay us!" (Exod. 5:21)[18]

Among Moses' accusers, according to a tale in the Midrash, are Dathan and Abiram, the very men who betrayed him to Pharaoh for slaying the taskmaster so many years before. "You are responsible for the widespread stench now issuing from the Israelitish corpses used as bricks for building when our quota was not complete," they say. "The Egyptians had but a faint suspicion that we were waiting for our redemption. It is your fault if they are fully conscious of it now."[19]

Moses has nothing to say in his own defense. He knows that the condemnation of the Israelites is thoroughly justified and his disastrous encounter with Pharaoh has resulted only in greater suffering for the very people he is struggling to save. The good shepherd is heartbroken by the peril that has befallen his flock. "His spirit almost rebelled," the rabbis imagined. "His people were like a sheep that had been carried away by a wolf—the shepherd pulled it one way, whilst the wolf pulled it the other way, and thus the poor sheep was torn to pieces. Such was the position of Israel between Moses and Pharaoh."[20]

Still, as the Bible confirms, Moses did not exactly blame himself for the failure of his scheme and the fresh cruelties that had been visited upon his fellow Israelites as a result of his clumsy efforts. Remarkably, the Bible makes it clear that Moses blamed God, who had sent him to speak the words that so enraged Pharaoh, and did not hesitate to tell him so at their very next encounter.

"Lord, why hast Thou dealt ill with this people?" Moses scolded Yahweh, apparently too angry and too indignant to restrain himself. "For since I came to Pharaoh to speak in Thy name, he hath dealt ill with this people—and neither hast Thou delivered Thy people at all." (Exod. 5:23)

An even harsher accusation was put into the mouth of Moses by the rabbinical storytellers: "Thou didst tell me that Thou art called Compassionate and Gracious, Longsuffering and Merciful," Moses says with elaborate sarcasm, "but as soon as I pronounced this Name before Pharaoh, misfortune descended upon the people of Israel."[21] And they imagined that Moses is condemned for his boldness: "For such audacious words," says the "angel of justice" to God, "Moses deserves to be punished." God himself complains like a much-put-upon father about a rebellious and insolent son. "Alas for the departed who no longer are here!" God retorts. "Many a time did I appear and manifest myself to Abraham, Isaac, and Jacob, but never did they venture to question My acts."[22] Yet God declines to punish Moses, the rabbis wrote, "for He knew that only out of his great love for his people and his compassion with the sufferers had he uttered such words."[23]

God was already familiar with the mood swings of Moses, the impudence and open defiance that Moses sometimes displayed. He would have been justified in pointing out that he had warned Moses back on Mount Horeb that Pharaoh would refuse to let the people go. But it appears that God endured the latest tantrum without a moment of anger or a murmur of argument. And when Moses had spent himself at last, God paused and then uttered an understated but solemn vow.

"Now shalt thou see what I will do to Pharaoh," said God to Moses—and the biblical text almost crackles with the icy resolve and ominous threat of his words. "For by a strong hand shall he let them go, and by a strong hand shall he drive them out of his land." (Exod. 6:1)

SECOND CALL

According to a literal reading of the Bible, God paused at that moment to deliver pretty much the same spiel that he had given once before on Mount Horeb.

"I appeared unto Abraham, unto Isaac and unto Jacob, as El Shaddai, but My name Yahweh I made not known to them," God says a second time. "And moreover I have heard the groaning of the children of Israel, whom the Egyptians keep in bondage, and I have remembered my Covenant. Wherefore say unto the children of Israel: I am the Lord, and I will bring you out from under the burdens of the Egyptians." (Exod. 6:2–3, 6)[24]

Given what had just transpired, Moses might have regarded God as a slightly senile deity who tended to repeat himself. Bible scholarship, however, provides a less blasphemous explanation: the second call of Moses in Exodus 6 is a "doublet" of the incident on Mount Horeb in Exodus 4, that is, a second version of the same story by a different biblical source. The first call is attributed to a conflation of the sources known as J and E while the second call is thought to be the work of the source known as P. The fingerprints of the Priestly source are clearly seen in the verses starting with Exodus 6:14, where the conversation between God and Moses is abruptly cut off and a long genealogical entry suddenly begins: "These are the heads of their fathers' houses: the sons of Reuben and the first-born of Israel. . . ." (Exod. 6:14) The Priestly source works his way through several generations of Israelites before focusing on the Levites in particular and ending with Aaron's son, Eleazar, who "took him one of the daughters of Putiel to wife; and she bore him Phinehas." (Exod. 6:25) Although P neglects to mention certain prominent members of the tribe of Levi—Miriam, the sister of Moses and Aaron, for example, or the wife and sons of Moses—he is careful to list the progeny of Aaron.

Here P betrays his ulterior motive: Aaron, Eleazar, and Phinehas are the first three high priests of Israel, all from the priestly tribe of Levi, and that is precisely why P thought to feature them so prominently. The same preoccupation with the priesthood and its prerogatives can be detected in all of the biblical passages attributed to P, who devoted much attention to the minutiae of ritual observance and sacred law and compiled those famous lists of who begat whom in order to legitimize the succession of both royal and priestly authority. That is why the Priestly source interrupted his version of the call of Moses to insert a lengthy family history that attested to the credentials of the Aaronite priesthood. As it turned out, Moses was no more enthusiastic about his chances of success during the second call than he had been during the first one, and no more hesitant to tell God so.

"Go in, speak unto Pharaoh, king of Egypt, that he let the children of Israel go out of his land," God commanded Moses, ignoring the fact that this is exactly what Moses had just done—and with such unfortunate consequences (Exod. 6:11, 29).

"Behold, the children of Israel have not hearkened unto me," Moses gently reminded God, resorting to ornate and euphemistic language and a certain diplomatic indirection that were hardly typical of his dealings with Yahweh. "How then shall Pharaoh hear me, who am of uncircumcised lips?" (Exod. 6:12, 30)

The reference to "uncircumcised lips" is generally understood by Bible scholars to be a yet more fanciful way of saying "slow of speech," which is itself a euphemism for some kind of speech impediment—that is, Moses was again arguing that he was not the right man for the job.

"See, I have set thee in God's stead to Pharaoh, and Aaron thy brother shall be thy prophet," God replied. "Thou shalt speak all that I command thee, and Aaron thy brother shall speak unto Pharaoh, that he let the children of Israel go out of his land." (Exod. 7:1–2)

The whole exchange must have prompted a sense of déjà vu in both God and Moses—but now God paused to go over a few of the more crucial details that Moses had clearly forgotten since their last conversation on Horeb. The whole enterprise was not going to be as straightforward as Moses might have wished, God reminded him, and God himself was not going to make things any easier.

"And I will harden Pharaoh's heart, and multiply My signs and My wonders in the land of Egypt," God declared. "But Pharaoh will not hearken unto you, and I will lay My hand upon Egypt, and bring forth My hosts, My people the children of Israel, out of the land of Egypt by great judgments." (Exod. 7:3–4)

God did not specify what he meant by "signs and wonders," but he promised that Pharaoh and the rest of Egypt would not fail to heed them in the end.

"And the Egyptians shall know that I am the Lord," God explained, "when I stretch forth My hand upon Egypt, and bring out the children of Israel from among them." (Exod. 7:5)

DUELING SORCERERS

When Moses and Aaron again presented themselves to Pharaoh, he demanded some proof that a god, *any* god, was sponsoring them. "Show a wonder," Pharaoh ordered, and Aaron promptly complied by performing the trick that God had taught Moses on Mount Horeb: "Aaron cast down his rod before Pharaoh and before his servants, and it became a serpent." (Exod. 7:10)

The reaction of Moses when he beheld the same trick on Mount

Horeb had been to turn and run. Pharaoh and his privy counselors, however, were frankly unimpressed by Aaron's legerdemain. "Then Pharaoh also called for the wise men and the sorcerers, and they also, the magicians of Egypt, did in like manner with their secret arts," the Bible reports. "For they cast down every man his rod, and they became serpents." (Exod. 7:11–12)

Indeed, the sign that God taught to Moses on the holy mountain "is made to look like a cheap juggler's trick," as Brevard Childs writes, "which a whole row of Egyptian magicians can duplicate with ease."[25] And the rabbis conveyed Pharaoh's contempt for the trick in a tale from the Midrash. "This is but poor magic for Egypt, a country steeped in the art of magic—our little children can do this!" sniffs Pharaoh, who summons his wife and children to perform the same feat, as if to emphasize it does not take a *real* sorcerer to do such silly tricks. "It is customary to bring to a place merchandise of which it is in need," Pharaoh cracks, "but you seem to bring brine to Spain and fish to Aacho."[26]*

A viper's nest of serpents now writhed on the floor of Pharaoh's palace, and Aaron contrived a big finish to his magic show: the snake that had once been his staff swallowed up each of the snakes that had once been the staffs of the Egyptians sorcerers. The Bible does not report the reaction of Pharaoh and his counselors to Aaron's bit of one-upmanship, although the rabbis imagined that Pharaoh is finally impressed. "When Pharaoh saw this miracle," goes the rabbinical tale, "terror seized him, and he was afraid lest Aaron's rod would swallow him up, too."[27] Still, Pharaoh was not yet moved to comply with the demands of Moses and Aaron. "And Pharaoh's heart was hardened, and he hearkened not unto them, as the Lord had spoken," the Bible repeats (Exod. 7:13).

"Pharaoh's heart is stubborn, he refuseth to let the people go," God reminded Moses, who was surely puzzling over the maddening paradox that confronted him—Pharaoh was only stubborn because God made him so (Exod. 7:14). But soon God would reveal a much more elaborate plan to afflict the Egyptians and their obstinate king. The curtain-raiser was over, and the show was about to begin.

---

*Other versions rendered the same passage as "bringing straw to Hafarayim." All of these phrases are equivalent to "carrying coals to Newcastle" and are meant to emphasize that Egypt was abundantly supplied with magicians and thus had no need of a couple of self-made sorcerers.

SECRET ARTS

Pharaoh was in the habit of a morning stroll along the Nile, the Bible continues, and God instructed Moses to intercept him there.

> Get thee unto Pharaoh in the morning; lo, he goeth out unto the water; and thou shalt stand by the river's brink to meet him; and the rod which was turned to a serpent shalt thou take in thy hand. (Exod. 7:15)

The rabbis, wondering why the god-king of ancient Egypt would be idling along the Nile, imagined that he is searching out a secret place where he will not be seen when he urinates and defecates. "Is there a god that hath human needs?" Pharaoh says to Moses in one rabbinical tale. "Verily, I am no god—I only pretend to be one before the Egyptians, who are such idiots, one should consider them asses rather than human beings."[28] And we may imagine Pharaoh's consternation when the persistent old man who keeps showing up at his palace now dogs him at the river's edge, too.

"Yahweh, the God of the Hebrews, hath sent me unto thee saying: Let My people go, that they may serve Me in the wilderness," Moses warned Pharaoh. "In this thou shalt know that I am Yahweh—behold, I will smite with the rod that is in my hand upon the waters which are in the river, and they shall be turned to blood." (Exod. 7:17–18)[29]

Yahweh proceeded to carry out his threat, although the Bible specified that it was *Aaron* who wielded the rod of God: "Take thy rod, and stretch out thy hand over the waters of Egypt," Moses instructed his brother, "over their rivers, over their streams, and over their pools, and over all their ponds of water, that they may become blood." (Exod. 7:19)

So began the first of the Ten Plagues. "And the fish that were in the river died," the Bible reports, "and the river became foul, and the Egyptians could not drink water from the river, and the blood was throughout the land of Egypt." (Exod. 7:21) Even water stored "in vessels of wood and in vessels of stone" turned into blood (Exod. 7:19), and the Egyptians were forced to dig new wells "for they could not drink of the water of the river." (Exod. 7:24) Seven days passed before the waters of the Nile ran clear again.

Predictably, Pharaoh was not much impressed by the feat. Just as they had done once before, his court magicians succeeded in duplicating the trick of turning water into blood "with their secret arts." (Exod. 7:22) Even if his subjects were thirsting for fresh water, Pharaoh contented himself with the abundant provisions that were readily available from the larders of the palace. "You don't trouble me," Pharaoh tells Moses in one Midrashic tale that anticipates the words of Marie Antoinette, "for if I can't have water, I'll have wine."[30] The Bible reports that Pharaoh "turned away, went into his house and dismissed the matter from his mind." (Exod: 7:23 NEB)

Next came the warning of a second plague. "Thus saith the Lord: Let My people go, that they may serve Me," said Moses. "And if thou refuse to let them go, behold, I will smite all thy borders with frogs, which shall go up and come into thy house, and into thy bed-chamber, and upon thy bed, and into the house of thy servants, and upon thy people, and into thine ovens, and into thy kneading-troughs." (Exod. 7:26–28) Again it was Moses who warned Pharaoh, but thanks to the Priestly source's tweaking of the text, it was Aaron who wielded the rod of God "over the rivers, over the canals, and over the pools." Just as Moses promised, "the frogs came up, and covered the land of Egypt." (Exod. 8:1–2) And, yet again, "the magicians did in like manner with their secret arts, and brought up frogs upon the land of Egypt." (Exod. 8:1–3)

Pharaoh must have quickly realized his folly in permitting his own magicians to conjure up yet more frogs at the very moment when the slimy creatures were already swarming out of the Nile and covering the land of Egypt. Indeed, the second plague seemed to have its intended effect on Pharaoh, who now summoned Moses and Aaron to the palace and delivered an urgent plea of his own.

"Entreat Yahweh," Pharaoh implored, "that He take away the frogs from me, and from my subjects; and then I will let the people go, that they may sacrifice to Yahweh." (Exod. 8:4)[31]

A sweet moment for Moses, at long last, and he must have relished the sight of the mighty Pharaoh reduced to begging a couple of slaves for the favor of removing the frogs from his bed and his breadbox. Indeed, the Bible suggests that Moses could not resist the impulse to prolong the moment of triumph by showing off a bit. Like a seasoned sideshow magician, Moses invited Pharaoh to specify exactly *when* the frogs should be taken away, as if to make the trick more difficult and thus even more astounding.

"I beg your royal favour," Moses improvised with a grand flourish.

"Appoint a time when I may intercede with Yahweh for you and your courtiers and the people of Egypt, so that you may be rid of the frogs, and none will be left except in the Nile, where they belong."

"Tomorrow," said Pharaoh.

"It shall be just as you say," replied Moses, "so that you will know that there is no one like our God, Yahweh—the frogs shall depart from you and your courtiers and your houses on the very day you have selected, and none will be left except in the Nile." (Exod. 8:5–7)[32]

Did Moses suffer a sudden wave of anxiety as he left the throne room in triumph? Had he gone a bit too far in making such a bold promise to Pharaoh? God had given specific instructions about how to start the plague of frogs, but he had said nothing at all about ending the plague, and he had not authorized Moses to leave it up to Pharaoh to specify when the frogs would be made to depart. "Moses appealed to the Lord to remove the frogs," goes the biblical account (Exod. 8:12 NEB), and he must have endured a few tense moments as he waited to see if God was going to make a liar out of him in Pharaoh's eyes.

Happily, God made good on the rash promise. "And the Lord did according to the word of Moses," the Bible reports, "and the frogs died out of the houses, out of the courts and out of the fields." But God played a trick of his own, perhaps as a rebuke to Moses as much as Pharaoh—the frogs were dead but not gone! "And they gathered them together in heaps, and the land stank." Still, it was Pharaoh who enjoyed the last laugh: "But when Pharaoh saw that there was respite, he hardened his heart; and hearkened not unto them; as the Lord had spoken." (Exod. 9:11)

"I WILL SEE THY FACE AGAIN NO MORE"

The third plague was to descend upon Egypt without warning. Aaron struck the soil with the rod of God, raising clouds of dust that turned into clouds of gnats, which proceeded to sting man and beast throughout the land (Exod. 8:13). Ominously, when the magicians of Egypt sought to duplicate this feat, they failed. "This is the finger of God," the magicians said to Pharaoh, as if to acknowledge a subtle intensification of Yahweh's punishing anger toward Egypt (Exod. 8:15).

Pharaoh himself was unmoved by the gnats—"Pharaoh's heart was hardened, and he hearkened not unto them" (Exod. 8:15)—and so God sent a plague of flies. Even if a swarm of flies was not much of an innovation after a swam of gnats, the fourth plague finally caught the attention of Pharaoh, and word was sent to Moses and Aaron: Pharaoh was ready to parley.

"Go ye, sacrifice to your God," offered Pharaoh, "but do it here in Egypt, not in the wilderness." (Exod. 8:21)[33]

"That we cannot do," countered Moses, "because the victim we shall sacrifice to the Lord our God is an abomination to the Egyptians. If the Egyptians see us offer such an animal, will they not stone us to death? We must go a three days' journey into the wilderness to sacrifice to the Lord our God, as he commands us." (Exod. 8:26–27 NEB)

Now Moses was apparently improvising again: God had not told him what kind of animal was to be sacrificed, and he could not have known whether or not the Egyptians would be put off by the sight of the ritual. For now, his motive was to secure permission for a three-day march into the wilderness—and then keep on going.

"I will let you go, and you shall sacrifice to your God in the wilderness—only do not go too far," allowed Pharaoh. "Now intercede for me!" (Exod. 8:28)[34]

Moses quickly agreed: "Behold, I go out from thee, and I will entreat the Lord that the swarms of flies may depart from Pharaoh, only let not Pharaoh deal deceitfully any more in not letting the people go to sacrifice to the Lord." (Exod. 8:25)[35]

The fear that Pharaoh would not keep his word was thoroughly justified, as Moses ought to have known. Moses dutifully entreated God to rid Egypt of the flies, and "there remained not one." But Pharaoh did not honor his end of the bargain: "And Pharaoh hardened his heart this time also, and he did not let the people go." (Exod. 8:27–28)

And so went the rest of the plagues in a disheartening round of demands and counterdemands, promises made and promises broken, threats uttered and threats carried out, each display of divine wrath followed just as surely by a display of imperial willfulness; and the Israelites were still slaves. The fifth plague was pestilence, "a very grievous murrain" that fell upon "the horses, upon the asses, upon the camels, upon the herds, and upon the flocks," with the result that "all the cattle of Egypt died" and the cattle belonging to the Israelites were miraculously spared (Exod. 9:3, 6). Then Moses threw handfuls of soot into the air, and when the dust settled over the land of Egypt, boils and blains broke forth "upon man and beast," including the Egyptian magicians, who were so stricken with boils that they could not even stand up before Moses, much less duplicate the sixth plague (Exod. 9:10).

The seventh plague was "a very grievous hail, such as hath not been in Egypt since the day it was founded even until now." God was thoughtful enough to spare the cattle and field hands by cautioning the Egyptians to get them under shelter, but only those "that feared the word of the Lord" heeded the kindly warning, and the rest watched as their cattle and crops and serfs were battered to death by "thunder and hail and fire." (Exod. 9:18–25) Only the land of Goshen was spared. (The Bible does not explain how there came to be any cattle left among the Egyptians after the murrain that was the fifth plague.) After the hail came the eighth plague, a swarm of locusts that devoured "every herb of the land, even all that the hail hath left" (Exod. 10:12), and after the locusts, the ninth plague was a darkness that settled over Egypt and extinguished every source of light except those in the houses of the Israelites—"a darkness that can be felt," as the Bible reports (Exod. 10:22).

None of the first nine plagues, however, made the slightest difference in the plight of the Israelites. Now and then, of course, Pharaoh would summon Moses and Aaron to the palace and make a great show of remorse and sudden resolve. "I have sinned this time; the Lord is righteous, and I and my people are wicked," said Pharaoh as the hail fell from the sky. "Entreat the Lord, and let there be enough of these mighty thunderings and hail, and I will let you go!" But as soon as Moses lifted the plague, Pharaoh "sinned yet more, and hardened his heart." (Exod. 9:27, 35)

The people of Egypt were not so indifferent to the ordeal. "How long shall this man be a snare unto us?" the royal counselors argued. "Let the men go, that they may serve the Lord their god; knowest thou not yet that Egypt is destroyed?" (Exod. 10:7) But Pharaoh was willing only to haggle endlessly and pointlessly with Moses and Aaron: first he agreed to let only the menfolk go, and then he allowed that women and children might accompany them, but not their flocks and herds.

Moses was no less obstinate than Pharaoh. "No, you must yourself supply us with animals for sacrifice, and our own flocks must go with us, too—not a hoof must be left behind," demanded Moses with sudden impudence that may have surprised both of them. "We may need animals from our own flocks to worship the Lord our God; we ourselves cannot tell until we are there how we are to worship the Lord." (Exod. 10:25–26)[36]

So the signs and wonders that God had vowed to send down on Pharaoh—or, at least, the first nine of them—ended in a standoff between two willful and stubborn men, one the ruler of a great and enduring empire and one the reluctant leader of a landless nation of slaves. All the palaver came to an end after the ninth plague, the plague of darkness, when Pharaoh and Moses exchanged harsh and ominous words.

"Out! Pester me no more!" Pharaoh said to Moses with cold contempt after Moses uttered his audacious demand that Pharaoh provide his slaves with cattle for the sacrifice to Yahweh. "See my face no more—for on the day thou seest my face again, thou shalt die."

"Thou hast spoken well," Moses replied with precisely the same coldness and the same contempt. "I will see thy face again no more." (Exod. 10:28–29.)[37]

ABOUT MIDNIGHT

"Yet one more plague will I bring upon Pharaoh and upon Egypt," God revealed to Moses in a phrase that hums with veiled threat and steely certitude, "and afterwards he will let you go." (Exod. 11:1)

The first indication that the signs and wonders were about to escalate from gnats and flies into something more fearful took the form of an exceedingly strange instruction by God to Moses. "Speak now in the ears of the people," God said, "and let them ask every man of his neighbour, and every women of her neighbour, jewels of silver and jewels of gold." Moses must have wondered why God expected the slave masters of Egypt to bestow gifts of silver and gold upon their slaves, but if God could harden the heart of Pharaoh, he could gladden the hearts of ordinary Egyptians and prompt them to bestow rich gifts on the Israelites. "And the Lord gave the people favour in the sight of the Egyptians," the Bible explains. "Moreover the man Moses was very great in the land of Egypt, and in the sight of Pharaoh's servants, and in the sight of the people." (Exod. 11:2–3)

But the plunder of the Egyptians was only a preface to the tenth and final plague.

"About midnight will I go out into the midst of Egypt," God told Moses, and Moses told the Israelites, "and all the first-born in the land of Egypt shall die, from the first-born of Pharaoh that sitteth upon his throne, even unto the first-born of the maid-servant that is behind the mill; even unto the first-born of the cattle." (Exod. 11:4–5)

The sideshow was over, and God was about to reveal the blood-thirsty aspect of his nature. Elsewhere in the Five Books of Moses, Yahweh is praised as merciful, compassionate, slow to anger and quick to forgive, a deity filled with fatherly love and loving kindness. But God makes no secret of his willingness to scourge and kill his own creatures when his patience is spent. God had once condemned all of humankind except Noah and his family to death by drowning; sent down hellfire and brimstone on the men, women, and children of Sodom and Gomorrah; sought to kill Moses himself—and now he was ready to rouse the Angel of Death from his long celestial slumber and put him back to work. Moses was "hot with anger," the Bible reports, but so was God himself (Exod. 11:9).

"And there shall be a great cry throughout all the land of Egypt, such as there hath been none like it before, nor shall there be like it anymore," God warned Moses about the night of carnage that was approaching. "But against any of the children of Israel shall not a dog whet his tongue, against man or beast; that ye may know that the Lord doth put a difference between the Egyptians and Israel." (Exod. 11:6–7)

Then Moses delivered one final warning to Pharaoh before the bloodletting began. At last Pharaoh himself would feel the sting of a plague, and he would respond not as a divine marionette whose heart had been hardened by God but as a flesh-and-blood human being—Pharaoh would beg Moses and the Israelites to leave Egypt so that *his* suffering would end.

"And all of thy servants shall come down unto me, and bow down unto me, saying: 'Get thee out, and all the people that follow thee,'" Moses said to Pharaoh. "And after that I will go out." (Exod. 11:8)

A NIGHT OF WATCHING

Long before the final plague, on the very eve of God's attack on Moses at the lodging place on the road to Egypt, God had predicted the momentous encounter between Moses and Pharaoh.

"Israel is My son, My first-born," God had instructed Moses to say to Pharaoh on his behalf. "And I have said unto thee: Let My son go, that he may serve Me; and thou hast refused to let him go. Behold, I will slay thy son, thy first-born." (Exod. 4:22–23)

God devised an elaborate ritual that would serve to warn him away from the dwellings of the Israelites on the night of the tenth plague. Every household was to select a lamb or a kid from the flock, an un-blemished male yearling, and slaughter it between dusk and nightfall. By night, the flesh was to be roasted over a fire and eaten with unleav-ened bread and bitter herbs, and the meal was to be taken within the four walls of each family's quarters: "[N]one of you shall go out of the door of his house until the morning." (Exod. 12:22) Still, even as they supped on the sacrificial flesh in the darkness and behind closed doors, the Israelites had to be prepared to leave Egypt on a moment's notice. "[Y]ou shall have your belt fastened, your sandals on your feet and your staff in your hand," God specified, "and you must eat in urgent haste." (Exod. 12:11 NEB) Most important, the blood of the sacrificial beast must be caught in a basin and then painted on the lintel and the side posts of each family's dwelling with a brush fashioned out of a bunch of hyssop.

> For I will go through the land of Egypt in that night, and will smite all the first-born in the land of Egypt, both man and beast; and against all the gods of Egypt I will execute judgments: I am the Lord. And the blood shall be to you for a token upon the houses where ye are, and when I see the blood, I will pass over you, and there shall be no plague upon you to destroy you, when I smite the land of Egypt. (Exod. 12:12–13)

Such a sign was essential if only because God was so hard to stop once he started to kill, as Moses had learned back in the wilderness of Midian when God sought to slay him. "The destroyer who will strike the first born of Egypt," one scholar wrote of God's night attack on Moses, "[was] already on his way"[38]—and Moses had been the first one the destroyer encountered. Indeed, the rabbis were willing to entertain the notion that when God goes on a rampage, he is perfectly capable of killing anyone and anything that crosses his path. "[O]nce the destroyer has been given permission to destroy," they warned, "he no longer dis-tinguishes between the righteous and the wicked."[39]

Sermons and Sunday school lessons tend to pretty up the tenth plague by suggesting it was the Angel of Death who actually did the dirty work. The rabbis imagined that God is assisted by "nine thousand myriads of the Angels of Destruction who are fashioned some of hail and some of flames, and whose glances drive terror and trembling to the heart of the beholder,"[40] and one rabbinical tradition even proposed to put the blame for "the frightful bloodshed" on Satan.[41] True enough, the Bible preserves a passing reference to "the destroyer" in the original account of the tenth plague (Exod. 12:23), but it is clear that God himself was the destroyer. "*I* will go through the land of Egypt in that night," God has already revealed to Moses, "and when *I* see the blood, *I* will pass over you." (Exod. 12:12–13)[42]

So the Bible conjures up one long night of terror, a dark night filled with strange sights and sounds, as Yahweh ranged through the land of Egypt, moving through the streets and alleys and striking down any living creature that was unfortunate enough to have been the firstborn of its mother. As in the blood ritual that Zipporah used to stave off God's attack on Moses at the lodging place, blood worked its magic again in Egypt, and only Moses and the Israelites who sheltered behind blood-smeared doors in the slave quarters were spared.

"And it came to pass at midnight that the Lord smote all the firstborn in the land of Egypt," the Bible confirms, "from the first-born of Pharaoh on his throne unto the first-born of the captive that was in the dungeon." (Exod. 12:29)

The death of the firstborn of Egypt managed to catch the attention of Pharaoh. No longer was his heart hardened to the affliction that God had sent down on Egypt; no longer did he sit in his palace in splendid indifference to the suffering of his fellow Egyptians. The Bible suggests that his own son, the crown prince of Egypt, was among the victims of the divine carnage. "And Pharaoh rose up in the night, he and all his servants, and all the Egyptians, and there was a great cry in Egypt," the Bible reports, "for there was not a house where there was not one dead." (Exod. 12:30) Indeed, the rabbis imagined that the death toll is multiplied by the sheer promiscuity of the men and women of Egypt. "[A]s the Egyptians led dissolute lives," goes one leering tale, "it happened not rarely that each of the ten children of one woman was the first-born of its father."[43]

The king of Egypt, who had vowed that Moses would die on the day he next saw the old man's face, hastened to find his old nemesis and plead for mercy.

"Rise up, get you forth from among my people, both ye and the children of Israel, and go serve the Lord as ye had said," Pharaoh begged Moses and Aaron. "Take both your flocks and your herds, as ye have said, and be gone—and ask God's blessing on me, too." (Exod. 12:31–32)[44]

Indeed, the panic seized all of Egypt, and the badly shaken survivors of the tenth plague joined their monarch in urging the Israelites to go. Just as God had directed, the Israelites asked to borrow the riches of their masters—"jewels of silver, and jewels of gold, and raiment"—and the riches were pressed upon them, willingly and even eagerly, if only to hasten their departure. After all, who could know whether the blood-thirsty God of Israel would stop with the firstborn of Egypt?

"And the Egyptians were urgent upon the people, to send them out of the land in haste," the Bible reports, "for they said: 'We are all dead men.' " (Exod. 12:33, 35)

Moses and the rest of the Israelites savored the sweet victory that God had bestowed upon them at the expense of the Egyptians, or so imagined the rabbis and sages in retelling the tale of the Ten Plagues. Pharaoh leaves his palace in the midst of the carnage to seek out Moses, they wrote, but when he pleads for help in finding the leader of the Israelites, the lads whom he encounters send him in the wrong direction and then laugh about it. "O my friend Moses!" Pharaoh cries out as he wanders like a madman through the slave quarters, "pray for me to God!"[45] At last, when he stumbles upon the house where Moses is keeping his vigil, Pharaoh is met with yet more derision.

"Who are thou," Moses teases from behind the barred door, "and what is thy name?"

"I am Pharaoh," the once mighty king replies miserably, "who stands here in humiliation."

"I will teach thee something and thou wilt learn," Moses lectures Pharaoh. "Raise thy voice and shout aloud: 'Children of Israel! Ye are henceforth your own masters, arise and depart from among my people!' "

The monarch complies, and his voice is miraculously heard throughout Egypt.[46] But he continues to fret: "I am a first-born myself," Pharaoh whimpers to Moses, "and I fear lest I, too, will die."

"I told thee already that thou needst not fear for thy life, for thou art destined for greater things," replies Moses, uttering a sly prophecy that alludes to Pharaoh's death at the Red Sea on a day of signs and wonders still to come. "Thou wilt live to manifest to the greatness of God."[47]

Pharaoh continues to implore Moses to leave Egypt at once, the rabbis wrote, but Moses insists on tarrying until morning, when the success of the slave rebellion and the moment of liberation will be plain for all to see.

"Are we thieves or burglars that we should sneak away under cover of darkness?" Moses taunts the king of Egypt. "The Lord hath commanded us not to leave our houses until the morning, and we will depart from the country, holding our heads high, and before the whole of Egypt."[48]

PLAGUE COUNTING

Only a single chapter of the Bible and not more than two dozen lines of text are taken up in telling the life story of Moses from the day of his birth, through childhood, adolescence, and young adulthood, the slaying of the taskmaster, the flight to Midian, the marriage to Zipporah, and the birth of his first son. But the various biblical authors and editors were so absorbed with the tale of the Ten Plagues that they devoted substantially all of seven chapters to the saga.

For that reason, perhaps, the biblical account of the Ten Plagues is riddled with variations and inconsistencies. Sometimes it is Moses who brings down a plague, at other times it is Aaron, and God himself delivers the decisive tenth plague. Sometimes Moses stalks Pharaoh along the banks of the Nile, and sometimes Pharaoh summons Moses and his brother to the palace. Sometimes Pharaoh is warned before a plague begins, sometimes not. Sometimes a plague affects all of Egypt, sometimes the Egyptians but not the Israelites, sometimes only "he that regarded not the word of the Lord." (Exod. 9:20) Some of the plagues seem repetitive; after all, is a plague of gnats—or were they lice, according to some translations, or mosquitoes or even maggots?[49]—really much different from a plague of flies? Sometimes the end of a plague is specified—the locusts, for example, were blown into the Red Sea by a "strong west wind" (Exod. 10:19)—and sometimes we are left to wonder. Exactly when and how, for instance, was the plague of darkness finally lifted from Egypt after Moses and Pharaoh broke off their negotiations?

In fact, two separate and contradictory versions of the plague saga can readily be teased out of the biblical text.[50] In one version, the plagues are intended to coerce Pharaoh into permitting a three-day march into the wilderness—a ruse that will put the Israelites beyond the reach of Pharaoh and allow them to keep on marching out of Egypt—but Pharaoh's heart has been hardened and the plagues are unavailing; the Israelites are forced to slip out of Egypt by night, and they are pursued all the way to the Red Sea by the armies of Pharaoh. In the other version, only a single plague—the slaying of the firstborn of Egypt—is required to bend the will of Pharaoh, who not only consents to the departure of the Israelites but pleads with them to go in haste. "[W]hen he shall let you go," God predicted, "he shall surely thrust you out hence altogether." (Exod. 11:1)

The most obvious explanation for these flaws lies in the multiple authorship of the Bible. Even something so basic as the number of plagues is probably the work of the Redactor who combined the writings of the Yahwist, the Elohist,[51] and the Priestly source. "[N]one of the three sources of the Pentateuch has more than seven," one Bible scholar notes, "and only the first and last are common to all."[52] The Yahwist recalled a hasty and secret departure from Egypt under cover of darkness, while the Priestly source described a long and even leisurely period of preparation for a highly public departure in the light of day. The Yahwist presented Pharaoh as a man whose free will is intact—he hardens his own heart against the plight of the Israelites and the threat of the plagues—while the Priestly source regarded Pharaoh as not much more than a straw man who was so thoroughly manipulated by God that we cannot say that he had a heart at all. And, intriguingly, the Deuteronomist did not bother to mention *any* of the ten plagues that are recounted in such detail and at such length in the Book of Exodus, contenting himself with a passing reference to "signs and wonders, great and sore, upon Egypt" (Deut. 6:22), an omission that offers yet another clue to the deeper mystery of whether the life of Moses and the events of the Exodus are history or legend.

Still more troubling are some of the theological mysteries in the sacred text. Moses taught the Israelites a revolutionary new faith that is purged of magic and paganism, a faith that rejects sorcery and superstition and worships Yahweh not as the most powerful of the gods but as the one and only God—or so goes the conventional wisdom of Bible scholarship. Yet Moses is also depicted as a wonder-worker and even a kind of sideshow sorcerer in his dealings with the Israelites and Pharaoh himself, and the rod of God becomes a magic wand in his hands. The

Bible readily concedes that the gods of Egypt and the "secret arts" of Pharaoh's own sorcerers were sufficiently powerful to match the first three plagues. *Hartumim*, conventionally translated from the Hebrew as "magicians," is a loan-word from the Egyptian language that originally referred to "scribes who kept the ritual texts," and thus suggests that the biblical author was crediting these "religious functionaries" with authentic mystical power and not mere sleight of hand.[53] Above all, the blood ritual that attended the slaying of the firstborn of Egypt and protected the Israelites from the hand of their own God—the smearing of blood on the doorposts—is hardly the stuff of the "ethical monotheism" for which Moses is celebrated.

"[W]as not all this sacrifice and ceremonial at bottom only magic and black art," Freud observed, "such as the old doctrine of Moses had unconditionally condemned?"[54]

Some of the uglier aspects of the plague saga are even harder to explain away. All of Egypt was made to suffer for the stubbornness of Pharaoh, for example, and the rabbis struggled to justify the notion of collective punishment. "The plagues that God sent upon the Egyptians corresponded to the deeds they had perpetrated against the children of Israel," the rabbinical tradition holds. "Because they forced the Israelites to draw water for them, and also hindered them from the use of the ritual baths," for example, "He changed their water into blood."[55] The tenth and most bloodthirsty of the plagues posed the most troubling moral dilemma, but the sages insisted that the firstborn of Egypt were condemned to death en masse because of the cruelties that had been practiced on the Israelites by the entire population over many years, starting with the mass murder of babies that nearly cost Moses his life and ending with one last infanticide on the eve of liberation.

"On the day of the exodus, Rachel the daughter of Shuthelah gave birth to a child, while she and her husband together were treading the clay for bricks," goes the rabbinical tale. "The babe dropped from her womb into the clay and sank out of sight. Gabriel appeared, moulded a brick out of the clay containing the child, and carried it to the highest of the heavens, where he made it a footstool before the Divine Throne. On that very night, God looked upon the suffering of Israel, and smote the first-born of the Egyptians."[56]

Perhaps most perplexing of all is the notion that the people of Egypt were forced to endure a series of plagues not because Pharaoh was stubborn and cruel but because God made him so by "hardening" his heart. "Pharaoh's destruction is not self-destruction, for Pharaoh is no longer a 'self,' " Bible scholar David Gunn points out. "Yahweh has split his mind, stolen his will."[57] Moses himself became " 'the silenced messenger,' " as another Bible critic puts it, "whose own voice melts into the words of God."[58] That's the real subtext of the plague saga in the hands of the Priestly source, who sought to celebrate the primacy of God's will in the history of humankind.[59]

Contemporary theologians, however, have been willing to challenge the disturbing subtext of the plague saga. "Superficially, the story provides a glorious tableau of deliverance with great signs and wonders, from slavery into freedom," writes Gunn. "The more one looks into it, however, the more muted that picture appears. The signs and wonders conceal destruction and suffering, deserved and undeserved—an excess of havoc, we might be tempted to argue."[60]

The crowning irony, then, is that the theology of the Ten Plagues denies the very theme that is regarded as the shining moral example of the Exodus—the theme of liberation. If God determines exactly how a human being will act and react, then there is no place for free will and no real freedom at all. "In a sense, then, the real issue throughout the narrative is not slavery vs. freedom," writes one revisionist theologian, "but merely the identity and character of the master whom Israel must serve."[61]

God himself was candid with Moses about the ordeal that Egypt and Israel were required to endure, and he was equally blunt in disclosing the reason why. By hardening Pharaoh's heart, God would have the excuse to inflict one plague after another so that, as God put it, "My wonders may be multiplied in the land of Egypt." (Exod. 11:9) In other words, God did not want the liberation of the Israelites to appear *too* easy; rather, God was thinking of his place in history and he knew that ten plagues would make a better story than one. If Moses was something of a sideshow magician, God was the ringmaster—and he knew how to put on a show that would stay in the memory of the crowds who witnessed it.

"I have hardened his heart, so that I may show these signs," God explained to Moses in a passage attributed to the Priestly source, "and so that you can tell your children and grandchildren the story: how I made sport of the Egyptians, and what signs I showed among them. Thus will you know that I am Yahweh." (Exod. 10:1–2)[62]

A NATURAL HISTORY OF THE PLAGUES

When Philo recapped the Ten Plagues, he drew upon some of the proto-scientific notions of his own era to explain what had happened. "For the elements of the universe, earth, water, air, and fire," he wrote, "were all by the command of God brought into a state of hostility against them, so that the country of those impious men was destroyed, in order to exhibit the height of the authority which God wielded."[63] So began a long tradition of seeking an explanation in science for what is reported in the Bible as miracle and mystery.

An early and favorite suggestion was that the plagues were caused by the entry of a comet into the atmosphere of earth at some point in prehistory—a perfectly natural cataclysm that resulted in a shower of debris from the skies, which the biblical author remembers as hail. Perhaps the dense clouds of dust and ashes from the comet caused the plague of darkness that is preserved in the Bible—or was the real cause of the darkness, as other scholars have speculated, a massive eruption of a volcano on the island of Santorini in 1447 B.C.E. or perhaps a freakish cloud of dust carried on the trade winds?[64]

The effort to demystify the Ten Plagues reaches its highest expression in the work of a Bible scholar named Greta Hort, a kind of biblical ecologist, who concedes that the biblical account might have been built around a "historical core" but proposes an elaborate scheme by which the plagues may be explained in terms of natural phenomena.[65] Suppose the first plague on Egypt resulted from the flooding of the tributaries of the Nile, which carried the red soil of the Abyssinian plateau into the Nile itself and reddened the river as it flowed through Egypt, she suggests. The flood waters would have washed out the dams, sluices, and wells on which the Egyptians relied for their water supply—and so they would have been forced to dig new wells, just as the Bible reports. "Perhaps nothing in the whole of the Biblical account of Israel in Egypt betrays so intimate a knowledge of the actual conditions in Egypt and of the events in that country," enthuses Hort, "as this description of all the Egyptians having to dig for water, and not only those who lived near the river."[66]

The floodwaters would have filled the river with flagellates that washed down from the mountain lakes, Hort speculates, and these flagellates would have intensified the redness of the water, created a terrible stench, killed off the fish, and rendered the water undrinkable—all conditions described in the biblical account of the first plague. The second plague followed from the first, according to Hort: the rotting bodies of dead fish, deposited along the banks of the Nile, polluted the habitat of the frogs and drove them out of the river in search of refuge on dry land. The death of the frogs was the result of infection by the anthrax bacillus that they contracted by consuming the insects that feasted on the dead fish—and the overpopulation of insects explains the third and fourth plagues. The fifth plague, a cattle pest, was caused by the grazing of livestock on lands that were still covered with the anthrax-infested corpses of dead frogs. And the sixth plague—of boils—can be explained as pustules caused by skin anthrax that had been spread to human beings by the flies.

"In these circumstances," Hort urges, "it would be unwarrantable scepticism not to accept the Biblical account of these phenomena as historically true."[67]

Ironically, the whole enterprise of explaining the signs and wonders of the Bible by reference to forces of nature can be seen as an effort by devout Bible scholars to convince the skeptical reader of the truth of Holy Writ. Much the same impulse drives the strong interest in biblical archaeology among literalists and fundamentalists, as if they believe that the minds of those who regard the Bible as myth and legend would be changed if they could uncover a scrap of parchment that proved once and for all the historicity of Moses and the events of the Exodus.

Yet all the elaborate speculation about the natural causes of the Ten Plagues and other biblical wonders misses the point that the biblical authors were trying to make in the first place. The miracles reported in the Bible were supposed to strike the reader as miraculous. Even if some natural phenomena can be found at the heart of the Ten Plagues, it is the theology rather than the natural history of the plagues that intrigued the biblical authors and inspired them to tell the tale of the plagues as they did. To hear the biblical authors tell it, God brought down "signs and wonders" on Egypt to inspire faith in the power of God, not the power of nature, and it hardly mattered to them how God chose to work the miracles that they set down in the Bible.

SITZ IM LEBEN

Sitz im Leben, a German phrase that means roughly "setting in life," is the technical term used by scholars to describe the original function of a given text in the Bible—the reason why it was written down, and the uses to which it was put by the original readership of the Bible. For example, the *Sitz im Leben* of the erotic love poetry of the Song of Songs is thought to have been the celebration of marriage; that is, the verses may have been recited as part of wedding festivities to encourage and sanctify the passions of the newly joined husband and wife. The Ten Commandments, as another example, were probably used as a kind of catechism and a confession of faith by the Israelites. And the *Sitz im Leben* of the Ten Plagues—the reason why the plague story was told—can be discerned in the biblical text that frames the crucial tenth plague.

When God is shown to order Moses and the Israelites to carry out an elaborate and prolonged ritual in preparation for the tenth plague, it was the Priestly source who provided detailed instructions for the proceedings: the selection and slaughter of an unblemished male yearling as a sacrificial offering,[68] the eating of the roasted flesh with bitter herbs and the unleavened bread known as *matzah,* and so on. But the ritual meal was not to take place only on the night of tenth plague; rather, it was a sacred observance that was to be repeated every year. "And this day shall be unto you for a memorial, and ye shall keep it a feast to Yahweh," the Bible specifies. "Throughout your generations ye shall keep it a feast by an ordinance for ever." (Exod. 12:14)[69] Indeed, the Priestly source breaks off his retelling of the plague saga and sets out still more detailed and exacting laws and rituals, all of them presented as God's instructions to Moses on the eve of the tenth plague.

When the Israelites celebrate the feast in the future, they must eat only unleavened bread—*matzah*—for seven days, a rule that would apply to the native-born and the "sojourner" in the land of Israel. The Israelites were to observe "a holy convocation" on the first day, and on that day "no manner of work shall be done." As for anyone who defied the prohibition against eating leavened bread, "that soul shall be cut off from Israel." (Exod. 12:15–16) Although the biblical text specifies that these instructions were being given to the Israelites at a time when they had not yet witnessed the tenth plague, the Priestly source emphasized that the rituals and observances were designed to remind future generations of what was about to happen.

"And it shall come to pass, when your children say unto you: What mean ye by this rite? that ye shall say: It is the sacrifice of the Lord's passover *[Pesach]*, for that He passed over the houses of the children of

Israel in Egypt, when He smote the Egyptians, and delivered our houses." (Exod. 12:26–27)[70]

The rituals and observances specified in Exodus 12, of course, define what came to be celebrated throughout Jewish history as Pesach, or Passover. The feast reportedly prepared by Moses and the Israelites in Egypt on the first Passover is still reenacted every year in Jewish homes around the world in the form of the seder, the ritual meal of the Passover observance. "This same night is a night of watching unto the Lord for all the children of Israel throughout their generations," the biblical author instructs. (Exod. 12:42)* Even the ritualistic questions and answers of Exodus—"What mean ye by this rite?"—are repeated, quite literally, in the enduring traditions of the seder. And it is exactly here, among the rules and rituals for the observance of Passover, that we find the real origin and function of the biblical account of the Ten Plagues.

What the Bible presents as the feast of the Passover, Bible scholars propose, is actually a relic of *two* ancient observances that may have no direct link to the life of Moses or the events of the Exodus, real or imagined. One such observance is believed to date back to the earliest years of settlement in the land of Canaan by the tribes of Israel; the other is thought to be far older and may reach all the way back to the earliest wanderings of the Israelites (or their predecessors) when they were still nomads who followed their herds and flocks through the wilderness. Bible scholars suggest that the ancient Israelites combined these two feasts into the single ritual observance we know as Pesach or Passover— and the authors and editors of the Bible gave us the text for the celebration of the ritual in Exodus 12.[71]

The more recent of the two rituals described in Exodus 12 is the feast of unleavened bread, which is believed by some scholars to have originated in the land of Canaan long before the arrival of the Israelites. The farmers of ancient Canaan would prepare and eat cakes of unleavened bread as a gesture of thanksgiving before the cutting of the first sheath of new grain. Clearly it was a harvest festival, a rite performed by settled tribes whose sustenance came from farming—and for that reason some scholars have concluded that the Israelites could not have cele-

---

*The Last Supper was a Passover seder celebrated by Jesus and the disciples, and the wine and unleavened bread of the Passover are linked to the Christian ritual of the Eucharist. "Should there not then be a common sharing of God's joy," proposes Brevard Childs, "which links the *seder* and the Eucharist into common praise?" (Childs, 1974, 214)

brated the ritual when they were still slaves in Egypt or wanderers in the wilderness, as the Bible suggests. Rather, it seems likely that the Israelites borrowed the observance from their neighbors *after* they settled in Canaan and began to cultivate the land.[72]

The older of the two observances described in Exodus 12, by contrast, may have originated as a sacrificial feast celebrated by the Israelites *before* they first arrived in Egypt. The feast may have originated among nomadic herdsmen as a celebration of the crucial moment in the life of a nomad when the spring rains ended and the herds and flocks were moved from winter pasturage to summer pasturage, a time of special danger because of the frailty of newborn lambs and kids and the uncertainty of finding sufficient water and fodder at their destination. A beast would be selected, slaughtered, roasted, and eaten in a solemn ritual meant to appease God (or the gods) and ensure the safety and fertility of the herds and flocks in the coming season, and the blood of the sacrifice would be smeared on the tents as a talisman against the demonic forces that were thought to bring starvation, illness, and death.[73]

The earliest form of the sacrificial feast, scholars speculate, may have included human offerings. "As with the fruits of the land, so too with living beings, each first produce is claimed by the deity who is the giver of the blessing which lies in fertility," suggests Noth.[74] At some primal moment in human history, however, the sacrifice of beasts replaced the sacrifice of human beings, and the observance of Passover required only the sacrifice of animal surrogates. "Sanctify unto Me all the first-born, whatsoever openeth the womb among the children of Israel, both of man and of beast, it is Mine," goes the ritual law of the Passover (Exod. 13:1)—but it was the sacrifice of the firstborn animal that "redeemed" the firstborn son. "I sacrifice to the Lord all that openeth the womb," Moses instructed every Israelite father to tell his son, "but all the first-born of my sons I redeem." (Exod. 13:15)*

When Moses, a man who had tended flocks and herds back in

---

*The tradition of redeeming firstborn male babies is still observed among the Jewish people in the ceremony known as *pidyon ha'ben*, a ritual in which parents make a symbolic payment of silver coins to a *kohen*, that is, a man who traces his ancestry to the priests, or *kohanim*, of ancient Israel. The rite of circumcision, so fundamental in Judaism and so prominent in the story of God's night attack on Moses, may represent another form of surrogate human sacrifice in which the cutting of a tiny bit of human flesh and blood replaced the taking of a life. See *The Harlot by the Side of the Road*, chapter nine, "The Bridegroom of Blood," and chapter eleven, "A Goddess of Israel."

Midian, begged permission of Pharaoh to sacrifice in the wilderness, perhaps he was envisioning precisely such a shepherd's ritual offering.[75] "The historical memory handed down in this account can be summarised in the following way," argues the renowned Bible scholar Roland de Vaux. "One spring, when the feast ensuring the well-being of the flocks and herds before they were taken to their summer pastures was being celebrated, at a time when a scourge was laying Egypt waste, the Israelites left Egypt, led by Moses in the name of their God, Yahweh."[76]

But even if such primal memories are preserved in the Bible, the biblical text itself is of much more recent vintage. The feast of the Passover and the feast of unleavened bread may have been combined for the first time as late as the seventh century B.C.E., when Deuteronomy was probably first composed and the religious practices of ancient Israel were reformed and regularized. By the sixth century B.C.E., after the land of Israel had been conquered, the Temple at Jerusalem destroyed, and much of the population exiled to Babylon, the site of the Passover observance was shifted from the temple[77] to the family home, where the sacrifice and the feast of Passover are shown to take place in the account that we find in the Book of Exodus[78] (Exod. 12:22). Indeed, it is possible that *all* of the rituals of Passover prescribed in Exodus and Deuteronomy may have been written into the text of the Bible at a relatively late date in the authorship of the sacred text by priests and scribes seeking to create an aura of antiquity and authenticity for the new-fangled observance by backdating the ritual law to Moses and the events of the Exodus.[79]

The *Sitz im Leben* of the Passover texts, then, may have been a kind of historical pageant in which the ritual observances associated with the Exodus were reenacted by successive generations of Israelites—"a constantly repeated cultic representation of the one great 'departure,' " as Martin Noth explains, "namely the departure from Egypt."[80] Indeed, the biblical account of the tenth plague can be read as the script and stage directions for precisely such a reenactment by generation after generation of Israelites who would gather around the family table, dine on roasted lamb and unleavened bread and bitter herbs, and recall the distant "night of watching" on which their forefathers did exactly the same.[81]

"And thou shalt tell thy son in that day," the Bible instructed a readership that lived centuries after the events described in the Book of Exodus, "saying: It is because of that which the Lord did for me when I came forth out of Egypt." (Exod. 13:8)

SING A NEW SONG

Yet another intriguing clue to the origin and function of the plague saga is found in one of the most awkward and embarrassing passages in the life story of Moses—"the despoiling of the Egyptians," as the passage is known among Bible scholars. At God's instruction, Moses directed the Israelites to ask their neighbors for fine clothing and jewelry of silver and gold, and the sense of the Hebrew text is that these precious objects were being "borrowed" even though Moses and the Israelites believed (and God surely knew) that they would not be coming back to Egypt to return them.[82]

Bible commentators over the centuries have found the despoiling of the Egyptians to be awkward and embarrassing because the biblical text can be read to suggest that Moses encouraged the Israelites to engage in the wholesale plunder of their kindly neighbors by plain fraud, a reading that has exerted special appeal for anti-Semites of every era. As Elias Auerbach points out with some chagrin in his own writings on the life of Moses, one influential turn-of-the-century exegete named Eduard Meyer, "who, it is well-known, was no friend of the Jews, deals with this episode with particular relish."[83]

So the apologists, Jewish and Christian alike, have struggled to come up with excuses and explanations for the incident. A favorite argument is that God intended the plunder to serve as reparations for centuries of slavery. "[The Israelites] were requiting [the Egyptians] with an affliction far slighter than any one of all they had endured themselves," the rabbis insisted,[84] and one modern scholar discerns in the biblical account "the custom of providing some type of gift for a slave released from bondage."[85] Still more fanciful explanations can be found in the rabbinical literature. "Pharaoh and his people . . . desired to pretend before the world that they were vastly rich," goes one tale, "as everybody would conclude when this wealth of their mere slaves was displayed to observers."[86] And Bible scholar George Coats argues that the despoiling of the Egyptians is a bit of exuberant propaganda that was meant to celebrate "a slave people who trick their masters and by virtue of their wit win the spoils of war which their cunning victory deserves."[87]

But there is quite another way to understand the text that comes down to us as the despoiling of the Egyptians, according to a mid-twentieth century Bible scholar named Julian Morgenstern. The borrowing of jewelry and clothing, he argues, was an ancient and honorable custom among nomadic tribes on certain festive occasions. Rather like the bride who wears "something borrowed, something blue," the womenfolk would borrow finery from their neighbors to bedeck themselves on the occasion of a wedding or some other festival, especially one in which a circle dance performed by the womenfolk was the focus of the celebration. "Manifestly, the Israelite women, when going forth from Egypt," he concludes, "were to be garbed as brides."[88]

The same custom is described in Book of Judges, Morgenstern suggests, where it is reported that the warriors of the tribe of Benjamin lay in wait at a vineyard in the Samaritan town of Shiloh to claim their brides from among the maidens who came out to perform a ritual dance at "the feast of the Lord." (Judg. 21:19–21) Still later, a passage in the portion of the Talmud known as the Mishnah describes a similar vineyard festival where "maidens of Jerusalem used to go out, clad in white garments, which had been borrowed, in order not to shame those who had none (of their own)." And Morgenstern argues that the tradition can be traced all the way back to the festival that was to be celebrated at the moment of liberation from Egypt: "Seven days thou shalt eat unleavened bread," God instructed, "and in the seventh day shall be a feast to the Lord." (Exod. 13:6) The Hebrew word translated as "feast" is *hag*, and "here the word cannot mean aught but a sacred dance."[89]

Another element of what may be the same dimly recalled ritual can be discerned in Exodus 13:9, a passage that is characterized by scholars as a "Deuteronomic addition" to the Book of Exodus and is understood to be largely metaphorical. "And it shall be for a sign unto thee upon thy hand, and for a memoral between thine eyes," Moses said of the "feast to the Lord." Later Jewish tradition was inspired to literalize these references by fabricating the ritual objects known as *tefillin*, or "phylacteries," a pair of little black boxes of leather containing fragments of scripture written out on parchment—the *tefillin* are strapped to the arm and the forehead by observant Jews during morning prayer. But the original biblical reference may have been just as literal-minded. "A sign upon thy hand" may have referred to "tattooing on the hand," Noth suggests, and "a memorial between thine eyes" may have identified "jeweled ornaments which hung over the forehead down as far as the bridge of the nose."[90]

So these fragments of memory and meaning make the curious scene that we find in the Bible come fully alive. On the glorious day when Egypt had been humbled by the tenth plague and the liberation of the Israelites was assured, Moses presided over a sacred ritual of thanksgiving among the people of Israel. The whips of the Egyptian taskmasters were now broken and discarded; the voices of the rumormongers and naysayers among the Israelites who had condemned Moses for his audacity were now silent. The festival that Moses had demanded of Pharaoh—the festival that Pharaoh had refused to permit for so long—would take place at last. And the savor of the moment was only heightened by the fact that the Egyptians themselves provided the finery that the women of Israel wore as they sang and danced in praise of Yahweh, the long-slumbering deity who had finally awakened and remembered his Chosen People.

"We can easily picture the happy scene," Morgenstern writes. "Miriam and the maidens are arrayed like brides, in the garments and jewels which they had borrowed from the Egyptian women. They are equipped with timbrels (*tuppim*), and they dance, precisely like the maidens of Samaria . . . or those of Jerusalem."[91]

The rabbis preserved a tale which presented something of the same scene—and they insisted that the sounds of singing and dancing reached all the way to the throne of God. "The angels in heaven learnt what was happening on earth," they wrote of the night when God had slain the firstborn of Egypt and set the children of Israel free. "When they were about to begin their song of praise to God, He silenced them with the words, 'My children on earth are singing now,' and the celestial hosts had to stop and listen to the song of Israel."[92]

Chapter Seven

EXODUS

*In the freshness of the dawn, I understand why Moses
received God's command in the morning. In the mountains, the question arises of itself: "Whom shall I send?"
Send me. . . .*

—HANNA SENESCH, FROM *BLESSED IS
THE MATCH,* BY MARIE SYRKIN

When the sun rose on the morning after the tenth plague, the
Egyptians who had survived the night of slaughter woke up to
yet another unsettling sight. The man called Moses, a shepherd's staff in
his hand, walked slowly and solemnly down the dusty road that led out
of Goshen, and behind him followed the men, women, and children of
the slave nation of Israel. The vast procession moved raggedly but without pause in the direction of the border of Egypt and the wilderness that
stretched out to the flat horizon and far beyond.

The men now carried weapons of war, and the women followed with
kneading troughs and a supply of unleavened bread dough slung over
their shoulders. As instructed by God, Moses urged the Israelites to ask
their former masters for the loan of "jewels of silver, and jewels of gold,
and raiment," and, remarkably, "the Lord gave the people favour in the
sight of the Egyptians, so that they let them have what they asked."
(Exod. 12:35–36) With swords slapping against their thighs, and their
wives and daughters draped in finery, the once humbled slaves "went up
armed out of the land of Egypt" (Exod. 13:8) "with a lifted hand" (Exod.
14:8), that is, "confidently and fearlessly" and even "defiantly."[1]

Somewhere in the throng of departing Israelites were Miriam and
Aaron, the brother and sister of Moses, and perhaps his wife and children were there, too, although the Bible mentions none of them in its

description of the moment of liberation. But the Bible does note that the procession included an honor guard that carried the ancient coffin holding the embalmed remains of Joseph. Four centuries had passed since Jacob followed Joseph into Egypt, but the Israelites had not forgotten the man who reigned as viceroy over Egypt in the golden days that preceded their enslavement. "God will surely remember you, and ye shall carry my bones away hence with you," Joseph had predicted long ago (Gen. 49:25), and now his words of prophecy were acted out by a distant generation.

"And it came to pass the selfsame day," the Bible author reports, "that the Lord did bring the children of Israel out of the land of Egypt by their hosts." (Exod. 12:51)

The Exodus from Egypt, long anticipated and long delayed, had begun at last.

THE MOSES PEOPLE

The Bible reports that six hundred thousand Israelites lined up behind Moses. But the biblical head count includes only "men on foot, not counting dependants" (Exod. 12:37 NEB), which is understood to mean "able-bodied infantrymen"[2] or men capable of bearing arms in battle.[3,4] A rough calculation of the women, children, and old folk who must have accompanied the men of fighting age brings the total to 2.5 million—"a fantastic number," as one Bible scholar pointed out.[5] Another figured that "[m]arching ten abreast, the numbers would have formed a line over 150 miles long, and would have required eight or nine days to march by any fixed point."[6] Indeed, as Noth renders Exodus. 5:5, Pharaoh complained to Moses that the Egyptians were a minority in their own country: "They [the Israelites] are now more numerous than the (native) people of the land."[7]

"With such a figure the Israelites would not have been obliged to emigrate from Egypt," observes Elias Auerbach. "They could have conquered it without much trouble and subjected their oppressors."[8]

The biblical census of Israelites on the day of the Exodus cannot be accurate, however, when measured against the population figures found elsewhere in the Bible itself. The very old fragment of biblical text known as the Song of Deborah gives the number of arms-bearing men as forty-thousand a century or so *after* the Israelites left Egypt and settled in Canaan (Judg. 5:8). Recent scholarship proposes that only a few of the tribes of Israel actually sojourned in Egypt—the rest of the Israelites in the tribal confederation may have remained in Canaan throughout the period of enslavement. So the actual number of Israelites who marched out of Egypt on that day, according to the cold-eyed calculations of Auerbach, may have amounted to as few as eight or nine thousand men.[9] In fact, some Bible critics are daring enough to suggest that only Moses himself and a tiny band of his followers—"the Moses people," as they are sometimes called in scholarly literature—actually experienced the ordeal of slavery in Egypt and the struggle for liberation that was later embraced by all twelve tribes as the great national myth of Israel.[10]

Along with Moses and the Israelites came what the Bible calls a "mixed multitude." (Exod. 12:38) Philo took the phrase to describe both the dependents who followed after the men of fighting age—"elders, and children, and women"—and "promiscuous persons collected from all quarters" such as "those who had been born to Hebrew fathers by Egyptian women."[11] Other Bible commentators understood the "mixed multitude" to include slaves and serfs of other races and nationalities who saw an opportunity to escape from their own servitude and attached themselves to the Israelites on their way out of Egypt. But the Bible has nothing more to say about the mixed multitude, and we are left to wonder whether the Exodus was the miraculous liberation of a single nation, or a general uprising of slaves, or perhaps both at once.

THE MYSTERY OF THE HABIRU

During one brief but spirited era of biblical scholarship in the early twentieth century, the fact that the Israelites are sometimes called "Hebrews" in the Bible provoked a frenzy of speculation among scholars and theologians who were convinced that the word Hebrew (*ibri*) is equivalent to "Habiru," a word of Akkadian origin that is found in various extrabiblical writings of the ancient Near East. Since precious little of what is described in the Bible—and virtually nothing about Moses and the events of the Exodus—can be found in any ancient source *other* than the Bible, the notion that the "Hebrews" and the "Habiru" were one and the same people generated real excitement. Here, at last, was the prospect of proving, once and for all and with solid documentary evidence, that the Bible is a work of history rather than myth and legend.

The mystery of the Habiru begins with the observation that the Chosen People are identified by two different terms in the pages of the Bible. The Bible generally refers to the Israelites as the "Children of Israel" (*b'nai yisroel*), a phrase that harks back to the patriarch Jacob, whose name was changed to Israel after he wrestled with (and bested) an angelic figure who may have been God himself (Gen. 32:29). But, now and then, the authors of the Book of Exodus call the Israelites by an entirely different name: "the Hebrews" (*ibrim*). Nowadays, of course, "Hebrew" is used to identify a language—the original language of the Bible, the sacred tongue that has always been used in Jewish liturgy around the world, and, more recently, the modernized version of Hebrew that is the national language of the State of Israel. When the word *ibri* appears in the Bible, however, it refers not to the *language* but to the *people* of Israel—and it is used only in passages of the Bible where non-Israelites are speaking about the Israelites or where the Israelites are distinguishing themselves from non-Israelites.

For example, when the enslavement of the Israelites in Egypt is first mentioned, the Bible notes that "the Egyptians made the *children of Israel* to serve with rigour"—but when Pharaoh imposed a death sentence on the firstborn of Israel, he summoned "the *Hebrew* midwives" and instructed them to murder the babies of "the *Hebrew* women." (Exod. 1:13, 15) So, too, when God first sent Moses on his mission of liberation in Egypt, he instructed Moses to use two different ways of identifying the Israelites, one when addressing the Israelites themselves and another when addressing Pharaoh. "Thus shalt thou say unto the *children of Israel*," God told Moses, "Yahweh hath sent me unto you." But when it came to the king of Egypt, "ye shall say unto him, Yahweh, the God of the *Hebrews*, hath met with us." (Exod. 3:16, 18)[12]

The Habiru are not mentioned in the Bible, but as references to these enigmatic people began to turn up in the writings of the ancient world, Bible scholars wondered if the term "Hebrews" might be used in the Bible to identify the people who are called Habiru in extrabiblical sources. The most provocative evidence was discovered in the late nineteenth century at an otherwise unremarkable little village in Egypt known as El-Amarna, where archaeologists uncovered a cache of clay tablets that date back to the fifteenth century B.C.E. Some 350 tablets were retrieved, each one covered with writing in the cuneiform (wedge-shaped) alphabet of the Akkadian language, the tongue used in international commerce and diplomacy throughout the ancient Near East.

The tablets turned out to be the royal archive of imperial Egypt during the reigns of several pharaohs, including the reformer-king Akhnaton, who imposed an early form of monotheism on polytheistic Egypt.[13] Among the correspondence found at El-Amarna were letters sent to the pharaohs by various allies and vassals throughout the domains of Egypt, and scribal copies of the letters that the pharaohs wrote in response. To the amazement and delight of scholars, the so-called Amarna Letters included correspondence from the warlords and chieftains of the land of Canaan that, intriguingly, contained intelligence reports about the threat of a newly arrived band of marauders called the Habiru (or Apiru, as the term is sometimes rendered in English) who were waging a war of conquest throughout Canaan.

"The Apiru plunder all the lands of the king," complained a Canaanite chieftain named Abdu-Heba, who ruled the city-state of Jerusalem as a vassal of Pharaoh and who now begged the Egyptian king to send an expeditionary force to protect him from the plunderers. "If there are archers here in this year, the lands of the king, my lord, will remain intact; but if there are no archers here, the lands of the king, my lord, will be lost!"[14]

Suddenly and dramatically, the archaeological record seemed to corroborate some of the crucial events described in the Bible. The existence of the Habiru in Egypt had already been reported in a few provacative pieces of evidence—two papyri from the reign of Ramses II, for example, depict a work-gang of Habiru "dragging up stone for temples built by [the pharaoh]"[15]—and now the Amarna Letters placed the Habiru in Canaan at a date that was consistent with the chronology of the Exodus as reported in the biblical text. Some scholars began to argue that the Habiru of the Amarna Letters and the Hebrews of the Bible were one and the same. When the Canaanite ruler of Jerusalem complained to Pharaoh about the threat of the Habiru invaders, as T. Eric Peet wrote in 1922 in *Egypt and the Old Testament*, "we are to see the Hebrews under Joshua entering Palestine."[16]

Such enthusiasm, however, was short-lived. Later research— including the discovery of yet more ancient writings in which the Habiru are also mentioned—began to erode the confidence of scholars who once saw the identification of the Hebrews as Habiru as "a virtual certainty."[17] The Habiru are mentioned in documents from throughout the ancient Near East over a period of several centuries, and eventually "Habiru" came to be understood as a generalized term of convenience that did not narrowly refer to the Israelites or any other specific tribe or race. Rather, "Habiru" is best rendered as "fugitives" or "refugees" and was loosely and generally applied to *any* people who lived outside the settled communities of the ancient world.

The Habiru might show up as bandits and brigands in one place, soldiers of fortune under hire to a local potentate in another, and what we would call illegal aliens or guest workers almost anywhere in the ancient Near East during the second millennium B.C.E. The most desperate among them might have sold themselves into slavery for the certainty of a place to sleep and a daily meal.[18] Like the Habiru mentioned in the Amarna Letters, some were marauders who ranged across the settled lands of the ancient world and occasionally descended upon towns and farms that offered the prospect of easy plunder.

"Habiru means not a tribe or a people but a human type," writes Martin Buber in an effort to debunk the myth of the Hebrews as Habiru. "They are people without a country, who have dissociated themselves from their national connections and unite in common journeys for pasture and plunder; semi-nomadic herdsmen they are, or freebooters if opportunity offers."[19]

So we are left with no greater assurance of the historical reality of the Exodus than when the Amarna Letters were first excavated from the shifting sands of Egypt. The Israelites of the Book of Exodus might be characterized as Habiru in the sense that they were landless wanderers who found their way to Egypt, but they were almost certainly *not* the Habiru of the Amarna Letters. Indeed, as Buber points out, the Habiru of the ancient Near East were not different in kind or nature from the Hyksos who briefly overran and ruled ancient Egypt, or the Huns against whom the emperor of China erected the Great Wall, or, we might add, the nomadic hordes of Central Asia whose distant descendants conquered Byzantium and established the Ottoman Empire in its place.[20]

Still, an important clue to the mystery of Moses and the events of the Exodus can be found in the very fact that the Israelites are presented by the Bible as dispossessed people of the kind that were once known in the ancient world as Habiru. To the pharaohs of ancient Egypt and their vassals throughout the ancient Near East, all nomadic peoples were objects of fear and loathing. But the Bible embraces and celebrates the nomadic ideal with the same romantic nostalgia that has enchanted and enthralled urbanites in every age and every land, including the Bible era as well as our own.

The sultans of the Ottoman Empire, for example, so revered the horse nomads from the steppes of Asia who were their distant ancestors that they insisted on pitching tents in the garden of the imperial palace of Topkapi in Istanbul to celebrate the fact that their forebears had once lived in goat-hair tents rather than gilded halls. "Planted as it was in the capital city of the Eastern Roman Empire," writes military historian John Keegan, "the Topkapi remained a nomadic camp."[21] The same reverence is still extended in the Arab world to the Bedouins, who are thought to preserve the purest form of the Arabic language; the strictest notions of justice, morality, and nobility; and the most cherished qualities of Arab civilization—hospitality, generosity, courage, honor, dignity, and self-respect. Even in our own century, wealthy families in Damascus and other Arab cities sent their sons to sojourn with a desert tribe in order to acquire these lofty qualities, and "even in the poorest suburbs of Baghdad, where swarms of people live in frightful congestion in primitive huts, people take great pride in keeping up . . . their Bedouin heritage."[22]

The very same glorification of the "nomadic ethos" suffuses the Bible, and so we might imagine that the priests and scribes who worked amid the opulence of the palace and the splendors of the temple in Jerusalem and elsewhere in ancient Israel were under the same thrall that so captured the imagination of the Ottomans. "I will let you dwell in your tents again," God promised the citified and corrupted Israelites in the Book of Hosea, "as in the days of old." (Hos. 12:10 New JPS) And the heroic qualities of the nomadic life would have exerted an even sharper and more poignant pull on the Israelites who witnessed the conquest of Jerusalem and the destruction of the Temple in 586 B.C.E. and were carried into captivity by the Babylonian emperor Nebuchadnezzar. The dispossessed aristocracy and priesthood of Israel lived in exile in the heart of Babylon, the greatest urban center of the ancient world, and they must have been haunted by the freedom enjoyed by the nomad. Since much of what we read in the Bible was composed, compiled, or edited during or shortly after the Babylonian Exile, it is there that we might look to find what the saga of slavery and liberation, wandering and conquest, really meant to the original authors of the Bible.

"By the rivers of Babylon, / There we sat down, yea, we wept, /

When we remembered Zion," goes the poignant song of exile preserved
in the Book of Psalms (Ps. 137:1), and the Bible suggests that they wept,
too, for the days when Moses and the Israelites wandered through the
wilderness and answered to no one but the restless God who journeyed
along with them.

INTO THE WILDERNESS

The wanderings recorded in the Book of Exodus began in Ramses, one
of the treasure-cities that had been built by the enslaved Israelites.
Then the procession headed toward Succoth, then Etham, and then Pi-
hahiroth, a place located somewhere near Migdol and Baal-zephon in
the vicinity of a body of water we know today as the Red Sea (Exod.
12:37, 13:18, 20, 14:2). But scholarship cannot determine where most
of these supposed stopping-places were actually located, if they existed
at all. Even the stretch of wilderness called Sinai in the Bible, for example, cannot be located with precision on the landscape of the ancient
Near East.[23] The peninsula between the modern states of Egypt and Israel that is today known as the Sinai did not acquire that name until
long after the Bible era, and the identification of a rather unimpressive
desert peak in the southern stretches of the peninsula as *the* Mount
Sinai of biblical fame "can only be traced back to about the third century A.D.," according to one Bible historian, "when certain colonies of
Christians who lived there, anxious to increase the importance of their
home, made it the scene of the wanderings of the Israelites."[24]

Yet much effort and imagination have been invested in fixing the
actual route of the Israelites on their way through the wilderness of
Sinai. Philo described the ultimate goal of the Israelites as Phoenicia,
Palestine, and "hollow Syria," "which was at that time called the land of
the Canaanites, the borders of which country were three days' journey
distant from Egypt."[25] Josephus read the same biblical text and came
up with "Letopolis, a place at that time deserted, but where Babylon
was built afterwards."[26] Some modern scholars believe that the place
called Baal-zephon, which probably was a sanctuary of the Canaanite
god Baal, may be a low hill near the Mediterranean coast of the Sinai
Peninsula where a shrine to the god Zeus was known to exist in later antiquity. Martin Noth wonders whether the biblical text "reproduces a
very old and perhaps even authentic local tradition" about the route of

the escaping Israelites or merely preserves the speculation of later Bible writers who sought to place the momentous event at the sea "in what seemed to be an appropriate place near the road connecting Palestine with Egypt which was much traveled at all times." But Noth shrugs at his own question: "No certain answer can be given."[27]

Similarly, the name and location of the body of water where Moses so famously parted the waves is still a puzzle. The familiar reference to the "Red Sea" is the result of an error in translation by the ancient scribes who first rendered the Hebrew Bible into Greek. The original Hebrew text of the Book of Exodus, using a word that is probably derived from ancient Egyptian, actually refers to the *Reed* Sea *(yam sup)*, not the *Red* Sea.[28] The erroneous place-name found its way into the New Testament, whose writers relied largely on the Septuagint, a Greek translation of the Hebrew Bible, rather than the original Hebrew text, and early translators of the Bible into English perpetuated the error. Today, the misidentification of the "Reed Sea" as the "Red Sea" is so familiar to Bible readers that "Red Sea" is used even by Bible translators who know better.[29]*

The "Red Sea" that figures so crucially in the events of the Exodus was *not* the Red Sea we know today as an extension of the Indian Ocean that separates Africa from the Arabian Peninsula. Nor was it the Gulf of Aqaba, which is what the author of the Book of Kings had in mind when he used the term "Red Sea" (1 Kings 9:26) to describe the home port of the royal navy of King Solomon.[30] More likely, the "Sea of Reeds" was a lake, a lagoon, or perhaps even a salt bog somewhere along the western fringe of the Sinai Peninsula. One translator renders the Hebrew word for "Sea of Reeds" as "papyrus marsh."[31] Others have speculated that the Sea of Reeds is actually the Gulf of Suez on the western edge of the Sinai,[32] one of the so-called Bitter Lakes to the north of Suez,[33] or perhaps "some piece of water on the edge of the Mediterranean fresh enough to allow reeds to grow in it."[34] Among Bible historians, the favorite site of the Reed Sea is the body of water known to the ancients as the Sirbonian Sea (now called Lake Sirbonis), which is actually a lagoon fed by the waters of the Mediterranean and separated from the sea by a "narrow spit of land" that may have been an alternate route between Egypt and Canaan even in antiquity.[35]

Even if we conclude that the biblical Sinai and the place we now

---

*I will use "Red Sea," "Sea of Reeds," or sometimes simply "the sea" in referring to the site of what scholars tend to call "the sea event."

call the Sinai Peninsula are one and the same, the itinerary of Moses and the Israelites during their forty years of wandering in the wilderness, as reported in meticulous and even tedious detail in the Bible, is so convoluted that it is almost certainly a fiction. Even at the time of the Exodus, the journey from Egypt to Canaan required only ten or eleven *days* of travel over well-established military highways or caravan routes. For the Israelites to spend forty *years* knocking around the confines of the Sinai, as the Bible reports, can mean only one thing—God and Moses were conspiring to make sure that the Israelites did *not* take the most direct route out of Sinai and into the Promised Land. The Bible concedes as much in describing the first leg of their long journey, although we will later discover a theological rationale for sending the Israelites on a forty-year ramble through the wilderness.

At first, God directed the Israelites to turn away from their line of march and head into the wilderness near the Sea of Reeds in order to spare them the necessity of battling their way through the territory of the warlike Philistines, who reportedly controlled the most direct route from Egypt to Canaan.* Although the Bible plainly states that "the children of Israel went up armed out of the land of Egypt" (Exod. 13:18), God apparently felt that these former slaves, newly liberated and wholly untutored in the arts of war, were not yet ready to fight for their own freedom. Indeed, God feared that they would turn and run all the way back to Egypt at the first skirmish, rather like Moses turned and ran when God first turned his staff into a snake on Mount Horeb.

> God led them not by the way of the land of the Philistines, although that was near; for God said: "Lest peradventure the people repent when they see war, and they return to Egypt." But God led the people about, by the way of the wilderness by the Red Sea. (Exod. 13:17–18)

To guide the Israelites through the trackless wastes of the Sinai Peninsula, God manifested himself in an entirely new and marvelous

---

*The reference to the Philistines in Exodus 13:17 is an anachronism that was inserted in the text of the Bible by a late author or editor, since these invaders from the Aegean did not establish themselves in Canaan until *after* the events depicted in the Book of Exodus, at least according to the strict chronology of the Bible. "Palestine" as a place-name is derived from "Philistine" and recalls the long period of primacy of the Philistines and other so-called "Sea Peoples" in the land of Canaan.

way: "And the Lord went before them by day in a pillar of cloud, to lead them the way, and by night in a pillar of fire, to give them light, that they might go by day and by night." (Exod. 13:21) Some scholars have speculated that the images of cloud and fire harked back to some primal recollection of a volcanic eruption or a particularly violent storm that burned itself into the collective memory of the ancient Israelites.[36] Or perhaps the biblical author was invoking a scene that was quite familiar to his own contemporaries—clouds of incense rising over the sacrificial fires were a daily feature of the rituals at the Temple at Jerusalem a thousand or so years after the events depicted in Exodus.[37] No matter what scene or memory inspired the passage, the image of the pillars of cloud and fire was meant to depict God in constant attendance as both guide and protector of the Israelites: "[T]he pillar of cloud by day, and the pillar of fire by night, departed not from before the people." (Exod. 13:21–22)

No longer did Moses have to persuade the Israelites of his legitimacy with long speeches or showy displays of magic. If the first nine plagues and the death of the firstborn and the fact of their liberation were not enough to convince them, those ever present pillars of cloud and fire surely eliminated any doubt that God himself was always at hand. Still, God continued to consult privately with Moses, and the Bible suggests that he briefed Moses on what to expect and what to do throughout the wanderings. Once Yahweh had drawn the Israelites into the wilderness, he gave a curious instruction to Moses. "Speak unto the children of Israel," he commanded, "that they turn back and encamp before Pi-hahiroth, between Migdal and the sea." (Exod. 14:2)

Based on purely tactical considerations, these new marching orders were an open invitation to disaster and defeat—God wanted the Israelites to halt their march in the direction of Canaan, turn back toward Egypt, and then stop and set up an encampment with their backs against the sea. As even an amateur tactician could readily have seen, the maneuver would put the Israelites at the mercy of any armed force that might come upon their encampment, trapping them between the attacking army and the sea with no line of escape. Indeed, God intended to put the Israelites in precisely such a predicament—Yahweh would use the Israelites to bait a trap for the Egyptians, and then, once again, he would punish and humble the Egyptians in a display of divine flash-and-dazzle. God even went to the trouble of "hardening" Pharaoh's heart yet again to make sure that the Egyptians played their appointed role in the set-piece battle at the Red Sea.

"And Pharaoh will say of the children of Israel: They are entangled in the land, the wilderness hath shut them in," God told Moses in perfect candor. "And I will harden Pharaoh's heart, and he shall follow after the children of Israel; and I will win glory for myself at the expense of Pharaoh and all his army; and they shall know that I am the Lord." (Exod. 14:3–4)[38]

SIX HUNDRED CHARIOTS

And so it happened that the moody and mercurial monarch, who could never quite make up his mind about the Israelites, suffered yet another change of heart. As if he hadn't seen the sight with his own eyes, as if he hadn't begged Moses to go, Pharaoh responded to the intelligence reports from his adjutants like a man who had awakened from a trance to discover the folly he committed while his heart was "hardened" and his mind was clouded by the God of the Hebrews.

"And it was told the king of Egypt that the people were fled," the Bible reports. "What is this we have done?" exclaimed a baffled Pharaoh, "that we have let Israel go from serving us?" (Exod. 14:5)

More than one explanation for Pharaoh's sudden change of heart can be discerned in the biblical text, which embodies the work of several sources with different points of view. The Yahwist suggests that Pharaoh finally realized that Moses had been fibbing when he asked for permission to lead the Israelites on a three-day round-trip into the wilderness, and he understood at last that Moses and the Israelites intended to keep marching.[39] By contrast, the Priestly source suggests that Pharaoh intended all along to let the Israelites go, but God "hardened his heart" at the last minute in order to give himself an opportunity for yet another confrontation with the king of Egypt.[40] In either case, Pharaoh now resolved to go after the Israelites and put an end to their insurrection once and for all.

> And he made ready his chariots, and took his people with him. And he took six hundred chosen chariots, and all the chariots of Egypt, and captains over all of them. (Exod. 14:6–7)

The Roman-era chronicler Philo imagined an army of professional soldiers in battle order, "all his force of cavalry, and his darters, and his slingers, and his equestrian archers, and all the rest of his light-armed troops."[41] Josephus, a former general himself, pointed out that the Egyptians were confident that they would easily defeat the fleeing Israelites, "as they had no armour, and would be weary with their journey."[42] The Bible makes the point that Pharaoh outfitted his picked troops with the state-of-the-art military technology of the ancient world—the chariot, an innovation of the detested but admired Hyksos that became the weapon of choice throughout the ancient Near East.[43] Rather like Hitler, who sent tanks armed with machine guns and cannon against mounted Polish cavalry officers bearing sabers and wooden lances in the opening hours of World War II, Pharaoh intended to engage in a display that was meant to overwhelm his enemies and extinguish any notion of resistance once and for all.

The approach of six hundred war chariots across the desert floor must have announced itself to the Israelites long before the first chariot, bristling with spear-points and bearing Pharaoh himself and two other warriors, appeared on the far horizon. Twelve hundred wooden wheels would have raised a cloud of dust and a sustained rumble that only grew louder as the army approached. Those who had pitched their tents on the leading edges of the vast encampment would have been the first to perceive the ominous sights and sounds, and word must have spread throughout the camp that some terrible force was approaching. Finally, the Egyptian chariots overtook the Israelites and closed upon them, trapping the fugitive slaves between their lance-points and the sea.

> And when Pharaoh drew nigh, the children of Israel lifted up their eyes, and, behold, the Egyptians were marching after them, and they were sore afraid; and the children of Israel cried out to the Lord. (Exod. 14:10)

Now Moses witnessed for the first time a characteristic of the Israelites that he would come to know with heartbreaking and sometimes maddening intimacy. They might "cry out to the Lord" now and then, but at moments of danger or deprivation, they were all too quick to whine and complain, to rise up in open rebellion against the authority of God and Moses. Panic-stricken and utterly demoralized at the sight of the Egyptian army bearing down on them, they thronged around Moses and hurled bitter words at him.

"Because there were no graves in Egypt, thou hast taken us away to die in the wilderness?" the rabble-rousers shouted with sharp and unsubtle sarcasm. "Is not this the word that we spoke unto thee in Egypt, saying: 'Let us alone, that we may serve the Egyptians?' For it were better for us to serve the Egyptians, than that we should die in the wilderness." (Exod. 14:11–12)

Four centuries of slavery had tainted the souls of the Israelites, weakened their will, and left them cowardly, cynical, and calculating. The Israelites were armed, but they dared not fight, even though they vastly outnumbered the Egyptians. After all, six hundred thousand men-at-arms ought to have been able to repulse six hundred chariots. Instead they complained about the peril into which Moses had led them. At that moment, the clamoring Israelites displayed what would come to be called the slave mentality, a craven spirit that God himself would burn out of the Chosen People with cruel resolve in the days ahead.

"Wherefore criest thou unto Me?" God rebuked the Israelites, and then he issued an order to Moses: "Speak unto the children of Israel, that they go forward." (Exod. 14:15)

But when Moses tried to shout down the panic-mongers and assert his authority over the mob, he seemed to scold them for their cowardice even as he soothed their fear.

"Fear ye not, stand still, and see the salvation of the Lord, which he will work for you to-day," sermonized Moses, "for whereas ye have seen the Egyptians to-day, ye shall see them again no more for ever."

And then, we might imagine, his eye fell on the weapons that the men carried but refused to use, and Moses uttered a few words of apparent reassurance that actually seethed with sarcasm of his own and carried a sharp rebuke.

"The Lord will fight for you," Moses told his people, "and ye shall hold your peace." (Exod. 14:13–14)

GOD OF WAR

God now manifested himself in plain view of the Israelites in the new and terrible role of Yahweh Sabaoth—God of Hosts, according to the traditional English translation, or God of Armies, a more accurate rendering that identifies Yahweh as a god of war. Here, for the first time in the Bible, Yahweh introduced the Israelites and the rest of humankind to holy war, a crusade in which God himself sent men into battle against each other and decided the outcome. A champion might be selected to lead an army into battle—here it was Moses, later it would be Joshua, and then others—but Yahweh always accompanied the crusaders into the fray. Thus, we are taught to believe, every victory and every defeat in a holy war is ordained by God. Then and now, even the worst atrocities are imagined by true believers to be blessed from on high.

To position himself for the coup de grâce that he intended to deliver to the Egyptians, Yahweh performed a field maneuver worthy of von Clausewitz. The pillar of cloud by which God had been leading the Israelites through the wilderness—or perhaps it was "the angel of God," according to the Elohist's version[44]—now removed itself from the vanguard and reappeared *behind* the throng of refugees, "between the camp of Egypt and the camp of Israel," thus shielding the Israelites from their attackers (Exod. 14:19–20). A mysterious void separated the two camps, a darkness not unlike the one that had been visited upon Egypt during the Ten Plagues, but now it functioned as a barrier that prevented the Egyptians in their war chariots from descending upon the Israelites and slaughtering them. Magically, the cloud shrouded the Egyptians in darkness while casting a divine glow on the Israelites.

And there was the cloud and the darkness here, yet gave it light by night there, and the one came not near the other all the night. (Exod. 14:20)

Next, God instructed Moses to perform what is far and away the most memorable and momentous of all the feats of magic attributed to him in the Bible, a miracle that would end the threat from Pharaoh once and for all.

"And lift thou up thy rod, and stretch out thy hand over the sea, and divide it," God commanded Moses, "and the children of Israel shall go into the midst of the sea on dry ground." (Exod. 14:15)

What happened next is actually told in several different versions by the various biblical sources. Indeed, the account of the miracle at the sea is perhaps the best evidence that the Bible was composed by several different authors with very different understandings of the event. When the text is fully deconstructed, and the various sources are teased out, what we find in Holy Writ is a set of parallel narrations, some of which allow us to see the saga of the Exodus in ways that bear little resemblance to the Sunday school version of the most famous Bible story of all.

In the Yahwist's version of the story, the miracle at the sea was a battle between God and the Egyptians in which the Israelites played no role at all except that of innocent bystanders. Yahweh manifested himself in some fearful manner over the camp of the Egyptians just as the sun was rising, and the battle-hardened soldiers who stood the morning watch were so spooked by what they saw that they broke and ran. Indeed, the army was put to rout by the sight of the divine visage that peered down at them, and the men charged headlong into the sea. Notably, the Yahwist did not mention the crossing of the Red Sea by the Israelites; rather, they simply stood their ground—and watched their former masters drown.[45]

"And it came to pass in the morning watch, that Yahweh looked down on the Egyptian army through the pillar of fire and cloud, and he threw them into a panic," goes the Yahwist's account, "so that the Egyptians said: 'Let us flee from the face of Israel, for the Lord fighteth against Egypt.' " The sea had already "returned to its accustomed place" (Exod. 14:27 NEB), and so "the Egyptians fled against it; and Yahweh swept them out into the sea." (Exod. 14:24–25, 27)[46]

A second and more familiar version of the incident at the Red Sea is the one told by the Priestly source, who was probably at work on the Bible several centuries after the Yahwist. While the Yahwist described how God divided the waters by means of "a strong east wind [that blew] all the night and turned the sea-bed into dry land," the Priestly source credited Moses with parting the waters of the Sea of Reeds by once again using his shepherd's staff as a magic wand[47]—"Then Moses stretched out his hand over the sea, and the waters were divided." (Exod. 14:21)[48]

Here the Priestly source described the miracle at the Red Sea in its classic formulation. "And the children of Israel went into the midst of the sea upon the dry ground; and the waters made a wall for them to right and to left." (Exod. 14:21) A fragment from the Elohist comes next in the biblical text: "All Pharaoh's horses, his chariots, and his horsemen" pursued the Israelites across the exposed seabed (Exod. 14:21–23),[49] but the wheels of their chariots bogged down in the mud.[50] Then the account of the Priestly source resumes, and God issued the crucial order to Moses that put an end to the long oppression of the Israelites at the hands of Pharaoh once and for all.

"And the Lord said unto Moses: 'Stretch out thy hand over the sea, that the waters may come back upon the Egyptians,' " goes the account of the Priestly source. "And the waters returned, and covered the chariots, and the horsemen, even all the host of Pharaoh that went in after them into the sea." (Exod. 14:26, 28)[51]

All of these narrative fragments—the Yahwist, the Priestly source, and even a fragment of the Elohist—were cobbled together at some unknown point in the long and gradual authorship of the Bible, a process that may have started as early as 1000 B.C.E. and continued through the fifth century B.C.E. The composite text that we find in the pages of the Bible was given a final polish by the biblical editor known as the Redactor sometime in or after the fifth century B.C.E., but the fingerprints of the underlying sources are still visible. That is why the biblical life story of Moses—and, in a real sense, all of the Bible—is "a combination of the wonderful and the ordinary," as one scholar puts it,[52] rather than a seamless and purely heroic saga.

The patchwork quality of the Bible also explains why Moses seems to wander in and out of the biblical account of the Exodus and sometimes very nearly disappears from sight. Scholars have identified several major themes in the story—the Exodus from Egypt, the miracle at the Red Sea, the making of the covenant between God and Israel on Sinai, the wanderings in the wilderness, and the conquest of Canaan— and they suspect that these so-called traditions may have originated among the Israelites as separate stories. The figure of Moses was used by the various biblical authors and editors as a narrative device to link the disparate themes into one long saga, but he may not have appeared in all of the traditions in their original form. Thus, for example, one version of the miracle at the Red Sea features God parting the waters with a gust of wind while another version, almost as an afterthought, assigns the same task to Moses.

THE SONG OF THE SEA

The point was not lost on the balky and cynical Israelites that the miracle at the sea was meant to be seen as a momentous test of faith in Yahweh. Now God would find out whether the Israelites were worthy of his divine favor—would they rise to their feet and walk into the sea, or would they halt at the last moment and allow the Egyptians to descend upon them? As far as the Israelites could tell, death threatened them ahead *and* behind, and only blind faith would motivate them to obey the orders that Moses shouted at them amid the clamor of the onrushing chariots. On that day, both God *and* the Israelites passed a test of faith at the Red Sea, according to the biblical author who clearly sought to offer his readership in ancient Israel a lesson on how God rewards the faithful.

> Thus the Lord saved Israel that day out of the hand of the Egyptians, and Israel saw the Egyptians dead upon the sea-shore. And Israel saw the great work which the Lord did upon the Egyptians, and the people feared the Lord. And they believed in the Lord, and in His servant Moses. (Exod. 14:30–31)

At the moment of Yahweh's glorious victory over Pharaoh, the Israelites gathered in their wilderness encampment and joined Moses in a triumphant chorus. "Then sang Moses and the children of Israel this song," the Bible reports (Exod. 15:1), and there follows a long and leisurely psalm of praise and thanksgiving.

> The Lord is my strength and song
> And He is become my salvation;
> This is my God, and I will glorify Him;
> My father's God, and I will exalt Him.
> (Exod. 15:1)

"Even the sucklings dropped their mothers' breasts to join in singing," the rabbis insisted. "[Y]ea, even the embryos in the womb joined the melody, and the angels' voice swelled the song."[53] Indeed, the Song of the Sea, as the passage is known, is grand and even grandiloquent, full of ornate phrases and martial flourishes.

Elsewhere in the Bible, God is praised as merciful and mild, full of compassion and loving-kindness, slow to anger and quick to forgive, but here Moses saluted Yahweh, the God of Armies, as "a man of war" whose "lust" is satisfied only when he has drawn the blood of his enemies. "Terror and dread" seized the enemies of Israel when God unsheathed his sword—"Thy right hand, O Yahweh, glorious in power," sang Moses, "Thy right hand, O Yahweh, dashed in pieces the enemy"—and the earth literally swallowed up the slain infidels (Exod. 15:3–16).[54] So stirred was Moses by the sight of the dead Egyptians and their shattered chariots that he seemed to entertain the faintly pagan notion, so alien to his own teachings, that Yahweh was the greatest of all gods rather than the one and only god. Indeed, some scholars speculate that the faith of Moses was hardly the strict and unsullied monotheism with which he is traditionally credited. Rather, the Song of the Sea can be read to suggest that Moses acknowledged the existence and even the efficacy of other gods and goddessses, claiming that Yahweh had bested them in combat against the Egyptians.

> Who is like unto Thee, O Yahweh, among the gods?*
> Who is like unto Thee, glorious in holiness?
> Fearful in praises, doing wonders?
> (Exod. 15:11)[55]

Thus ends the biblical account of the miracle at the Red Sea, the one that the Redactor intended his readership, then and now, to embrace as Holy Writ. But the text offers yet another way of understanding the encounter between the Egyptians and the Israelites at the Red Sea, a brief intelligence report that may be the most authentic of all. As we have noted, the so-called Song of Miriam, a fragment of ancient Hebrew poetry that follows the Song of the Sea, is seen by scholars as the oldest passage in the Book of Exodus, perhaps even the oldest in all of the Bible.[56] Indeed, the couple of lines of biblical text known as the Song of Miriam is thought to be so ancient that it cannot be reliably attributed to *any* of the conventional sources of biblical authorship. And so, even if we regard the Bible as a work of myth and legend, it is possible to imagine that the Song of Miriam was created and sung by a flesh-and-blood woman at some unknowable place and time in the distant past.[57]

Here we find an oblique reference to what happened at the Red

---

*Here the original text of the Bible uses the word *elim*, which literally means "the gods," and that's how the word is rendered in the King James Version and more recent translations based on the KJV. Jewish translations tend to be more circumspect—*elim* is rendered as "the mighty" (JPS) or "the celestials" (New JPS) in order to downplay the polytheistic implications of the original text—and the New Jerusalem Bible, a Catholic translation of recent vintage, renders the word as "the holy ones."

Sea in the exalted words and phrases that were supposedly uttered by Miriam, who is described elsewhere in the Bible as the sister of Moses and a prophet in her own right.

"And Miriam, the prophetess, the sister of Aaron, took a timbrel in her hand," goes the introductory passage, "and all the women went out after her with timbrels and with dances." (Exod. 15:20)

> And Miriam sang unto them:
> Sing ye to the Lord, for He is highly exalted:
> The horse and his rider hath He thrown into the sea.
> (Exod. 15:20–21)

Philo imagined that these two war chants, the Song of the Sea and the Song of Miriam, are sung on the shore of the Red Sea by "two choruses, one of men and the other of women," with Moses leading the male chorus "and his sister that of the women."[58] Bible scholars, however, suggest that the two songs reflect the work of separate and distinct biblical sources, and they describe the miracle at the sea from two very different points of view. And the single most intriguing feature of the Song of Miriam is what is left out.

THE SONG OF MIRIAM

A cherished maxim of Bible scholarship holds that "shorter is older."[59] For this reason, the two spare lines of the Song of Miriam are generally regarded as older than any of the tales told by the Priestly source, the Yahwist, or the Elohist, and even older than the Song of the Sea, which has been dated all the way back to the thirteenth century B.C.E.[60] Since it is so much older than the other sources, goes the conventional wisdom, it must be more accurate and reliable. In the Song of Miriam, insists Auerbach, "we are confronted with a genuine historical piece of news from Mosaic days," an intelligence report in which the destruction of an Egyptian army on the field of battle "is proved to be a confirmed historical fact."[61]

The two lines of verse in Miriam's song, which also appear in a slightly different form in the Song of the Sea, were once thought to be a fragment of a longer work that was lost to the various authors and editors of the Bible or, possibly, excluded by them from the final text.

Today, however, most scholars are convinced that the Song of Miriam is a short call-and-response song that is preserved in the Bible in its entirety. So we are invited to imagine a scene in the wilderness of Sinai on the day of victory over the Egyptians: Miriam stood at the center of a circle of women who danced around her as they beat out a simple rhythm on drums and tambourines. Again and again, Miriam called out: "Sing ye to Yahweh, for He is highly exalted." And each time Miriam's voice was heard, the other women responded in chorus: "The horse and his rider hath He thrown into the sea."[62] (Exod. 15:21)[63]

Here, at last, the Israelites were able to celebrate the feast (or *hag*)[64] that Moses had in mind when he first conveyed God's demand to Pharaoh back in Egypt: "Let My People go, that they may a hold a feast unto Me in the wilderness." (Exod. 5:1) Here is what Moses meant when he called upon the Israelites to "keep it a feast to the Lord throughout your generations." (Exod. 12:14) Dressed in the finery that they had "borrowed" from their former masters on their way out of Egypt, striking drums and shaking tambourines as they danced in a circle around the song-leader, the women of ancient Israel sang a song of praise and thanksgiving to Yahweh for the victory that he had bestowed upon them in battle against the Egyptians. But it was Miriam, not Moses, who presided over the ritual, and it was the sound of Miriam's voice that stirred the Israelites to a kind of ecstasy. Almost inadvertently, the Bible author betrays the fact that Miriam was a familiar and powerful person in her own right, a prophetess and perhaps a priestess, too, whose word was obeyed and even revered by the Israelites.

By long and pious tradition, of course, Miriam has been regarded as the sister of both Moses and Aaron, the very same sister who watched over the infant Moses as he floated down the Nile in his little boat of reeds. Although Jewish tradition explains Miriam's name by reference to the Hebrew word for "bitterness," scholars suggest that her name, like that of her brother, actually derives from an ancient Egyptian word— *mri*, which means "beloved (of the deity)," thus suggesting that both of them were born in Egypt just as the Bible reports.[65] But the Bible itself casts doubt on these old certainties, and Miriam remains a profoundly mysterious woman whose real origin and role in the history of ancient Israel can only be glimpsed through the cracks of the biblical text.

For example, when the birth of Moses is announced in Exodus 2:2, he seems to be the firstborn and only child of his mother and father. "[T]his passage not only does not mention other brothers and sisters but, indeed, makes their existence very improbable," argues Auerbach.[66] A sister conveniently showed up to watch over Moses on the Nile, but she is not named in those passages, and only "pure assumption" allows us to conclude that she and Miriam are the same person.[67] The Bible does not mention Miriam by name until the moment of victory at the sea—and then, intriguingly, Miriam is introduced as the sister of Aaron, not Moses! (Exod. 15:20)

Some scholars take the absence of Moses at this crucial point in the narrative as proof that neither Miriam nor Aaron was actually related to Moses at all. "[O]therwise Moses would surely have been named there instead of Aaron," Martin Noth points out, "or at least alongside him." Auerbach suggests that only "a later development of tradition" in ancient Israel proposed a blood relationship between Moses and Miriam.[68] A careful reading of the biblical text "eliminates not only the possibility that she was Moses' sister but also that Aaron was Moses' brother."[69] Miriam and Aaron may have been each other's sibling, Auerbach concludes, "but not the brother and sister of Moses."[70]

Still, Aaron and Miriam are given crucial, if sometimes controversial, roles to play in the history of ancient Israel. Aaron is introduced in the Bible as the first high priest of ancient Israel and the founder of a priestly dynasty; indeed, the Priestly source displays a much livelier interest in Aaron's bloodlines than in those of Moses. Miriam, too, is credited with stirring qualities of leadership—the Bible author calls her a *nebhia'ah*, the Hebrew word that is usually translated as "prophetess" but can also be rendered as "the ecstatic, the enthused," thus suggesting that she was a compelling and charismatic figure who was uniquely capable of inspiring the people and moving them to spirited worship.[71] So some scholars argue that Miriam may have originated in "a more primitive tradition" that predates the saga of Moses.[72] What we find in the Song of Miriam may be the faint remnants of "an originally much richer tradition" in which both Aaron and Miriam stood apart from Moses— and perhaps even against him—as spiritual and political leaders of ancient Israel in their own right.[73]

As we have already seen—and will see again—there is an odd and artificial quality to the depiction of these three supposed siblings. Aaron, for example, seems to have been written in (and out) of various scenes in the life of Moses by different biblical authors; he is given the role of "a vital prop for Moses" in the early encounters with Pharaoh, but he falls silent during the Ten Plagues and disappears entirely by the time the Israelites reach the Red Sea.[74] So, too, is Miriam presented as a crucial and dynamic figure at first—the Israelites rallied around her at the moment of victory and thrilled at the sound of her voice. But later on both Miriam *and* Aaron are depicted as rivals of Moses, fully deserving of the punishment they will be made to endure for their rebelliousness.

Moses himself is sometimes depicted as strong and heroic, sometimes as needy and even cowardly, and sometimes as a kind of marionette whose strings are yanked from on high. He is often shown as a rather passive figure who relies on others for his sheer survival. If not for the courage of his older sister, he might have perished in infancy on the waters of the Nile. On Mount Horeb, Moses begged to be excused from the mission to Egypt because he was "slow of speech," and Yahweh was moved to deputize Aaron as bearer and user of the rod of God and as spokesman to both the Israelites and the Egyptians. Moses relied on Zipporah to spare him from God's murderous attack on the road to Egypt. During the Ten Plagues, he comes across as "a rather characterless instrument in Yahweh's hands," as one scholar puts it, and he is given no role at all in at least one version of the miracle at the Red Sea.

Thus it is tantalizing to conjure up the "much richer tradition" of Miriam and Aaron, a lost and perhaps even forbidden tradition that suggests Miriam and Aaron were historical figures who played a crucial role in the spiritual life and political destiny of ancient Israel. Perhaps they were unrelated to Moses by any blood ties, and the family relationships were written into the biblical text to create an imaginary link between otherwise separate figures in the pantheon of national heroes. Or perhaps Moses himself is purely the stuff of myth and legend, and only Miriam and Aaron were real people. Just as Haile Selassie, the last emperor of Ethiopia in the twentieth century, claimed descent from King Solomon, is it possible that the court historians of ancient Israel imagined a blood relationship between a mythic Moses and a flesh-and-blood Miriam?

"[S]ome tradition in the Old Testament knows of God's mighty acts accomplished for the benefit of Israel without giving any role to Moses," George Coats points out. "[T]he so-called Song of Miriam recounts the occasion of salvation for Israel in the wilderness without reference to any contribution from Moses."[75]

Indeed, the most intriguing and important feature of the Song of Miriam is the fact that Miriam did not seem to know—or, at least, chose not to mention—the most colorful and memorable details of the miracle at the sea that so captivated the later authors of the Bible. She said nothing of the parting of the waters, nothing about the crossing of the seabed between walls of water. Neither did she utter the name of Moses or make even an oblique reference to any role he might have played in the miracle at the sea, which raises the provocative notion that he played no role at all because he was not there.

THE ANGEL OF THE SEA

The miracle at the sea is "the real nucleus of the Exodus theme," as Martin Noth says, "not only the end but also the goal and climax of the whole." The victory of Israel over the Egyptians "is the very act which was first and chiefly meant when Israel confessed Yahweh as 'the God who led us up out of Egypt.' "[76] And the Song of the Sea, a hymn of praise and thanksgiving to Yahweh, was a centerpiece of the ritual life of the ancient Israelites: "[W]e may imagine that wherever the Exodus was recalled in the oldest Israelite worship, this hymn had a principal place."[77] Yet the overlapping layers of tradition in the biblical text, each one different in crucial details, obscures what really happened there. "The incident itself," Noth shrugs, "remains veiled from our sight."[78]

Behind the veil so artfully woven by the biblical editors may be something primal and perhaps even purely mythic. Ironically, the myth at the heart of Holy Writ may have been borrowed by the Israelites from the Canaanites, the dreaded and despised people so passionately condemned in the pages of the Bible as pagans and idolaters. The Song of the Sea reminds some scholars of the "Canaanite epic style"[79] and the cosmology of ancient Canaan that found its way into the Bible in several places—the Canaanites imagined a battle at the beginning of the world between the deity known as Baal and the sea-god known as Yamm, a conflict in which Baal represented divine order and Yamm represented the chaos that preceded the creation of the world.[80]

Some theologians are willing to speculate that the biblical depiction of God engaged in battle at the Red Sea harkens back to the old Canaanite myth. "[T]he sea crossing of the Exodus is being associated with the primordial act of creation,"[81] as Brevard Childs puts it. "Thus the victory over Pharaoh reflected the victory of order over the primordial dragon of chaos, which was followed by the mythical battle with the sea."[82] Even the use of a rod by Moses to part the waters is thought to recall a scene from Canaanite myth in which Baal uses a club to subdue the sea-god.

Such speculation puts an unsettling spin on the rhetorical question that Moses asked aloud in the Song of the Sea: "Who is like thee, O Lord, among the gods?" (Exod. 15:11 NEB) Perhaps he was simply engaging in a bit of irony—the credo of the monotheistic faith of Moses, after all, is "the Lord is One"—or perhaps he assumed that there *were* rival gods and praised Yahweh not as the one and only god but merely as a god who is "unique among the circle of 'gods.' " When Noth read the Song of the Sea, he concluded that "its ultimate origin is in non-Israelite polytheistic ideas."[83] And Childs insisted that, although the Priestly source censored "the crasser mythological imagery" of the Canaanites, certain key elements of the pagan cosmology of Canaan—the striking of the sea and the drying up of its waters— became the "stereotyped vocabulary for describing the event."[84]

Elements of the pagan myth seem to have found their way even into the tales of the Midrash. The rabbis, for example, imagined a standoff between Moses and Rahab, the "Angel of the Sea,"[85] at the moment when Moses seeks to divide the waters and allow the Israelites to cross. Like the Canaanite sea-god known as Yamm, Rahab is said to personify the restless power of the primordial waters of the earth. "I will not do according to thy words, for thou art only a man born of woman, and, besides, I am three days older than thou, O man, for I was brought forth on the third day of creation, and thou on the sixth," Rahab taunts Moses, alluding to the seven days of Creation described in Genesis. When Moses asks God for advice on how to handle the insolent sea-spirit, Yahweh recommends a sharp blow with the sapphire rod that symbolizes the divine authority bestowed upon Moses.

"Moses, what does a master do with an intractable servant?" asks God.

"He beats him with a rod," answers Moses.

"Do thus!" God instructs. "Lift up thy rod, and stretch out thine hand over the sea, and divide it."[86]

The rabbis, of course, delighted in dressing up the miracle at the sea with even more miraculous flourishes. Not only do the waters of the Red Sea divide at God's command, they imagined, "but all the water in heaven and on earth, in whatever vessel it was, in cisterns, in wells, in caves, in casks, in pitchers, in drinking cups, and in glasses, and none of these waters returned to their former estate until Israel had passed through the sea on dry land."[87] God wants to make a great show of the miracle at the sea, and so "[t]he waters were piled up to the height of sixteen hundred miles, and they could be seen by all of the nations of the earth."[88]

As the Israelites cross the Red Sea between shimmering walls of crystalized water, they see that God has provided for their every need. "Whatever their hearts desired, the Israelites found in the middle of the sea," goes another rabbinical tale. "There was sweet water to slake their thirst, and . . . when a child cried, the mother had only to stretch out her hand and pluck an apple, a pomegranate, or any other fruit to quiet the crying baby."[89]

When the Egyptians balk at pursuing the Israelites across the seabed, a mare ridden by an angel rears up in front of the army and gallops off between the walls of water; Pharaoh's stallion bolts after the mare, and the army follows the doomed king into the trap that has been prepared for them by God himself.[90] The bodies of the drowned Egyptians wash up on the shore, where the Israelites recognize the faces of their former oppressors. "This one was my taskmaster, who beat me with those fists of his at which the dogs are now gnawing," they are imagined to say, "and yonder Egyptian, the dogs are chewing the feet with which he kicked me."[91] The Bible is quite clear that *every* Egyptian died in the Sea of Reeds—"Not one man remained alive" (Exod. 14:28)—but the sages imagined that God spares Pharaoh from death by drowning and grants him eternal life so that the defeated oppressor of Israel might stand at the gates of hell and scold each wicked king who shows up there: "Ye ought to have learned from my example."[92]*

Even in antiquity, some Bible readers saw mythmaking at work in *all* of the stories that have attached themselves to "the sea event." "[I]n dealing with a crowd of women, at least, or with any promiscuous mob, a philosopher cannot influence them by reason or exhort them to reverence, piety and faith," observed Strabo, a Greek geographer and historian of the first century B.C.E., who was no less cynical on the subject of religion than such famous doubters as Karl Marx and Sigmund Freud.

---

*When the mummy of the pharaoh Merneptah was found to contain a high concentration of salts, some nineteenth century Bible historians were moved to declare that he must have been the pharaoh who drowned at the Red Sea. However, the salt residues proved nothing, since a salty substance called natron was commonly used in the process of mummification in ancient Egypt.

"Nay, there is need of religious fear also, and this cannot be aroused without myths and marvels."[93] So the skeptics have always argued that whatever happened at the Red Sea can be explained by some freakish but hardly miraculous mechanism of the natural world.

One of the earliest examples was Artapanus, a Jewish Hellenistic author of the second century B.C.E., who attributed the crossing of the sea to the skills of Moses as a wilderness guide: "Moses, knowing the country and observing the tide, took advantage of the low water and led the Israelites through it at low tide."[94] Josephus allowed as how the parting of the sea could have been caused by "by the will of God or maybe by accident,"[95] and Philo chose to put the whole incident in purely metaphorical terms: the casting of horse and rider into the sea meant only that "God cast to utter ruin and the bottomless abyss the four passions and the wretched mind mounted on them."[96]

More recently, scientists using computer simulations have proposed that a sustained wind might have lowered the water level to a point where the Israelites could have crossed the sea on an exposed ridge.[97] The "strong east wind" of the biblical account might have been "a sirocco, such as used to appear in spring and autumn in Syria-Palestine."[98] Others have proposed a tidal wave following a volcanic eruption as the cause of the supposed miracle, and Martin Noth entertains the frank notion that the whole spectacle might have been nothing more than a mirage.[99]

The biblical authors would have been puzzled and surprised to hear such speculation, since the Bible "is clearly speaking here of a divine miracle," as Noth points out,[100] and the ancients were thoroughly at ease with the notion that a deity might work his will through wholly natural phenomena—something as unremarkable as a "strong east wind" might be regarded as miraculous. And they were untroubled by the ambiguous role of Moses, who may have used his staff or may have relied on the wind to part the waters of the Red Sea. "[T]he children of Israel understood this as an act of their God, as a 'miracle,' " writes Martin Buber, "which is assuredly to be attributed to the personal influence of Moses."[101]

Still, a worldly reader might come away from the biblical text with the impression that what happened at the Red Sea was neither a divine miracle nor a freak of nature but an act of courage by a band of slaves who rose up against their masters and, like Spartacus in ancient Rome, Nat Turner in the antebellum South, or the fighters of the Warsaw

Ghetto during the Holocaust, won a tactical victory by force of arms. And yet the simplest and most straightforward explanation of what happened on the shores of the Red Sea was the most troubling of all to the guardians of Holy Writ.

DISHONORED CORPSES

The notion that Moses and his army of ex-slaves stood their ground against the Egyptians at the Red Sea—"a military encounter in which Israel defeated the pursuing chariotry of Pharaoh," as one revisionist Bible historian puts it[102]—would have struck the rabbis and sages of late antiquity and the Middle Ages as no less blasphemous than the suggestion that the biblical account was something borrowed from pagan myth. Even though the Bible depicts Moses as a man of action, even a man of violence who was capable of ordering his own praetorian guard to carry out bloodthirsty purges and scorched-earth campaigns against his enemies, the militant Moses has been mostly written out of Judeo-Christian tradition by clergy who prefer to see him as a good shepherd rather than a man of war.

The Midrash preserves a cautionary tale about a descendant of Joseph from the tribe of Ephraim who declares after only 180 years of servitude in Egypt that God has called him to lead the Israelites in a war of self-liberation and the conquest of Canaan. Only the Ephraimites rally to his call to arms, and they rise up against their masters, provision themselves with gold and silver and weapons of war, and march out of Egypt in the direction of the Promised Land, "expect[ing] to buy food and drink on the way or capture them by force if the owners would not part with them for money."

But, according to the Midrashic tale, these Bible-era partisans are exterminated "root and branch" in their first skirmish with the Philistines, who stand between them and the Promised Land, and only ten survivors manage to make their way back to the relative safety of slavery in Egypt. When Moses finally leads the nation of Israel out of Egypt more than two hundred years later, God chooses a roundabout itinerary through the wilderness to spare the Israelites the sight of the "dishonored corpses" of the Ephraimites that still litter the highway to Canaan. "As for the disaster of the Ephraimites, it was well-merited punishment because they had paid no heed to the wish of their father

Joseph, who had adjured his descendants solemnly on his deathbed not to think of quitting the land until the true redeemer should appear."[103]

The same horror of war finds expression in another rabbinical tale that describes how the various tribes of Israel respond to the appearance of the Egyptians at the Red Sea. The tribes of Zebulun, Benjamin, and Naphtali want to turn around and march back to Egypt. Reuben, Simeon, and Issachar propose to martyr themselves by marching into the sea. Dan, Gad, and Asher fancy they can "shout and raise a great clamour" and thereby frighten off the Egyptians. Alone among the twelve tribes of Israel, Judah and Joseph "advised an open battle with the Egyptians," but Moses rejects all of these proposals, and especially the notion of armed resistance against the oppressor.

"And the Israelites remembered the words of Jacob, when he blest his sons: 'It is not for Israel to fight and use weapons of war,' " the rabbis concluded. " 'Prayers are its swords, and supplications its bows.' "[104]

The rabbinical literature reflects the strategies for survival that were embraced by the Jewish people throughout the centuries of exile from their ancient homeland in the land of Israel. The Jews of the Diaspora were taught that armed resistance was futile. Only a patient and long-enduring faith in God—combined with the protection of the rich and powerful men under whose rule they lived—would preserve the Jewish people until the coming of the Messiah. Against the threat of pogrom, inquisition, forced conversion, expulsion, and mass murder, the Jewish people sought to protect themselves by shunning violence and, instead, making the best deals they could with princes and kings throughout Christendom and the Islamic world. Although isolated incidents of self-defense and even open resistance can be found throughout history,[105] Jewish soldiery of the kind that would have been so familiar to Moses was not seen again until the stirrings of political Zionism in the late nineteenth century and, especially, World War II and its aftermath. So startling was the sight of Jewish men and women bearing arms in battle that Menachem Begin hailed them as nothing less than "a new speci-men of human being . . . completely unknown to the world over 1800 years, 'the fighting Jew.' "[106]

Of course, the pacifism that permeated Judaism in the Diaspora was not always a characteristic of the Jewish people or their ancestors in an-cient Israel. Indeed, the history of the Israelites, much of it told in the Bible itself, is a chronicle of open insurrection against foreign invaders and conquerors, starting with the Assyrian conquest of the northern kingdom of Israel in the eighth century B.C.E. and continuing for nearly a thousand years. Armed resistance to Roman occupation of Palestine was so intense, so sustained, and so effective that Jewish sovereignty was not fully extinguished until the second century C.E., when the Roman armies finally put down the rebellion of Simon Bar Kochba, a revolutionary leader who more closely resembles the warlike Moses of the Sinai campaign than the mild Moses who dickered with both God and Pharaoh. And, significantly, Bar Kochba was anointed as the leader of a Jewish national liberation movement by the greatest sage of his era, Rabbi Akiba, who entertained the notion that the man of war was, in fact, the Messiah.

THOUSANDS AND TENS OF THOUSANDS

Even the rabbis and sages who compiled and edited the Talmud and the Midrash conceded that there are times when piety is simply not enough and action must be taken. They conjured up a faintly comical scene in which Moses prays fervently and at tedious length to God on high as the Egyptian chariots thunder ever closer.

"O Lord of the world!" Moses implores. "I am like the shepherd who, having undertaken to pasture a flock, has been heedless enough to drive his sheep to the edge of a precipice, and then is in despair how to get them down again."[107]

"Moses, My children are in distress—the sea blocks the way before them, the enemy is in hot pursuit after them, and thou standest here and prayest," God scolds his wordy prophet. "Sometimes long prayer is good, but sometimes it is better to be brief."[108]

The rabbis did not mean to suggest that God was instructing Moses and the armed Israelites to unsheathe their swords and face their enemy. Rather, God is reminding Moses that he need only wield the rod of God to save the Israelites. "For thee there is naught to do," God tells Moses, "but lift up thy rod and stretch out thine hand over the sea, and divide it."[109] But a few contemporary Bible scholars with revisionist tendencies wonder whether the Bible preserves a faint remnant of a resort to arms by a band of runaway slaves in the wilderness of Sinai. Frank M. Cross, for example, sees in the Song of the Sea a veiled account of an amphibious assault by soldiers whose landing craft were swamped in the rough waters. "So far as we can tell, the Egyptians are cast out of barks or barges into the stormy sea," Cross explained. "[T]hey sink in the sea like a rock or a weight and drown."[110] As Brevard Childs puts it, "the enemy being described is an historical one, rather than mythological."[111]

A battle rather than a miracle is suggested by the very setting of the Song of Miriam. In the brief prologue, the Israelite women were apparently waiting in camp; the men are not mentioned at all,[112] and we might deduce that the men of fighting age had marched out of the encampment to face their attackers. When the first man staggered back into camp with a bloodied weapon and reported the defeat of the Egyptian army, what he described must have seemed so unlikely that the victory could only have been achieved with the miraculous intervention of Yahweh. The Bible confirms that Miriam and the women of Israel "went out" of the camp, presumably to greet the returning heroes and sing a song in praise of both God and the triumphant slave army just as women of the nomadic tribes of the ancient Near East always greeted victorious warriors, long before and long after the events of the Exodus.

In fact, the Song of Miriam depicts much the same scene that we find in the biblical account of the throngs of women who welcomed King Saul and his favorite warrior, David, when they returned from a victorious campaign against the Philistines, an event that came several hundred years later in the chronology of the Bible: "[T]he women came out of all the cities of Israel, singing and dancing, to meet king Saul, with timbrels, with joy, and with three-stringed instruments." Just as Miriam led the women of Israel in a call-and-response song to greet the warriors at the Red Sea, the women who gathered to greet Saul and David "sang to one another in their play, and said, 'Saul hath slain his thousands, and David his tens of thousands.' " (1 Sam. 18:6–7)

There is an unmistakable barb in the song of victory sung to Saul and David—the shepherd is praised as a greater hero than the king because he has slain so many more men—and so, too, does the Song of Miriam deliver a subtle slur on a great leader. The prophetess Miriam lavished praise on Yahweh for allowing the slave army to prevail against the "horse and rider" of imperial Egypt, but she pointedly ignored the role of Moses in the victory. If the Song of Miriam is the oldest fragment of the Bible, if these two spare lines of praise and thanksgiving recall what actually happened in the distant past, then we might wonder why Miriam neglected to mention the man who was supposedly her own brother, the chosen prophet of Yahweh, and the wielder of the rod of God.

GENERALISSIMO AND GRAND INQUISITOR

One explanation for the absence of Moses in the Song of Miriam, of course, is that Miriam chose to praise Yahweh and ignored his human emissary out of simple piety, and that is exactly how the passage has been explained in traditional Bible commentary. As we have seen, Jewish tradition has always been uncomfortable in lionizing Moses out of a concern for suggesting that he was even faintly divine. The text used by observant Jews in the celebration of the seder, the ritual meal of Passover, does not mention the name of Moses at all. Like Miriam, the Haggadah credits only God with the miracles that brought about the liberation of the Israelites, and Moses remains a missing person.

But there are other ways, far more daring ways, to explain why Moses is absent from the Song of Miriam. Perhaps Moses is a mythic figure, a Hebrew counterpart to Hercules or Romulus, a character who had not yet been dreamed up at the time when a flesh-and-blood prophetess called Miriam celebrated a military victory over the Egyptians at the Sea of Reeds. Or perhaps Moses and Miriam were both real people who lived at different times and places in the long history of Israel. Maybe they ended up together in the pages of the Bible only because their lives were interwoven by the bards who preserved the legends and fables of ancient Israel from generation to generation.

Even if we read the Bible literally, and regard Moses and Miriam as a brother and sister who shared the struggle for liberation in the wilderness of Sinai, the biblical text still suggests a deadly tension between the siblings, a rivalry for power that eventually reached a flash point when both Miriam and Aaron openly challenged the leadership of Moses. As we shall see, Moses was not only and not always the Good Shepherd—the Emancipator was also the Generalissimo and the Grand Inquisitor, and anyone whom Moses regarded as an enemy, foreign or domestic, was at risk of scourging or liquidation or both. Not even Miriam, so charismatic and so beloved of her people, would escape the punishment that Moses inflicted on those who dared to defy his authority.

Still, at the moment when the song of victory was sung on the shores of the Red Sea, the Bible author allows us to witness a rare moment of unsullied and uncomplicated triumph for "the man Moses." He had managed to survive the wrath of a homicidal god and had suffered the sting of an ungrateful people, and he would encounter both again soon enough. As he looked out over the men and women who sang and danced in such frenzy under the desert sky, he may have suffered a moment of fear and doubt: How would he manage to move the horde across the wilderness? Where would he find food and water for such a multitude? Could these unruly ex-slaves make themselves into an army and defeat the peoples who stood between them and the Promised Land? And how much longer could he count on the assistance of the moody and impulsive god who called himself Yahweh?

The answers to these troubling questions would present themselves soon enough. Today, however, Moses, could enjoy a brief moment of rest at the pinnacle of divine grace and worldly power. Tomorrow, Moses and the Israelites would rise and move on.

Chapter Eight

THE SORCERER AND THE SORCERER'S APPRENTICE

"Poetry embroidered magic, and transformed it into theology. . . ."
—WILL DURANT, *THE STORY OF
CIVILIZATION: OUR ORIENTAL HERITAGE*

When the song that Miriam and the women of Israel sang by the shores of the Red Sea finally ended, Moses rallied the Israelites for the next stage of their journey toward Canaan. The people lumbered to their feet, folded their tents and packed up their belongings, and trudged after him. Almost immediately, they found themselves in a predicament that threatened not only the success of their trek toward Canaan but their very survival in the wilderness.

> And Moses led Israel onward from the Red Sea, and they went into the wilderness of Shur; and they went three days in the wilderness, and found no water. (Exod. 15:22)

The sages imagined an incident at the Red Sea that symbolizes the maddening lack of resolve and self-discipline that the Israelites would display in confronting each new crisis in the wilderness. Before setting out from the Red Sea, according to a tale from the Midrash, the Israelites hike down to the shore to see for themselves the site of the miraculous victory. They find that the sea has cast up not only the corpses of the drowned Egyptians but also the treasure that they carried with them. So the Israelites pick their way among the corpses, searching out the gold and silver and gemstones that lie scattered in the sand or hidden away in the cloaks of the dead men. Moses despairs at the sight. God has granted them a victory over Pharaoh, of course, but a long march lies ahead, and stern discipline will be required if they are to survive. Yet the Israelites now content themselves with easy pickings.

"Do you imagine," Moses scolds the Israelites, "that the sea will for ever cast out upon the shore precious stones, gems, and pearls?"[1]

Not that the booty will do them much good in the wilderness, the rabbis seemed to suggest. Food and water are far more precious than gold to the desert traveler, and the treasure is just so much dead weight. The Israelites might spend their time more profitably by abandoning the bounty and instead filling up their goatskins with water. God and Moses, as we shall see, were forced to contend with the same stubbornness, the same lack of discipline, the same failure of courage and imagination, throughout the years of wandering in the wilderness. The Israelites were an unruly flock, much to the consternation of both God and Moses.

"Ye are a stiff-necked people," cried God, thus summing up the character flaws of the unruly Israelites (Exod. 33:5). One of the little-noticed revelations of the Bible is that God and Moses were bested by human nature—the Israelites remained defiant, obstinate, headstrong, and free-spirited despite every promise of divine reward and every threat of divine punishment. As we shall see, Moses became so sick of these maddening people that he asked God to put an end to his ordeal by killing him. God himself, although he never fully withdrew his blessing from the Chosen People, threatened to kill *them* and start all over again with Moses as the founder of a new race. So the fact that the Israelites survived at all must be seen as a miracle in itself.

THE BREAD OF AFFLICTION

The Bible confirms that the provisions carried by the Israelites were spare indeed. Their departure from Egypt on the morning after the tenth plague had been so sudden—"[T]hey were thrust out of Egypt," the Bible reports, "and could not tarry" (Exod. 12:39)—that they carried only a meager supply of dough, which had been prepared in such haste that they did not bother to leaven the dough and allow it to rise. So, instead of baking loaves of bread, they rolled out the dough into round cakes and baked them into the hard, dry, crackerlike stuff that is called *matzah*—"the bread of affliction," as the Bible later describes it

(Deut. 16:3), ostensibly because it recalls the suffering of the enslaved Israelites in Egypt but perhaps also because a prolonged diet of the stuff is something of an affliction in itself, as every observant Jew who has celebrated Passover knows from personal experience.*

Like desert travelers in every age and every wilderness, the Israelites must have trekked from one source of water to another, always watching out for an oasis or even just a well, always scanning the horizon for some sign of pasturage for their beasts of burden, always measuring the precious supply of foodstuffs in their sacks and saddlebags. One day the last few crumbs of *matzah* would be handed around to the hungry multitude; one day the goatskins would supply only droplets of water and then no water at all. On that day, as the Israelites surely anticipated, they would confront the hunger and thirst that would kill them just as surely and just as cruelly as Pharaoh and his soldiers had threatened to do.

By tradition, the supply of *matzah* lasted exactly thirty-one days,[2] but the goatskins ran dry after only three days and they found no source of water to refill them (Exod. 15:22). When at last Moses led the Israelites to a sparse oasis, they must have broken ranks, rushed headlong to the shallow pool surrounded by a few sorry palms, fallen to their knees on the muddy banks, scooped up water with their bare hands or lapped it up with their tongues like dogs. But even then, the Israelites must have felt only a sharp stab of despair as they tasted salt on their tongues and something even fouler at the back of their throats—and then spit the vile stuff out.

And when they came to Marah, they could not drink of the waters of Marah, for they were bitter. (Exod. 15:23)

Marah, a Hebrew word that means "bitterness," is a byword of the life of Moses and the experience of the Israelites in the Exodus. For example, "Meror" ("the Bitter One") is the title given by the rabbis to the pharaoh who enslaved the Israelites,[3] and the name of Miriam, whose rivalry with Moses would soon end in her own bitter defeat, was given a similar reading in the rabbinical literature. One of the ritual foods of the traditional Passover seder is a dish of bitter herbs called *maror*, a symbol

---

*"[S]even days shalt thou eat unleavened bread," goes the biblical instruction that still applies to the observance of Passover, "that thou mayest remember the day when thou camest forth out of the land of Egypt all the days of thy life." (Deut. 16:3–4)

of the oppression that the Israelites suffered in Egypt. And here in the wilderness of Shur, the Bible author tells us, the nameless spring to which Moses led them was called Marah in recollection of the bitter and undrinkable water that they found there.

Bitterness, too, was the response of the Israelites to every moment of adversity and uncertainty in the wilderness, and Moses was always the target of their complaints. God had anointed Moses as his personal emissary, armed him with magical and even miraculous powers, and charged him with the mission of leading the Israelites to the Promised Land—and yet his every step was dogged by the snarling of the Israelites. At the first taste of brackish water from the spring at Marah, for example, they seemed to forget their salvation at the Red Sea only a few days earlier, and they were ready to rise up against Moses in rebellion.

"And the people murmured against Moses," the Bible reports, "saying, 'What shall we drink?' " (Exod. 15:24)

SWEET WATER

If the Israelites were quick to complain to Moses, he was equally quick to address his own plaints to the deity who had put him in charge in the first place. "And he cried unto Yahweh," the Bible reports—"What do I do now?" we might imagine him to say—and Yahweh worked yet another miracle. "[A]nd Yahweh showed him a tree, and he cast it into the waters, and the waters were made sweet." (Exod. 15:25)[4]

There is something faintly druidical about the scene at Marah as described by the Yahwist.[5] The biblical text appears to preserve some primitive folk wisdom about the curative power of a particular desert flora; some ancient manuscripts of the Bible suggest that what Moses tossed into the water was not a whole tree but a piece of wood or a shrub, and Bible scholars speculated that the wholly natural properties of the plant were what purified the tainted waters.[6] Even the rabbis were willing to entertain the faintly scandalous notion that God tutors Moses in some arcane ritual that seems more appropriate to a medieval alchemist than to the man who will hand down the Ten Commandments. "God bade him take a piece of a laurel tree, write upon it the great and glorious name of God, and throw it into the water," goes one rabbinical tale, "whereupon the water would become drinkable and sweet."[7]

But one or more later authors, probably the Deuteronomist and perhaps the Priestly source,[8] insisted on putting a theologically correct interpretation on the magic trick at Marah. "There he made for them a statute and an ordinance," goes a biblical aside, "and there he proved them" (Exod. 15:26)—that is, God offered the Israelites a bargain at Marah, divine healing in exchange for compliance with divine law, and waited to see if they took him up on his offer. "If thou wilt diligently hearken to the voice of the Lord thy God, and wilt do that which is right in His eyes, and wilt give ear to His commandments, and keep all His statutes," God told them, "I will put none of the diseases upon thee, which I have put upon the Egyptians; for I am the Lord that healeth thee." (Exod. 15:26)

The fussiness and formalism of the priests and scribes can be detected in the biblical report of the next stopping-place on the way toward the Promised Land. "And they came to Elim," the Bible continues, "where were twelve springs of water, and three score and ten palm-trees, and they encamped there by the waters." (Exod. 15:27) Here we are no longer witnessing a moment of magic *or* miracle; instead, the text is given over to the abstract symbolism of numbers so favored by the Priestly source: twelve is the number of the tribes of Israel, and seventy is the traditional count of the Israelites who followed Jacob into Egypt, the languages spoken by the peoples of the world, the members of the rabbinical assembly known as the Sanhendrin, and the translators who created the first Greek translation of the Hebrew Bible. Even so, the magical quality of the landscape did not escape the attention of the rabbis of Midrashic tradition, who imagined that God paused during the six days of Creation to place the bountiful oasis of Elim and its numerologically meaningful wells and trees on the very path that the Israelites would travel countless generations later.[9]

ONION, RADISH, AND GARLIC

The next stopping-place brought the next crisis of leadership for Moses and his brother Aaron, who was written into the scene by the Priestly source but given no role of his own to play. Somewhere between Elim and Sinai, in a place that the Bible calls the wilderness of Sin, the Israelites began to murmur yet again. The objects of their latest grievance were both Moses *and* Aaron, and not merely a few rabble-rousers but "the whole congregation of the children of Israel" joined in the chorus of complaint (Exod. 16:2). Although the Bible does not plainly say so, it appears that the sparse supply of *matzah* had run low or run out, and now the Israelites bellyached about their empty stomachs, blaming Moses and his brother for their woes. Yet again they yearned openly for slavery or even death in preference to the ordeal of the wilderness.

"Would that we had died by the hand of the Lord in the land of Egypt, when we sat by the flesh-pots, when we did eat bread to the full," goes the memorable biblical refrain, "for ye have brought us forth into this wilderness, to kill this whole assembly with hunger." (Exod. 16:3)

Moses must have found the complaint even more maddening because it was so palpably false. Meat was a rarity and a delicacy even among ordinary peasants and workers in ancient Egypt—Herodotus, for example, came upon an inscription on one pyramid that inventoried the precise quantities of onion, radish, and garlic that sustained the men who had labored to quarry and raise the stones. Mere slaves, and especially foreign slaves, would have tasted the savory contents of the flesh-pot even less often. "In their exasperation they spoke untruths," the rabbis explained, "for in reality they had suffered from want of food in Egypt, too, as the Egyptians had not given them enough to eat."[10]

Yahweh quickly reassured Moses that he would yet again come to the rescue of the Israelites—and, not incidentally, Moses himself, whose leadership was constantly threatened. "I have heard the murmurings of the children of Israel," Yahweh told Moses. "Speak unto them, saying: At dusk ye shall eat flesh, and in the morning ye shall be filled with bread; and ye shall know that I am the Lord your God." (Exod. 16:12) At day's end, flocks of quail would alight at the encampment in such vast profusion that every man, woman, and child would sate himself or herself on generous portions of flesh roasted over the fire—"The quails came up, and covered the camp" (Exod. 16:13)—and, at dawn, when the morning dew evaporated, a miraculous foodstuff would be left behind, "a fine, scale-like thing, fine as the hoar-frost on the ground." (Exod. 16:14)

"Behold, I will cause to rain bread from heaven for you; and the people shall go out and gather a day's portion every day," God instructed Moses, "that I may prove them, whether they will walk in My law, or not." (Exod. 16:4)

So strange was the sight of the stuff that appeared with the morning dew that the Israelites were dumbfounded. "They said one to another:

'What is it?' " the Bible reports, "for they knew not what it was." And Moses answered: "It is the bread which the Lord hath given you to eat." (Exod. 16:15) The question on the lips of the astounded Israelites— *Man hu,*[11] a Hebrew phrase rendered in English as "What is it?"—is the origin of the Hebrew word *man* and its English equivalent, "manna," the name by which the "bread from heaven" came to be known. The curious substance "was like coriander seed, white, and the taste of it was like wafers made with honey" (Exod. 16:31) or "a cake baked with oil" (Num. 11:8), and once gathered up, it proved to be a highly versatile foodstuff.

> The people went about, and gathered it, and ground it in mills, or beat it in mortars, and seethed it in pots, and made cakes of it. (Num. 11:8)

The daily feast in the wilderness was intended as yet another demonstration by Yahweh of his power and generosity. Rather like the Wizard of Oz, he used a bit of flash-and-dazzle to catch the attention of his audience—"[T]hey looked toward the wilderness, and, behold, the glory of Yahweh appeared in the cloud" (Exod. 16:10)—and, again like the Wizard, God bestowed upon the Israelites exactly what they yearned for. All that he wanted in return was a little respect. "At dusk ye shall eat flesh, and in the morning ye shall be filled with bread," God told Moses, and Moses told the assembled Israelites, "and ye shall know that I am Yahweh your God." (Exod. 16:12)[12] But as it turned out, the Israelites were no more credulous than Dorothy and Toto, and no display of divine magic, no act of divine grace, was ever enough to convince them, once and for all, that Yahweh ought to be obeyed on faith alone. Thus did the Israelites teach God and Moses a lesson about the restlessness of human nature, which is never satisfied with dictates from on high and always seeks to probe the outermost boundaries of freedom.

For example, God issued a set of detailed instructions about the gathering of the manna to "prove" the Israelites—that is, to extract from them a concrete gesture of compliance with divine law. Although the manna fell in abundance, the Israelites were ordered to gather only "a day's portion every day." Miraculously, even though some gathered more and some gathered less, "he that gathered much had nothing over, and he that gathered little had no lack." A double portion was to be gathered on the sixth day because no manna fell on the seventh day, "a holy sabbath unto the Lord"—and here we find the very first use of the word "sabbath" in the Bible.[13] The daily harvest of manna must be completed in the morning hours because "as the sun waxed hot, it melted," and what was gathered had to be prepared and eaten the same day; hoarding was futile because any manna kept overnight "bred worms, and rotted." The extra portion that was gathered on the sixth day, however, was still wholesome and good to eat on the Sabbath (Exod. 16:4, 16–18, 20, 21, 23).

As if bread falling from heaven to feed a desperate band of escaped slaves were not astounding enough, the rabbis elaborated upon the miracle of manna with special passion. Manna was created in the twilight between the sixth day of Creation and the first Sabbath, they rhapsodized,[14] and the stuff is milled in the third heaven by the angels "for the future use of the pious."[15] Anyone fortunate enough to live on a diet of manna acquires the strength of angels and no longer need bother himself with bowel movements since "manna is entirely dissolved in the body." Only if the manna-eater lapses into sin will he once again feel the need to "ease himself," as the sages so delicately put it.[16] And one never tires of the taste of manna because "[o]ne had only to desire a certain dish, and no sooner had he thought of it, than manna had the flavor of the dish desired," the rabbis imagined. "The same food had a different taste to every one who partook of it, according to his age; to the little children it tasted like milk, to the strong youths like bread; to the old men like honey; to the sick like barley steeped in oil and honey."[17] On the Sabbath, the stuff "sparkl[ed] more than usual, and it tasted better than usual."[18]

Yet the unruly Israelites were not content even with the food of angels. A few obstinate Israelites insisted on keeping a little hoard of manna overnight—sure enough, the stuff was wormy and rotten by morning, "and Moses was wroth with them." (Exod. 16:20) The rabbis imagined that the hoarders are Dathan and Abiram, two biblical characters who always seem to show up in the rabbinical literature as the adversaries of Moses. Their crime is revealed when the worms that infest their cache of forbidden manna "moved in a long train from their tents to the other tents, so that everyone perceived what these two had done."[19] And the Bible reports that some of the Israelites refused to eat day-old manna on the Sabbath and insisted on going out in search of fresh manna—but found none, of course. Now it was Yahweh himself whom they managed to make wroth.

"How long refuse ye to keep My commandments and My laws?" God railed to Moses in reproach to the Israelites (Exod. 16:28–29). The same note of exasperation, the same ache of disappointment, the same bitter reproach will characterize Yahweh's troubled relationship with his Chosen People throughout the Exodus and long after.

MANNITE AND EXHAUSTED BIRDS

Still, no matter how boldly the Israelites defied the will of Yahweh, no matter how wroth he waxed, Yahweh did not withdraw the gift of manna. Throughout all that was yet to come in the wilderness, despite every insult and disappointment that Yahweh was forced to endure from his own Chosen People, bread fell from heaven every day. "And the children of Israel did eat the manna forty years," goes the biblical account, "until they came to the borders of the land of Canaan." Even then, a cache of the bread from heaven was safely ensconced along with the other holy relics of Israel in the temple that came to be built in Jerusalem. "Take a jar, and put an omerful* of manna therein, and lay it up before the Lord," God told Moses, and Moses told Aaron, "to be kept through your generations." (Exod. 16:33, 35) Only when Moses died, the rabbis insisted, did the daily ration of manna cease to fall from the heavens.[20]

Although the Bible insists that manna fell from heaven every day, the oldest account of the miracle may have been much more restrained—perhaps the manna fell only once. Elias Auerbach suggests that it was the Priestly source who insisted that God kept it up throughout the wanderings in the Sinai, thus making the miracle seem even more miraculous and emphasizing both the glory and the generosity of God. "To consider the manna as a habitual food of the people for forty years is a

---

*An omer was a clay vessel that held six and a half pints and came to be used as a unit of measurement. The Priestly source, always so interested in measuring and counting, paused to point out that "an omer is the tenth part of an ephah." (Exod. 16:36) The late authorship of the passage is betrayed by the writer's suggestion that Aaron dutifully placed the jar of manna alongside the tablets of the Ten Commandments, which had not yet been given to Moses at this point in the biblical narrative, both of which lay in the Tabernacle, which had not yet been erected (Exod. 16:34). No explanation is given for the fact that the jarful of manna did not go rotten and wormy over the generations.

grotesque exaggeration of the miracle," writes Auerbach, "which belongs to a later strata only."[21] As it turns out, however, it is not necessary to invoke Yahweh at all to explain the "miracle" of quails and manna, which might have been the result of thoroughly natural phenomena. Among all the scientific explanations for the miracles of the Exodus, the one that accounts for the food that rained down from heaven is the most convincing of all.

The quail that submitted themselves so meekly to the appetites of the Israelites, according to Martin Noth, may have been the migratory birds that are known to gather in flocks along the Mediterranean coast of the Sinai during the seasonal migrations between Europe and Africa in spring and autumn.[22] Josephus reported that the flocks were so spent from their long flight that they could be caught by hand, and, more recently, the Bedouins of the Sinai have been known to gather up unresisting birds at will for an easy meal. "[R]eports of migratory birds flying up from Africa and arriving exhausted in the peninsula have been repeatedly verified in modern times," writes Werner Keller.[23]

Manna, too, might owe nothing to divine intervention. From the description in the Bible, manna appears to be the sweet-tasting, yellowish-white, resinous substance that is exuded when the plant lice known as *Trabutina mannipara* and *Najococcus serpentinus* feed on the fruit of the tamarisk tree, a native plant of the Sinai Peninsula. "During the warmth of the day it melts, but it congeals when cold," reports one scholar, confirming the biblical account. "These pellets or cakes are gathered by the natives in the early morning and, when cooked, provide a sort of bread. The food decays quickly and attracts ants."[24] Manna was a cash crop in the Sinai as early as the fifteenth century, when a German pilgrim reported that "the monks and the Arabs gather, preserve and sell [manna] to pilgrims and strangers who pass that way," and the stuff was still being harvested commercially and exported from the Sinai in the twentieth century under the brand name Mannite as a delicacy for the pious gourmet. "In good years," one biblical historian insists "the Bedouins of Sinai can collect 4 pounds per head in a morning."[25]

Such down-to-earth explanations would not have bothered the biblical authors, who were capable of seeing the hand of God in *every* event in the life of Moses, from birth to death, and *every* experience of the Israelites during the Exodus, no matter how mundane or even profane. What made Yahweh unique in the eyes of the ancient Israelites was not merely that he claimed to be the one and only God or that he disdained the idols and images demanded by other deities. Rather, Yahweh was something new and revolutionary in the history of religion precisely because, more often than not, he manifested himself and worked his will through the sweep of history rather than periodic bursts of divine legerdemain through the agency of Moses.

Indeed, the miracles that decorate the biblical text are always offered by the sources to make some theological point, which is how the commentators of both Jewish and Christian tradition have explained the miracle of quails and manna to their congregants over the centuries. The rabbis taught that manna was delivered to the Israelites every day, thus sparing them the burden of collecting and carrying the stuff through the wilderness, so that "they might day by day depend on God's aid, and in this way, exercise themselves in faith."[26] The church fathers went even further, arguing that the feeding of the thankless multitudes was evidence that the grace of God does not depend on faith or good works. "If a generation of Israelites deserved to be abandoned by Yahweh in the hour of peril, it was the generation of the Exodus," writes one Catholic scholar. "Not only were they completely lacking in the faith and confidence that were demanded of Israel in the holy war, but they complained against Moses (and Yahweh) in a way that was little short of blasphemous."[27]

A crucial but mostly overlooked point about God, Moses, and the Exodus is buried away in one of the countless parables and homilies that were offered by the rabbis to point out the marvelous qualities of manna. Two Israelites present themselves to Moses and demand that he resolve a bitter dispute between them over the ownership of a certain slave. The first man insists that his slave has been stolen from him by the second man, and the second man insists just as stoutly that he has purchased the slave from the first one. Moses reserves judgment until the next morning—he knows that manna always appears in precisely the right measure for each family, and so he watches to see where the slave's daily ration of manna will appear. When Moses measures the manna that piles up at the first man's tent, he finds that it includes a portion for the slave, too. "It was a clear proof that the slave still belonged to him and had never been sold," goes the rabbinical tale. "Moses consequently commanded the thief to return the property to the rightful owner."[28]

The "property," of course, is a human being, which reminds us that the abolition of human slavery was never the goal of God *or* Moses in the biblical account of the Exodus—the Israelites owned and used slaves of their own throughout the biblical era, and the Five Books of Moses are indifferent to the fact of human slavery, even if some of the more progressive laws handed down by Moses would serve to improve the conditions of servitude. Although Moses the Emancipator has been regarded in more recent centuries as a shining symbol of freedom, the flesh-and-blood Moses as depicted in the Bible never bothered himself with such gentle and sentimental notions. Once he had succeeded in leading the Israelites to a place where they were able to worship God in the way that Moses demanded of them—once he had given the Israelites the freedom to submit to the god called Yahweh—he was more concerned with asserting his authority over the Israelites and punishing his adversaries for their defiance of that authority than with setting men free.

"YE HAVE BEEN REBELLIOUS"

Starting in distant antiquity, Moses was made over into a charismatic leader, a mild and merciful lawgiver, a proto-democratic figure who embraced the ideal of liberty and ruled by common acclaim. "Moses was elected the leader," insisted Philo, "not having gained it like some men who have forced their way to power and supremacy by force of arms and intrigue, and by armies of cavalry and infantry, and by powerful fleets, but having been appointed for the sake of his virtue and excellence and that benevolence towards all men which he was always feeling and exhibiting. . . ."[29] The same reverential attitude toward Moses can be traced through two thousand years of sermons and homilies, political propaganda and stump speeches, sacred art and popular culture.

Yet an open-eyed reading of the biblical text reveals that Moses was no more beloved than any other autocrat in history. As the Bible never fails to remind us, the people of Israel were "stiff-necked"—that is, unruly, ungrateful, brimming with grievance and complaint, quick to demand favors and quick to forget that favors had been done for them, stubbornly insisting on the right to go and do as they pleased, and perfectly capable of challenging and even condemning their leader at the slightest disappointment. In other words, the Israelites were human beings, ordinary and unremarkable, and they behaved just as mortal men and women have always behaved toward those who try to rule them without their consent.

"Ye have been rebellious against the Lord," Moses complained of the Israelites, "from the day that I knew you." (Deut. 9:24)

Of course, it is also possible to look on the Israelites with more compassion and insight than the biblical authors were able to muster. Moses, after all, had not been elected by anyone except an unheard and unseen God, and so far God had not deigned to speak to anyone other than Moses and his brother. Yet Moses had urged them out of the relative safety and comfort of Egypt into an empty and threatening wilderness, all on a vague promise that someday they would reach a distant land of "milk and honey." Such rhetoric had surely been heard before among the poor and oppressed, and history assures us that it would be heard again and again through the centuries. The Bible encourages its readers to regard the skepticism and defiance of the Israelites toward Moses as an appalling lack of faith, but the modern reader might take a very different view of any man who claimed to speak for an invisible deity and sought to rule a nation through a harsh theocracy.

Indeed, the tension between Moses and the Israelites steadily mounted on the long trek through the Sinai. Sometimes the Israelites complained about too little food and water; sometimes they carped about too much of the same old stuff—a steady diet of quails and manna soon grew tedious. And like leaders in every age who have faced a hungry mob, Moses sought to shift the blame for the lack of provisions in the wilderness to someone other than himself. Remarkably, it was God himself against whom Moses chose to direct the anger of the Chosen People.

"[I]t is not against us that you bring your complaints, we are nothing," Moses and Aaron hastened to tell the Israelites. "It is against Yahweh that you bring your complaints, and not against us." (Exod. 16:7–8)[30]

Thus did Moses attempt to impugn those who challenged his political authority by characterizing them as apostates and heretics—defiance of God's messenger, Moses insisted, was defiance of God. Although Moses has long been celebrated as an icon of liberation and freedom, his words of reproach are the same ones that have always been invoked with bloody results by inquisitors in service to autocracies and theocracies throughout history. And as we shall see, Moses was willing to go far beyond mere rhetoric in purging and putting down the rebellions of those who murmured against him.

THE ANTI-MOSES TRADITION

Moses is made to play a godlike role himself at certain moments in the Bible. "See, I place you in the role of God to Pharaoh, with your brother Aaron as your prophet," God declared when he first sent Moses on his mission to Egypt. "Thus he shall serve as your spokesman, with you playing the role of God to him." (Exod. 4:16, 7:1 New JPS) Yet the Bible does not make Moses into a demigod or a superhero—a fact that sets the Bible apart from other sacred writings of the ancient Near East—and he is presented as a thoroughly flawed human being rather than a plaster saint. As noted earlier, some scholars detect an "anti-Moses tradition" that runs just beneath the surface of the biblical text and sometimes erupts into open condemnation of Moses.

The Bible, for example, is candid about the flaws and frailties of Moses—his slowness of speech, his moments of timidity and even cowardice, his fits of anger and his spells of depression, his willingness to commit ghastly atrocities, and the slow deterioration of his relationship with Yahweh from trust and intimacy to defiance and sheer dysfunction. At the end of his tumultuous and troubled life, as we shall see, Moses suffered the ultimate punishment at the hands of God: he was condemned to die without reaching the Promised Land—perhaps even put to death—by the very God who had once befriended him. Moses died alone, and God went to the trouble of secretly burying Moses so that "no man knoweth of his sepulchre unto this day." (Deut. 34:6)

The biblical passages that seem to denigrate Moses are probably the remnants of a political rivalry between the various priestly castes of ancient Israel, one that traced its descent from Aaron, another that claimed to descend from Moses. The Priestly source was probably an Aaronite priest, for example, and the Elohist may have been a priest of the so-called Mushite line. Each of the biblical sources felt at liberty to put his or her own spin on the sacred history of ancient Israel, even if it meant disparaging a figure as central and commanding as Moses. What was at stake in the treatment of Moses was less a matter of theology than of politics, and that is why he was caught in a cross fire of priestly rhetoric.

The roots of the anti-Moses tradition probably reach back to the period of the divided monarchy in ancient Israel, when the empire of David and Solomon split in two and rival kings reigned in what was left, one in the southern kingdom of Judah and one in the northern kingdom of Israel. Jerusalem remained the capital of Judah, where the descendants of King David continued to reign, and the site of the principal shrine of Yahweh—and, significantly, the priests who served in Jerusalem traced their ancestry back to the first high priest of Israel, Aaron. The cities of Dan and Bethel in the northern kingdom of Israel were designated as shrines to Yahweh—and the priests who served at the sanctuary in Dan claimed descent from Moses. After the destruction of the northern kingdom in 722 B.C.E., all of the various priestly castes ended up in Jerusalem, where the old rivalries continued to simmer and sometimes boiled over.

The rival factions took very different views of Moses. For example, the Elohist, who is thought to have been a priest from the northern kingdom, revered and exalted Moses, while the Yahwist, who is linked to the royal court of the southern kingdom, regarded him as nothing more than "an inspired shepherd whom Jahweh used to make his will known to men."[31] Some of the biblical sources were apparently willing to entertain even harsher judgments of Moses, which may explain why he is depicted at certain moments in the Bible as a coward, a defeatist, a rebel against God himself.

The less savory details that found their way into the Bible are regarded by some scholars as "a polemic against the claims of the northern kingdom" by the priests who were natives of Jerusalem,[32] an effort to show that "the ancestors of the northern kingdom [had] forfeited the privileges of divine election, leaving the door open to a new act of election for David. . . ."[33] The ancient biblical propagandists did not feel at liberty to simply write Moses out of Holy Writ, of course, but they were perfectly willing to show him as deeply flawed.

Priestly politics aside, some imaginative readers have come up with an even more startling account of the life—and death—of Moses. The favorite text of the biblical conspiracy buffs is the Book of Hosea, where the irascible prophet from the northern kingdom worked himself into a frenzy over the appalling misconduct of his fellow Israelites. "They break all bounds," railed Hosea, "and blood toucheth blood." (Hos. 4:2) To a few revisionists, the obscure words and phrases of Hosea conceal the faint memory of a conspiracy against Moses by his enemies among the Israelites.

The most famous of the conspiracy theorists was Sigmund Freud, who read the Book of Hosea and came up with a far more shocking (and thoroughly Freudian) speculation. Hosea, he argued, preserves "unmistakable traces of a tradition to the effect that [Moses] met a violent end in a rebellion of his stubborn and refractory people." The anti-Moses tradition, as Freud saw it, was not a matter of a few disgruntled priests who sought to blacken the reputation of Moses to serve their own political motives. Rather, Freud entertained the scandalous idea that the Israelites did not merely murmur against Moses, they murdered him.

THE MURDER OF MOSES

"The great deed and misdeed of primeval times, the murder of the father, was brought home to the Jews," Freud wrote in *Moses and Monotheism*, "for fate decreed that they should repeat it on the person of Moses, an eminent father substitute."[34] Freud suggested that the collective guilt of the Israelites over the murder of Moses prompted a powerful yearning for the miraculous rebirth of the man they had slain, a yearning that Freud regarded as the font of the powerful tendency toward messianism that is mentioned nowhere in the Five Books of Moses but later came to be the essential theology of Judaism.[35]

"Towards the end of the Babylonian exile the hope arose among the Jewish people that the man they had so callously murdered would return from the realm of the dead," Freud concluded, "and lead his contrite people—and perhaps not only his people—into the land of eternal bliss."[36]

More temperate scholars were (and remain) unpersuaded. Even Ernest Sellin, the scholar whose speculation on the murder of Moses first inspired Freud, eventually renounced his own theory.[37] "[T]he alleged murder of Moses cannot be adequately supported by the biblical sources," adds Jay Y. Gonen, a psychohistorian who has found the supposed evidence in Hosea to be "at best far-fetched." Still, even a critic like Gonen concedes that the murmurings of the Israelites against Moses, so thoroughly documented in the biblical text, may reflect "a murderous rage [that] is as important as an actual murder," and he agrees that the Bible preserves more than one moment when "the children of Israel 'have had it' with their father in heaven and with their leaders on earth, not the least of whom was Moses,"[38] though he refuses to entertain the notion that the Israelites actually acted on their "murderous rage" toward Moses.

Remarkably, Freud went on to argue that the Israelites buried the man they had slain, recruited a new man to lead them out of the wilderness, and gave the new chieftain the same name as the old one! The first Moses, Freud proposed, was a renegade Egyptian prince, a follower of the pharaoh Akhenaton and a worshiper of the sun-god Aton, who made himself the liberator of the slave nation of Israel and marched them into the wilderness, where they tired of his strict and imperious leadership, rose up against him, struck him dead, and buried him in an unmarked grave somewhere in the shifting sands of the Sinai. The second Moses, according to Freud, was a Midianite, the son-in-law of Jethro, and the man whom the Israelites drafted to lead them out of the wilderness.

"We know nothing personal, however," Freud admitted, "about this other Moses—he is entirely obscured by the first, the Egyptian Moses— except possibly from clues provided by the contradictions to be found in the Bible in the characterization of Moses." All of the ambiguities and inconsistencies of the biblical text amounted to proof in Freud's eyes that two very different men were being depicted: "[Moses] is often enough described as masterful, hot-tempered, even violent, and yet it is also said of him that he was the most patient and 'meek' of all men," explained Freud, who suggested that "tradition or legend [made] the two people into one."[39] So Freud concluded that "the Egyptian Moses . . . had never heard the name of [Yahweh], whereas the Midianite Moses never set foot in Egypt and knew nothing of Aton."[40]

Freud's speculations about the murder of Moses have come to be regarded as the excesses of an otherwise gifted mind. "That a scholar of so much importance in his own field as Sigmund Freud could permit himself to issue so unscientific a work, based on groundless hypotheses," huffs Martin Buber, "is regrettable."[41] Indeed, the founder of psychoanalysis appeared to suffer from something of a Moses complex, as Freud himself might have put it—he explicitly compared himself to Moses and regarded Jung as his own Joshua, at least until the two men fell out. On holidays in Rome, he would always make what he called a pilgrimage to Michelangelo's statue of Moses: "I stood daily in the church in front of the statue, studied it, measured it, drew it. . . ."[42] Even Freud called the notion of a second Moses "wholly my invention," and he briefly considered disclaiming the dubious scholarship of *Moses and Monotheism* with the subtitle "A Historical Novel."[43]

But even if Freud was wholly wrong, even if Moses managed to survive the muttered threats of his own followers, he lived in fear of them throughout the wanderings of the Exodus. The Bible, for example, reports that the Israelites were ready to rise up again when they reached the next stopping-place at Rephidim and found no water to drink.

"WHAT SHALL I DO WITH THIS PEOPLE?"

"Why did you bring us up from Egypt," the mob shouted at Moses yet again, "to kill us and our children and livestock with thirst?"

"Why do you quarrel with me?" retorted Moses in exasperation. "Why do you try the Lord?" And he addressed a shrill plea of his own to Yahweh: "What shall I do with this people? They are almost ready to stone me." (Exod. 17:2–4)[44]

God whispered a reassuring promise to Moses in his moment of terror, instructing him to gather a few of the elders, pick up his trusty staff, and trek out to the same mountain on which God first recruited a reluctant Moses.

> Behold, I will stand before thee upon the rock in Horeb, and thou shalt smite the rock, and there shall come water out of it, that the people may drink. (Exod. 17:6)

Moses did as he was told. A fountain of fresh water spouted from the dry rock at the first blow of his staff, and the Israelites quenched their thirst. Yahweh, too, watched from his perch atop the rock, although the Bible suggests that God was invisible to everyone, perhaps even to Moses. But the water was palpable enough, and the sullen Israelites were sated yet again. According to the Bible, the Israelites dubbed the place both Massah ("spring of trial") and Meribah ("spring of contention")[45] "because they had quarreled and because they had tried the Lord, saying, 'Is the Lord present among us or not?'" (Exod. 17:7 New JPS) Scholars suggest that the spring was an ancient site where the nomadic tribes traditionally resolved their "disputes at law" by trials, ordeals and other "proofs,"[46] and so the place-names may have predated the traditions that found their way into the Bible. But, in a real and urgent sense, it was Moses no less than God who was on trial before the thirsty mob, and the biblical author reports that Moses feared for his life: "They are almost ready to stone me."

Even the sages, not unlike Freud, were capable of imagining the murder of Moses by the Israelites. "O Lord of the World! I am surely doomed to die," Moses is made to cry out in one of the Midrashic tales inspired by the incidents at the dry water holes. "Thou biddest me not to be offended with them, but if I obey Thy words, I shall certainly be killed by them."

"Try thou to act like Me," God replies, "as I return good for evil, so do thou return to them good for evil, and forgive their trespass; go on before the people, and We shall see who dares touch thee."[47]

God would not always be so easygoing. The Bible will later disclose yet another incident of near-rebellion by the Israelites over the lack of water, yet another plea by Moses to Yahweh for divine rescue, yet another miracle in which water was drawn from a dry rock with a blow from the rod of God. The rabbis imagined that the spring at Massah-Meribah wandered along with the Israelites and showed up again later, but Bible scholars suggest that the matching pair of miracle stories are "doublets." But there is one crucial difference between the two tales: when Moses struck a rock and brought forth water a second time, as we shall see, the mercurial god called Yahweh regarded it as an act of insufferable arrogance and defiance. The miracle of water from the rock at Massah is the first faint augury of the appalling punishment that Moses will be made to suffer, and that's why the question posed by God in the rabbinical tale—"We shall see who dares touch thee"—is stained with cruel irony.

"YAHWEH WILL BE AT WAR"

Among the perils of the wilderness was one that took the form of flesh and blood. The trackless stretches of the Sinai were forbidding but not empty; the nomadic tribes who ranged through the rocky wasteland were quick to set upon any stranger who dared to invade their territory or merely erred in crossing some invisible boundary of rock and sand. As the Israelites idled in their tents at Rephidim, freshly supplied with water and sated with quail and manna, a raiding party of Amalekites rode into sight and set up a war camp.

The Israelites had not yet been called upon to use the weapons they had carried out of Egypt. Now Moses turned to one of his lieutenants—a young man named Joshua, who was destined to succeed Moses as leader of the Israelites and whom we now meet for the first time in the biblical account[48]—and issued a sharp command that must have taken all of them aback.

"Choose us out men, and go out—fight with Amalek," Moses barked. "Tomorrow I will stand on the top of the hill with the rod of God in my hand." (Exod. 17:9)[49]

The next morning, Joshua rallied his troops and marched out of camp while Moses ascended to the peak of a hill overlooking the ground where the Israelites and the Amalekites would meet each other in battle. With him were Aaron and another elder of the Israelites named Hur, and all three of these old men watched as the soldiers of Israel, all of them former slaves, raised their weapons and closed with the Amalekites. First the Israelites and then the Amalekites enjoyed a brief advantage in the fighting, and Moses soon noticed a curious cause-and-effect relationship between the course of battle and the position of his hand.

And it came to pass, when Moses held up his hand, that Israel prevailed, and when he let down his hand, Amalek prevailed. (Exod. 17:11)

So it went, hour upon hour, and Moses struggled to keep both his hands held high as a signal to the warriors. But he was a man in his eighties, and he grew weary at the effort of standing for so long with upraised arms. Aaron and Hur noticed the way his arms would sink despite his grim effort to keep them up. The two of them searched out a nearby stone and rolled it to the top of the hill so Moses would have a place to sit, and they stood on either side of the old man and supported his arms in the gesture that seemed to stir the Israelites to victory.

Thus his hands remained steady until the sun set, and Joshua overwhelmed the people of Amalek with the sword. (Exod. 17:12–13 New JPS)

Something remarkable but often overlooked happened at Rephidim: the Israelites formed themselves into disciplined battalions, closed with a fierce enemy in pitched battle, and held the line without breaking and running. The burden of fighting the enemies of Israel had been delegated by God to humankind, and holy war now became a human enterprise. Indeed, as Brevard Childs observes, the biblical text that describes the victory over the Amalekites "became one of Augustine's warrants by which to defend the theory of the 'just war.' "[50] The desert wilderness "in which Moses kept the Jews wandering until he had made a fighting people of them," Robert Graves writes of the Sinai in his biography of "Lawrence of Arabia,"[51] became the anvil on which a nation of slaves was hammered into sovereignty. A profoundly new kind of liberation had taken place: the slaves had become warriors, and the warriors had won their first battle. Many more battles would be fought before they claimed the prize that Yahweh had promised them, but none of them would ever forget the day the sword of Israel was first blooded.

"Write this for a memorial in the book, and read it aloud to Joshua," an exultant Yahweh told Moses, thus affirming the authorship of at least a fragment of the Five Books of Moses by Moses himself,[52] "for I will utterly blot out the remembrance of Amalek from under heaven." (Exod. 17:14)[53]

AMALEK

The Amalekites were only the first of a great many adversaries whom the Israelites would face in battle, sometimes in victory and sometimes in defeat, over the next several hundred years of biblical history. "[A] wild tribe of Bedouins" is how Martin Buber describes them,[54] and more recent scholarship suggests that they were a confederation of nomadic tribes who ranged through the Sinai.[55] Among all the enemies of Israel over its long history, however, the Amalekites are remembered—and condemned—with unique fervor in the Bible itself and throughout Jewish tradition.

The Bible does not reveal the atrocities that inspired such fear and loathing, but the rabbis managed to imagine a few. According to one rabbinical tale, the Amalekites reveal to Pharaoh that the three-day trek into the wilderness is only a ruse, thus provoking the angry monarch into pursuing them.[56] And according to another tale, the Amalekites play an especially cruel and dastardly trick on the Israelites during the battle at Rephidim. Somehow the Amalekites have gotten their hands on a roster of slaves from the archives of imperial Egypt— every brick fashioned by an Israelite slave has been marked with the name of its maker, and the scribes of Pharaoh have gone to the trouble of carefully noting the output of each man. So the Amalekites are able to lure the soldiers of Israel out of the safety of their camp by addressing

each one by name with "kindly" words. "Those who answered the enticing call found certain death at his hands, and not only did Amalek kill
them, but he also mutilated their corpses by cutting off a certain part of
the body, and throwing it toward heaven with the mocking words, 'Here
shalt Thou have what Thou desirest.' " Clearly, a "certain part" was the
male sexual organ: "In this way did he jeer at the token of the Abrahamic covenant."[57] Joshua, by contrast, was praised in the same story
because he "did not repay like with like" at this moment of victory, and,
instead, treated the enemy "humanely"—that is, he contented himself
with lopping off their heads with a sharp sword, "an execution that does
not dishonor."[58]

An intriguing passage in the Book of Deuteronomy suggests that
the Israelites may have skirmished with the Amalekites on an earlier occasion and suffered a treacherous and humiliating defeat at their
hands.[59] "Remember what the Amalekites did to you on your way out of
Egypt," Moses recalled during the long farewell speech that constitutes
the Book of Deuteronomy, "how they met you on the road when you
were faint and weary and cut off your rear, which was lagging behind exhausted." (Deut. 25:17–18 NEB) The matter-of-fact account suggests
that the Amalekites rode up from behind and slaughtered the strag-
glers while the main force of the Israelites marched on—"a common
practice in desert warfare," according to Auerbach, and one that "no
doubt frequently happened elsewhere."[60] But it was enough to prompt a
blood feud that apparently spanned several centuries of biblical history.
"The failure to spare the weak and defenseless was an act of barbarism
and provided for Israel's continued hatred," offers Brevard Childs, who
points out that God later ordered Saul to exterminate the Amalekites—
"men and women, children and babes in arms, herds and flocks, and
camels and asses"—in specific retaliation "for what they did to Israel,
how they attacked them on their way up from Egypt." (1 Sam. 15:2–3
NEB)[61]

"It shall be, when the Lord thy God hath given thee rest from all
thine enemies round about, in the land which the Lord thy God giveth
thee for an inheritance to possess it, thou shalt blot out the remembrance of Amalek from under heaven," Moses will tell the Israelites on
the eve of his own death. "Thou shalt not forget." (Deut. 25:19)[62]

By contrast, Sir Flinders Petrie, a storied British archaeologist of the
early twentieth century who conducted excavations throughout the
Near East, speculated that the Amalekites were merely a local tribe of

Bedouins who were defending their own territory, especially the oasis around which they lived, from the throng of strangers who appeared one day from out of the wilderness and helped themselves to the precious springs.[63] So it is possible to regard the Israelites as aggressors in the battle of Rephidim rather than the victims of aggression, an invading army that expelled the Amalekites from their tribal lands by force of arms, satisfied their own need for water, and then moved on.[64] Indeed, as we shall see, God approved even more brutal treatment of the Midianites during the march through the wilderness. And Moses, who had been so timid about undertaking his commission in the first place, conducted the Sinai campaign with real passion once he had been blooded in battle against Amalek.

So memorable was the victory over the Amalekites at Rephidim that Moses paused to build an altar called Adonai-nissi, "The Lord is my banner."[65] (Exod. 17:15) But Moses predicted that the Amalekites, whether literally or metaphorically or both, were not yet utterly defeated. "The hand upon the throne of Yahweh," he recited in what may have been a ritual incantation or a cry of war. "Yahweh will have war with Amalek from generation to generation." (Exod. 15–16)[66] For that reason, "Amalek" became a kind of catchphrase in Jewish tradition across the centuries for whatever oppressor was currently spilling Jewish blood, from the Romans during the Hadrianic persecution to the Nazis during the Holocaust. "So long as the seed of Amalek exist, the face of God is covered," as the rabbis put it, "and will only come to view when the seed of Amalek shall have been entirely exterminated."[67]

JETHRO

Word of what had happened to the Israelites in the Sinai reached all the way to the land of Midian, perhaps from the surviving Amalekites or witnesses to the battle, thus illustrating how a seemingly empty wilderness fairly buzzed with gossip. One man who listened with special interest was Jethro, the father-in-law of Moses, who was moved to a grudging admiration of the stranger whom he had once sheltered as a fugitive. "Jethro heard of all that God had done for Moses, and for Israel His People, how that Yahweh had brought Israel out of Egypt." (Exod. 18:1)[68] And so Jethro decided to trek out into the wilderness of Sinai in search of Moses.

Along with Jethro came Zipporah and her two sons, Gershom and Eliezer. When we last encountered Zipporah, she was in the company of Moses and one or both of their sons* on the way out of Egypt.[69] Nowhere does the Bible reveal exactly when, how, or why they had returned to Midian. In fact, the text of Exodus 18 conflates two versions of the same story: the Elohist suggested that Zipporah had returned to her father's household while the Yahwist suggested that Zipporah had been with Moses all along; the Elohist referred to two sons but the Yahwist knew only one.[70] A later biblical author tried to resolve the conflict by explaining that Moses "had sent her away" to his father-in-law at some point in the past, and now Jethro went to the trouble of bringing Zipporah and her sons to rejoin Moses in the wilderness (Exod. 18:2). To remind us of the long, strange trip that brought Moses to the reunion with his family in the Sinai, the biblical author paused to reflect on the meanings assigned to the names of his sons: Gershom ("stranger") harks back to the lonely exile of Moses in Midian, where he had been "a stranger in a strange land"; Eliezer ("God helps")[71] signifies that "the God of my father was my help, and delivered me from the sword of Pharaoh." (Exod. 18:3–4)

Strangely enough, Moses did not bother to greet Zipporah, the woman who had once saved his life by courageously standing up to Yahweh during the night attack on the road from Midian to Egypt, or his two sons, one of whom figured so crucially in the ritual of blood magic that Zipporah performed on that fearful night. If Moses felt any affection for his little family, the biblical author does not deem it worthy of mention, and nothing more is seen or heard of them after the reunion in Sinai. Later, as we shall see, Miriam complained bitterly about the wife of Moses without letting on whether it was Zipporah or some other spouse to whom she referred. But neither the Bible nor the rabbinical literature suggests that Moses enjoyed the company of Zipporah or *any* woman once he had sired a couple of sons back in Midian. "Ever since he has chosen to receive Divine revelation," Zipporah complains to her

---

*The Bible suggests but does not state outright that both Gershom and Eliezer accompanied Moses and Zipporah to Egypt, although only one son is mentioned in the account of the night attack in Exodus 4:24–26. The biblical text does not name the son who underwent an emergency circumcision by Zipporah, and as we have seen, rabbinical tradition is divided on whether it was Gershom or Eliezer.

sister-in-law Miriam in a tale told by the rabbis, "he no longer knows his wife."[72]

If so, Moses was unique among the famous men of the Hebrew Bible in practicing celibacy—David's carnal appetites were sometimes perverse and always insatiable, Solomon was barely content with the favors of a thousand wives and concubines, and the other kings of Israel were not shy about supplying themselves with the comforts of a harem. Even Hosea, so quick to scold his fellow Israelites for their excesses, took a whore to wife, if only to make an ironic point about their promiscuity. But Moses was apparently too old or too fatigued by the duties of leadership or too distracted by his demanding relationship with Yahweh to show much interest in sex.

A profoundly mystical explanation for his abstinence was offered by the sages, who did not fail to notice that Moses was not much interested in physical pleasure. They harked back to the scene on Mount Horeb where Moses was commanded by Yahweh to take off his shoes, a gesture that signified "the desire of God that he cut asunder every bond uniting him with earthly concerns," as the rabbis explained. "[H]e was even to give up his conjugal life." Alarmed at the notion of a monastic Moses, the angel Michael dares to express his concerns to God: "O Lord of the world, how can it be Thy purpose to destroy mankind? Blessing can prevail only if male and female are united." But God sternly decrees that the only conjugal partner whom Moses will enjoy from now on is the Shekhinah, a queenly figure of Jewish mystical tradition. Moses displays a possessiveness toward the Shekhinah that is almost husbandly, cherishing the wish "that the Shekhinah might dwell with Israel" to the exclusion of the other nations of the world.[73] Yet the notion of an intimate bond between Moses and the Shekhinah is far more unsettling than mere celibacy since it suggests that Moses would enter into some kind of divine intercourse with a figure who was regarded as the consort of God or perhaps even God himself in a feminine manifestation.

"Moses has begot children, he has done his duty toward the world," God scolds Michael. "I desire him to unite himself now with the Shekhinah, that she may descend upon earth for his sake."[74]

If Moses was indifferent toward Zipporah and his sons at the moment of reunion, however, he made a great show of respect and deference, perhaps even a display of real affection, for Jethro. "And Moses went out to meet his father-in-law, and bowed down and kissed him."

The two men exchanged a few pleasantries—"They asked each other of their welfare" (Exod. 18:7)—and then Moses ushered the old priest of Midian into his tent for a private conversation that he did not want to be overheard by his wife and children, the tribal elders, or even his trusted lieutenants.

MOSES AND HIS MENTOR

What did Moses say to Jethro in the privacy of his tent? The Bible suggest that Moses was eager to convince Jethro that the tribal deity of the Israelites was as powerful as the gods of Midian and perhaps even more powerful.

> And Moses told his father-in-law all that Yahweh had done unto Pharaoh and to the Egyptians for Israel's sake, all the travail that had come upon them by the way, and how the Lord delivered them. And Jethro rejoiced for the goodness which Yahweh had done to Israel. (Exod. 18:8–9)[75]

Notably, Moses did not try to convince Jethro that Yahweh was the one and only God, whether out of delicacy and diplomacy in dealing with his pagan father-in-law or simply because Moses, too, regarded Yahweh as merely one god among many. "Blessed be Yahweh," the old pagan said at last. "Now I know that Yahweh is the greatest of all gods, because he has delivered the people from the power of the Egyptians who dealt so arrogantly with them." (Exod. 18:8–11 NEB)[76] Devout Bible commentators warn against "misunderstand[ing] the Old Testament idiom by being too literal," but John Calvin was not alone in concluding that Jethro's words "smacked of polytheism."[77]

The Bible does not disclose what else was said during the tête-à-tête, and something crucial appears to be missing from the text. For we are next told that it was Jethro, the priest of Midian, not Moses, the chosen emissary of Yahweh, or Aaron, the high priest of Israel, who performed the Bible's first recorded ritual of sacrifice to Yahweh in the wilderness of Sinai. When the knife was wielded on the sacrificial beast, when blood was spilled on the altar, when flesh was burned as an offering to Yahweh, it was a pagan who presided over the sacred event. Indeed, Moses is not mentioned at all.

And Jethro, Moses' father-in-law, took a burnt-offering and sacrifices for God, and Aaron came, and all the elders of Israel, to
eat bread with Moses' father-in-law before God. (Exod. 18:12)

The conventional explanation for Jethro's curious role—and the
one embraced over centuries of rabbinical commentary—is that Jethro,
impressed by what God had done for his Chosen People, was inspired to
embrace the faith of Israel.[78] According to the Midrash, Jethro recognizes the primacy of God long before he meets Moses and thus is already
regarded as an apostate by his own people. Jethro's apostasy, the rabbis
suggested, explains why he is forced to put his own daughters to work in
caring for the flocks and why his daughters are abused by the shepherds
at the well of Midian.[79]

The rabbis were even willing to honor Jethro above Moses as the
initiator of the sacrifice to God: "In truth," goes one tale, "it reflects
shame upon Moses and the sixty myriads of Jews that they had not
given thanks to God for the release from Egypt, until Jethro came and
did so."[80] Even so, the old priest of Midian did not actually conduct the
sacrifice to the god of Israel, but merely " 'fetches' it or has it fetched,"
Martin Buber insists. "And the reason why Moses is not mentioned is—
as rabbinical exegesis recognized—very simply that the spot where the
sacrifice is brought 'before God' lies at the entrance to the leader's tent,
to which Moses had led his father-in-law, and which Aaron and the elders now enter as well."[81]

A more worldly reading of the same text suggests that the encounter between Moses and Jethro was a moment of high diplomacy,
the formal greeting of a potentate by "a political fugitive taking refuge
in a foreign country and under the protection of a 'national' leader."[82]
In the scene in which Moses warmly hails his father-in-law but mentions nothing of his wife or children, the strict protocol of the desert
tribes may have dictated the form of greeting, elevating Jethro to the
position of honor and relegating his daughter to a secondary role. Indeed, some scholars speculate that the realpolitik of the ancient Near
East explains the relationship between Jethro and Moses, two tribal
leaders who were mindful of the threat that Egypt represented to both of
them and who found a way to live in peace with each other in the Sinai
and the land of Canaan. Perhaps the tribes had entered into a strategic
alliance, and the two chieftains had sealed the treaty with that most
ancient of diplomatic rituals—marriage. The sacrifice to Yahweh for

which Jethro generously provided the livestock may have been nothing more than a courtesy extended by a political leader to his ally.

But there is a third and rather less tortured way of looking at the same text. What if it was Moses and the Israelites who had converted to the faith of Midian and the tribe called the Kenites,* and not the other way around? What if the shared ritual of sacrifice described in the Bible was the rite of initiation by which Jethro welcomed Moses and the Israelites into the cult of Yahweh? "Some scholars regard Jethro and his tribe, the Kenites, as the first worshipers of YHWH," observes one commentator, summing up the so-called Kenite (or Midianite) Hypothesis. "Moses is supposed to have learned from his Kenite relatives both the name of the God and the location of his holy mountain. . . ."[83] The site of the sacrifice was "a proper Midianite sanctuary,"[84] and the pleasure that Jethro displayed at hearing what Yahweh had done for the Israelites "gives expression to his proud joy that *his* God, Yahweh, the God of the Kenites, has proved himself mightier than all the other gods," according to Karl Budde,[85] one of the Bible critics who gave the Kenite Hypothesis its "classic formulation."[86] Indeed, an intriguing bit of evidence for just such an argument can be detected in the simple fact that *Aaron's* attendance at the sacrifice is reported but *Moses* is missing.

"There must have been something about Moses which was so objectionable to the later redactor," argues Elias Auerbach, "that he deleted it."[87] And what the redactor found too hot to handle was the suggestion that Jethro, the priest of Midian, "either consecrated Moses a priest or instructed Moses in the offering up of the sacrifice." That the first sacrifice to Yahweh should have been performed by a pagan priest, "which the most ancient account probably related with ingenuous truthfulness, would appear so incredible and shocking to a later writer that he would delete it," Auerbach concludes.[88] The role of Jethro was further obscured by ancient translators of the Bible who rendered the Hebrew word for "priest" *(kohen)* as "chief," thus hiding the fact that Jethro was, above all, a religious rather than a political figure.[89]

The sense of mystery that surrounds Jethro is only heightened by the fact that the Bible itself appears to be so confused about his real identity. As mentioned earlier, the father-in-law of Moses is dubbed

*The father-in-law of Moses is described in the Bible both as a Midianite (Exod. 3:1) and a Kenite (Judg. 1:16, 4:11).

Jethro by the Elohist, but the Yahwist knows him as Hobab and he is called Reuel (Exod. 2:18) in yet another passage that may represent a blending of both J and E.[90] To make the whole matter still more baffling, both Josephus[91] and the translators of the King James Version (Num. 10:29) sometimes know him as "Raguel." A few simple explanations for these ambiguities have been offered. Perhaps Reuel was Jethro's clan name, rather than his personal name, and a slight correction of the Hebrew text would identify the man named Hobab as the brother-in-law or the son-in-law rather than the father-in-law of Moses. According to Julian Morgenstern, who subscribed to a variant of the Midianite Hypothesis, Hobab was the "priest-chieftain" of the Kenites and the brother-in-law of Moses, and "it was from Hobab that Moses must have learned of Yahweh and of the manner of His worship."[92]

At the heart of the mystery of Jethro is a plain and poignant truth that is conveyed in the biblical narrative. Jethro alone befriended Moses at his moment of greatest need; he harbored the fugitive from Pharaoh's justice for forty years; he betrothed his eldest daughter to Moses and welcomed the Israelite into his clan; he joined Moses in the ritual of animal sacrifice by which Yahweh preferred to be worshipped; and he tutored Moses in the art of governing a nomadic tribe on the move through the wilderness. And so it is conceivable that Moses learned something even more arcane from the man who was his patron and protector, his mentor and friend—perhaps Jethro was a sorcerer, too, and Moses his apprentice.

MOSES THE MAGICIAN

Amalek was condemned in Midrashic tradition as a "magician and enchanter"[93]—an accusation freighted with the contempt with which the rabbis and sages regarded sorcery and superstition. The same charge was laid against Pharaoh and his courtiers, who were said to be "adept in magic,"[94] and against Balaam and his sons, Jannes and Jambres, who used "magic contrivances" to slay the angels of heaven at the Red Sea.[95] Alone among the nations of the ancient Near East, the priesthood of ancient Israel displayed an "official hostility" toward the black arts. The Bible itself reflects a "condemnation of diviners as well as of magicians of all kinds" that Bible scholar W. F. Albright calls "characteristically Israelite."[96]

"The faith of the Old Testament carried on this warfare with special bitterness in one direction," observes Gerhard von Rad, "against belief in the spirits of the underworld, against demons and spirits of the dead, against soothsaying and necromancy, against every occult practice of this kind."[97]

"Thou shalt not suffer a witch to live," goes the famous injunction (Exod. 22:17 KJV) in the so-called Mosaic code, a compendium of law that is scattered through the Five Books of Moses and includes stern prohibitions against using "enchantments" and consulting "wizards" and "familiar spirits" as well as against tattooing, body-piercing, and other practices that struck the priests as dangerously close to magic and superstition (Lev. 19:26, 28, 31). The Book of Deuteronomy is clear and comprehensive on the subject: "There shall not be found among you," decreed Moses to the Israelites, "one that useth divination, a soothsayer, or an enchanter, or a sorcerer, or a charmer, or one that consulteth a ghost or a familiar spirit, or a necromancer," all of whom he condemned as "an abomination to the Lord." (Deut. 18:10–11) Even the Third Commandment—"Thou shalt not take the name of the Lord thy God in vain" (Exod. 20:7)—can be understood as a specific injunction against the kind of "name-magic" that is common to all primitive religion.

"Anyone who knows a divine name can make use of the divine power present in the name to effect blessings and curses, adjurations and bewitchings and all kinds of magical undertakings," explains Martin Noth. "[T]he Divine name was revealed for the praise of God and for calling upon him, but it must be protected from possible misuse."[98]

The Bible is harsh on those who defy these prohibitions—Saul forfeited the favor of God, the crown of Israel, and eventually his own life after he dared to prevail upon the witch of Endor to raise the spirit of the prophet Samuel from the dead (1 Sam. 27:6 ff.). Even the study and practice of mysticism were actively discouraged by the rabbis, who decreed that no man could delve into the mysteries of the Kabbalah until he had reached the age of forty. Throughout the long history of Judaism, ritual magic, no matter how soul-stirring, has been rejected in favor of the elaborate and sometimes brittle legalisms that reach their most elaborate expression in the Five Books of Moses.

"That is the religion of Moses," insists Martin Buber, "the man who experienced the futility of magic."[99]

Yet, as we have seen, the Bible is soaked with magic, and never more so than in the life story of Moses. Moses used his shepherd's staff as a magic wand to work signs and wonders in Egypt. Zipporah's defense of Moses against Yahweh's night attack on the road to Egypt can be seen as a grotesque ritual of blood magic, and the same can be said of the smearing of blood on the doorposts of the Israelites to ward off Yahweh on the night of the tenth plague. More paraphernalia of magic is yet to come in the biblical account: Moses, after handing down the commandment against the making of graven images, fashioned a serpent of bronze that supposedly cured the ill effects of snakebite in anyone who looked upon it, and God was regularly consulted by means of the mysterious equipage known as the Urim and Thummim, which were probably designed for obtaining oracles from Yahweh by the casting of lots.

The law of Moses preserves a few rituals that can only be described as the crudest of sympathetic magic. If a woman was suspected of cuckolding her husband, according to one especially bizarre passage in the Book of Numbers, the priest was instructed to write down a series of harrowing curses on a scroll, wash the words off the page and into a vessel filled with holy water and dust from the floor of the Tabernacle, and then make the accused woman drink the strange brew. If the woman was innocent of adultery, the potion would do her no harm. If, however, the woman *was* an adulteress, then the brew would "[bring] out the truth" by causing afflictions that would disfigure the woman and prevent her from bearing children: "Her belly shall distend and her thigh shall sag; and the woman shall become a curse among her people." (Num. 5:27)[100]

So Moses, the ethical monotheist who supposedly purged ancient Israel of superstition, comes across at moments as a "cult magician,"[101] and the Bible preserves a "peculiar duality," as Elias Auerbach puts it, a juxtaposition of "the loftiest and purest ideas" and "remnants of magical witchcraft."[102] Nor does the Bible deny that magicians in service to pagan gods were capable of working wonders—when Aaron turned the rod of God into a serpent, for example, the magicians of Egypt did exactly the same. "Here then is granted the reality of supernatural miracle-working among the 'heathen' which can be achieved through 'secret arts,' i.e., 'magic,'" allows Martin Noth, "and which on occasion can be just the same as the effects produced by the wonderful power of the God of Israel."[103]

The rabbis made a few rather dutiful efforts to explain away the magic that suffuses the biblical text. When the court magicians of Egypt duplicate the first few signs and wonders of the Ten Plagues, it is "only because Moses willed them to do it,"[104] according to one tale. Yet even the rabbis were apparently enchanted by Moses and his undeniably Merlin-like qualities, and their piety was sometimes overwhelmed by a certain childlike sense of wonder; another tale preserved in the rabbinical literature suggests that the sorcerers of Pharaoh's court fail in their efforts to duplicate the plague of lice not because they lack magical powers but only because they bump up against the outer limits of those powers.

"The demons could not aid them, for their power is limited to the production of things larger than a barley grain, and lice are smaller," reasoned the rabbis. "The magicians had to admit, 'This is the finger of God.' "[105]

So a plain reading of the Bible and the pious rabbinical literature presents an image of Moses as "the sorcerer," as one Bible scholar put it, "the healer, the dispenser of oracles, the Faustian magician."[106] And, at certain vivid moments, the manual of priestcraft that is embodied in the Five Books of Moses, with its detailed instructions for ornate but bloody rituals of animal sacrifice, is raw, dark, and primitive, starkly at odds with the lofty ethical teachings that are offered elsewhere in the Bible.

"[W]as not all this sacrifice and ceremonial at bottom only magic and black art," taunted Freud, "such as the old doctrine of Moses had unconditionally condemned?"[107]

At one point during their long trek through the wilderness, for example, the Israelites took up their familiar chorus of complaint. "Wherefore have ye brought us up out of Egypt to die in the wilderness?" they cried to Moses yet again. "For there is no bread, and there is no water." The ungrateful Israelites even spat upon the manna that Yahweh had bestowed upon them: "We loathe this worthless food." (Num. 21:5)[108] So God afflicted the thankless Israelites with a plague of "fiery serpents" whose bite was fatal. Suddenly the Israelites took up a new cry: "We have sinned," they implored, "pray unto the Lord that He take away the serpents from us." (Num. 21:6–7)[109] What Moses did next, at the supposed bidding of Yahweh, was a plain violation of the Second Commandment, which sternly forbids the making of graven images.

And Moses made a serpent of brass, and set it upon the pole; and it came to pass, that if a serpent had bitten any man, when he looked unto the serpent of brass, he lived. (Num. 21:9)

Centuries later, the Bible reports, the serpent of bronze, known as the Nehushtan, had come to be regarded as an object of worship in the Temple at Jerusalem, where it was displayed and venerated along with other paraphernalia of paganism such as the carved wooden poles and standing stones that symbolized the deities of the dreaded Canaanites. The fact that the relic had been crafted by Moses with his own hands must have given it a rare aura of sanctity in ancient Israel, but its sanctity did not prevent the reformer-king Hezekiah from hauling the bronze serpent of Moses out of the Temple and breaking it into pieces in order to prevent the offering of sacrifices to it (2 Kings 18:4). Perhaps it was Hezekiah, not Moses, who ought to be credited with purging the faith of Israel of the magic that so enthralled the Israelites and maybe even Moses himself.*

THE SORCERER AND THE SORCERER'S APPRENTICE

The Bible reports that Moses was raised and educated in the court of Pharaoh, where magic and religion were seen as one and the same thing. Even if Moses fancied himself as one who shunned superstition and sorcery, surely he picked up a few tricks in Egypt, "a country steeped in the art of magic," as Pharaoh was imagined to tell Moses in a tale from the Midrash.[110] Among the many mentors of Moses, however, none was quite so beloved or revered as the old priest of Midian. If we can entertain the notion that Jethro initiated Moses into the worship of the god called Yahweh, we might wonder what *else* Jethro taught his son-in-law during the long years of exile when Moses lived under his protection and tutelage.

Indeed, as we have seen, Jethro comes across as a Merlin-like figure in one tale with a curiously Arthurian twist. Jethro tests every man who

---

*Some scholars trace the Nehushtan all the way back to Egypt and suggest that the Israelites brought it with them into the wilderness. Others argue that the passage in the Book of Numbers that describes the making of the bronze serpent by Moses himself is yet another "pious fraud" that was inserted into the Bible to explain how it came to be found in the Temple at Jerusalem during the reign of Hezekiah. Bible scholar H. H. Rowley suggests that the Nehushtan was a Jebusite icon that was already the object of worship in Jerusalem when David conquered the city several centuries after the events of the Exodus.

courts his daughter by calling upon him to uproot a tree that grows in his garden. Moses succeeds where all the others fail—and Jethro, like Merlin with young Arthur, marks him as a man of destiny.* And perhaps even more intriguingly, the Bible itself plainly depicts a scene in which Jethro offered advice and instruction to Moses in the art of government, if not the art of magic. Significantly, it was the priest of Midian, rather than Yahweh, who taught Moses how to rule the often unruly Israelites and prescribed an elaborate system for imposing the law of Yahweh on his Chosen People.

"Why sittest thou thyself alone, and all the people stand about thee from morning unto evening?" demanded Jethro, who was aghast at the way his son-in-law insisted on judging every trivial controversy among the Israelites. "Thou wilt surely wear away, both thou, and this people that is with thee; for the thing is too heavy for thee; thou art not able to perform it thyself alone." (Exod. 18:14, 17–18)[111]

So Jethro instructed his son-in-law in statecraft. Moses ought to shift some of his burdens of office to trusted subordinates—"able men," as Jethro put it, "such as fear God, men of truth, hating unjust gain." Adapting the conventional command structure of ancient armies, Jethro prescribed the appointment of "rulers of thousands, rulers of hundreds, rulers of fifties, and rulers of ten." The word of Moses would be law—"And thou shalt teach them the statutes and the laws," Jethro told him, "and shalt show them the way wherein they must walk, and the work that they must do" (Exod. 18:19–21)—but the task of administering the law was to be handed over to a many-tiered bureaucracy that must have reminded Moses of the one that served the pharaohs of Egypt. Indeed, the newly minted judges numbered 78,600, if we take at face value the population of Israel at the time of the Exodus as reported in the Bible and apply the formula prescribed by Jethro.[112]

"And let them judge the people at all seasons," Jethro concluded. "Every great matter they shall bring unto thee, but every small matter they shall judge themselves, so shall they make it easier for thee and bear the burden with thee." (Exod. 18:22)[113]

Moses, who had previously taken his instructions solely and directly from Yahweh, now looked to the priest of Midian to reveal what the God of Israel demanded of him. "If thou shalt do this thing, and God command thee so, then thou shalt be able to endure, and all this people

---

*See chapter four.

also shall go to their place in peace," concluded Jethro. "So Moses hear-kened to the voice of his father-in-law, and did all that he had said." And then the old man, his daughter restored to her husband, his son-in-law properly instructed in the arts of government, his work done, packed up and "went his way into his own land." (Exod. 18:23–24, 27) At least according to the Book of Exodus, the "wildly-experienced sheikh and his daring disciple,"[114] as Buber calls Jethro and Moses, parted company for what may have been the last time.

From now on, the only one to whom Moses could turn for advice, instruction, or even just a few moments of friendly conversation was Yahweh. And God would often visit Moses in the days to come, de-scending from heaven for an occasional chat in the privacy of his tent or summoning him to the sacred mountain for more weighty conversa-tions. All of these encounters between God and Moses were supposedly intimate: Yahweh spoke with Moses "face to face," as the Bible puts it, "as a man speaketh unto his friend." (Exod. 33:7–11) Yet Yahweh showed himself to be a cranky and demanding friend, a friend given to sudden fits of anger and abrupt changes of heart, a friend whose rage might turn murderous at any moment. Surely there were moments of loneliness and despair in the days and years ahead when Moses sorely missed Jethro—the warm embrace, the easy smile, the friendly banter, and perhaps, too, the forbidden wisdom that the old sorcerer imparted to him.

Chapter Nine

GOD OF THE MOUNTAIN, GOD OF THE WAY

Perhaps—I wondered, as I watched the priest being clothed, as the incense climbed indolently to the apse, as the chant lifted the spirit high above the rue Daru—perhaps God should be thought of as a spiritual Point of Aries. Insubstantial, without a material presence, but nonetheless our focal point and our security.
—GEOFFREY MOORHOUSE, *THE FEARFUL VOID*

In the third month after departing from Egypt, the Israelites moved out of Rephidim and pitched their tents at the foot of a mountain in the wilderness of Sinai, the same holy mountain where Moses had first encountered Yahweh. Promptly upon their arrival, Moses found himself called by a voice "out of the mountain"—and now Yahweh announced that he was ready to make himself known to the rest of the Israelites. Alone with Moses on the peak of Sinai, Yahweh instructed him to carry back a formal offer to "the house of Jacob."

> Ye have seen what I did unto the Egyptians, and how I bore you on eagles' wings, and brought you unto Myself. Now therefore, if ye will hearken unto My voice, and keep My covenant, then ye shall be Mine own treasure from among all peoples: for all the earth is Mine, and ye shall be unto Me a kingdom of priests, and a holy nation. (Exod. 19:4–6)

So far, everything God had bestowed upon the Israelites had been given freely, but now he wanted something in return: a covenant, a formal contract that obliged the Israelites to obey Yahweh's as-yet-undisclosed law. Nothing in their experience of the restive and unruly

Israelites had quite prepared Moses *or* Yahweh for their answer to God's proposition—the Israelites said yes.

"All the Lord hath spoken," replied the people in a single affirming chorus, "we will do." (Exod. 19:8)

So Moses made his way back up the mountain and reported the surprising affirmation to Yahweh, who promptly issued another set of instructions for his octogenarian emissary to carry down the mountain again.

"Lo, I come unto thee in a thick cloud, that the people may hear when I speak with thee, and may also believe thee forever," he told Moses, who would no longer be forced to rely on magic and miracle to convince the cynical Israelites of his authenticity as the deputy of Yahweh. But first the people were to prepare themselves for the momentous experience of encountering God: "Go unto the people, and sanctify them to-day and to-morrow, and let them wash their garments, and be ready against the third day; for the third day the Lord will come down in the sight of all the people upon Mount Sinai." (Exod. 19: 9–11)

Three days of ritual purification must be completed before God would consent to appear, Moses told the Israelites. Only freshly laundered clothing must be worn on the day of the visitation. "Come not near a woman," Moses sternly admonished the menfolk (Exod. 19:15). A barrier was erected around the base of the holy mountain to hold back the throngs. Only Moses himself was permitted to actually set foot on Sinai to speak with God.

"Take heed to yourselves, that ye go not up into the mount, or touch the border of it; whosoever toucheth the mount shall be surely put to death," warned Moses, and he allowed them to understand that the punishment would be both sudden and mysterious: "No hand shall touch him, but he shall surely be stoned, or shot through; whether it be beast or man, it shall not live." (Exod. 19:12–13)

A sure sense of what makes for good theater was at work in the instructions that Moses passed along to the Israelites under Yahweh's direction: "Be ready against the third day," Moses warned the Israelites (Exod. 19:15), and surely they were filled with both anticipation and fear at the thought of what they might see and hear on that momentous day.

THE THIRD DAY

At dawn on the third day, just as Moses had promised, the camp was suddenly awakened from its slumber by a sudden flurry of "thunders and lightnings" that rumbled and flashed atop the sacred mountain. Then the harsh sound of a ram's horn was heard, plaintive and piercing, a sound so harsh and so penetrating that one almost hears it in his heart rather than his ears, "and all the people that were in the camp trembled." As the Israelites crept out of their tents, they looked up to see that a thick cloud had settled over the sacred mountain, and smoke and fire seemed to rise from the peak of Sinai "as the smoke of a furnace." (Exod. 19:16–18)

Now Moses summoned the people to follow him, and they thronged behind him as he approached the holy mountain. The ground beneath their feet rumbled and roiled, "the whole mountain quaked greatly," so that they must have lurched after Moses with unsteady steps. High above their heads, the clouds above Sinai seemed to burn from within, and a thick column of smoke rose into the sky from the mountaintop— all because Yahweh had descended upon the mountain "in fire." The shriek of the ram's horn, which seemed to come from nowhere and everywhere at once, grew steadily louder until the sound of the trumpet transformed itself into something else, something strange and unearthly. Yahweh, who had kept his distance from his Chosen people for four centuries, was about to make himself heard, not only by Moses but by all of Israel (Exod. 19:18–19).

The Bible is careful to point out that what the Israelites actually perceived were "the thunderings and the lightnings, and the voice of the horn, and the mountain smoking," but even these oblique manifestations of Yahweh were enough to scare the wits out of them: "When they saw it, they trembled, and stood far off." (Exod. 20:15) If they were disappointed at not seeing Yahweh himself with their own eyes, they gave no sign of it; indeed, they begged Moses to act as their go-between.

"Speak thou with us, and we will hear," the Israelites cried to Moses, "but let not God speak with us, lest we die." (Exod. 20:16)

"Fear not, for God is come to prove you," Moses reassured them, "so that the fear of him may remain with you and keep you from sin." (Exod. 20:17–18) Then, as the Israelites waited at a safe distance, Moses disappeared into "the thick darkness where God was," and the unearthly din and clamor reached a sudden climax (Exod. 20:17–18).[1]

"And when the voice of the horn waxed louder and louder," the Bible reports, "Moses spoke, and God answered him by a voice." (Exod. 19:19)

"LEST THEY PERISH"

Yahweh settled himself at the peak of Sinai, concealed from sight by cloud and smoke but plainly audible to the multitude of people who ringed the mountain. Moses presented himself to Yahweh, all ready to carry back the terms of God's covenant to the waiting Israelites, but he was surprised to find a distressed and distracted deity. Rather than getting down to business, Yahweh fussed over the protocol of his visit to Sinai like the moody and mercurial potentate that he truly was.

"Go down, charge the people, lest they break through unto Yahweh to see him, and many of them perish," God said. "And let the priests that come near to Yahweh sanctify themselves, lest Yahweh break forth upon them." (Exod. 19:21)[2]

These cranky words were puzzling to Moses. No priesthood yet existed in Israel, at least according to the biblical account, since Aaron and his sons had not yet been consecrated as priests. Still more perplexing was God's apparent obsession with his own security and sanctity— Yahweh repeatedly threatened to kill anyone who looked upon him or even set foot on the holy mountain while he was in residence there. Moses had to remind Yahweh that the security arrangements for his much ballyhooed appearance on Sinai had already been put into place.

"The people cannot come up to Mount Sinai," Moses gently reminded his omniscient yet somehow forgetful master, "for thou didst charge us, saying: 'Set bounds about the mount, and sanctify it.'" (Exod. 19:23)

"Go, get thee down, and thou shalt come up," God replied, apparently reassured, "thou, and Aaron with thee—"

And then God was seized once again with his concerns about crowd control.

"—but let neither priests nor people force their way up to Yahweh for fear that he may break out against them." (Exod. 19:24 NEB)

Moses descended the mountain yet again to deliver the latest word from Yahweh to the waiting Israelites down below. In fact, the biblical text depicts an elderly Moses as shlepping up and down Sinai no less than three times on that hectic day. But surely Moses took God's latest threat of violence quite seriously; after all, God had once tried to kill him on the road to Egypt, and the all-knowing and all-seeing deity had needed a smear of blood on the houses of the Israelites to remind him not to kill them, too, on the night of the tenth plague. So Moses delivered yet another dire warning to the people, then made it back to the top of the holy mountain in time to hear Yahweh's next words.

God, at long last, was ready to bestow his blessing on the Israelites, but only on the condition that they agree to restrain their unruly impulses and obey the divine law that he was about to reveal to them. The elaborate legal code that Yahweh detailed to Moses, which is scattered in bits and pieces throughout the pages of Exodus, Leviticus, Numbers, and Deuteronomy, bulks up to a total of 613 commandments, according to Jewish tradition. But when Yahweh and Moses finally got down to business on Mount Sinai, God started with only ten.

THE TEN WORDS

"I am the Lord thy God, who brought thee out of the land of Egypt, out of the house of bondage," Yahweh began, reminding Moses of everything he had already done for Israel, and then he began counting off the basic laws that are known to the biblical author by an elegant shorthand phrase, "the ten words" (Exod. 34:28, Deut. 4:13), and to the rest of the world as the Ten Commandments.

"Thou shalt have no other gods before Me," goes the first and most fundamental of the Ten Commandments. And then Yahweh continued: "Thou shalt not make unto thee a graven image"; "Thou shalt not take the name of the Lord thy God in vain"; "Remember the Sabbath day"; "Honour thy father and mother"; "Thou shalt not murder"; "Thou shalt not commit adultery"; "Thou shalt not steal"; "Thou shalt not bear false witness"; and "Thou shalt not covet thy neighbor's house." (Exod. 20:3–14)

Of course, Yahweh elaborated at some length upon a few of "the ten words." The crimes that a human being might commit against the deity were especially important to Yahweh, and he took care to explain them in some detail. The prohibition against graven images, for example, extended to "any manner of likeness" and specifically forbade the making of statues of "any thing that is in heaven above, or that is in the earth beneath, or that is in the water under the earth," all out of fear that the

Israelites would "bow down unto them and serve them"—a well-founded anxiety, as it turned out, since the Bible confirms that the Israelites were quick to succumb to the seductions and corruptions of paganism (Exod. 20:4–5). Here God paused to make it clear that he wasn't kidding by pointedly reminding Moses that he was capable of Godfather-like vengeance.

"For I the Lord thy God am a jealous God, visiting the iniquity of the fathers upon the children unto the third and fourth generation of them that hate Me," Yahweh said of himself, "and showing mercy unto the thousandth generation of them that love Me and keep My commandments." (Exod. 20:5–6)

The Bible is freighted with laws, some exalted and inspiring, some mundane and practical, some exceedingly strange and even downright bizarre; but nothing else has equaled the Ten Commandments for sheer staying power. "The ten pearls" is how the so-called Decalogue is described in the Midrash,[3] and contemporary Bible commentators are no less ardent. "They are the kernel and the soul of Moses' life work," enthuses Elias Auerbach, "the foundation stone of the religion of Israel through which they have become the basic law for the moral development of all mankind."[4]

Some scholars argue that the form of the Ten Commandments—a series of unconditional orders and prohibitions rather than a more elaborate "if-then" legal formula—reveals that they were early and authentic, dating back to the distant era when the Israelites were still a nomadic people.* Even the number of commandments in the Decalogue is thought to be evidence of its primitiveness, "for the Israelite could recite the words of the covenant on his ten fingers."[5] But not every Bible critic shares the traditional enthusiasm for the antiquity and authenticity of the Ten Commandments, and even the simple and enduring moral instruction of the Decalogue cannot be reliably attributed to Moses. In fact, the age and authorship of the Ten Commandments, along with their original and authentic meaning and even their order and number, are still the subject of controversy among Bible scholars.

---

*The Ten Commandments have been described as absolute (or "apodictic") law: "Thou shalt not murder." (Exod. 20:13) Much of the rest of biblical law is conditional: "If one man's ox hurt another's, so that it dieth, then they shall sell the live ox, and divide the price of it." (Exod. 21:35) A Bible scholar named Albrecht Alt argued that apodictic law is characteristically Israelite and thus dates back to the wilderness period, while conditional law is borrowed from the Code of Hammurabi and other sources.

By now we should not be surprised to discover that the Bible contains not one but three versions of the Decalogue. The classic formulation of the Ten Commandments in Exodus 20 is credited to the Elohist, but the Deuteronomist came up with a version of his own (Deut. 5:6–18), and an alternate list of commandments in Exodus 34 is known by Bible scholars as the Yahwistic Decalogue, even though, by some counts, it actually includes *twelve* commandments.[6] Even the familiar version of the Ten Commandments, in referring to Yahweh, shifts abruptly from the first person—"Thou shalt have no other gods before Me" (Exod. 20:3)—to the third person—"Thou shalt not take the name of the Lord thy God in vain" (Exod. 20:7)—a fact that "arouses the suspicion that the beginning of the Decalogue is no longer in its original form."[7] The text of the Ten Commandments is not exactly the same in every version of the Bible; the Masoretic Text, the authoritative version of the Hebrew Bible in Jewish tradition, differs slightly from the text found in the Septuagint, the Greek translation that was used by the authors of the New Testament.[8] Even the numbering of the Ten Commandments is obscure; Jewish tradition starts counting with the phrase "I am the Lord thy God" (Exod. 20:1), but Christian tradition regards "Thou shalt have no other gods before Me" as the First Commandment.*[9]

As simple (perhaps even simplistic) as they may seem, the Ten Commandments probably meant something different to the ancient Israelites than what they mean to us today. "Thou shalt have no other gods before Me," which seems to allow for the existence of more than one god, was not necessarily the credo of strict monotheism that is traditionally attributed to Moses. Yahweh apparently demanded only that the Israelites worship him to the exclusion of other gods and goddesses without giving an opinion on whether or not the rival deities also possess divine powers.[10] Indeed, some scholars argue that strict monotheism—the notion that Yahweh was not merely the exclusive god of Israel but the one and only god in the cosmos—was an innovation of the prophets, not Moses, and thus "the First Commandment was unthinkable before Hosea."[11]

"Thou shalt honor thy father and mother" was originally intended

---

*Because it is more commonly used and thus more familiar, I have followed the numbering system that regards "I am the Lord thy God" as a prologue and "Thou shalt have no other gods before Me" as the First Commandment.

to afford a kind of social security to elderly parents who were commonly "driven out of the home or abused after they could no longer work."[12] "Thou shalt not kill" was not a complete prohibition against the taking of human life; the verb used in the Hebrew text referred specifically to "a type of slaying which called forth blood vengeance." Originally, the commandment applied only to "one who kills out of enmity, deceit, or hatred," according to Brevard Childs, but did not rule out capital punishment or the killing of a soldier in battle.[13] "Thou shalt not steal" was originally directed against the crime of kidnapping or slave-taking rather than theft in general.[14]

Somewhere beneath the surface of its familiar text, the Decalogue may preserve the nomadic ideal that was so stirring to the citified priests who recorded and preserved the sacred writings of the Israelites. Thus, for example, the Tenth Commandment—"Thou shalt not covet thy neighbor's house"—can be seen as a rejection of *all* houses by a tent-dwelling people who cherished the freedom of movement that a house-dweller never knows. "It is the brief expression of the 'desert-ideal,' the tenacious adherence to the forms of nomadic life that alone were considered worthy of men and pleasing to God," writes Elias Auerbach, drawing a familiar analogy between the Israelites of antiquity and the Bedouin of more recent times. "[T]he possession of a solid house draws other evils to it, not only restraint but also possessiveness, proneness to a life of ease, cowardice, relaxation of tribal loyalty, dissolution of pure moral customs."[15]

The same sentiment apparently prompted the prophet Jeremiah, writing in the seventh century B.C.E. and later, to invoke a desert tribe called the Rechabites, who were thought to have descended from Jethro himself, as a challenging moral example to the corrupted city-dwellers of ancient Israel. "Ye shall drink no wine," railed Jeremiah, quoting the words of the desert-dwelling Rechabites, "neither shall ye build house, nor sow seed, nor plant vineyard, nor have any; but all your days ye shall dwell in tents." (Jer. 35:6–7)

So, too, does the Third Commandment—"Thou shalt not take the name of the Lord thy God in vain"—conceal a hidden and long-forgotten meaning behind its deceptively simple text. Some commentators understood it to be a prohibition against swearing falsely under oath, others saw it as a ban on cursing, and one contemporary scholar confessed that he did not know what it meant: "I freely admit that for me the words are not understandable," writes Auerbach. But a faint clue to the real meaning of the commandment can be found in a rabbinical tale in which Moses ascends to heaven from atop Sinai but is prevented from approaching God by the guardian angel Kemuel and his army of twelve thousand angels of destruction who stand at the gates of heaven: Moses destroys his angelic adversary simply by uttering the Name of God.[16] Here, once again, we find Moses, the supposed enemy of superstition and sorcery, invoking the holy name as a magical weapon—and it may have been precisely such name-magic that the Third Commandment was originally intended to prevent.

"Thereby everything 'magical' was banished into the sphere of the unlawful and prohibited," writes Auerbach of the Third Commandment. "That this was possible, that Moses in one of the basic commandments undertook to eradicate this general belief of his time and of the following centuries by forbidding its practice, is an astonishing sign of how far ahead of his time he was in his inner religious development."[17]

Not every Bible critic has been quite so credulous. The pioneering nineteenth century Bible scholar Julius Wellhausen denied that Moses had anything to do with the Ten Commandments, arguing that the Decalogue was no older than the eighth century B.C.E. and embodied the same commitment to social justice that found its fullest expression in the writings of Amos, Isaiah, and Micah.[18] More recent (and more temperate) scholars are willing concede that if anything in the Five Books of Moses* can legitimately be credited to Moses, it is the Decalogue—Auerbach characterizes the Ten Commandments as "the only written document of which it can be said that it goes back directly to Moses."[19] But even Auerbach feels compelled to admit that we cannot know with certainty whether *any* portion of the biblical text comes down to us as it was written or uttered by Moses himself, if only because the text has been left so misshapen—"grotesque" is the word he uses—by the "many hands [that] worked over the oldest, simple narrative."[20]

---

*The first five books of the Hebrew Bible (Genesis, Exodus, Leviticus, Numbers, and Deuteronomy) are known variously as the Five Books of Moses, the Pentateuch ("five scrolls"), and the Torah ("law" or "instruction").

AND TEN THOUSAND MORE

Yahweh did not stop with "the ten words." Once he finished dictating the Decalogue, he proceeded to offer up a wild miscellany of sacred law that continues in fits and starts throughout the Bible. The body of law that God transmitted to Moses on Sinai addresses subjects ranging from the law of divorce to the rules of war and just about everything in between.

According to pious tradition and true belief, all of these 613 commandments—and, indeed, each and every word of the first five books of the Bible—passed directly "from the mouth of God to the hand of Moses," as Jewish congregations recite after the reading of the Torah in the synagogue. Rabbinical tradition holds that the entirety of the sacred law in all of its particulars was miraculously inscribed between the lines of the Ten Commandments on the two tablets of stone that Moses carried down from Sinai, "although the table[t]s were not more than six hands in length and as much in width."[21] At the same time, the traditionalists insist, God gave Moses the so-called Oral Law, a vast compendium of rules and regulations that were first recorded in the Talmud, and the rich accumulation of legend and lore *(haggadah)* that is preserved in both the Talmud and the Midrash, none of which was actually collected and written down by human hands until sometime around and after 500 C.E.

An open-minded reading of the Bible, however, suggests something quite different about its composition. Regardless of its actual authorship, whether human or divine, the Bible is a fantastic patchwork of law, legend, history, politics, propaganda, poetry, prayer, ethics, genealogy, dermatology, hygienic practices, military tactics, dietary advice, and carpentry instructions, among many other things, and the bits and pieces of Holy Writ were composed at different times and places and for different purposes by the various biblical authors and editors. Nowhere are the motives of a biblical author more clearly discernible than in the laws that were supposedly handed down on Sinai, a collection of priestly rules and regulations that were backdated and inserted into the account of the Exodus by a source who lived centuries later.

That is why Yahweh prescribed a punishment for starting a fire that spreads to standing corn even though the people of Israel were still homeless wanderers who tilled no crops of any kind. Taxes and tithes and fines were specified in shekels and other kinds of money at a time when coinage and currency had not yet been invented anywhere in the ancient Near East. Rituals were described for sacrifices to be conducted by a priestly caste in a magnificent temple at a time when no temple had yet been built and no priesthood yet existed.

In fact, Bible scholarship has identified no less than three separate and distinct codes of law embedded in the Five Books of Moses: the Book of the Covenant (Exod. 20.22 ff.), the Holiness Code (Lev. 17.1 ff.), and substantially all of the Book of Deuteronomy. All of these laws are collectively known as the Mosaic code, and yet not one of them likely dates as far back as the supposed era of Moses. They are concerned with the practical problems of a settled community of farmers and city-dwellers in the land of Canaan rather than a nomadic tribe wandering through the wilderness of Sinai. The very form of the covenant that Yahweh supposedly offered to Israel on Sinai bears a striking resemblance to diplomatic treaties of the eighth century B.C.E. by which the rulers of the Hittite and Assyrian empires made peace with the princes and peoples whom they conquered.[22] Even the oldest codes of law probably did not find their way into the Bible until the priests and scribes of ancient Israel fixed the text of the Five Books of Moses in their final form as late as the fourth century B.C.E. For that reason, the Bible has been called "a veritable anthology of Israelite covenant law representing seven hundred years of development, yet all of it is introduced by words such as 'And the LORD said to Moses . . .' "[23]

Some of the laws are famous—and famously misunderstood. "Thou shalt give life for life, eye for eye, tooth for tooth," goes perhaps the most familiar clause of the Mosaic code, "hand for hand, foot for foot, burning for burning, wound for wound, stripe for stripe." (Exod. 21:23–25) The *lex talionis* ("law of retaliation"), as it is called, resembles and may be derived from the celebrated Code of Hammurabi from nearby Mesopotamia. But the biblical version was actually far less harsh in practice than the laws of neighboring civilizations of the ancient Near East because it was not interpreted literally and meant only that punishment should be in proportion to the wrongdoing that was being punished. "Let the punishment fit the crime" is a good way of summing up the moral imperative of the *lex talionis*.

Although much of the sacred law may seem odd and obsolete, many of its clauses are still in full force and effect today among observant Jews. "Thou shalt not seethe a kid in its mother's milk" (Deut. 14:21), a rather obscure passage that might be understood as a moral parable, was the starting point for the elaborate body of law that governs kosher, or "clean," dietary practices and requires Jews to avoid preparing or eating milk and meat products at the same time. The ritual of circumcision (Gen. 17:10), the wearing of fringed prayer shawls (Num. 15:38), the use of phylacteries in prayer (Exod. 13:9), and the affixing of a mezuzah—a small box containing verses from the Torah—on the doorposts of Jewish homes (Deut. 6:9) are all derived from elaborations upon various passages of the Five Books of Moses. "Six days shall work be done; but on the seventh day is a sabbath of solemn rest" (Exod. 31:15), for example, has come to be understood to prohibit a pious Jew from riding in an automobile, turning on a light, carrying money in his or her pocket, or putting pen to paper from sundown to sundown on the Sabbath. To this day, the blessing that Yahweh dictated to Moses for the purpose of consecrating Aaron as the first high priest of Israel is still recited by rabbis over their congregations and parents over their children in Jewish communities throughout the world.

> The Lord bless thee, and keep thee;
> The Lord make His face to shine upon thee, and be gracious unto
> thee;
> The Lord lift up His countenance upon thee, and give thee
> peace.
>
> (Num. 6:24–26)

Some of the most celebrated provisions of the Mosaic code embody an admirable sense of caring and compassion and a fierce commitment to social justice, even if these values are sometimes expressed only obliquely. Slavery is taken for granted as a fact of life, but the conditions of servitude were somewhat softened in biblical law—a man was subject to punishment for beating a slave to death, and a woman who was sold into slavery by her father was to be set free if her master married her and then failed to honor her "conjugal rights." (Exod. 21:7–11, 20) The wages of a hired servant had to be paid before the end of each day of labor (Lev. 19:13), and if a man pledged his cloak as collateral for a loan, the garment had to be returned each night to keep him warm (Exod. 22:25–26). Merchants were held to honest business practices: "Just balances, just weights shall you have." (Lev. 19:36) And just as the Sabbath day was set aside as a day of rest for man and beast, master and slave, the land itself was to be left fallow in the seventh year and the crops were to be left in the field "that the poor of thy people may eat, and what they leave the beast of the field shall eat." (Exod. 23:10–12)

Some of the Mosaic legislation expresses a kind of Bible-era utopianism. A yearlong celebration of freedom was to take place every fiftieth year, the year of the jubilee (Lev. 25:10). Slaves were to be set free en masse. Land and other possessions were to be restored to their original owners. The fields were to be abandoned: "Ye shall not sow, neither reap that which groweth of itself in it, nor gather the grapes in it of the undressed vines." (Lev. 25:11) Charity was a sacred obligation, rather than merely a worthy goal, and any man who "be waxen rich" was ordered to share his wealth with the poor (Lev. 25:26). The arrival of each jubilee was to be announced by the sounding of a horn by which Yahweh commanded the Israelites to "proclaim liberty throughout the land unto all the inhabitants thereof." (Lev. 25:10)

But often even the most compassionate laws were given a sharp and punishing edge by a stern and sometimes bloodthirsty Yahweh. A man who was found gathering firewood in the wilderness on the day of the Sabbath was dragged before Moses and Aaron, and God commanded the entire congregation to stone him to death for his transgression (Num. 15:32–36). So, too, was a rebellious son who failed to properly honor his mother and father subject to the death penalty (Deut. 21:20–21). A man who committed any sin "worthy of death" was to be hung from a tree after execution so that his dangling corpse would be a caution to other potential sinners (Deut. 21:22).

Now and then, the law of Moses reaches a fervor and even a grandeur that fairly thunders with stern morality and yet, at the same time, glows with the sense of social justice that we have come to regard as the essential teaching of the Judeo-Christian tradition. "Ye shall not afflict any widow, or fatherless child," Yahweh declared atop Sinai. "If thou afflict them in any wise—for if they cry at all unto Me, I will surely hear their cry—My wrath shall wax hot, and I will kill you with the sword, and your wives shall be widows and your children fatherless." (Exod. 22:21–23) Paradoxically, the same deity who gave orders for the "ethnic cleansing" of the land of Canaan is also shown to command that the Israelite and the non-Israelite live in peace and harmony with one another.

And if a stranger sojourn with thee in your land, ye shall not do him wrong. The stranger that sojourneth with you shall be unto you as the home-born among you, for ye were strangers in the land of Egypt: I am the Lord your God. (Lev. 19:34)

God moved on from the fundamental ethical concerns of the Ten Commandments to a series of pronouncements that reflect his apparent obsession with the modesty of the priests who would offer sacrifices at the altar of a temple yet to be built—no steps shall lead up to the altar, God took care to decree, lest the worshippers be afforded an opportunity to look up the tunics of the priests and gawk at their "nakedness"! (Exod. 20:23) Indeed, the sheer bulk of ritual law suggests one of the reasons the Bible was written in the first place. The biblical authors who showed such a compelling interest in the fine points of priestcraft, known collectively as the Priestly source, or "P," pressed Moses into service as a mouthpiece to promulgate a code of law that Moses himself would have found bizarre.

GOLD AND SILVER, TONGS AND FLESH-HOOKS

P lingered long and lovingly over the biblical passages that describe the consecration of Aaron and his sons as the first priests of Israel. Ironically, though scholars credit Moses with the intent to replace the opulent paganism of Egypt with something austere, the Bible suggests that the Israelites emulated and perhaps even exceeded the worst excesses of ritual and adornment. Thus, long and rather tedious passages of the Bible are devoted to an inventory of the sacred objects that the Israelites were ordered to make—an altar of gold, lamps and candlesticks, snuff dishes and fire pans, tongs and flesh-hooks, pans and bowls, bells and curtains and veils, and priestly vestments laden with precious ornaments. The materials to be used in the making of the priestly paraphernalia were rare and costly: "Gold and silver, and brass; and blue, and purple, and scarlet, and fine linen, and goats' hair; and rams' skins dyed red, and sealskins, and acacia-wood; oil for the light, spices for the anointing oil, and for the sweet incense; onyx stones and stones to be set for the ephod and the breastplate." (Exod. 25:3–7) Even the fine points of carpentry were described in meticulous detail: "According to all that I show thee," God said, "the pattern of the tabernacle, and the pattern of the furniture thereof, even so shall ye make it." (Exod. 25:9)

Some of the most sacred objects demanded by God on Sinai, however, remain obscure despite (or because of) the lengthy descriptions in the biblical text. For example, the Bible frequently refers to something called an "ephod," but we still do not know with certainty what it was or how it was used. The first time an ephod is mentioned by Yahweh, it is described as an elaborate outer garment to be worn by the high priest, first Aaron and then his successors, so that he "may minister unto Me in the priest's office." (Exod. 28:3) The ephod was embellished with two onyx stones on which the names of the tribes had been engraved, and a breastplate was set with more precious stones—carnelian, topaz, carbuncle, sapphire, emerald, jacinth, agate, amethyst, beryl, onyx, jasper, all enclosed in pure gold. (Exod. 28:17–20)

Elsewhere in the Bible, however, we are given the impression that the ephod is "a small piece of cloth, apparently girded about the waist, serving as a kind of apron, and really leaving the wearer practically naked, worn by priests or persons functioning as priests."[24] So abbreviated was the ephod worn by King David during the ritual procession that brought the Ark to Jerusalem that he inadvertently exposed himself to the crowd as he danced in a spiritual frenzy—an indiscretion that led to considerable marital discord back at the palace (2 Sam. 6:23). And the same term is used yet elsewhere in the Bible to identify *something* fashioned out of precious metal (Judg. 8:27), perhaps an idol of gold or silver, a housing in which to store and display an idol, or some other "cult-object" that symbolized authority and could be used to consult with Yahweh to obtain oracles.[25] (1 Sam. 14:3, 18, 20).

The kind of ephod worn by the high priest included a place for storing something known as the Urim and Thummim, a pair of profoundly mysterious objects even more baffling to contemporary scholarship. As best we can make out, the Urim and Thummim were somehow used by the priest to communicate with God and obtain his advice and direction (or "oracle") on important questions, although "Yes," "No," and "No Comment" were probably the only available answers. Some scholars suspect that they were inscribed with holy words and used for divination by the casting of lots, although "just what was cast, whether an arrow with a peculiar marking or a lot of some other kind, is far from certain."[26] What *is* certain, however, is that the Urim and Thummim were yet another example of the ritual magic that persisted in ancient Israel long after Moses supposedly purged the faith of such faintly paganistic practices.

By far the most sacred and revered objects described in the Mosaic code are the Ark of the Covenant, a box in which the tablets of the law were to be stored and carried, and the Tabernacle, a "dwelling-place" where Yahweh sojourned on his visits to his people and the place where the Ark and other sacred objects were to be kept. The Ark is depicted in the Bible as a richly decorated chest fashioned of acacia-wood, covered in gold, and surmounted by two graven images of cherubim, not the plump little angels of Renaissance art and contemporary Christmas cards, but grotesque creatures with human heads, the bodies of four-legged beasts, and outstretched wings.[27] But the Ark was not merely a container for transporting the stone tablets from place to place; it was thought to be the throne of Yahweh, although, "as far as the human eye could tell, it was an *empty* throne upon which Yahweh was invisibly present."[28] More precisely, the extended wings of the gilded cherubim atop the Ark were the seat of Yahweh—"the mercy seat," as it was known—and the Ark itself was his footstool.[29]

> And when Moses went into the tent of meeting that He might speak with him, then he heard the Voice speaking unto him from above the ark-cover that was upon the ark of the testimony, from between the two cherubim, and He spoke unto him. (Num. 7:89)

The Ark was fitted with rings and poles that allowed the Israelites to carry it with them through the wilderness, and they imagined that God rode along with them atop the mercy seat. "Rise up, O Lord, and let Thine enemies be scattered," Moses cried to the invisible Yahweh each time the Ark was lifted up for another day of marching, as if to invite God to bestir himself from his sedan chair and drive away any adversary whom his Chosen People might encounter on the way. And when the Ark was lowered to the ground at the end of the day, Moses invited God to seat himself once again: "Return, O Lord, unto the ten thousands of the families of Israel." (Num. 10:35–36)

Some thoroughly practical concerns can be discerned through the veil of ritual that is spun out in the revelation on Sinai. The rites that Moses was ordered to perform were intended to strike both fear and awe into the hearts of the Israelites while, at the same time, elevating Aaron and his sons to positions of unchallenged authority and providing them with a comfortable livelihood. The Priestly source, who is credited with these passages, was clearly concerned with justifying and assuring the privileges and prerogatives of his own caste.

"Thou shalt kill the ram, and take of its blood, and put it upon the tip of the right ear of Aaron, and upon the tip of the right ear of his sons, and upon the thumb of their right hand, and upon the great toe of their right foot, and dash the blood against the altar round about," goes one of the lengthy instructions for the consecration of Aaron and his progeny (Exod. 28:20). The garments that they are to wear are described in loving detail: "Tell all the craftsmen whom I have endowed with skill to make the vestments," God ordered Moses, "a breast-piece, an ephod, a mantle, a chequered tunic, a turban and a sash." (Exod. 28:3–4) Even their most basic needs were not ignored in the elaborate rituals of sacrifice that are prescribed in the Bible: the blood of the firstlings, oxen and sheep and goats, was to be splashed on the altar, the fat was to be burned in the fire, but the savory roasted meats and the aromatic loaves of fresh-baked bread were to be put aside for the sustenance of the priesthood, "all the best of the oil, and all the best of the wine, and of the corn, the firstfruits which are given to the Lord," and everyone in the priestly household who was ritually pure was permitted to enjoy the bounty (Num. 18:12–13, 18).[30]

"I, the Lord, commit to your control the contributions made to me, that is all the holy-gifts of the Israelites," God was made to say to Aaron by the Priestly source. "I give them to you and to your sons for your allotted portion due to you in perpetuity." (Num. 18:8 NEB)

Indeed, the real motive of the Priestly source is disclosed when God announced the special calling of Aaron and his brood. "And bring thou near unto thee Aaron thy brother, and his sons with him, from among the children of Israel" God told Moses, "and thou shalt anoint them, and consecrate them, and sanctify them, that they may minister unto Me in the priest's office." (Exod. 28:1, 41) Here is a fateful moment in the history of Israel and a very revealing clue to the authorship of the Bible—the high priesthood is bestowed not only upon Aaron himself, not only upon his sons, but upon "his seed after him." (Exod. 28:1, 41, 43) The priestly dynasty that claimed descent by blood from Aaron included P and the Deuteronomist, and the text that they contributed to the Bible betrays their urgent concern for preserving their own power and position in the hothouse of court and temple politics that was ancient Israel.

"I KNOW THEE BY NAME"

After listening to Yahweh dictate the first set of laws, Moses trudged back down the mountain and recited "all of the words of the Lord, and all of the ordinances," and the people once again assented to the covenant that God had offered them. "All the words which the Lord hath spoken," they said a second time, "will we do." (Exod. 24:3) An elaborate blood ritual sealed the covenant between God and Israel. "Moses wrote all the words of the Lord," the Bible reports, and then he built an altar at the foot of Sinai, an arrangement of twelve pillars that represented each of the twelve tribes of Israel. He summoned a corps of young men and set them to the task of sacrificing "burnt-offerings" and "peace-offerings" to Yahweh, a ritual that required them to slaughter the sacrificial animals and collect the blood that spilled from their severed necks (Exod. 24:4–6).

"And Moses took half of the blood, and put it in basins, and half of the blood he dashed against the altar." Then he picked up the scroll on which he had written down the sacred law, and again read "the book of the covenant" out loud to the gathered tribes, as if to make sure they understood exactly what was required of them. For a third time, they agreed to submit to God's terms: "All that the Lord hath spoken will we do, and obey." (Exod. 24:7) Finally, Moses solemnly sprinkled the gathered multitude with blood: "Behold the blood of the covenant, which the Lord hath made with you in agreement with all these words." (Exod. 24:6–8)

Now Yahweh summoned Moses to a feast to celebrate the sealing of the covenant. Aaron was invited, too, and so were two of his sons, Nadab and Abihu, and seventy of the elders of Israel (Exod. 24:1). Although Yahweh had repeatedly threatened to kill anyone who dared to set foot on the sacred mountain other than Moses himself—"for man shall not see Me and live," as God liked to remind Moses (Exod. 33:20)—the guests at the dinner party on the slopes of the Sinai were permitted a glimpse of their elusive God:

And they saw the God of Israel, and there was under His feet the like of a paved work of sapphire stone, and the like of the very heaven for clearness. And upon the nobles of the children of Israel He laid not His hand; and they beheld God, and did eat and drink. (Exod. 24:10–11)

What the elders saw, as best as we can make out from this phantas-magoria, were the feet of Yahweh planted firmly on paving stones of pure sapphire. The rest of the Israelites had to content themselves with less intimate manifestations of God—the pillars of fire and cloud, the thunder and lightning above Sinai, the trumpeting voice of Yahweh that sounded from atop the holy mountain. Moses alone would be permitted to see God "face to face, as a man speaketh unto his friend" (Exod. 33:11)—and live. And yet it is not clear exactly what Moses saw when he looked upon Yahweh.

Frustrated at God's game of hide-and-seek, Moses finally demanded an opportunity to see what God looked like once and for all.

> Thou hast said: I know thee by name and thou hast also found grace in My sight. Now therefore, I pray Thee, if I have found grace in Thy sight, show me now Thy ways, that I may know Thee— show me, I pray Thee, Thy glory. (Exod. 33:12–17)[31]

God was quick to reassure Moses of his warm and caring feelings— "My presence shall go with thee," said Yahweh in a moment of tenderness, "and I will give thee rest" (Exod. 33:14)—but there were limits to his largesse. "Thou canst not see My face," said God to Moses, "for man shall not see Me and live." Why an all-powerful deity could not do what he wanted to do is not explained, here or elsewhere in the Bible, but Yahweh came up with an elaborate compromise.

> Behold, there is a place by Me, and thou shalt stand upon the rock. And it shall come to pass, while My glory passeth by, that I will put thee in a cleft of the rock, and will cover thee with My hand until I have passed by. And I will take away My hand, and thou shalt see My back; but My face shall not be seen. (Exod. 33:17–23)

God's display of his backside, of course, squarely contradicts the biblical text that depicts God and Moses speaking "face to face" (Exod. 33:11) and even "mouth to mouth" (Num. 12:8). Renaissance art rendered the scene quite literally—Moses sees the back of an old man's head, draped in silver-gray locks and framed in a shimmering gold halo—but the scene can be understood in rather less subtle ways. For example, the Hebrew word used in the text to describe the physical appearance of God and conventionally rendered as "glory" (*kavod*) also means "liver" and is sometimes used idiomatically to refer to the male reproductive organ. "The fact that the Lord wants to be seen only from behind," explains Jack Miles in *God: A Biography*, "may suggest that he is concealing his genitalia from Moses."[32]

Of course, the rabbis, who dared not entertain the notion that God *had* genitalia, imagined that God is rather coy about showing himself to Moses. "When I revealed Myself to thee in the burning bush, thou didst not want to look upon Me," God says to Moses in one rabbinical tale, "now thou art willing, but I am not."[33] So profoundly forbidden is the sight of God that even the angelic hosts are not permitted to gaze upon him. So when God reveals himself to Moses for a brief moment, the angels are so jealous of Moses—"he, who is born of woman"—that they conspire to murder him. And they would have succeeded "had not God's hand protected him."[34]

When it comes to the nagging question of what God looks like, the Bible leaves us with a profound and persistent mystery—and that is doubtless what its authors intended. The essential revelation of Moses seems to have been that God detested images because he was imageless. All of the manifestations described in the Bible were metaphors and nothing more. Thus, for example, the sight of God's feet on sapphire-blue paving stones meant simply that the view from the heights of Sinai was sublimely and even divinely beautiful: "The sapphire proximity of the heavens," Martin Buber writes, "overwhelms the aged shepherds of the Delta, who have never before tasted, who have never been given even the slightest idea, of what is shown in the play of early light over the summits of the mountains."[35] Plainly, the authors of the Bible did not really know what Moses saw when he beheld God "face to face," apparently did not care to know, and certainly did not intend their readers to know—because, as Bible scholar James Plastaras puts it, "there was really nothing to see."[36]

TABLETS OF STONE

When the meal on the slopes of Sinai ended at last, Yahweh was ready to go back to work. "Come up to Me into the mount, and be there," he told Moses, "and I will give thee the tables of stone, and the law and the commandment, which I have written, that thou mayest teach them."

(Exod. 24:12) "Tarry ye here for us, until we come back unto you," Moses told the elders, "and, behold, Aaron and Hur are with you; if anyone has a dispute, let him go to them." (Exod: 24:12–14)[37] Then Moses turned and set off in the direction of the mountain, followed by young Joshua, the hero of the battle against the Amalekites, a confidant whom Moses apparently preferred to his own brother. At last, even the trusted Joshua went no farther, and Moses continued alone to the peak of Sinai once again. For six days, Moses waited on the mountaintop, and on the seventh day he was finally summoned into the presence of Yahweh by a voice that thundered from somewhere within the cloud.

> And the appearance of the glory of the Lord was like devouring fire on the top of the mount in the eyes of Israel. And Moses entered into the midst of the cloud, and went up into the mount; and Moses was in the mount forty days and forty nights. (Exod. 24:17–18)

God spent those forty days and forty nights dictating the fine points of the Torah. At last, when Yahweh finished, he bestowed upon Moses a relic so holy that it could not fail to impress even the most cynical of the Israelites—a pair of stone tablets on which were inscribed "the ten words," the first and most important of the many laws of Yahweh, each one "written with the finger of God." (Exod. 31:18) The rabbis imagined that the tablets are cut from a diamond quarry, "and the chips that fell, during the hewing, from the precious stone made a rich man of Moses."[38] Still, an even greater treasure was bestowed upon both Moses and the Israelites—the Law itself. Moses was "the most admirable of all the lawgivers who have ever lived in any country either among the Greeks or among the barbarians," enthused Philo, "and his are the most admirable of all laws, and truly divine."[39]

That such a blessing should be bestowed upon a landless nation of former slaves was unlikely in itself, as the rabbis were willing to concede, and the sheer surliness that the Israelites had earlier displayed toward God and Moses made it even more remarkable. Indeed, one of the most cherished tales in the rabbinical literature holds that God offers the Law to each nation of the world, and he only settles on the Israelites because everyone else turns it down—the sons of Esau because they do not want to submit to the commandment against taking human life, the sons of Moab and Ammon because they refuse to refrain from adultery, the sons of Ishmael because they object to the commandment against theft, and so on. At last, God approaches the Israelites, and they alone agree to submit themselves to every one of the Ten Commandments.[40]

A certain irony can be detected in the rabbinical tale: the Israelites agree to be obedient, but the Bible reports that their obedience lasts barely overnight. Indeed, the rabbis suggested that their hasty embrace of the Torah is compelled by threat rather than true belief—God tears Sinai from the earth and holds the mountain over their heads. "If you accept the Torah, all is well," God was imagined to say, "otherwise you will find your grave under this mountain."[41] Once the divine threat is withdrawn, the Israelites are quick to forget the First Commandment and all the others.

Indeed, at precisely the most exalted moment of the Exodus, the very moment at which God was giving the Ten Commandments to Moses, Yahweh was distracted by something that only he was able to see and hear from high atop Mount Sinai. Suddenly, Yahweh broke off the solemn ceremony of law-giving and addressed Moses with new urgency and unmistakable anger.

"Go, get thee down," Yahweh abruptly ordered Moses, "for thy people, that thou broughtest up out of the land of Egypt, have dealt corruptly and turned aside quickly out of the way which I commanded them." (Exod. 32:7–8)

"THIS IS YOUR GOD"

"All that God has said will we do," the people of Israel had cried out, not once but three times; but their enthusiasm for the law of Yahweh had quickly subsided even as Moses began to ascend Sinai yet again. Without Moses to hector and scold them, the Israelites reverted to their old ways, forgetting about their pledge of obedience to Yahweh and his many laws. Rather, they began to fret, to murmur, to carp and complain. With each passing day, the thunder and lightning atop Sinai must have seemed more remote and unremarkable, and the terror of Yahweh began to wane. And, since Moses was gone, they turned to Aaron, the man whom Moses had left in charge, and directed their grievances to him.

This man Moses, the man that brought us up out of the land of Egypt, we know not what is become of him. Up, make us a god who shall go before us. (Exod. 32:1)[42]

Aaron did not think to scold the Israelites for their fickleness and infidelity. Rather, he cowered before the crowd and quickly complied with their demands—Aaron, the brother of Moses and the high priest of Israel, turned into an apostate with alarming suddenness, breaking the First and Second Commandments that God had just handed down. Even though the Bible insists that the Israelites were "set on evil" and so Aaron acted out of fear for his life (Exod. 32:22), it appears that he completed the task of idol-making with a certain ardor and ingenuity.

"Break off the golden rings, which are in the ears of your wives, of your sons, and of your daughters," cried Aaron to the mob, "and bring them unto me." (Exod. 32:2)

Jewelry of fine gold was heaped up before Aaron, and he set to work making a new god for the Israelites to worship, melting the stuff down over a fire and then shaping the lump of molten gold with a graving tool. Before long, he had fashioned the figure of a beast. "Calf" is the familiar but misleading word used in most English translations to describe the graven image that Aaron made, but the word resonates much differently in biblical Hebrew, where it suggests a potent and powerful young bull rather than a frail and spindly calf—"bull-calf" is how the word is rendered by the plainspoken translators of the New English Bible. The bull was revered throughout the ancient Near East as the symbol of fertility, and the bull-calf was the sign of the supreme god in the pantheon of the pagan Canaanites, El (or Bull-El, as he was sometimes called).[43] For that reason, the sight of the golden calf that Aaron offered the Israelites seemed to inspire a worshipful impulse in the men and women who had just sworn their fidelity to Yahweh as the one and only God.

"This is your god,* O Israel," Aaron cried out to the mob as he presented the golden calf, "who brought you up out of the land of Egypt!" (Exod 32:4 New JPS)

---

*The original Hebrew text is actually plural: "These are your *gods*, O Israel. . . ." The phrase is sometimes rendered by Bible translators in the singular in order to resolve a contradiction in the original text—Aaron refers to "gods" but makes only a single golden calf. But Aaron's use of the plural is a clue to what may be the real reason why the incident of the golden calf appears in the Bible, as we shall soon see.

Then Aaron built up an altar out of gathered stones and addressed the Israelites with a paradoxical command—"Tomorrow shall be a feast to Yahweh!" (Exod. 32:5)—as if to suggest that the veneration of a graven image was perfectly compatible with the worship of God.

The Israelites, who had always been balky and halfhearted when it came to obeying the will of Moses and Yahweh, showed no such reluctance toward the new god whom they had demanded of Aaron. The very next morning, they rose at dawn and gathered around the altar to offer sacrifices to the golden bull-calf, burnt-offerings and peace-offerings, all in a twisted mimicry of the ritual of sacrifice to Yahweh that Moses had offered only days earlier. When they had satisfied their momentary urge toward prayer, the men and women of Israel—perhaps in the frenzy of spiritual ecstasy, perhaps out of a certain fatalism brought on by guilt over their apostasy—indulged a very different impulse.

"The people sat down to eat and drink," goes the spare biblical report that inspired Cecil B. DeMille and countless other movie moguls to depict a scene of orgiastic excess, "and gave themselves up to revelry." (Exod. 21:6)[44]

"NOW LET ME ALONE, THAT MY WRATH MAY WAX HOT AGAINST THEM"

"Wherefore the children of Israel shall keep the sabbath throughout their generations for a perpetual covenant," Yahweh apparently was saying to Moses, according to the biblical chronology, at the very moment when the Israelites were about to shatter the covenant they had just made with him. "It is a sign between Me and the children of Israel forever." (Exod. 31:16–17)

At that very moment, the all-seeing and all-knowing Yahweh noticed the apostasy of the Israelites, and he revealed to Moses exactly what was happening at the foot of Sinai. "They have made them a molten calf, and have worshipped it, and have sacrificed unto it." (Exod. 32:7–8)[45] And, displaying the jealous wrath of which he regularly boasted, Yahweh vowed to work rough justice on the Israelites.

"I have seen this people, and, behold, it is a stiff-necked people," Yahweh raged at Moses. "Now therefore let Me alone, that My wrath may wax hot against them, and that I may consume them." (Exod. 32:9–10)

God impulsively offered Moses the very deal he had made with Noah—God would exterminate the people he had just chosen as his "special possession," and he would start all over again with Moses and his two sons. "And I will make of thee a great nation," God promised Moses as he had promised Abraham, Isaac, and Jacob (Exod. 32:10).

Moses responded to Yahweh's offer with remarkable boldness and courage, scolding the Almighty for his ill-considered threats and pointing out the appalling public relations problem that mass murder of the Chosen People would represent.

> O Lord, why shouldst thou vent thy anger upon thy people, whom thou didst bring out of Egypt with great power and a strong hand? Why let the Egyptians say, "So he meant evil when he took them out, to kill them in the mountains and wipe them off the face of the earth"? (Exod. 32:11–12)[46]

Moses seemed to detect a shadow of self-doubt in his jealous and wrathful god, and so he moved quickly to exploit his momentary advantage.

"Turn from Thy fierce wrath, and repent of this evil against Thy people," he implored Yahweh. "Remember Abraham, Isaac, and Israel, Thy servants, to whom Thou didst swear by Thine own self, and saidst unto them: 'I will multiply your seed as the stars of heaven, and all this land that I have spoken of will I give unto your seed, and they shall inherit it forever.' " (Exod. 32:12–13)

The man who had once complained to Yahweh that he was slow of speech now proved himself to be a clever and highly effective advocate. Or perhaps Yahweh was bluffing all along—the rabbis, always eager to put God in the best light, insisted that he was only toying with Moses when he threatened to destroy the Israelites because he "liked to hear Moses pray."[47] In any event, the Bible reveals that God cooled off, calmed down, and "repented of the evil which He said He would do unto His people." (Exod. 32:14)

So the moment of danger passed, at least for now, and Moses "turned and went down from the mount," carrying the two stone tablets on which God had inscribed the divine law that the Israelites had just broken (Exod. 32:14–15).

PURGE

Joshua met Moses on his way down the mountain, and as the two of them descended together, a strange sound reached their ears from far below.

"There is a noise of war in the camp," observed Joshua, who had been blooded in battle against the Amalekites and now heard the clamor from below as the sound of a new assault on the Israelites by yet another enemy (Exod. 32:17).

"This is not the clamour of warriors, nor the clamour of a defeated people," said Moses, who already understood the meaning of the sounds that reached their ears from afar, "it is the sound of singing that I hear." (Exod. 32:18 NEB)

> And it came to pass, as soon as he came nigh unto the camp, that he saw the calf and the dancing; and Moses' anger waxed hot, and he cast the tables out of his hands, and broke them beneath the mount. (Exod. 32:19)[48]

Moses next destroyed the golden calf and then literally shoved it down the throats of the faithless men and women who had been dancing around the mute idol only moments before. Indeed, the Bible reports that Moses "burnt it with fire, and ground it to powder, and strewed it upon the water," and then, not unlike a punishing father who washes out a child's mouth with soap, Moses "made the children of Israel drink of it." (Exod. 32:20)

Finally, he turned on his brother, Aaron, with a bitter accusation. "What did this people unto thee," Moses demanded, "that thou hast brought a great sin upon them?" (Exod. 32:21)

"Let not the anger of my lord wax hot; thou knowest the people, that they are set on evil," Aaron said. "So they said unto me: Make us a god, which shall go before us; for as for this Moses, the man that brought us out of the land of Egypt, we know not what is become of him." (Exod. 32:22–23)

Moses cannot have failed to notice the self-serving spin that Aaron put on his confession, subtly blaming his brother for leaving him alone for forty days with the ungovernable multitude. But Aaron went even further in excusing himself from blame by suggesting, remarkably enough, that the golden bull had made itself! "And I said unto them: Whosoever hath any gold, let them break it off," Aaron continued, "so they gave it to me; and I cast it into the fire, and there came out this calf."

Finally, Moses resolved to put an end to the revelries and rebelliousness of the Israelites. He strode to the gates of the encampment and issued a challenge to the raucous men and women who had gathered there to worship the golden calf.

"Whoever is on the Lord's side," Moses called, "let him come unto me." (Exod. 32:26)[49]

Here was the latest moment of crisis and peril in the leadership of Moses—who would answer his call? The dancing Israelites had voted with their feet against his authority, and they had made themselves a new leader in the guise of the golden bull-calf. As it turned out, however, a goodly number of the men of his own tribe, the tribe of Levi, hastened to his side—and Moses was ready to set the Levites to a bloody task. Only moments before, Moses had pleaded with Yahweh *not* to start killing the men, women, and children of Israel, but now he issued orders of his own that were no less bloodthirsty.

> Thus saith the Lord, the God of Israel. Put ye every man his sword upon his thigh, and go to and fro from gate to gate throughout the camp, and slay every man his brother, and every man his companion, and every man his neighbour. (Exod. 32:27)

So began the purge of the Israelites. A stray passage in the biblical text reports that it was Yahweh who "smote" the people for making the calf of gold (Exod. 32:35), a line that is sometimes interpreted to mean that he sent down a divine plague rather like the ones that afflicted the Egyptians. But elsewhere the Bible makes it clear that the work of smiting the Israelites was taken up by the praetorian guard of Levites who rallied around Moses, unsheathed their swords, and starting killing their fellow Israelites. When the killing was finally done, the camp of the Israelites was littered with three thousand corpses (Exod. 32:28), and the rabbis imagined that each one of the sinners had suffered "the lawful punishment of decapitation."[50]

Then, as the fortunate survivors cowered in their tents, the Levites gathered around Moses to celebrate the brutal success of the purge. The authority of Moses had been restored, and he had learned a crucial lesson about the necessity of surrounding himself with a corps of armed men who were both reliable and ruthless—here was the first but not the last time that terror would be used to punish the faithless and put down the defiant among the Israelites. So Moses blessed the Levites who had anointed their swords with the blood of their own kin and who now constituted an elite corps in the most intimate kind of holy war.

"Consecrate yourself to-day to the Lord, for every man hath been against his son and against his kin," Moses cried, "that He may also bestow upon you a blessing this day." (Exod. 32:29)

"THESE ARE YOUR GODS, O ISRAEL"

The greatest act of apostasy in the history of ancient Israel—the making and worship of an idol in the shape of a golden calf—was repeated several hundred years later by Jeroboam, the monarch who ruled over the northern tribes of Israel when the united monarchy of David and Solomon split in two after the death of Solomon in the tenth century B.C.E. According to the account in the First Book of Kings, Jeroboam established sanctuaries for the worship of Yahweh in various cities of the northern kingdom in order to discourage his subjects from traveling to the rival kingdom of Judah to worship at the Temple of Solomon in Jerusalem. At two of these sanctuaries, the ones in Dan and Bethel, Jeroboam installed figures of young bulls cast in gold—the very same image that the Israelites had worshipped in the wilderness. Remarkably, Jeroboam echoed the words of Aaron when he presented the golden calves to the Israelites: "Behold thy gods, O Israel, which brought thee up out of the land of Egypt." (1 Kings 12:28) A careful reading of the texts reveals no less than thirteen points of commonality between the two tales, including the fact that the names of two of Aaron's sons, Nadab and Abihu, pointedly resemble those of Jeroboam's sons, Nadab and Abijah. (Exod. 6:23, 1 Kings 14:1, 20)[51]

The traditional explanation for the striking similarities between the two biblical accounts is that Jeroboam was such a dedicated sinner that he reveled in reenacting the very worst sin in the collective memory of ancient Israel—the "sin *par excellence*"—and doing so no less than twenty-one times, according to a count by Bible scholars Moses Aberbach and Leivy Smolar.[52] So we are asked to believe that Jeroboam was so diabolical that he simply did not care that he was defying the first two commandments and the most hallowed traditions of his people, which regarded idol worship as an abomination.

Somewhat more convincing is a scholarly apologia for Jeroboam: the ritual use of a young bull had once been an acceptable practice in ancient Israel, one that both Aaron and Jeroboam felt at liberty to embrace, and so Jeroboam was "a reviver of an ancient cult first introduced by Aaron."[53] The calf itself may have been a familiar emblem of leadership among the Israelites in the era before their arrival in Canaan—a *Führersymbol*, according to an unfortunate technical term used by Bible scholars[54]—and *not* a deity in itself; after all, Aaron characterized the golden calf as "the god which brought thee up out of the land of Egypt" (Exod. 32:4), thus suggesting it as "a replacement for Moses, not for God,"[55] and he used the golden calf as a ritual object in the worship of Yahweh: "To-morrow shall be a feast to the Lord." (Exod. 32:5)

Most convincing of all, if also more challenging to pious assumptions about the authorship of the Bible, is the rather subversive notion that the story of Aaron and the golden calf was written into the Bible *after* Jeroboam's reign as a veiled attack on the king who was the first in the history of ancient Israel to install a calf of gold in a place of worship. The priests of Jerusalem promoted the idea that Yahweh accepted worship and sacrifice only in the Temple of Jerusalem, and they condemned Jeroboam as a sinner because he established rival places of worship and sacrifice in Dan and Bethel. "[O]ne must consider the possibility that the polemic against the golden calf derives not from the primary shape of the Moses traditions," offers Coats, "but rather from the Jerusalem court in reaction to the rebellion of Jeroboam."[56] To put it more bluntly, the incident of the golden calf at Sinai may have been a bit of black propaganda, "a fabrication," as one scholar put it, "a projection back into the desert era of the 'Sin of Jeroboam.' "[57]

Such a reading is supported by some intriguing bits of evidence in the biblical text. For example, Jeroboam did not come up with the idea of using a pair of golden figurines to adorn a sanctuary where Yahweh was worshipped—Yahweh himself had ordered Moses to decorate the Ark with golden cherubim. When Jeroboam built his own places of worship in northern Israel, he used calves instead of cherubim to adorn his sanctuaries, and what the Jerusalem priesthood found objectionable were the sanctuaries themselves rather than the golden calves that were installed there. The suggestion that the golden calves at Dan and

Bethel were idols while the cherubim at Jerusalem were merely decorations was a way of putting a spin on the deeds of Jeroboam that served the ulterior motive of the biblical sources.

Why was Aaron chosen as the fall guy by the biblical propagandists? Although the most important and influential faction of the priestly caste of ancient Israel claimed descent from Aaron, several elements of the priesthood did not. The priests of Shiloh and Dan, for example, appear to have descended directly from Moses,[58] and the priests of Jerusalem known as Zadokites were not regarded as descendants of Aaron until a very late period in the history of ancient Israel.[59] One scholar speculated that Zadok, the founder of the priestly line, was actually a Jebusite—not an Israelite—who was first recruited for priestly service by King David when he conquered the Jebusite city of Jerusalem.[60] Perhaps it was a faction of these non-Aaronite priests who cast Aaron in his paradoxical role of prophet and apostate when they made up the tale of the golden calf as an attack on Jeroboam—and they may even have gone so far as to depict the punishment of Aaron for the sin of the golden calf in a long-suppressed passage of biblical text now lost to us.*

Some scholars are convinced that the original text of the Bible actually reported the scourging or perhaps even the death of Aaron in a passage that was later excised.[61] If so, Aaron was saved from the indignity of divine punishment by the Aaronite priests who were final editors and ultimate custodians of Holy Writ. So offensive was the "sin of Jeroboam," so dangerous was the notion of sacrifice at a sanctuary other than the one in Jerusalem, that even the Aaronite sources were willing to leave in the incident of the golden calf as a way of attacking Jeroboam—but, some scholars suggest, they were unwilling to depict the founder of the priesthood of Israel as worthy of divine punishment, and so they left out the original ending of the story.

Moses, of course, is nowhere to be found in any of these counter-readings of the biblical text. The figure of Aaron, as we have already noted, seems to have been written into the Bible in a highly artificial manner, and scholarship suggests that he was put there by the priests of ancient Israel who descended from Aaron as a way of validating their

---

*The Deuteronomist, for example, indicates that Yahweh was ready to slay Aaron, and only the intervention of Moses spared his life: "The Lord was very angry with Aaron to have destroyed him," Moses recalled in Deuteronomy, "and I prayed for Aaron also the same time." (Deut. 9:20)

power and privilege in the court and temple of Jerusalem. Here, as elsewhere in the Bible, the various priestly factions who were the final editors and guardians of Holy Writ apparently felt at liberty to tamper with the text in order to serve their own interests and motives.

JUST KILL ME!

On the day after the purge of the Israelites at the foot of the holy mountain, Moses addressed the survivors in stern but compassionate words. With his authority apparently restored, and a personal bodyguard at his side just in case he was wrong, Moses could afford to strike a statesmanlike stance even as he reminded the Israelites that they were sinners whose only faint hope for redemption was the influence Moses himself might be able to wield in private consultation with the angry and jealous Yahweh.

"Ye have sinned a great sin," Moses said to them, "and now I will go up unto the Lord; perhaps I may be able to secure pardon for your sin." (Exod. 32:30–31)[62]

So Moses mounted Sinai yet again, and the Bible reports a remarkable encounter with Yahweh in which these two moody and mercurial figures struck sparks off each other as they debated the fate of the Israelites.

"Oh, this people have sinned a great sin, and have made a god of gold," said Moses to Yahweh, telling him nothing he did not already know. "Yet now, if Thou wilt forgive them, forgive. But if not, blot out my name, I pray, from Thy book which Thou hast written." (Exod. 32:31–32)[63]

His words amounted to an audacious challenge to Yahweh—"If you won't do what I want, just kill me!"—and now God responded in curiously ambiguous terms that did not rule out the possibility that he would do exactly that.

"Whosoever hath sinned against Me," Yahweh said to Moses, "him will I blot out of My book."

Both of them were perfectly capable of histrionics, especially when bickering with each other, and now Yahweh displayed the same sullenness that Moses had just shown. Yahweh would stop killing his Chosen People, at least here and now. He would even allow them to continue their journey to the land of Canaan, "a land flowing with milk and honey," and he would even spare them the trouble of conquering the Promised Land by driving out the many tribes and nations that already lived there, "the Canaanite, the Amorite, and the Hittite, and the Perizzite, the Hivite, and the Jebusite." (Exod. 33:2) But Yahweh would be damned if he'd go with them.

"Depart, go up hence, thou and thy people, unto the land which I swore unto Abraham, to Isaac, and to Jacob, and I will send an angel before thee," Yahweh ranted at Moses, "for I will not go up in the midst of thee; for thou art a stiff-necked people; lest I consume thee in the way." (Exod. 33:1–3)[64]

Moses, of course, hastened to relay the harsh words of Yahweh to the chastened Israelites—"If I go up into the midst of thee for one moment, I shall consume thee" (Exod. 33:5)—and the Israelites responded just as Moses had intended, mourning the "evil tidings" from Yahweh and readily complying with his demand that they prove the sincerity of their remorse by stripping themselves of their jewelry: "Put off thy ornaments from thee." (Exod. 33:5) From the day they departed from the holy mountain, the Bible suggests, the Israelites were too ashamed of themselves to adorn their bodies with the baubles that they had borrowed from their Egyptian masters or plundered from the dead bodies of the Egyptian soldiers.

Still, the Bible insists that God did not absent himself entirely from the Israelites once they resumed their journey through the wilderness of Sinai. Even if he found them to be insufferable in their sweaty multitudes, Yahweh was perfectly willing to closet himself with Moses in the tent that was set aside for their tête-à-têtes, the tent of meeting. But Yahweh waited until Moses shlepped the tent out of the camp and pitched it at some distance from the rest of the Israelites, who "rose up, and stood, every man at his tent door, and looked after Moses, until he was gone into the Tent." (Exod. 33:8) Only then did Yahweh deign to enter the tent of meeting, his presence marked by a pillar of cloud standing at the door and a fiery glow from within, and spend a few moments in intimate conversation with Moses.

"And Yahweh spoke unto Moses face to face, as a man speaketh unto his friend," the Bible so famously states, although no explanation is offered on what Moses saw when he beheld the face of God (Exod. 33:11).

So long as the cloud lingered at the tent of meeting, so long as the "glory" burned within, the Israelites sought refuge in their tents and watched from afar. Yahweh, they had learned, was just as jealous and wrathful as Moses had advertised him to be, and so they were content to let Moses deal with him. "And whenever the cloud was taken up from over the tabernacle," the Bible reports, "the children of Israel went onward, throughout all their journeys." (Exod. 40:35–36)

THE HORNS OF MOSES

Once the wrathful Yahweh had cooled off, he agreed to provide a new set of stone tablets to replace the ones that Moses had cast down in anger at the sight of the golden calf—and he decided to add a few more laws that had apparently slipped his mind during their earlier sessions. So Yahweh invited Moses to return to the top of Mount Sinai. No one should accompany him, God was careful to warn Moses yet again, and no living creature, man or beast, should be allowed to set foot on the slope of the holy mountain. So Moses spent another forty days and forty nights in the company of Yahweh, patiently listening to another recitation of "the ten words" and many more besides, and, throughout the long ordeal, "he did neither eat bread, nor drink water." (Exod. 34:28) At the end, God replaced the two tablets that Moses had destroyed when he first beheld the golden calf.

> Hew thee two tables of stone like unto the first; and I will write upon the tables the words that were on the first tables, which thou didst break. (Exod. 34:1)

Then Moses took the two new tablets in hand—by tradition, God had inscribed "the ten words" on the first pair of tablets and Moses inscribed the second pair—and headed down the mountain once more.

Something exceedingly strange had happened to Moses during his long sojourn in the presence of Yahweh, although he did not yet know it. Unbeknownst to Moses, his face had been somehow charged with light, and a kind of celestial glow shone from his face as he approached the camp. When Aaron and the rest of the Israelites laid eyes on Moses, the sight of his shining face was so unsettling that they stood at a distance and gaped at him in horror.

Behold, the skin of his face sent forth beams, and they were afraid to come nigh unto him. (Exod. 34:30)

At first, Moses "knew not that the skin of his face sent forth beams" (Exod. 34:30), and the Bible suggests that it was only the fearful response of the Israelites that made him aware of his disfigurement. So brightly did it shine, imagined the sages, "that if even to-day a crack were made in his tomb, the light emanating from his corpse would be so powerful that it could not but destroy all the world."[65] But he spoke reassuringly to Aaron and the elders, soothing their fears and coaxing them nearer, and when they finally edged up to him, Moses conveyed to them the latest batch of sacred ordinances from on high. Then he summoned the rest of the Israelites to hear his recitation of "all that Yahweh had spoken with him in mount Sinai" (Exod. 34:32)—and the multitudes must have stared with both fright and fascination at what had become of the familiar face of old Moses.

At last, Moses realized that the strange glow from his face was so off-putting that he could not go about the camp without scaring the wits out of the Israelites. So he resorted to the same ploy that was later used by the Elephant Man to hide *his* disfigurement: "And when Moses had done speaking with them, he put a veil on his face." (Exod. 34:33) Indeed, the Bible suggests that Moses was veiled for the rest of his life, a period of forty years, removing it only when closeting himself with Yahweh in the tent of meeting or when making a formal address to the Israelites. Only on these rare ceremonial occasions did Moses permit the Israelites to see exactly what happened to a man who spoke "face to face" with Yahweh.

No single line of biblical text has been quite so mangled or misunderstood as the reference to the shining face of Moses and the way he tried to conceal it. The Hebrew phrase that actually describes the appearance of Moses in the biblical text includes a word (*qaran*) that derives from the word for "horn," and so the translators of the Vulgate, the first Latin translation of the Bible, rendered the phrase to mean that "the skin of his face sent forth *horns*." But earlier translators understood the Hebrew text as a metaphorical phrase that meant "to radiate with light," and the ancient Greek translation known as the Septuagint gives the same phrase a much different meaning—the face of Moses "sent forth beams [of light]."[66] A couple of thousand years later, the meaning of the biblical text is still being debated by scholars, and the question of what the Israelites actually saw when they looked on the face of Moses is no less baffling.

The authors of the New Testament, who appeared to rely on the Septuagint for their references to the Hebrew Bible, concluded that the face of Moses was suffused with celestial light on his return from Sinai, and they were inspired to depict a similar scene in which Jesus, attended by Moses and Elijah, was transfigured with the same divine light (Matt. 17:3). The rabbis, too, envisioned Moses with a shining face, and one tale reports that the glow emanates from the traces of heavenly ink that are somehow smeared on his face as he writes down the words of the Torah.[67] Centuries later, however, the Renaissance artists who relied on the Vulgate—including Michelangelo—would depict Moses with a pair of faintly satyric horns projecting from atop his head. Indeed, the notion that all Jews are horned, a slur that has been favored by anti-Semites over the ages because it suggests both bestiality and devilry, probably started with what may have been an innocent mistranslation.

A more recent commentator argues that the enigmatic text was meant to suggest that the skin on Moses' face "[dried] up and [became] toughened like leather from overexposure to the light and heat of the divine countenance." Another suggests that the biblical authors meant to depict Moses as literally horned, at least according to "a suppressed tradition in which Moses is a deity, the offspring of the horned moon god Sin of Sinai."[70] And a third entertains the notion that the biblical author may have intended to liken Moses to the golden calf. "Would the horns connect Moses to a bovine element in the Yahweh religion?" George Coats wonders aloud. "Was the Calf in fact a symbol of Moses rather than an idol or even a symbol of God?"[71]

Even the face-covering used by Moses is the subject of some heated controversy among Bible scholars. The Hebrew word conventionally translated as "veil" (*masweh*) may in fact refer to a mask of the kind commonly worn by priests of pagan cults when addressing their gods and goddesses. If so, the text may preserve a faint remnant of a ritual in which the priests of prebiblical times donned a cultic mask in order to approach Yahweh and ask him for advice. "[T]he history of Moses' mask has now become perfectly clear," enthuses Elias Auerbach. "When Moses entered the tent of God to consult the deity, he put on the face mask. . . ." So embarrassing was the spectacle of Moses in the mask of a pagan priest, Auerbach suggests, the priestly redactors of the Bible tried to hide the real purpose of the mask by simply reversing the original meaning of the text—the Bible reports that Moses donned the mask only when moving among the people, and he took it off when address-ing Yahweh.[70]

No matter what it was originally intended to mean, the image of Moses as a man in a mask is so odd and so unsettling that it has been left out of the iconography of Moses, in both sacred art and pop culture. But the Bible reports that the Israelites rarely saw the unveiled face of Moses throughout their forty years of wandering through the wilderness. For them, the veil itself must have been "a visible and concrete symbol of Mosaic authority derived from his intimacy with God," as Coats puts it. "The veil might then be defined as a symbol for Mosaic authority, de-rived from Moses' presence with God, and thus ranked alongside the rod as a symbol of Moses' stature."[71] At the same time, the mask must have made Moses a stern and even a scary figure among the Israelites—aloof and unapproachable, no less mysterious than the god he served.

GOD OF THE VOLCANO, GOD OF THE MOON

At last, the chastened Israelites struck their tents, packed away the newly inscribed stone tablets in the newly constructed Ark, and then moved off into the wilderness. The Bible suggests that Yahweh rose from his perch atop the holy mountain of Sinai and seated himself on the outstretched wings of the golden cherubim atop the Ark of the Covenant. Despite all of his threats and ultimatums, God moved with them, a pillar of cloud by day, a pillar of fire by night.

The very image indicates something subtly but profoundly revolu-tionary in the faith of Israel and, in a sense, the history of religion. The gods and goddesses of the ancient world were sometimes regarded as sedentary deities who were rooted in one place—a mountain, a grotto, a grove of trees, a pool of water—and sometimes as restless wanderers who meandered through the world in the company of the tribe that worshipped them. A stationary god was thought to enjoy divine au-thority only in the place where he dwelled, and a wandering god exer-cised his authority over the clan or tribe with whom he moved. But Yahweh was both, a god of the holy mountain called Sinai *and* a god who rode along with the Israelites throughout their forty years of wan-dering in a wilderness that was also called Sinai.

The dual nature of Yahweh suggests to some Bible critics that the

Israelites (or, perhaps, the various biblical authors) were inspired by the example of other gods and goddesses of the ancient world in conceiving and describing the god with whom they made their covenant. The borrowing of other people's gods was nothing new or remarkable in the ancient world; it was a common practice for a conquered people to adopt the more appealing deities of their conquerors, and sometimes it worked the other way around. Indeed, the syncretism of the ancient world—the combining of the best qualities of various gods and their rituals of worship—resulted in a rather easygoing and eclectic attitude toward religion. The very notion of a god who insisted that he was the one and only, a god who demanded holy war against his enemies, is something that began with Moses. Somewhere in the far-distant past, however, the Israelites were apparently not so choosy, and the god called Yahweh appears to embody the qualities of several other gods of the ancient world.

Sometimes Yahweh manifested himself in the phenomena of a volcanic eruption—smoke, fire, and seismic tremors. Since the only active volcanoes of the Near East in the biblical era were found not in the Sinai but rather in the Arabian Peninsula, the likely location of the land of Midian, some scholars believe the holy mountain on which Yahweh revealed himself was actually a volcanic peak somewhere along the road between Mecca and Medina in what is now Saudi Arabia.[72] If so, the depiction of Yahweh as a volcano god prompts some critics to wonder if he was originally a god of Midian who only later came to be worshipped by the Israelites.*

At other times Yahweh appeared as a sky god who wandered through the heavens and manifested himself now and then in the brief but violent phenomena of a thunderstorm, the flashes of lightning and peals of thunder that heralded his sojourn on the holy mountain. Or perhaps one of the biblical authors meant to conjure up the fire and smoke of

---

*Indeed, as we have already noted, the tradition that identifies Sinai as one of a couple of mountains in what is now called the Sinai Peninsula—the so-called Mountain of Moses (Jebel Musa, 7,497 feet) or, more popularly, Mount St. Catherine (Jebel Qaterin, 8,649 feet)—dates back only to the Byzantine era and may have had less to do with authentic biblical tradition than with an interest in promoting tourism to the Greek Orthodox monastery of St. Catherine. Ironically, some ancient inscriptions on the approaches to these promontories suggest that they may have been sacred in pagan tradition, and, if one of these mountains was the biblical Sinai, it is possible that Moses and the Israelites were drawn to these sites for precisely that reason.

"the smelting fires" of the wandering metalsmiths known as the Kenites,[73] the tribe to which the in-laws of Moses belonged. Yet another speculation is that Yahweh was patterned after a Mesopotamian god called Sin. Intriguingly, the symbol of the god Sin was the moon, a celestial light that wanders restlessly through the skies, an eternal companion to one who treks across an otherwise empty wilderness. Did the pagan deity called Sin bestow his name upon the wilderness of Sin, one of the stretches of wilderness named in the Bible, and a variant of his name upon Sinai, the holy mountain where Yahweh entered into his covenant with Israel?

"Jahweh, in origin, is a God of the Way," observes the writer Bruce Chatwin, himself an inveterate wanderer for whom Moses was an object of fascination. "His sanctuary is the Mobile Ark, His House a tent, His Altar a cairn of rough stones. And though He may *promise* His Children a well-watered land—blue and green are a bedouin's favorite colours—He secretly desires for them the Desert."[74]

The crucial fact, however, is that Yahweh manifested himself as both kinds of god, and many more besides. If Moses can be credited with working a revolution in the faith of humankind, if he was truly the first man to teach that God is not merely a tribal deity but a cosmic one, then the Mosaic revolution began at Sinai, where Yahweh universalized himself by decamping from the holy mountain and leading his people into the wilderness and beyond. "For a spirit like Moses'," offers Elias Auerbach, "just such an experience could be the means of freeing himself from the age-old belief in the locally restricted nature of the deity and of advancing toward the idea of the universality of God."[75]

But at the moment of revelation at Sinai, Yahweh was not yet what he would become in Judeo-Christian tradition, the King of the Universe, and the champion of the poor and oppressed. For now, Yahweh was still "a brutal, partial and murderous god," as Karen Armstrong points out in *A History of God*, a "passionately partisan" god of war who sided only with the tribe that carried him into battle atop the Ark of the Covenant. "If Yahweh had remained such a savage god," she argues, "the sooner he vanished, the better it would have been for everybody."[76] But the fact is that Yahweh had not yet satisfied his taste for human blood, and the god who bestirred himself from the holy mountain and set off toward the land of Canaan was directing his people toward a holy war.

"I WILL SEND MY TERROR BEFORE THEE"

Atop the holy mountain, Yahweh now announced a new mission for Moses and issued a new set of marching orders for the Israelites.

> I will send an angel before thee unto a land flowing with milk and honey. (Exod. 33:2–3)[77]

Of course, the land of milk and honey was teeming with people who considered that they had every right to stay there, and Yahweh never bothered to conceal the fact that the Israelites would be forced to drive out the native-dwelling peoples by force of arms. But Yahweh was the God of Armies, as we have already seen, and he promised to join the Israelites in a holy war against anyone who stood in their way.

"I will send My terror before thee," vowed Yahweh. "I will be an enemy unto thine enemies, and an adversary unto thine adversaries. Behold, I am driving out before thee the Amorite, and the Canaanite, and the Hittite, and the Perizzite, and the Hivite, and the Jebusite." (Exod. 23:22, 27; 34:10–11)[78]

And then Yahweh rose up from Sinai and moved off into the distance, a pillar of cloud by day and a pillar of fire by night, always visible to the multitude of Israelites in these manifestations but always beyond their firm grasp and always out of plain sight, as he led his people onward toward the land of Canaan. As Moses and the Israelites were soon to discover, what had begun as an escape from slavery would soon become a campaign of conquest that could be understood as holy war, or genocide, or both.

Chapter Ten

MAN OF WAR

*Suddenly, at a turn in the terrain, I spied some tiny lights
shining palely in the far distance, near the bottom of a
gorge. It must have been a small village whose inhabitants were still awake. At that point an astonishing thing
happened to me. I still shudder when I recall it. Halting,
I shook my clenched fist at the village and shouted in a
furor, "I shall slaughter you all!"*
    —NIKOS KAZANTZAKIS, *REPORT TO GRECO*

After a year of wandering in the Sinai, as if to confirm that the band
of runaway slaves had finally turned itself into an army of conquest, Moses announced that Yahweh had ordered him to conduct a
census of every man "twenty years old and upward, all that were able to
go forth to war." (Num. 1:45) To credit the census-takers of Sinai with
the precise results that are reported in the Bible, the army of Israel numbered exactly 603,550 men of fighting age (Num. 1:46).

Aaron and his sons and the whole tribe of Levi were exempt from
the first census and the general conscription. Moses detailed them to
the care of the Tabernacle, which was erected at the very center of the
encampment, and ordered them to pitch their tents in a protective circle around it. So sacred were the precincts of the Tabernacle, Moses
warned, that the other tribes must stay "a good way off" in their assigned camping grounds and "the common man who draweth nigh shall
be put to death." (Num. 1:51, 2:2)

The scene that is described in almost obsessive detail in the Bible
suggests both the strict order and the bright color of an army on parade
in full regalia and, at the same time, the elaborate rituals of a pilgrimage
festival at a splendiferous temple. "The Israelites shall encamp each under his own standard, by the emblems of his father's family," goes the

biblical account (Num. 2:3 NEB). Typically, the rabbis later added colorful details: "Judah's flag was azure, and bore the form of a lion," the rabbis suggested; Reuben's flag was red; Simeon's was green; Naphtali's was "the color of wine, and on it was the figure of a hind," and so on.[1] As the tribes gathered around the Tabernacle for a sacrificial offering to Yahweh Sabaoth, the God of Armies, the Levites were made to undergo a ritual of purification that required "a razor to pass over all their flesh" (Num. 8:7), and an altar was erected, anointed, and consecrated with a "dedication-offering" that lasted a full twelve days.

Wagonloads of precious objects were turned over to Aaron and the Levites. "Twelve silver dishes, twelve silver basins," goes the biblical inventory, "and twelve golden pans, full of incense." The sands of the Sinai were soaked with the blood of the livestock that was offered up in abundance as a sacrifice to Yahweh. "Twelve bullocks, the rams twelve, the he-lambs of the first year twelve," the account continues, "the males of the goats for a sin-offering twelve, and all the oxen for the sacrifice of peace-offerings twenty and four bullocks, the rams sixty, the he-goats sixty, the he-lambs of the first year sixty." (Num. 7:84–88)

The pomp and circumstance reported in the Bible, however, are probably nothing more than the grand confabulation of the Priestly source. The biblical count of the Israelites in the wilderness is no more credible than the one offered at the outset of the Exodus from Egypt; the multitudes would have filled to overflowing even the empty stretches of the Sinai. No effort is made to explain how a mob of refugees that fed itself on manna and the occasional quail managed to round up the herds and flocks that were sacrificed to Yahweh, or where they found the stores of silver and gold that would have been required to fashion the objects and ornaments that P inventoried with such exacting precision and apparent pleasure.

One such object, however, is evidence that the Israelites were now a nation at war in enemy territory. Yahweh ordered Moses to make a pair of silver trumpets "for the calling of the congregation, and for causing the camps to set forward." (Num. 10:2) God specified exactly what trumpet calls were to be used to signal the various tribes to break camp and move out, to summon the "heads of thousands" and the Israelites en masse to the tent of meeting, to announce the new moon and the changes of season, to celebrate the sacrifices at the altar (Num. 10:3–7). But Yahweh understood that the Chosen People now constituted a fighting force, an army engaged in a holy war, and so he specified when the trumpets were to be sounded as a call to arms.

"And when ye go to war in your land against the adversary that oppresseth you, then ye shall sound an alarm with the trumpets," God instructed Moses, "and ye shall be remembered before the Lord your God and ye shall be saved from your enemies." (Num. 10:9)

DOING GOOD AND SPEAKING EVIL

Moses and the Israelites moved in fits and starts across the wilderness, sometimes pausing for a night's rest, sometimes for a day or two, sometimes for "a month, or a year." (Num. 9:22) By the second month of the second year, they had moved out of the Sinai and crossed into a new and forbidding stretch of wilderness called Paran (Num. 10:11, 13). At each stopping place, Yahweh manifested his presence in the familiar ways—a cloud by day, a fire by night—and issued his daily marching orders to the Israelites (Num. 9:14).

> So it was always: Whenever the cloud was taken up from over the Tent, then after that the children of Israel journeyed; and in the place where the cloud abode, there the children of Israel encamped." (Num. 9:16–17)[2]

The Bible suggests that Moses and the Israelites were lost in a vast and trackless wilderness, but in reality the Sinai Peninsula was and is a confined and well-traveled place that could easily have been crossed in ten or eleven days. "The Egyptians, the Patriarchs, the Jews, the Romans, the Crusaders and the Arabs all passed over these tracks," observed C. Leonard Woolley and T. E. Lawrence, archaeologist and soldier, after their own sojourn in the Sinai, "and [t]he careless traveler who piles up four stones in a heap by the roadside here erects an eternal monument to himself."[3] If the Israelites bumped around the Sinai for forty years, as reported in the Bible, then the real miracle is that they did not find their way out by accident.

Still, Moses betrayed a certain anxiety about making his way through the empty stretches of Paran and, remarkably, a distinct lack of confidence in Yahweh's willingness or ability to lead them out of the wilderness and into Canaan. So far, Moses had relied on the directions given to him by Yahweh, but now he resorted to a more down-to-earth source of intelligence. Just as Lewis and Clark recruited Sacagawea to lead them through the wilderness of North America, Moses called upon a savvy native to guide him across the unknown terrain. The man to whom Moses turned for advice is identified in the Bible as "Hobab, the son of Reuel the Midianite, Moses' father-in-law." (Num. 10:29)

"We are journeying unto the place of which the Lord said: I will give it to you," Moses explained to Hobab, as if to remind his Midianite in-law* that the Israelites were embarked on a divine mission. "Come thou with us, and we will do thee good." (Num. 10:29)

At first, Hobab refused: "I will not go, but I will depart to mine own land, and to my kindred." (Num. 10:30) And so Moses was reduced to begging his highly reluctant in-law.

"Leave us not, I pray thee, forasmuch as thou knowest how we are to encamp in the wilderness, and thou shalt be to us instead of eyes," pleaded Moses in ornate phrases that barely concealed his desperation (Num. 20:32). Then he resorted to unabashed bribery: "If you will go with us, then all the good fortune with which the Lord favours us we will share with you." (Num. 20:32 NEB)

The fact that a near relation of Hobab was living in Canaan after its conquest by the Israelites (Judg. 4:11) is taken by some scholars as evidence that Hobab finally agreed to lead the Israelites into Canaan and "was rewarded for his services with a homestead in the Promised Land,"[4] but the text does not actually say so. Rather, the Bible seems to suggest Moses used the Ark as a tool for divination to find the way.

> And they set forward from the mount of the Lord three days'
> journey, and the ark of the covenant of the Lord went before
> them three days' journey, to seek out a resting-place for them.
> (Exod. 10:33)

What is entirely clear, however, is the fact that the Israelites had once again lapsed into a mutinous mood.

---

*The uncertain phrasing of the biblical text makes it impossible to know whether the man named Hobab was known to the Bible author as the father-in-law or brother-in-law of Moses.

And the people were as murmurers, speaking evil in the ears of the Lord, and when the Lord heard it, His anger was kindled; and the fire of the Lord burnt among them, and devoured in the uttermost part of the camp. (Num. 11:1)

Whether the latest affliction from on high was literally a divine fireball or a metaphorical reference to a plague, the Israelites resorted to another old habit: "And the people cried unto Moses, and Moses prayed to the Lord, and the fire abated." (Num. 11:2) The experience was memorable enough to give a name to the stopping place where it all happened: "And the name of that place was called Taberah"—the Hebrew word is understood to mean "burning"[5]—"because the fire of the Lord burnt among them." (Num. 11:3) But the latest affliction sent down by a disappointed and embittered God was no more effective in changing the nature of the Israelites than anything that had come before, and the patience of both God *and* Moses would be taxed yet again.

CUCUMBERS AND MELONS, GARLICS AND LEEKS

Soldiers and sailors in every age have complained about their rations, whether they dined on hardtack or K rations, and so did the army that marched behind Moses. The "mixed multitude" that had followed the Israelites out of Egypt "fell a lusting" for something other than manna to eat, and the Israelites, too, were reduced to tears of frustration and yearning.

Who shall give us flesh to eat? We remember the fish, which we did eat in Egypt freely; the cucumbers, and the melons, and the leeks, and the onions, and the garlick. But now our soul is dried away: there is nothing at all, beside this manna, before our eyes. (Num. 11:4–6 KJV)

So the old song of self-pity was heard again in the camp of the Israelites, whose maddening lack of appreciation for God and Moses is one of the fundamental theological themes of the Bible and, at the same time, one of its most acute insights into human nature. Yahweh was provoked to fresh rage by these food fantasies, but it was Moses who felt even more bitterly aggrieved. In fact, Moses appeared to blame God rather than the unruly Israelites for the new problem that had presented itself, and he preempted any expression of divine anger by a sudden temper tantrum of his own.

"Wherefore has thou afflicted thy servant?" Moses railed at Yahweh, "and wherefore hast I not found favour in thy sight, that thou layest the burden of all this people upon me?" (Num. 11:11 KJV)

Perhaps dumbfounded by the sheer audacity of Moses, or perhaps correctly assuming that these questions were merely rhetorical, Yahweh was uncharacteristically silent in the face of the tirade.

"Have I conceived all this people?" Moses continued to rage and sputter, "have I brought them forth, that Thou shouldest say unto me, Carry them in thy bosom, as a nursing-father carrieth the sucking child, unto the land which thou did swear unto their fathers?" (Num. 11:11)

So distraught was Moses that he invited God to regard him as a grotesque, a man with breasts, but Yahweh still said nothing as Moses stoked himself into yet a greater frenzy. "Whence should I have flesh to give unto all this people? For they trouble me with their weeping, saying: Give us flesh, that we may eat," ranted Moses. "I am not able to bear all this people myself alone, because it is too heavy for me." (Num. 11:13–14)

Then Moses spent himself in a final plea to Yahweh, an unwholesome and unholy demand that bespoke the weariness that now replaced his anger. Once before he had pleaded with God, "blot me, I pray Thee, out of Thy Book which Thou hast written" (Exod. 32:32). Now Moses made the same demand in much blunter terms.

"And if Thou deal thus with me, kill me, I pray Thee, out of hand, if I have found favour in Thy sight," Moses implored, "and let me not see my wretchedness." (Num. 11:15)

Moses, who had earlier tried and failed to convince God to send someone else on the mission of liberation, now sought to resign his commission with a simple if desperate plea: Kill me! But God was not ready to relieve Moses of his duties, and he seemed to ignore all of his bluster and bravado. Indeed, God abruptly changed the subject.

"Gather unto Me seventy men of the elders of Israel, and bring them unto the tent of meeting, that they may stand there with thee," Yahweh instructed Moses, "and I will come down and talk with thee there." (Num. 11:16–17)[6] Yahweh seemed to be offering to shift some of the workload from the harried Moses to the elders: "I will take of the spirit which is upon thee, and will put it upon them," Yahweh explained, "and they shall bear the burden of the people with thee, that thou bear it not thyself alone." (Num. 11:17)

But as Yahweh continued his instructions, a certain rage of his own began to reveal itself in the words he instructed Moses to speak to the gathered elders. "Sanctify yourselves against to-morrow, and ye shall eat flesh," Yahweh told Moses to say, "for ye have wept in the ears of the Lord, saying: Would that we were given flesh to eat! for it was well with us in Egypt. Therefore the Lord shall give you flesh, and ye shall eat." (Num. 11:18)

Yahweh's words fairly hummed with a subtle threat. If the Israelites hungered for flesh, then flesh they would eat—but they would soon regret that they had dared to ask.

"Ye shall not eat one day, nor two days, nor five days, neither ten days, nor twenty days," Yahweh instructed Moses to say, "but even a whole month, until it come out at your nostrils, and it be loathsome unto you, because that ye have rejected the Lord which is among you, and have troubled Him with weeping, saying: Why, now, came we forth out of Egypt?" (Num. 11:19–20)

Moses demanded to know how he was supposed to come up with enough butchered meat to feed six hundred thousand soldiers and their dependents, and for a whole month at that. "Shall the flocks and the herds be slain for them, to suffice them?" asked Moses, "or shall the fish of the sea be gathered together for them, to suffice them?" (Num. 11:21 KJV)

Yahweh was understandably astounded and perhaps even aghast at the sudden dullness of the man who had witnessed so many signs and wonders and ought to have known perfectly well that Yahweh was capable of working a miracle whenever he chose.

"Is the Lord's hand waxed short?" replied Yahweh, indulging in a bit of divine sarcasm. "Now shalt thou see whether My word shall come to pass unto thee or not." (Num. 11:23)

Then the latest bit of divine legerdemain began. "And there went forth a wind from the Lord, and brought across quails from the sea, and let them fall by the camp," the Bible reports. So abundant were the fallen quail that they piled up around the camp to a depth of two cubits* for a distance equal to a day's march in any direction (Num. 11:31–32). The people stuffed themselves with roasted flesh, but Yahweh exacted a cruel revenge on them.

---

*A cubit is equivalent to approximately eighteen inches or a half meter, although the precise measurement varied through history.

While the flesh was yet between their teeth, before it was chewed, the anger of the Lord was kindled against the people, and the Lord smote the people with a very great plague. (Num. 11:33)[7]

The survivors of the plague, sickened at the sight of dead quail and dead kinfolk, packed up and marched off to a new camping ground. The stopping place that they left behind was dubbed Kibroth-hattaavah—"the graves of lust"[8]—"because there they buried the people that lusted." (Num. 11:34)

A WOMAN OF COLOR

Yet again was murmuring against Moses heard in the camp of the Israelites, but the source of the latest sedition must have surprised and shocked Moses. The words of condemnation fell from the lips of his own sister and brother: "And Miriam and Aaron spoke against Moses because of the Cushite woman whom he had married" (Num. 12:1), as if to suggest that the man who had been anointed by God to lead the Israelites ought to have chosen a bride from one of the twelve tribes.

By "Cushite," Miriam and Aaron were apparently referring to the people of Cush, a biblical term used to identify the land later known as Ethiopia, and suggesting that Moses had married not only a foreigner but also a woman of color.* Such was the meaning given to their complaint by Martin Luther, who translated "Cushite" as "Negress."[9] But the whole controversy is something of a mystery, since the only wife of Moses actually named in the Bible is Zipporah, a Midianite. The rabbis tried to solve the mystery by supplying Moses with an Ethiopian wife in an elaborate yarn about his adventures as a mercenary-king before coming to Midian and marrying Zipporah, and contemporary scholarship has proposed a less fanciful solution by suggesting that the second wife of Moses came not from Ethiopia (or Cush) but from a place called

---

*More recently, Moses himself has come to be regarded as a man of color in certain folk traditions, possibly because he was born on the African continent. "As black as Moses" is how Mark Twain described the black-skinned Africans he saw in Morocco in *The Innocents Abroad*. Nothing in the Bible or biblical traditions, however, suggests that Moses was black.

Cushan, "a tribe or confederacy of tribes" that may have been related in some way to the Midianites.[10] "I see the tents of Cushan in affliction," goes an enigmatic line in the Book of Habakkuk. "The curtains of the land of Midian do tremble." (Hab. 3:7)

The real motive of Aaron and Miriam in attacking Moses, however, had nothing to do with the race or tribe of his wife. What really bothered them was the power that their brother wielded as leader of the Israelites and spokesman of God. Miriam, as the Bible makes clear, was a prophetess in her own right (Exod. 15:20); Aaron was the anointed high priest; both of them were older than Moses—and the Bible suggests they resented the prerogatives of their younger brother, who routinely betook himself to the tent of meeting and came out again with elaborate accounts of his long conversations with God.

"Hath the Lord indeed spoken only to Moses?" they dared to ask out loud. "Hath He not spoken also with us?" (Num. 12:2)

The rabbis depicted the attack on Moses by Aaron and Miriam as sibling rivalry of the pettiest kind. Miriam has been told by Zipporah that Moses abstains from sexual relations with her in order to purify himself for his dealings with God. But Miriam and Aaron remark to each other that they receive their own divine revelations even though they continue to enjoy the sexual companionship of their spouses. "Moses abstains from conjugal joys only out of pride," they murmur against Moses, "to show how holy a man he is."[11]

What remains unspoken in the biblical text is an even harsher accusation that may have occurred not only to Aaron and Miriam but to other Israelites too. How did they know that Moses conversed with Yahweh at all? Nobody else was privileged to witness his supposed encounters with an invisible deity in an empty tent. What Moses reported about his intimate relationship with Yahweh could only be embraced on blind faith—and, as we have seen, faith was not found in abundance among the Israelites.

Moses did not seem especially riled up by the accusations of Aaron and Miriam; nor did he show any jealousy when Yahweh allowed his "glory" to be seen by the men and women of Israel or his "spirit" to descend on the elders of Israel from time to time. When Yahweh agreed to bestow the gift of prophecy on the elders (Num. 11:25), it was Joshua rather than Moses who panicked when two of them, Eldad and Medad, continued to sit in the middle of encampment and spout words of prophecy long after the others had fallen silent.

"My lord Moses," Joshua had cried out, "stop them!" (Num. 11:28 NEB)

"Are thou jealous for my sake?" replied Moses. "Would that all the Lord's people were prophets, that the Lord would put His spirit upon them!" (Num. 11:29)

Moses remained silent and self-effacing in the face of the accusations of Miriam and Aaron: "Now the man Moses was very meek," the Bible insists, conveniently ignoring his bad temper and poor impulse control, "above all the men that were upon the face of the earth." (Num. 12:3) But, as far as Yahweh was concerned, Miriam and Aaron had openly challenged his authority, and so he took the matter in hand. God spoke "suddenly" to the three siblings, summoning them to assemble at the tent of meeting, then manifested himself in a pillar of cloud at the door of the tent. Yahweh singled out Aaron and Miriam, and they stepped forward. "Hear now My words," said Yahweh to the two of them.

> If there be a prophet among you, I the Lord do make Myself known unto him in a vision, I do speak with him in a dream. My servant Moses is not so; he is trusted in all My house; with him do I speak mouth to mouth, even manifestly, and not in dark speeches; and the similitude of the Lord doth he behold. Wherefore then were ye not afraid to speak against My servant, against Moses? (Num. 12:6–8)

With these words, Yahweh disappeared from the tent of meeting, but he left behind an unmistakable sign of his wrath toward the rebellious siblings.

"And when the cloud was removed from over the Tent," goes the biblical account, "behold, Miriam was leprous, as white as snow." (Num. 12:10)

Staring in horror at his sister's suddenly foul and disfigured flesh, Aaron promptly repented of his challenge to the authority of Moses. Curiously, he suffered no punishment of his own, but he issued a plea on behalf of Miriam. "Oh my lord, lay not, I pray thee, sin upon us, for that we have done foolishly, and for that we have sinned," pleaded Aaron, addressing not God but Moses and adopting the abject stance of a slave toward his master. "Let her not, I pray, be as one dead, of whom the flesh is half consumed when he cometh out of his mother's womb." (Num. 12:11–12)

A miraculous cure, Moses must have understood, would only confirm his victory and their defeat. So Moses addressed an urgent prayer to Yahweh: "Heal her now, O God, I beseech thee." (Num. 12:13)

God resolved to grant the prayer, but not before making a public display to show what happened to a woman who dared to claim for herself the right of prophecy. "If her father had but spit in her face, should she not hide in shame seven days?" Yahweh mused out loud to Moses. "Let her be shut up without the camp seven days, and after that she shall be brought forth again." (Num. 12:14)

So Miriam was sent out of the encampment to endure her seven days of public humiliation. Then, as God had promised, she was cured of leprosy. The point had been made that God was on the side of Moses, and Miriam and Aaron would never again dare to place themselves in opposition to him. But their rebellion, which may have been the most intimate challenge to the authority of Moses, would not be the last one.

"EVERY ONE A PRINCE"

The next order that Yahweh dispatched to Moses was a sure sign that the aimless wanderings were coming to an end and the war of conquest was about to begin. Moses was to recruit one man from each of the twelve tribes, "every one a prince," for a dangerous mission of espionage in Canaan that would prepare the Israelites for the full-scale invasion. "Send thou men," Yahweh instructed Moses, "that they may spy out the land of Canaan, which I give unto the children of Israel." (Num. 13:2)

The men were to infiltrate the land of Canaan from the south, where an empty desert and barren mountains formed a kind of no-man's-land, and then press on to the hill country, the farm country, the towns and cities, all the way to the northernmost reaches of the land. They would carefully survey "the people that dwelleth therein, whether they are strong or weak, whether they are few or many; and what the land is that they dwell in, whether it is good or bad; and what cities they are that they dwell in, whether in camps, or in strongholds; and what the land is, whether it is fat or lean, whether there is wood therein, or not." (Num. 13:18–20)

And then Moses concluded his briefing and sent off the spies with a final word of encouragement: "And be ye of good courage, and bring of the fruit of the land." (Num. 13:20)

Forty days passed before the spies returned from their mission. As the twelve men approached the camp, they carried a cluster of grapes so fat and abundant that it required the strength of two men to bear up the pole on which it hung. Others brought bundles of figs and pomegranates that must have seemed sweetly irresistible to men and women who had tired of the daily ration of manna long before. And the tales that they told of their adventures were even more astounding than the bounty they had carried back from Canaan—astounding, yes, and alarming, too.

"We came unto the land whither thou sent us, and surely it floweth with milk and honey, and this is the fruit of it," they said, gesturing toward the gargantuan bunch of grapes taken from a place called Eshcol. "But the people that dwell in the land are fierce, and the cities are fortified, and great; and moreover we saw the children of Anak there." (Num. 13:27–29)

The spies were referring to a legendary race of giants who were thought to be descendants of the Nephilim, the fearful offspring of the "sons of God" who descended to earth soon after the Creation and bedded down the "daughters of men" who caught their fancy, as we read in one of the most enigmatic passages of the Bible (Gen. 6:4). And then the spies listed the flesh-and-blood tribes and nations whom the Israelites would be forced to fight on their way into the Promised Land—the Amalekites in the south, the Hittites and the Jebusites and the Amorites in the mountains, the Canaanites by the shores of the Mediterranean Sea and the banks of the Jordan River. (Num. 13:28–29)

Moses must have despaired at the fearful report, but one of the twelve spies, a man named Caleb from the tribe of Judah, boldly stepped forward and addressed the crowd with bracing words. "We should go up at once and possess it," Caleb called out, "for we are well able to overcome it." (Num. 13:30)

"We are not able to go up against the people, for they are stronger than we," retorted Caleb's comrades, who proceeded to spin out even more terrifying tales about what they had seen in Canaan. "The land, through which we have passed to spy it out, is a land that will swallow up any who go to live in it. All the people we saw there are men of gigantic size, and we were in our own sight as grasshoppers, and so we were in their sight." (Num. 13:31–33)[12]

The horror stories of the other spies stoked the fear of the Israelites, and the whole of the encampment "lifted up their voice, and cried, and the people wept that night." (Num. 14:1) Then, as the night passed, the keening and moaning of the terrified crowd were replaced by the purposeful noise of murmuring against Moses and Aaron.

"Would that we had died in the land of Egypt!" cried the panic-mongers. "Or would that we had died in this wilderness! And wherefore doth the Lord bring us unto this land, to fall by the sword? Our wives and our little ones will be a prey; were it not better for us to return to Egypt?" (Num. 14:2–3)

"Let us make a captain," the crowd roared back at the rabble-rousers, "and let us return to Egypt." (Num. 14:4)

Moses and Aaron fell on their faces in the sight of the crowd, as if to emphasize how devastating was the sin of cowardice and defeatism. Caleb and Joshua, the only two spies who remained unafraid, "rent their clothes" in a primal expression of grief and mourning—but the two of them stayed on their feet and tried to rally the crowd.

"The land, which was passed through to spy it out, is an exceeding good land," Caleb insisted once again. "If the Lord delight in us, then he will bring us into this land and give it unto us—a land which floweth with milk and honey." (Num. 14:7–8)

"Only rebel not against the Lord, neither fear ye the people of the land," added Joshua, "for they are bread for us, their defence is removed from over them, and the Lord is with us; fear them not." (Num. 14:9)

The crowd may have been afraid to fight the native peoples of Canaan, but they showed no fear of Moses and Aaron, Joshua and Caleb. Indeed, they were ready to answer the sweet words of encouragement with a shower of stones, and they would have done so if Yahweh had not descended once again and manifested himself in the tent of meeting where all of Israel was able to see his "glory" (Num. 14:10).

"How long will this people despise me?" God asked Moses, "and how long will they not believe in Me, for all the signs which I have wrought among them?" (Num. 14:11)

CARCASSES IN THE WILDERNESS

"I will smite them with the pestilence, and destroy them," Yahweh raged to Moses, "and make of thee a nation greater and mightier than they." (Num. 14:12)

Did Moses offer up a sigh of weariness and frustration at that moment? Yahweh was back to his old threats, and Moses repeated the very same speech that he had given on previous occasions when Yahweh was in the mood to exterminate the Chosen People.

"Now if Thou shalt kill this people as one man," Moses said to Yahweh, reprising his earlier arguments against Yahweh's threats of mass murder against the Israelites, "when the Egyptians shall hear, they will say to the inhabitants of the land, and the nations which have heard of the fame of Thee will speak, saying: Because the Lord was not able to bring this people into the land which He swore unto them, therefore He hath slain them in the wilderness." (Num. 14:13–16)[13]

So, once again, Moses played on Yahweh's concern for his own reputation and his own place in history, flattering him and soothing him.

"And now, I pray Thee, let the power of the Lord be great, as Thou hast spoken, saying: The Lord is slow to anger, and plenteous in lovingkindness, forgiving iniquity and transgression," Moses continued. "Pardon, I pray Thee, the iniquity of this people according to the greatness of thy lovingkindness, and as Thou hast forgiven this people, from Egypt even until now." (Num. 14:17–19)[14]

The words worked the intended magic on Yahweh, and once again he relented.

"I have pardoned according to thy word," Yahweh conceded—but he was not willing to let the latest act of defiance go unpunished. "Surely all those men that have seen My glory, and My signs, which I wrought in Egypt and in the wilderness, yet have put Me to proof these ten times, and have not hearkened to My voice, surely they shall not see the land which I swore unto their fathers, neither shall any of them that despised Me see it." (Num. 14:21–23)

The Israelites would not be slain here and now, but neither would they be allowed to enter the land of Canaan. Their punishment, then, was to "wander to and fro in the wilderness forty years"—one year for every day the faithless spies spent on their mission in the land of Canaan, as God pointed out in a gesture of poetic justice. At the end of forty years, the men and women who had been born in slavery, "the generation that had done evil in the sight of the Lord," would have died out. (Num. 14:34, 32:13)

> As I live, surely as ye have spoken in Mine ears, so will I do to you. Your carcasses shall fall in this wilderness, and all that were numbered of you, from twenty years old and upward, ye that have murmured against Me, surely ye shall not come into the land. (Num. 14:28–29)

A very different fate awaited the children of the Israelites who had been raised in the wilderness, who had not known slavery in Egypt and who were not tainted with the faithlessness and cowardice of the slave generation.

> And your children shall be wanderers in the wilderness forty years, and shall bear your strayings, until your carcasses be consumed in the wilderness. But your little ones, that ye said would be a prey, them I will bring in, and they shall know the land which you have rejected. (Num. 14:31–33)[15]

Of the slave generation, only the intrepid Joshua and the faithful Caleb—"because he had another spirit with him, and hath followed Me fully" (Num. 14:24)—would be permitted to live long enough to set foot on the soil of the Promised Land. The spies who had played on the fears of the Israelites and prompted the latest rebellion were struck down then and there with a divine plague (Num. 14:38).

On the fate of Moses and Aaron and Miriam—would they end up like the faithful Joshua and Caleb or the godforsaken Israelites?—Yahweh remained utterly and pointedly silent.

YE SHALL FALL BY THE SWORD

Thus chastened, the Israelites grimly resigned themselves to the fate that awaited them under the leadership of Moses. But an impulsive few responded to the harsh decree of Yahweh with an odd and quixotic gesture—they suddenly and paradoxically resolved to march on Canaan after all. Rising early in the morning, they strapped on their swords and set out in the direction of the hill-country near Beersheba in the southern stretches of Canaan, where they intended to fight their way into the Promised Land.

"Lo, we are here, and will go up unto the place where the Lord hath promised," they told each other, "for we have sinned." (Num. 14:40)

The self-appointed conquerors of Canaan vowed to drive into the Promised Land directly from the south.[16] Yahweh, however, had already selected a different line of march for the army of Israel, a much more circuitous route that would carry the Israelites all the way around the southern border of Canaan and into Moab for an assault on Canaan from its eastern frontier. If the little band of warriors thought to redeem themselves by marching into battle, they were mistaken. Their act of courage was seen as an act of treason, according to the Bible, and they condemned themselves yet again as rebels against the authority of God and Moses.

"Go not up, for the Lord is not among you," sniggered Moses, who remained in camp with the Ark of the Covenant and the rest of the sacred relics that were customarily carried into battle, and he offered a dire prophecy to these latest rebels: "For there the Amalekite and the Canaanite are before you, and ye shall fall by the sword; forasmuch as ye are turned back from following the Lord, the Lord will not be with you." (Num. 14:42–43)

The warriors ignored the warning and insisted on ascending into the hill-country of Canaan, but the whole affair ended just as Moses had predicted. "Then the Amalekite and the Canaanite, who dwelt in the hill-country, came down, and smote them and beat them down, even unto Hormah." (Num. 14:45) An ominous meaning could be read in the defeat—God had promised to sweep away the native-dwelling people of Canaan and open the land to the Israelites, but here was the first suggestion that the victory of the Israelites was not assured.

REVOLUTION

Far from the tent of meeting, out of sight and earshot of the inner circle of Moses, a few unhappy men were bent in whispered conversation. Although they had witnessed the public humiliation of Miriam and Aaron at the threshold of the tent of meeting, the scourging of the camp with plague, the rout of a detachment of Israelites in their first skirmish in Canaan, they were undeterred by these signs of divine disfavor, and they dared to plot an uprising of their own. Two of the plotters were Dathan and Abiram, and the third man was a Levite named Korah.

The plotters first came to the attention of Moses only when Korah and his co-conspirators—"princes of the congregation, the elect men of the assembly, men of renown," 250 of them in all (Num. 16:2)—declared their defiance of the man who had always insisted that God was on his side. Suddenly, Moses found himself in a face-to-face confrontation with Korah and his cohorts.

"Ye take too much upon you, seeing all the congregation are holy, every one of them, and the Lord is among them," the rebels declared, piously invoking the name of Yahweh and alluding to his solemn statement on Sinai that Israel was "a kingdom of priests, and a holy nation." (Num. 16:3, Exod. 19:4–6) And then they openly challenged the authority that Moses and Aaron had wielded over the rest of the Israelites for so long and with such pious self-assurance: "Why, then, do ye lift yourselves up above the assembly of the Lord?" (Num. 16:3)[17]

Moses answered the challenge by falling to his face on the ground, a gesture that was apparently intended to demonstrate how appalling he found the defiance of Korah and, at the same time, to invoke the authority of Yahweh through a gesture of prayer. A moment later, Moses was back on his feet and ready to crush Korah and the band of renegade Levites who followed him (Num. 16:4).

"In the morning the Lord will show you who are His, and who is holy," taunted Moses, who proceeded to describe the rules of a contest that would decide, once and for all, who enjoyed the confidence of Yahweh and who did not. Moses invited Korah and his comrades-in-arms, all of them Levites in service to the priesthood, to load their fire pans with aromatic incense and set them afire as an offering to Yahweh. Aaron would do the same, and then the Israelites would see whether Yahweh favored the high priest of Israel or the Levites who followed Korah. "And it shall be that the man whom the Lord doth choose, he shall be holy," explained Moses, who added his own opinion on how the contest would turn out: "Ye take too much upon you, ye sons of Levi." (Num. 16:5, 7)

As it happened, a second conspiracy was at work in the camp of the Israelites under the leadership of Dathan and Abiram. According to rabbinical tradition, they are the same malefactors who had threatened to betray Moses to the authorities for striking down the Egyptian taskmaster, and now they rise up in open rebellion against Moses. Unlike Korah, who presented himself as a pious fellow who sought nothing more than equal access to God, Dathan and Abiram were wholly secular rivals who resented Moses for making himself the uncrowned king of Israel. And when Moses summoned them to answer for their sedition, the Bible reports, they refused to comply.

"Is it a small thing that thou hast brought us up out of a land flowing with milk and honey, to kill us in the wilderness, but thou must needs make thyself a prince over us?" they complained, audaciously characterizing Egypt rather than Canaan as a land of "milk and honey." "Moreover thou hast not brought us into a land flowing with milk and honey, nor even given us inheritance of fields and vineyards." (Num. 16:13–14)[18]

Because Dathan and Abiram accused him of political rather than theological offenses against the people of Israel, Moses did not fall on his face at their words. Rather, he raged against his accusers with raw fury. Moses was quick to answer the charges laid against him, to acquit himself of the accusation that he had aspired to power for its own sake and then misused the power that God had bestowed upon him; but he addressed his words to God.

"I have not taken one ass from them," Moses assured Yahweh, "neither have I hurt one of them." (Num. 16:15)

On the next morning, the rebels appeared as scheduled at the door of the tent of meeting, each one carrying his fire pan and a supply of incense. As the aromatic clouds of incense rose in the crisp morning air, the assembled tribes witnessed the sudden manifestation of the "glory" of God.

"Separate yourselves from among this congregation," Yahweh told Moses and Aaron, "that I may consume them in a moment." (Num. 16:21)

Moses and Aaron must have been well pleased at God's preference for them, but they did not want their entire assembly of Israelites to go up in flames along with the defiant Levites. "O God, the God of the spirits of all flesh," they pleaded in unison, "shall one man sin, and wilt Thou be wroth with all the congregation?" (Num. 16:22)

Once again, Yahweh responded to their plea for mercy, and he instructed Moses and Aaron to address the gathered Israelites. "Depart, I pray you, from the tents of these wicked men, and touch nothing of theirs, lest ye be swept away in all their sins." (Num. 16:26)

So it was that Dathan and Abiram and "their wives, and their sons, and their little ones" found themselves abandoned by the rest of the Israelites, who stood at a safe distance. Moses stood alone at the threshold of the tent.

"By this ye shall know that the Lord hath sent me to do all these works, and that I have not done them of mine own mind," Moses hastened to explain, anxious to shift both the credit and the blame for what was about to happen to Yahweh. "If these men die a natural death, then the Lord hath not sent me. But if the Lord makes a great chasm, and the ground opens its mouth and swallows them and all that is theirs, and they go down alive into the pit,* then ye shall understand that these men have despised the Lord." (Num. 16:28–30)[19]

As these words died on his lips, the ground beneath the feet of the rebels, apparently so solid, shuddered, groaned, and then cracked wide open, just as if the earth itself had opened its mouth, and all of the rebels who had stood so defiantly at the openings of their tents— Korah, Dathan and Abiram, their wives and sons and little ones— "went down alive into the pit, and the earth closed upon them, and they perished from among the assembly." (Num. 16:33) A moment later, as the Israelites fled in panic "lest the earth swallow us up" (Num. 16:34), a ball of fire fell from on high and incinerated the rest of the conspirators. "And fire came forth from the Lord," the Bible reports, "and devoured the two hundred and fifty men that offered the incense." (Num. 16:34–35)

KING MOSES

Moses is embraced in the traditions of all three Bible-based religions as the Emancipator, the Lawgiver, the Prophet. He is praised as the Good Shepherd who faithfully tended the flock of Israel, the Intercessor and

---

*The original Hebrew text of the Bible uses the term *sheol*, which is sometimes translated into English as "the pit." Sheol was vaguely understood by the Bible author as a murky underworld to which the dead are consigned. Sheol is not equivalent to the Christian concept of Hell as a place where the evil are punished after death, however, and the familiar notions of Heaven and Hell are entirely absent from the Five Books of Moses.

Mediator who pleaded with God for mercy on behalf of a weak and flawed people. At one or two places in the Bible, Yahweh even likened Moses to a god: "Aaron will be the mouthpiece, and you will be the god he speaks for." (Exod. 4:16)[20] Only one honorific is denied him by the biblical sources: Moses is never called a king. And yet the repeated acts of insurrection in the wilderness betray the fact that Moses was perceived as a monarch by the very people over whom he exercised such stern authority, and more than a few of them resented him bitterly.

Indeed, the Bible betrays a distinct fear and loathing of monarchy among the Israelites. Kingship always suggested oppression and enslavement for the nomadic tribes of Israel, and Pharaoh is not the only example of a monarch who sought to deprive an Israelite of his liberty. When, at long last, the Israelites clamored for a monarch of their own in the newly conquered but still chaotic land of Canaan—"Now make us a king to judge us like all the nations" (1 Sam. 8:5)—the prophet Samuel delivered a bitter denunciation of kings in general. "This will be the manner of the king that shall reign over you," warned Samuel. "He will take your sons for his chariots and to be his horsemen, to plow his ground, and to reap his harvest, and to make his instruments of war. And he will take your daughters to be perfumers, and to be cooks, and to be bakers. And he will take your fields, and your vineyards, and your olive-yards, even the best of them, and give them to his servants. And ye shall cry out in that day because of your king whom ye shall have chosen, and the Lord will not answer you in that day." (1 Sam. 8:11–17)[21]

Philo acquitted Moses of these kingly crimes in his biography, insisting that Moses neither aspired to power over the Israelites nor abused that power when it was bestowed upon him by God. "Of all these men, Moses was elected the leader . . . , not having gained it like some men who have forced their way to power and supremacy by force of arms and intrigue . . . , but having been appointed for the sake of his virtue and excellence," urged Philo. "[H]e alone of all the persons who have ever enjoyed supreme authority, neither accumulated treasures of silver and gold, nor levied taxes, nor acquired possession of house, or property, or cattle, or servants of his household, or revenues . . . , although he might have acquired an unlimited abundance of them."[22]

Even Philo, however, was willing to concede that a man who walks like a king and talks like a king ought to be called king: "[T]he king, and lawgiver, and high priest, and prophet" is how Philo listed the offices of

Moses.[23] And Moses *is* regarded as something of an autocrat—and condemned for it—in the biblical account of the uprisings that he faced and crushed in the last days of his life. The very grievances that Samuel cataloged a few centuries later were put in the mouths of the dissidents who rose up against Moses by the rabbinical storytellers. Although we have come to regard Moses as a champion of liberty and an embodiment of thoroughly democratic values, the Bible confirms that he ruthlessly suppressed even the faintest stirrings of insurrection by the Israelites.

Indeed, Korah and the Levites who rose up against Moses claimed to act out of purely egalitarian motives—"*All* the congregation are holy, every one of them, and the Lord is among them"—but the biblical author and the sages who came later did not regard Korah as praiseworthy. Korah is depicted as a rabble-rouser in one rabbinical tale, and his fellow dissidents spread rumors about the boundless sexual appetites of Moses, warning "their wives to keep far from him."[24] Not content with merely slandering Moses, the rabbis suggested, Korah's co-conspirators try to stone him to death.[25] Indeed, the essential message of the Bible is that defiance of Moses and defiance of God were one and the same, an equation that has been invoked by autocrats throughout the ages to justify their power and prerogatives. In that sense, the divine right of kings began with Moses.

Yet the rabbinical literature preserves at least a faint trace of sympathy for the democratic impulses that drove Korah. He sets about raising a rebellion by playing on the resentment of the Israelites toward Moses. "He has laid upon all the children of Israel heavy burdens," Korah tells the others, "and given them laws which are very severe." And Korah bemoans the fate of a poor widow who is so harried by the burdensome commandments of Yahweh that she faces starvation. The law of Moses forbids her to sow her field with two kinds of seed or to reap the corners of her field and yet commands her to tithe to the priests, and so she is forced to sell her land in order to meet her obligation. With what is left of the proceeds, she buys two sheep, but then Aaron shows up and demands the firstborn sheep for himself. "All the firstlings," he reminds her, citing the Mosaic code, "thou shalt sanctify unto the Lord thy God." When she slaughters the remaining sheep, he shows up again and demands "the shoulder, the two cheeks and the maw as his share." And when she seeks to evade his latest demand by declaring that the animal has already been devoted to God, Aaron seizes *both* sheep. "If such is the case, then *all* is mine, for everything devoted in Israel belongs to the priests," says Aaron to the poor widow.

"Thus, the priests are always despoiling the poor, the widows and the orphans," Korah declares. "When the children of Israel are asking them: why are ye acting thus? they reply: because such is the Law!"[26]*

At the heart of Korah's rebellion is an idea that strikes the contemporary reader as thoroughly appealing: Moses and Aaron ought not to lord it over the rest of the Israelites because every man and woman enjoys the right to address God without the permission or intercession of someone in authority. To justify his democratic rhetoric, Korah invoked the promise that Yahweh had once made to the Chosen People: Israel would be a "kingdom of priests" and a "holy nation," a promise that he interpreted to mean that all Israelites are created equal in the eyes of God. But the biblical author who was at work a couple of thousand years ago did not intend these words to carry a democratic message. A "kingdom of priests," as Bible scholars have suggested, was a purely elitist notion that meant only that the kings of Israel would be drawn from the ranks of the priesthood, or that the Israelites would be expected to maintain an especially high standard of piety and purity, or that Israel would be called upon to carry the word of God to the rest of the world as "a light unto the nations."[27] Only to the contemporary reader does God's promise appear to be an invitation for the individual to address himself or herself directly to God.

The rabbis who elaborated upon the rebellion of Korah were not democrats or egalitarians, and they were quick to insist that Moses and Aaron were right, and Korah was wrong—Moses may have been elected to his high office by no one except God, but God's vote was the only one that counted. "The death and destruction of Korah and his company ought to have convinced the children of Israel that Moses was only acting according to the will of God," and they hastened to reassure their congregants "that he had never usurped the power for himself or arbitrarily invested his brother Aaron with the priesthood."[28]

Still, even the biblical author was moved to report that Moses defended himself against the charges laid against him by Korah and the other rebels, and his apologia inevitably reminds the modern reader of

---

*Much the same story was used by opponents of the New Deal, who cast Roosevelt in place of Moses and imagined federal bureaucrats in place of the priesthood, and again during the Johnson presidency as a protest against the War on Poverty.

Nixon's "I am not a crook" speech: "I have not taken one ass from them." (Num. 16:15) Perhaps Moses protested too much when he protested at all, but even if he were innocent of any abuse of power, the fact remains that Korah and the other rebels do not appear quite as blameworthy to the contemporary reader as they did to the biblical sources. Indeed, if we prefer to see Moses as a man who "proclaimed liberty throughout the land," then we might begin to see Korah, Dathan, and Abiram, too, as freedom fighters.

BUDS, BLOSSOMS, AND ALMONDS

As if to remind the Israelites of the fate that awaited anyone who defied God and his prophet, Yahweh directed Moses to gather up the fire pans from among the ashes of the dead rebels, beat the pans into flat sheets of metal, and use the sheets to cover the altar "that they may be a sign unto the children of Israel"—a pointed reminder that "no common man, that is not of the seed of Aaron, draw near to burn incense before the Lord." (Num. 17:3–4) And yet, if the all-knowing and all-seeing Yahweh thought that the sudden death of Korah and his fellow rebels would be enough to inspire obedience in the Israelites, he was wrong again. On the very next morning, the camp was abuzz with yet more treasonous murmurings against Moses and Aaron.

"Ye have killed the people of the Lord," they dared to cry out, stubbornly siding with the rebels who were now only ash and charred bone and condemning Moses and Aaron for insisting *they* were the people of the Lord (Num. 17:6).

Yet again the cloud that signaled the presence of Yahweh descended over the tent of meeting, and yet again the "glory" of God was seen in the camp. "Get you up from among this congregation," Yahweh warned Moses and Aaron once again, "that I may consume them in a moment." (Num. 17:10) Moses and Aaron fell to their faces, pleading abjectly for mercy on behalf of the defiant crowd that refused to beg for itself, and Moses ordered Aaron to light up a fresh supply of incense as an urgent gesture of atonement. "The plague is begun," Moses cried out, and he saw that the Israelites were already falling where they stood. Fourteen thousand and seven hundred of them were dead before Aaron succeeded in stopping the spread of the plague by placing himself "between the dead and the living." (Num. 17:11, 13)

One last gesture was offered by Yahweh to the ever dubious Israelites to confirm the leadership of Moses and Aaron—and, surprisingly, it was a bit of legerdemain rather than an act of vengeance. Yahweh ordered that twelve rods be gathered, one from each of the twelve tribes, and that the name of the prince of each tribe be inscribed on the rods. When it came to the rod of the Levites, Aaron's name was to appear. All of the twelve rods were to be placed in the tent of meeting, and when the Israelites next beheld the bundle of sticks, they would find miraculous evidence of God's will. Somehow, Yahweh decided that sideshow magic would be more persuasive than plague and hellfire or the sight of the earth cracking wide open to swallow the enemies of Moses and Aaron.

"And it shall come to pass, that the man whom I shall choose, his rod shall bud," Yahweh explained, "and I will make to cease from Me the murmurings of the children of Israel, which they murmur against you." (Num. 17:19)

The next day, Moses entered the tent of meeting, "and, behold, the rod of Aaron for the house of Levi was budded, and put forth buds, and bloomed blossoms, and bore ripe almonds." Once the miracle had been displayed to the assembly of Israelites, Yahweh ordered that the rod of Aaron be placed in the tent of meeting along with the other sacred relics—the stone tablets on which the Ten Commandments were inscribed, the jarful of manna—and kept there forever as "a token against the rebellious children." Perhaps the Israelites would pause and reflect on the miraculous rod of Aaron before running amok and risking death from on high, Yahweh mused out loud to Moses, and "there may be made an end of their murmurings, against Me, that they die not." (Lev. 17:23, 25)

Yet again, God guessed wrong.

THE SIN OF MOSES

At the oasis of Kadesh in the wilderness of Zin, Moses called a halt and signaled the Israelites to make camp. Here they lowered the Ark, here they erected the tent of meeting, here they pitched their tents for what turned out to be a long rest. The Bible discloses only that they "stayed some time at Kadesh" (Num. 20:1 NEB), but rabbinical tradition and contemporary scholarship alike propose a much longer sojourn at

Kadesh, perhaps twenty years or even more, the life span of a full generation.[29] Here at Kadesh, Moses must have sensed that the long march we call the Exodus was coming to an end, and a new era was about to begin, an era of war and conquest. What role Moses himself would play from now on, whether he would see the day of victory toward which he had been struggling, was still an open question.

Yahweh had already disclosed the fate he had decreed for the generation of Israelites who had been born in Egypt and who had proved themselves better suited for slavery than freedom: God would make them wander aimlessly for forty years, and only when the slave generation was gone would the Israelites be permitted to enter the land of Canaan. Already, the old guard was dying in the wilderness. "Miriam died there," the Bible records, "and was buried there." (Num. 20:1) The Israelites must have mourned the loss of the beloved priestess of Israel, the woman who had led the song of victory at the Red Sea, although the biblical author offers nothing more than a brief death report. And here at Kadesh, too, the destiny of Moses was revealed in an incident that seemed trivial at first but turned out to be momentous.

The fateful incident began with precisely the kind of civil disorder that was a tiresome fact of life in the camp of the Israelites by now. When the springs and wells at Kadesh ran dry and the supplies of fresh water ran out, the Israelites assembled themselves and approached Moses and Aaron with words and gestures that must have struck them as deeply familiar.

> Would that we had perished when our brethren perished before the Lord! And why have ye brought the assembly of the Lord into this wilderness to die there, we and our cattle? And wherefore have ye made us to come up out of Egypt, to bring us unto this evil place? It is no place of seed, or of figs, or of vines, or of pomegranates; neither is there any water to drink. (Num. 20:3–5)

Moses and Aaron once again led the angry mob to the tent of meeting, fell down on their faces, and received a set of instructions from Yahweh. "Take the rod, and assemble the congregation," God told Moses and Aaron, "and speak ye unto the rock before their eyes, that it give forth to them water out of the rock; so thou shalt give the congregation and their cattle drink." (Num. 20:8)[30]

The words of Yahweh were simple and straightforward, and yet, as we shall shortly see, Moses and Aaron did not follow the precise instructions they had been given, much to their sorrow and grief. Did Moses and Aaron, both men of advanced years, fail to heed the words of Yahweh because they were hard of hearing? Did their attention wander as God spoke? Did they think back to the day at the place called Rephidim—another day, another place—when Yahweh first instructed them to draw water from a rock? Were they simply so weary and frustrated at repeating the task that they allowed their anger to overwhelm their judgment? Or, perhaps, was Moses guilty of the sin of pride, claiming for himself the miraculous powers that had been bestowed upon him by Yahweh? The biblical author does not answer any of these questions, but the lapse was to have catastrophic consequences for both Moses and Aaron.

"Hear now, ye rebels," Moses cried out to the thirsty mob, "are we to bring you forth water out of this rock?" (Num. 20:19)

Then Moses brought down his wooden staff against the rock—the same procedure that had worked so well at Rephidim—and "water came forth abundantly, and the congregation drank, and their cattle." (Num. 20:11)

One small detail ought to have alerted Moses to the fact that something was very wrong. Only a single blow had been necessary to draw water from the rock at Rephidim, but here at Kadesh the water flowed only on the second blow. Yahweh allowed Moses to understand that he had made a terrible mistake—Moses was supposed to *speak* to the rock, not *strike* it—and now Yahweh regarded both Moses and Aaron as rebels for failing to carry out his instructions with precision. The devil, as Moses was about to learn, is in the details.

"Because ye believed not in Me, to sanctify Me in the eyes of the children of Israel," declared Yahweh, harshly and impulsively, "therefore ye shall not bring this assembly into the land which I have given them." (Num. 20:12)

The spring at Rephidim had been called Meribah by the biblical author, and the spring near the oasis of Kadesh was given the very same name. *Meribah* means "strife,"[31] and the Bible explains that the place earned its name because it was there that "the children of Israel strove with the Lord." (Num. 20:13) But it was Moses and Aaron alone, the loyal servants of Yahweh, and not the unruly Israelites, who were made to suffer for what happened at the second Meribah—they would not be permitted to enter the Promised Land. Against the blow of a wooden staff upon a dry rock, a lifetime of struggle, hardship, and faithful service counted for nothing in the eyes of Yahweh.

THE SACRED OASIS

The line of march that the Israelites followed through the wilderness is carefully chronicled in some of the most tedious and baffling passages of the Bible: "And the children of Israel journeyed from Rameses, and pitched in Succoth. And they journeyed from Succoth, and pitched in Etham. And they journeyed from Etham, and turned back unto Pi-hahiroth, and they pitched before Migdol. . . ." (Num. 33:1–49)[32] Scholars have struggled without success to pinpoint these exotic place-names on a map of the Sinai Peninsula, but most of the sites where the Israelites pitched their tents are "no longer capable of being located at all," as Martin Noth flatly declares.[33]

But Kadesh (Num. 20:1), or as it is sometimes known, Kadesh-barnea (Num. 32:8) or Meribah-kadesh (Deut. 32:51)[34] has been identified with precision by contemporary Bible scholarship. The search for the historical reality behind the biblical references to Kadesh has been especially compelling because some scholars argue that it is Kadesh rather than Sinai or even the land of Canaan that figures most crucially in the history and theology that is hidden beneath the surface of the received text of the Bible.

The oasis known to the biblical author as Kadesh, insists Noth with utter self-confidence, "is to be identified with the region of the present-day spring 'en qdes [En-gedi], which lies about forty-six miles as the crow flies south-south-west of Beersheba."[35] If Kadesh is En-gedi, then it is the largest oasis in Sinai, several miles across, fifteen miles long, some sixty square miles in all, only a hundred miles or so from the border of Egypt.[36] "Murmuring brooks, rich vegetation of grasses, trees and shrubs and flowers, birds and insects conjure up a truly fairylike picture to the traveler who is arriving from the desert," writes Elias Auerbach about the real-life oasis of En-gedi. "For the poor Bedouin who knows hardly anything except severe privations, this too is 'a land flowing with milk and honey.' "[37]

Other sites in the same vicinity have been proposed as the real Kadesh. The renowned archaeologist C. Leonard Woolley, discoverer of the lost civilization of Ur, and T. E. Lawrence, the future "Lawrence of

Arabia," were sent into the Sinai shortly before World War I on an archaeological dig whose real purpose was to provide cover for a military expedition that had been assigned to map the terrain for use by the British Army in the event of hostilities in the Levant, and they proposed the district of Kossaima rather than the spring at En-gedi as the most likely site of Kadesh. "[A] dung-heap like [En-gedi]" was too barren to have supported the Israelites, write Woolley and Lawrence, and "only in the Kossaima district are to be found enough water and green stuffs to maintain so large a tribe for so long."[38]

Martin Buber, too, insists that Kadesh "should not be understood as meaning a single spot, but the entire group of level valleys lying south of Palestine on the way between Akaba and Beersheba." Here was found "a paradisical fruitfulness," a place where "the water bursts forth from the clefts and crannies of the rocks," as Buber reports. "To this day the soil, which is several feet deep, still provides the Arabs who till it with rich harvests of grain when there has been a good rainy season."[39]

The Bible itself confirms that Kadesh was the site of several crucial events in the life of Moses and the Exodus. As we have already seen, Miriam died at Kadesh, and the rock that Moses struck with his staff to draw water was located somewhere in the vicinity. By parsing out the biblical text, however, some scholars have come to believe that the sacred oasis of Kadesh, rather than the holy mountain called Sinai or Horeb, was the place where Yahweh first appeared to Moses in the guise of a burning bush[40] and where Yahweh made a covenant with Moses and handed him the Ten Commandments.[41] The battle between the Israelites and the Amalekites (Exod. 17:9) may have been fought for the possession of the oasis at Kadesh.[42] And Kadesh was where Moses reunited with his father-in-law and his own family; where Jethro offered the first sacrifice to Yahweh; where Miriam and Aaron, Dathan and Abiram, and Korah, too, rebelled against Moses; and where the manna and quails were miraculously provided to the Israelites.[43] Of seventeen biblical passages that recount the adventures of Moses during the Exodus, according to one scholar's count, thirteen are linked to Kadesh.[44]

A still more momentous significance for Kadesh has been proposed by scholars, one that undercuts the biblical account of the Exodus and the life of Moses. Perhaps the saga of liberation, law-giving, and conquest that we find in the Bible was grafted onto a far older tradition that had long existed among a tiny band of nomadic tribesmen who dwelled around the oasis of Kadesh—or so goes the argument of the revisionists in contemporary Bible scholarship. Did the Levites originate in Kadesh and claim the oasis as their tribal homeland? Or did they come upon Kadesh in their own wanderings, drive out the native tribe of Amalekites who dwelled there, and make it their own? Were the life-giving springs to be found at Kadesh always regarded as sacred? Was Kadesh, which means "sanctuary," the place where Moses officiated as the priest of a Yahweh shrine, as Geo Widengren suggests, or did Moses "[learn] his trade" as tribal chieftain and high priest from the old priest of Midian whom he first met there, as Hugo Gressmann argued?[45] Was it Kadesh and not Sinai that represented the most sacred site in the history of ancient Israel and the authentic goal of the Exodus in the "oldest strata of tradition" that found its way into the Bible?[46]

Thus does Kadesh become both the alpha and the omega of the Exodus in a fresh reading of the Bible. The tribal nomads who wandered into Egypt started out from Kadesh rather than Canaan, the revisionists propose, and it was to Kadesh that they returned upon their liberation from Egypt.[47] The original tradition did not mention that Moses was punished for striking the rock at Kadesh by being excluded from the Promised Land because Kadesh itself was "the promise and its fulfillment."[48] And most surprising of all, a counterreading of the Bible suggests that neither God nor Moses had anything to do with the departure from Kadesh—the Israelites packed up and moved on after a long sojourn only because they were driven out by local tribes who claimed the oasis as their own or, even more likely, because they had grown too numerous to survive on its springs and needed the more abundant resources of Canaan. "It was bitter necessity which impelled them toward cultivated land," explains Auerbach, "typical of all Bedouin migrations."[49]

"The goal of the exodus from Egypt was Kadesh and not Canaan. The plan for the conquest of Canaan arose only at a later time in Kadesh, presumably as a consequence of the overpopulation of the oasis," proposes Auerbach, neatly summing up the revisionist theory of the sacred oasis. "From the eastern border of Egypt the Israelite tribes headed immediately and directly for the oasis of Kadesh. Here they remained during the entire period of their stay in the wilderness. A 'desert-wandering' in the sense of the later traditions never took place. The departure from Kadesh, about a generation later, was followed immediately by the march into East Jordan territory and the conquest of Canaan."[50]

How, then, did Sinai replace Kadesh as the most important site in the saga of the Exodus as preserved in the Bible? The "oldest strata of tradition," writes Widengren, focused on Kadesh, not Sinai, and it was only much later in the authorship of the Bible that "the Sinai-traditions got the upper hand, and the Kadesh-traditions were pushed into the background." The authentic traditions were preserved in what Widengren regards as an ancient poem that found its way into the Book of Deuteronomy. "The Lord came from Sinai," Moses sang of Yahweh, and "rideth upon the heaven" (Deut. 33:2)—and here, Widengren insists, can be glimpsed a god who dwelled on a mountain but bestirred himself in order to rendezvous with the nomadic people of Israel at the oasis of Kadesh.[51]

"At last we can look through a rent in the curtain which has been concealing from us the prehistoric past of Israel and see in the ancient Levitic civilization of Kadesh," rhapsodizes Auerbach, "one of the spiritual roots from which grew the innovation of Moses in world history, the religion of Israel."[52]

Whether one prefers the plain text of the Bible or the imaginative readings of the scholars, Kadesh remains a fateful place in the life of Moses and the destiny of the Israelites. Sinai may have been the site where Moses was called and the Law was given, according to the biblical author, but Kadesh was the "workshop" where Yahweh undertook "to raise up to the Lord out of these hordes a sanctified group, a cleansed community," as Thomas Mann puts it. "He chiselled, blasted, planed, and smoothed at the rebellious block with sturdy patience, with repeated forbearance, often forgiving, sometimes blazing with scorn and lashing out ruthlessly." And it was at Kadesh where the King of the Universe, all-powerful and all-knowing, was forced to confront his own limitations. The Israelites—"so wilful, so forgetful, so unregenerate," Mann writes[53]—resisted every effort of God to change their nature and turn them from rebellious ex-slaves into faithful servants of the Lord.

THE KING'S HIGHWAY

Moses was not so distraught over the revelation of his fate at Kadesh that he could not tend to the diplomatic overtures and strategic planning that were necessary to prepare for the biblical equivalent of D Day—the invasion of Canaan and the conquest of the Promised

Land. Putting aside the fact that Yahweh did not intend him to set foot in Canaan, Moses began to conduct himself less like a prophet in the wilderness than a king on the throne.

He began by dispatching envoys from the encampment at Kadesh to the court of the king of Edom, whose lands lay in the path of the Israelites on their line of march into Canaan. "This is a message from your brother Israel," went the ingratiating dispatch that the messengers of Moses carried, as if to suggest that Moses and the king of Edom were royal brethren of equal rank (Num. 20:14 NEB). Moses reminded him of the troubled history of Israel and its miraculous salvation, "the travail that hath befallen us, how our fathers went down into Egypt, and we dwelt in Egypt a long time, and the Egyptians dealt ill with us, and our fathers, and when we cried unto Yahweh, he heard our voice, and sent an angel, and brought us forth out of Egypt." (Num. 20:15–16)[54] Then Moses reported that the Israelites were encamped on the border of Edom and asked for permission to use the royal road to cross his kingdom on the way to Canaan.

"Let us pass, I pray thee, through thy land," implored Moses in his diplomatic note, "we will not pass through field or through vineyard, neither will we drink of the water of the wells. We will go along the king's highway, we will not turn aside to the right hand nor to the left, until we have passed thy border." (Num. 20:17)

The king of Edom may have bridled at the temerity of Moses, or he may have been charmed by his courtly manners and deferential phrases, but the hordes of armed strangers who camped at his frontier represented a threat that he could not overlook—the pillage of crops, the sapping of wells, the destruction that was inevitable when six hundred thousand or more hungry nomads swarmed through town and country.

"Thou shalt not pass through me," the king decreed, "lest I come out with the sword against thee." (Num. 20:18)

Moses tried to dicker with the king, perhaps thinking him only a wily negotiator who wanted to exact a price for safe passage across his lands.

"If we drink of thy water, I and my cattle, then will I give the price thereof," Moses replied. "Let me only pass through on my feet; there is no hurt." (Num. 20:19)

But the king was unpersuaded by the earnest promise—"Thou shalt not pass through," was his final word (Num. 20:20)—and so the Israelites were forced to make their way around the border of Edom, a long and arduous detour that carried them from the southern border of Canaan to its eastern frontier.

On the way, Moses was reminded that Yahweh had not changed his mind about the punishment he had decreed for both Moses and Aaron back at Kadesh. As they skirted the border of Edom and passed Mount Hor, Yahweh summoned both Moses and Aaron to the mountaintop—and, rather ominously, instructed them to bring along Eleazar, the eldest surviving son of Aaron.

"Aaron shall be gathered unto his people," said Yahweh, "for he shall not enter into the land which I have given unto the children of Israel, because ye rebelled against my word at the waters of Meribah." (Num. 20:24)

Yahweh directed Moses to strip Aaron of his priestly vestments, and to put them upon Eleazar, thus assuring that the high priesthood would descend from Aaron to his son. And then the old man was made to suffer the ultimate penalty for disobedience to the divine will. Ironically, it was not the making of the golden calf or the murmuring against Moses for which Aaron's life was forfeited. Rather, Aaron was made to die because his brother struck the rock at Meribah rather than speaking to it—perhaps the original case of guilt by association.

The rabbis imagined a tender scene in which Moses leads his brother to a cave on Mount Hor where they find "a couch spread out by celestial hands, a table prepared, and a lighted candle on it." When Aaron is led to the couch, he finds himself surrounded by "ministering angels." And Yahweh himself eases Aaron from life to death, "luring away the soul of Aaron by a Divine kiss." Once a weeping Moses steps out of the death chamber, the cave vanishes from sight.[55] But the Bible itself is blunt and plainspoken: "Aaron died there in the top of the mount," goes the biblical death report in its entirety, and when the Israelites saw that Moses and Eleazar were returning to the encampment without Aaron, they understood at once that yet another one of the old guard had passed away. "And when all the congregation saw that Aaron was dead, they wept for Aaron thirty days, even all the house of Israel." (Num. 20:28–29)

Of course, the mourners included very few who actually remembered Aaron in his prime, the heady and fateful days when he boldly wielded the rod of God to work magic in the court of Pharaoh. Forty years had passed since the Israelites first came out of Egypt, and the slave generation was very nearly dead and gone. Of the three siblings who had led the Israelites out of Egypt, the three who witnessed the miraculous victory at the Red Sea, the three who had celebrated the covenant with Yahweh and the giving of the law at Sinai, only Moses remained.

A SERPENT OF BRONZE

Because they were denied safe passage through Edom, the Israelites were forced to fight their way into Canaan—and, remarkably enough, they proved themselves far more adept and courageous in battle than all of their cowardly murmurings would have suggested. The first campaign was fought against the Canaanite king of Arad, who heard that the Israelites were marching toward his kingdom and sent an army to intercept them. The first skirmish went to the Canaanites, and a number of Israelites were taken captive. "If Thou wilt indeed deliver this people into my hand," the Israelites prayed to Yahweh on their own initiative, "then I will utterly destroy their cities." (Num. 21:2) God heard the prayer and decided to grant it. "The Lord hearkened to the voice of Israel, and delivered up the Canaanites; and they utterly destroyed them and their cities." The site of the victory was Hormah, a place-name that means "utter destruction."[56] (Num. 21:3)

But even in the flush of victory on the battlefield, the Israelites persisted in making war on Yahweh, too. As they skirted the southern border of Edom and marched northward along the shores of the Red Sea, their weariness and impatience turned into open defiance once again.

"Wherefore have ye brought us up out of Egypt to die in the wilderness?" they muttered, directing their grievances against Moses and God. They signified their rejection of Yahweh by again turning away the manna that continued to appear in the camp every morning. "For there is no bread, and there is no water," they moaned, "and we are heartily sick of this miserable fare." (Num. 21:5)[57]

For their latest and most audacious expression of ingratitude, Yahweh resorted to an affliction that recalled the distant days when his ill will was directed at the Egyptians rather than the Israelites—he sent a plague of "fiery serpents" against the Israelites, "and they bit the people, and much people of Israel died." (Num. 21:5–6) Once again, it was only the intercession of Moses that prevented the decimation of the Israelites—and only after he followed some very strange orders from Yahweh.

And the Lord said unto Moses: "Make thee a fiery serpent, and sit it upon a pole, and it shall come to pass, that every one that is bitten, when he seeth it, shall live." And Moses made a serpent of brass, and set it upon the pole, and it came to pass, that if a serpent had bitten any man, when he looked unto the serpent of brass, he lived. (Num. 21:8–9)

Rabbinical tradition was mightily troubled by the biblical account of the Nehushtan, as the snake of brass was known, since the very act of fashioning it was a plain violation of the Second Commandment and the way it was put to use appears to be the crudest form of sympathetic magic. But the sages gamely tried to explain it all away: "It was not the sight of the serpent of brass that brought with it healing and life," they insisted, "but whenever those who had been bitten by the serpent raised their eyes upward and subordinated their hearts to the will of the heavenly Father, they were healed; if they gave no thought to God, they perished."[58]

But no such distinction appears in the Bible, which suggests that the bronze snake of Moses was preserved and revered by the Israelites for several centuries. It was not until the reign of Hezekiah in the eighth century B.C.E. that the Nehushtan was dragged from the Temple at Jerusalem, where it had enjoyed a place of honor along with the other relics of Moses, and destroyed it in the same way that Moses himself had destroyed the golden calf. "And he broke in pieces the brazen serpent that Moses had made," the Bible reports of the reformer-king, "for unto those days the children of Israel did offer to it." (2 Kings 18:4)

Still, the Nehushtan served its purpose in the wilderness, and the Israelites relied on its healing power until the plague of serpents abated. Then the Israelites lifted up the Ark and resumed their march, pushing north as far as the banks of Arnon, whose sluggish waters flowed between the land of the Moabites and the land of the Amorites and into the Salt Sea, lapping gently on the shore of the Promised Land.

"I HAVE DELIVERED HIM INTO THY HAND"

The Israelites paused at the Arnon and set up their encampment in the plains of Moab. Emissaries were dispatched to the court of King Sihon, ruler of the Amorites, with a plea and a promise: "Let me pass through thy land," went the message, "we will not turn aside into field, or into vineyard." (Num. 21:22) Like the king of Edom, the Amorite king refused to allow the Israelites to pass through his lands; but he took the precaution of sending an army to drive them off. In the end, though, the warrior-king may have regretted his decision: "And Israel smote him with the edge of the sword, and possessed his land," the Bible confirms, "and Israel dwelt in the cities of the Amorites." (Num. 21:24–25)[59]

Emboldened by the Israelites' first victory against the Amorites, Moses sent out spies to reconnoiter the towns in the vicinity. On their return, the spies were more encouraging than the ones who had infiltrated Canaan, and the Israelites resolved to push even deeper into the territory of the Amorites. One of the local chieftains—Og, the king of Bashan—rode out at the head of his own army to meet the Israelites in battle, but Yahweh was still favorably disposed to the Israelites and promised them another victory.

"Fear him not," Yahweh told Moses, "for I have delivered him into thy hand, and all his people, and his land." (Num. 21:34)

When the fighting was finally over—and the mighty Og, whom the Bible describes as a giant, was dead and buried in a sarcophagus measuring "nearly fourteen feet long and six feet wide" (Deut. 3:11 NEB)—the victorious Israelites established a vast encampment along the eastern bank of the Jordan River in the plains of Moab, where they apparently found a warm reception among the womenfolk: "And the people began to commit harlotry with the daughters of Moab." (Num. 25:1) But the Israelites did not plan to linger much longer in Moab. On the far side of the Jordan, shimmering in plain sight during the heat of the day, was the land of Canaan, the Promised Land. On a clear and moonless night, the Israelites might have glimpsed the far-distant lights of Jericho, the first objective of the invasion forces when the conquest began in earnest.

A STAR OUT OF JACOB

To assist the high command of Israel in marshaling their forces for D Day, Yahweh ordered a new census to be taken: "And it came to pass after the plague, that the Lord spoke unto Moses and unto Eleazar the son of Aaron the priest, saying: 'Take the sum of all the congregation of the children of Israel, from twenty years old and upward, by their fathers' houses, all that are able to go forth to war in Israel.' " (Num. 26:1–2) Fatefully, not a single man who had been counted in the first census was still alive—just as Yahweh had decreed, a whole generation had perished in the wilderness (Num. 26:1–2, 63–65). The army of Israel that would invade and conquer the Promised Land consisted of young men who had never known the deadening weight of slavery.

Moses was still in command, as far as we know, but the biblical author betrays a certain sense of decline in his authority and activity. When diplomatic letters were dispatched to the king of Edom, it was Moses who sent them, but when it came to the campaign against the king of Arad and the king of Bashan, Moses is not mentioned at all. "Israel vowed a vow," reports the Bible, using the word Israel in the collective sense, and it is *Israel's* voice to which Yahweh harkened. Israel, not Moses, "sent messengers unto Sihon king of the Amorites." (Num. 21:2–3, 21) Nor is Moses mentioned in the long and colorful account of Balaam the magician, who was commissioned by the king of Moab to curse the Israelites and ended up blessing them.

The Moabites were "sore afraid" of the Israelites, "a people come out from Egypt" who were now encamped among them in ominous numbers. "Now will this multitude lick up all that is round about us," cried the Moabites, "as the ox licketh up the grass of the field." (Num. 22:4) So the king of Moab summoned a sorcerer named Balaam to assist him in driving out the invaders, "for I know that he whom thou blessest is blessed, and he whom thou cursest is cursed." (Num. 22:6)

Balaam, as we have seen, was regarded in pious tradition as a powerful sorcerer. The rabbis imagined that Balaam and his two sons, Jannes and Jambres, play a decisive role in the life of Moses. In the tales told by the rabbis, they show up in the court of Pharaoh and the kingdom of Ethiopia, conspire to set the Egyptians in pursuit of the escaping Israelites at the Red Sea, and connive with the Amalekites to attack the Israelites in the wilderness. A certain grudging admiration of Balaam can be detected in the rabbinical literature, where he was held up as a counterpart of Moses. "In order that the heathens might not say, 'Had we had a prophet like Moses, we should have received the Torah,' " goes one discourse, "God gave them Balaam as a prophet, who in no way was inferior to Moses either in wisdom or in the gift of prophecy."[60] And yet all of these colorful incidents and asides in the rabbinical literature are merely fairy tales—Balaam, as far as the biblical author knew, had nothing at all to do with Moses.

The story of Balaam is a Sunday school classic. Balaam was persuaded by the king of Moab to make his way to the encampment of the Israelites and cast a spell on them, but he was hindered by a balky ass that refused to move forward despite Balaam's blows and curses. The dumb beast saw plainly what the mighty sorcerer could not see at all— "the angel of the Lord standing in the way, with his sword drawn in his hand"—and finally turned its head around and complained to Balaam in a human voice: "What have I done unto thee, that thou hast smitten me these three times?" (Num. 22:23, 28) At that moment, Yahweh "opened the eyes of Balaam," allowed him to see the sword-wielding angel, and sent the now repentant pagan to bless rather than curse the Israelites. "How goodly are thy tents, O Jacob," go the memorable words of Balaam when he looked down on the camp of the Israelites, "Thy dwellings, O Israel!" (Num. 24:5) And it was Balaam who was inspired by Yahweh to tell the king of Moab "what this people shall do to thy people in the ends of days." (Num. 24:14)

> There shall step forth a star out of Jacob,
> And a sceptre shall rise out of Israel,
> And shall smite through the corners of Moab,
> And break down all the sons of Seth.
> And Edom shall be a possession.
> Seir also, even his enemies, shall be a possession;
> While Israel doeth valiantly.
>
> (Num. 24:17–18)

Balaam was permitted by Yahweh to glimpse a distant future, a glorious era that would come long after the conquest of Canaan, when the crowned kings of Israel would enjoy sovereignty over an empire that included Moab (whose people are here dubbed "the sons of Seth") and Edom (including the mountainous region known to the biblical author as Seir). What Balaam described, of course, is the kingdom of David, the glorious monarch who would push the borders of Israel to the fullest extent of God's biblical promise, if only for a brief generation or two.[61] But Balaam sang not a single word of praise for Moses.

BELLY TO BELLY

Comfortably encamped at a place called Shittim in the plains of Moab, the men of Israel, idle and bored, had begun to dally with the flirtatious women of the locality. But the women of Moab were not content merely to seduce the men of Israel—they enticed the Israelites into their shrines as well as their beds, lured them to the rituals of sacrifice and sacred intercourse that celebrated the pagan gods of Moab, encouraged them to eat and drink their fill at the feasts that followed, and finally convinced them to bow down in open worship to the Baal of Peor, a local shrine that honored one of the principal gods of the pagan pantheon.

Yahweh waxed predictably wroth at the latest evidence of vice and corruption, and he decreed a punishment that was typically harsh, but novel in its details. Moses was ordered to take the chieftains of the twelve tribes of Israel and hang them up in the open, where they could be seen by all of their people and where the harsh desert sun would beat down on them from sunrise to sunset, so that "the fierce anger of the Lord may turn away from Israel." (Num. 25:4)

Not content with scourging only the chieftains, Moses took it upon himself to order a new purge of the camp, rallying the judges whom he had appointed back in Sinai and issuing an order of his own: "Slay ye every one of his men that have joined themselves unto the Baal of Peor." (Num. 25:5) As if to ratify the decree of Moses, the Bible suggests, Yahweh crowned the effort to cleanse the camp of apostates by sending down a plague that caused some twenty-four thousand of the Israelites to sicken and die.

But even the latest act of retribution was not enough to turn the men away from the alluring women of Moab. One day, for example, an Israelite man named Zimri strolled boldly and blithely through the camp with a strange woman in tow—she was a Midianite, as it turned out, not a Moabite—and then, in plain sight of Moses, his own wife and family, and the rest of the Israelites, and to their utter astonishment, the man and his lady friend slipped into the inner chamber of a tent for a moment of intimacy. Perhaps the philandering Zimri, a prince of the tribe of Simeon, had been so absorbed in his love affair that he had not noticed the new reign of terror that Moses had imposed on the Israelites, or perhaps he was so intent on sexual pleasure that he simply did not care. But the fact remains that Zimri and his lover did not bother to conceal their tryst from the teeming hordes that milled around the camp. Enraged at the knowledge of what was happening inside, an angry and mournful crowd began to gather outside the tent.

One man in the crowd was more angry than mournful, however, and he resolved to punish the prince of Simeon for his adultery and apostasy then and there. Phinehas, son of the high priest Eleazar and grandson of Aaron, pushed his way through the crowd, a long spear held upright in one hand, and then he followed Zimri and his lover into the tent they had chosen for their rendezvous. "And he went after the man of Israel into the chamber, and thrust both them through, the man of Israel, and the woman through her belly." (Num. 25:8) The Bible leaves it to the reader's imagination to supply the specific juxtaposition of a man's body and a woman's body that would permit both of them to be impaled with a single spear-thrust.

A cruel irony was at work here—both Zimri's lover, a woman of high birth named Cozbi, and Zipporah, wife of Moses, were Midianites. The rabbis imagined that Cozbi seduces Zimri by appealing to his jealousy of Moses. "My father ordered me to be obedient to the wishes of Moses alone, and to none other," Cozbi teases Zimri, "for he is a king, and so is my father, and a king's daughter is fit for none but a king." Prodded by her taunts but still mindful of the law of Israel, Zimri drags her before Moses and demands to know whether she is permitted or forbidden to him as a sexual partner—and when Moses answers, "Forbidden," Zimri is provoked to righteous indignation. "How then canst thou assert that she is forbidden to me," argues Zimri, "for then thy wife would be forbidden to thee, for she is a Midianite like this woman." Moses finds no answer to Zimri's taunt, and so the zealous Phinehas takes it upon himself to slay both of the lovers. "Moses is doomed to impotence because his wife Zipporah is a Midianite woman," Phinehas reflects. "Hence there remains nothing but for me to interpose."[62]

The slaying of Zimri and his Midianite lover was enough to appease an angry Yahweh, at least for the moment, and "so the plague was stayed from the children of Israel." (Num. 25:9) Moses singled out Phinehas for praise, and he passed along a commendation from Yahweh: "Behold, I give unto him My covenant of peace, and it shall be unto him, and to his seed after him, the covenant of an everlasting priesthood; because he was jealous for his God, and made atonement for the children of Israel." (Num. 25:12–13) But Yahweh was not yet done with the Midianites, and he issued one more order to Moses, the last one Moses would ever hear from the mouth of Yahweh, the last one he would ever carry out.

"Make the Midianites suffer as they made you suffer with their crafty tricks," Yahweh commanded Moses, "and strike them down." (Num. 25:16–18 NEB)

FIVE SISTERS

Even now, as the Israelites prepared for the final campaign, Yahweh decided to add one or two new clauses to the laws that had been handed down on Sinai. One of the last amendments to the sacred law was occasioned by a curious encounter between Moses and the daughters of a man named Zelophehad, five self-assertive sisters who protested against the tradition of the Israelites (and so many other peoples of the ancient Near East) that permitted a man's property to descend to his male children only.

"Our father died in the wilderness, and he had no sons," said the five women to Moses. They paused to remind Moses that their father had *not* been a follower of the rebellious Korah—"He was not among the company of them that gathered themselves together against the Lord in the company of Korah, but he had of his own sins"—and then they continued: "Why should the name of our father be done away from among his family, because he had no son? Give unto us a possession among the brethren of our father." (Num. 27:3–4)[63]

"The daughters of Zelophehad speak right," Yahweh counseled Moses. "Thou shalt cause the inheritance of their father to pass unto them. And thou shalt speak unto the children of Israel, saying, If a man die, and have no son, then ye shall cause his inheritance to pass unto his daughter." (Num. 27:3–8)[64]

Yahweh now took Moses aside to deliver yet another judgment, an intimate and momentous judgment on Moses himself.

"Get thee up into this mountain of Abarim, and behold the land which I have given unto the children of Israel," said Yahweh, pointing out a peak that offered a vista of the plains of Moab, the Jordan River, and the land of Canaan in the far distance. "And when thou hast seen it, thou also shalt be gathered unto thy people, as Aaron thy brother was gathered, because ye rebelled against my commandment in the wilderness of Zin." (Num. 27:12–14)[65]

"Gathered unto thy people" is a poignant biblical euphemism for death. Although we might conclude that Moses, at the age of 120, ought to have expected to die in the near future—he had already lived ten years longer than Joseph (Gen. 50:22)—the Bible emphasizes that he was still in hearty good health: "His eye was not dim, nor his natural force abated." (Deut. 34:7) We are meant to see his death as premature and thus tragic: Yahweh, who had managed to get over so many acts of apostasy and blasphemy by the Israelites, so many expressions of defiance and even open rebellion, was still holding a grudge against Moses about the fact that he struck the rock at Kadesh rather than speaking to it! Still, Moses did not argue with Yahweh, as he had done so many times before on behalf of the unruly Israelites, nor did he plead for his own life. Rather, he dutifully attended to the practical question of who would succeed him as the leader of the Israelites.

"Let the Lord, the God of the spirits of all flesh, set a man over the congregation, who may lead them out, and who may bring them in," Moses said—using a Hebrew phrase that actually means "to command the army"—"that the congregation of the Lord be not as sheep which have no shepherd." (Num. 27:16)

"Take thee Joshua, a man in whom is spirit, and lay thy hand upon him," Yahweh replied, "and set him before Eleazar the priest, and before all the congregation, and give him a charge in their sight." (Num. 27:18–19)[66]

At that moment, Yahweh permitted himself one oblique expression of the intimacy between him and the man with whom he had spoken "face to face." Joshua would bring the Israelites into the Promised Land, but he would not be granted the ready access to God that Moses had enjoyed for so long. When Joshua sought Yahweh's advice, he would have to go to the high priest, Eleazar—and Eleazar, in turn, would have to resort to the mute instructions of the Urim and Thummim to learn what God desired. "At his word shall they go out," Yahweh told Moses, "and at his word shall they come in." (Num. 27:21) The voice of Yahweh, in other words, would no longer be heard once Moses was gone, and the Israelites would be left only with the strange paraphernalia of the Urim and Thummim, the casting of lots and the reading of oracles.

At last, Yahweh issued his final order to Moses.

"Avenge the children of Israel against the Midianites," God told Moses. "Afterward shalt thou be gathered unto thy people." (Num. 31:2)[67]

"HAVE YE SAVED ALL THE WOMEN ALIVE?"

Moses called yet another mass meeting of the Israelites, and he addressed the multitude with his customary crispness and sternness. "Arm ye men from among you for the war, that they may go against Midian, to execute the Lord's vengeance on Midian," called Moses (Num. 31:3), although he did not pause to explain why they were being sent to slaughter the *Midianites* when it was the "daughters of Moab" who had first seduced the menfolk.

The muster was not especially large—"Of every tribe a thousand, throughout all the tribes of Israel, shall ye send to the war" (Num. 31:4)—and the field commander was not the battle-hardened Joshua but the zealous Phinehas, son of the high priest Eleazar, the man who had assassinated Zimri and Cozbi, the Israelite prince and his Midianite lover. Holy relics and sacred vessels were removed from the tent of meeting and sent along with the expeditionary force, and Phinehas carried the two silver trumpets in his own hands to sound the alarm that would send the soldiery into battle.

The first reports from the front confirmed a victory over Midian. Not a single Israelite soldier was killed in action, and yet every single man among the Midianites was slain,* including the five kings who reigned in the land of Midian and the sorcerer Balaam, too (Num. 31: 7–8, 49). As was the custom of all armies of the ancient world, the Israelites set fire to dwellings in both the fortified cities and the tent camps, and they claimed as spoils of war "the women of Midian, and their little ones, and all their cattle, and all their flocks, and all their goods." (Num. 31:9) When Phinehas and his twelve thousand troops appeared on the outskirts of the Israelite camp in the plains of Moab, they were followed by a long line of captive women and children, noisy herds and flocks, and creaking wooden carts piled high with booty.

Moses walked out to welcome the returning army, and with him were Eleazar and "all the princes of the congregation." But something about the sight of the triumphal march seemed to displease Moses, even

---

*The Bible reports that the Israelites "slew every male" in Midian (Num. 31:7). But at least some of the Midianites must have survived the slaughter because the Book of Judges reports that "the hand of Midian prevailed against Israel" after the conquest of Canaan (Judg. 6:2). Tradition explains that the campaign ordered by Moses exterminated every Midianite who was to be found in the vicinity of the Israelite encampment, but not the entire nation of Midian.

to offend him. When at last Moses spoke, he addressed a single pointed question to the triumphant officers who had captained the troops in battle: "Have ye saved all the women alive?" (Num. 31:15)

The words of Moses to his army were ominous but rich with irony. He had many Midianite relations of his own, and yet the fact that the women and children of Midian had been spared seemed to move him to a terrible rage.

"Behold, these caused the children of Israel to revolt so as to break faith with the Lord in the matter of Peor," Moses ranted. Then, he issued a command that would have sounded bloodthirsty on the lips of any battlefield commander in any war, but seems even more so on the lips of the Liberator and the Lawgiver. "Now therefore kill every male among the little ones," ordered Moses, "and kill every woman that hath known man by lying with him." (Num. 31:16–17)[68]

His order was chillingly precise. Only the virgin girls—"the women children that have not known man by lying with him" (Num. 31:18)— would not be put to the sword; but neither would they be wholly spared. "Keep them alive for yourselves," said Moses to his men-at-arms (Num. 31:18).[69]

"A RANSOM FOR OUR LIVES"

The slaughter of Midianite women and children is rationalized in pious tradition as a justified punishment for the scheme "to seduce the sons of Israel to unchastity and then to idolatry," a scheme that the rabbis attributed to the despised Balaam. And yet the Bible seems to acknowledge that the mass murder of the captive women and their young sons was something far beyond the justifiable bloodshed of a holy war, something that scarred and tainted the men who were commanded by Moses to carry out the killings. As if acknowledging the atrocity, Moses prescribed an elaborate ritual of purification.

"Every garment, and all that is made of skin, and all work of goats' hair, and all things made of wood, ye shall purify," Moses ordered. "And encamp ye without the camp seven days, whosoever hath killed any person, and whosoever hath touched any slain," he continued, "purify yourselves on the third day and on the seventh day, ye and your captives." (Num. 31:19–20)[70]

Then the high priest, Eleazar, added his own instruction on the ritual of purification to be carried out by "the men of war that went to the battle." Objects of metal—"the gold, and the silver, the brass, the iron, the tin, and the lead, every thing that may abide the fire"—were to be passed through a flame and then "it shall be purified with the water of sprinkling." (Num. 31:22) Everything else, including their garments, was to be immersed in water and washed to make them pure. "And ye shall wash your clothes on the seventh day, and ye shall be clean, and afterward ye may come into the camp." (Num. 31:24)

Yahweh, on the other hand, was less concerned with the ritual of purification than with the division of the flesh-and-blood plunder, both human and animal, which included precisely 32,000 virgins, 675,000 sheep, 72,000 head of cattle, and 61,000 asses. Half the sum was to be allotted to "the men skilled in war, that went out to battle," God ordered, and the other half to the congregation of Israelites at large. From the share allotted to the warriors, "one soul of five hundred, both of the persons, and of the cattle, and of the asses, and of the flocks" was to be turned over to the high priest "as a portion set apart from the Lord." From the share allotted to the rest of the Israelites, one in fifty was to be turned over to the Levites (Num. 31:25–30).[71] Of the virgin girls who were taken captive and left alive after the slaughter of their mothers and brothers, "the Lord's tribute was thirty and two persons," and these thirty-two young women were handed over to the Lord's representative on earth, Eleazar (Num. 31:41). Exactly what the high priest did with the Midianite girls is not disclosed in Holy Writ.

The whole tawdry affair of Zimri and Cozbi, and the war of extermination that resulted from their tragic liaison, remains an especially ugly stain on biblical tapestry. "It defames, for no apparent reason, an otherwise unknown Israelite clan as well as a Midianite tribe," observed Martin Noth, referring to the clan of Zimri and the tribe of Cozbi. Scholars agree that these passages are "a late element in the redaction of the Pentateuch" that was probably unknown to the older sources and was inserted into the biblical text in order to "legitimatize the descendants of Phinehas, in the face of any possible opposition, as the true heirs to 'Aaronite' privileges."[72] Even pious commentators who accepted the genocide of the Midianites as historical fact were stunned into embarrassed silence by the slaughter of innocents ordered by Moses himself.

"Perhaps the recollection of what took place after the Indian Mutiny, when Great Britain was in the same temper, may throw light on this question," offered J. H. Hertz, the late chief rabbi of Great Britain, who concedes that the sacred text presents "peculiar difficulties" and falls back on the faintly Kiplingesque apologia that he found in *The Expositor's Bible*: " 'The soldiers then, bent on punishing the cruelty and lust of the rebels, partly in patriotism, partly in revenge, set mercy altogether aside.' "[73]

So terrible was the mass murder of women and children that the soldiers who carried it out on orders from Moses regarded themselves as indelibly bloodstained, and even the offerings demanded by Yahweh did not relieve them of their feelings of guilt and self-reproach—or so we might conclude from what is reported next in the biblical account. For, as it turned out, the officers of the Israelite army came forward with a spontaneous guilt-offering by the men of war, something above and beyond what was demanded of them by Yahweh. The soldiers had stripped their victims and their captives of much precious loot—"jewels of gold, armlets, and bracelets, signet-rings, ear-rings, and girdles" (Num. 31:50)—and now they offered the booty to Yahweh, not just one precious bauble out of fifty but all of the treasure, "to make atonement for our souls before the Lord." (Num. 31:50)

Exactly why the warriors felt it necessary to atone—to offer their loot "as a ransom for our lives," as the New English Bible puts it (Num. 31:50)—is not explained in the Bible. The rabbis imagined that Moses himself is curious to know what inspires the extravagant act of contrition. The warriors describe how they frequently found themselves alone with the Midianite women during the pillage of their houses, and "even though we committed no sin with the Midianite women, still the heat of passion was kindled in us when we took hold of the women, and therefore by an offering do we seek to make atonement." Moses declares himself mightily impressed by their self-control, especially since an act of sexual excess in the heat of battle would have gone undetected. "Even the common men among you," Moses says to his soldiers, "are filled with good and pious deeds."[74]

But even the biblical author seems to have been aghast at the brutality and coldbloodedness of the slaughter. The Bible reports that Moses and Eleazar accepted the offering of gold and silver and wrought jewelry, but we might imagine that the stuff seemed as tainted to them as it did to the soldiers who had taken it by force of arms. And so they simply heaped up the treasure in the tent of meeting "for a memorial for the children of Israel before the Lord" (Num. 31:54)—a memorial to the slain innocents of Midian, and a reproach to the nation of liberated slaves in whose name the atrocity had been committed.

"A FRESH BROOD OF SINFUL MEN"

Still, the recent campaigns had enriched the Israelites with plundered cattle, booty, and slaves, and the Israelites finally stopped complaining to Moses about the lack of food and water. And yet, as Moses now discovered, the new wealth was even more corrosive of morale than the years of privation in the wilderness. So abundant were the cattle of the tribes of Reuben and Gad, and so rich was the pasturage in Moab, that the men lost the will to fight, and they petitioned Moses for permission to stay behind when the rest of the Israelites marched into Canaan.

"If we have found favour in thy sight, let this land be given unto thy servants for a possession," begged the men of Reuben and Gad. "Bring us not over the Jordan." (Num. 32:5)

Moses was appalled at the cowardice and avarice that seemed to lie hidden behind their simpering plea and self-serving arguments.

"Shall your brethren go to the war, and ye shall sit here? How dare you discourage the Israelites from crossing over to the land which the Lord has given them?" Moses reproached them, likening them to the spies who returned to Kadesh with such baleful reports of the Promised Land. "And now you are following in your fathers' footsteps, a fresh brood of sinful men to fire the Lord's anger once more against Israel, for if you refuse to follow him, he will again abandon this whole people in the wilderness, and you will be the cause of their destruction." (Num. 32:6–9, 14–15)[75]

But the Reubenites and Gadites were quick to answer his censure with a proposition.

"We will build sheepfolds here for our cattle, and our little ones shall dwell in the fortified cities, but we ourselves will be ready armed to cross the river and fight, according to your command," they offered. "We will not return unto our houses until the children of Israel have inherited every man his inheritance." (Num. 32:16–17)[76]

Suddenly the idea did not seem quite so objectionable. If the tribes of Reuben and Gad stayed on the land that had already been taken in battle from the defeated King Sihon and King Og, then there would be more land in Canaan for allocation to the other ten tribes. And Moses already sensed that the task of forging a nation out of twelve nomadic tribes would only grow more complicated and burdensome when the native dwellers were conquered and the land was ready to be divided up among the conquerors.

"If you will arm yourselves to go before the Lord to the war, and every armed man of you will pass over the Jordan, until He hath driven out His enemies from before Him, and the land be subdued, then this land shall be unto you for a possession," Moses allowed. "But if ye will not do so, behold, ye have sinned against the Lord, and know ye your sin which will find you." (Num. 32:20–23)[77]

Then the men of Reuben and Gad, having gotten from Moses exactly what they had asked for, flattered the old man by suggesting that the whole plan had all been *his* idea all along—and a good one at that.

"Thy servants will do," they said with a flourish, "as my lord commandeth." (Num. 32:25)

"AS THORNS IN YOUR EYES, AND AS PRICKS IN YOUR SIDES"

Yahweh, at last, was apparently well pleased with Moses and the Israelites. Sihon and Og and Arad had been defeated, and the campaign against the Midianites had resulted in the elimination of many thousands of idolators and seductresses. Now, on the very eve of the invasion of Canaan, Yahweh took Moses aside for one last briefing before the final assault. Their meeting took place in the plains of Moab, hard by the river Jordan, directly across from the town of Jericho. Here Yahweh disclosed the names of the second-generation leaders who would be given the privilege of taking Canaan from the Canaanites—Eleazar, Joshua, Caleb, and one prince from each of the rest of the tribes—and he reminded Moses of what was expected of the Israelites when they crossed the Jordan.

"Speak unto the children of Israel, and say unto them: 'When ye pass over the Jordan into the land of Canaan, then ye shall drive out all the inhabitants of the land before you and dwell therein, for unto you have I given the land to possess it,' " God instructed Moses. "Destroy all their figured stones, and destroy all their molten images, and lay their hill-shrines in ruins." (Num. 33:51–53)[78]

Then Yahweh paused and issued one final admonition: it was up to the Israelites to drive out the native-dwelling people of Canaan.

"But if ye will not drive out the inhabitants of the land from before you, then shall those that ye let remain of them be as thorns in your eyes, and as pricks in your sides, and they shall harass you in the land wherein ye dwell," said Yahweh, and he assured Moses that he would not be kindly disposed toward the Chosen People if they failed in their mission of conquest and extermination: "And it shall come to pass, that as I thought to do unto them, so will I do unto you." (Num. 33:55–56)

With these last few words from Yahweh to Moses, the saga that began on the banks of the Nile came to an end on the banks of the Jordan. The Exodus had already passed into the realm of myth, the wandering in the wilderness had come to an end, and all was ready for the invasion and conquest that had been the real but unrevealed goal of the divine scheme in which Moses was made to play such a decisive role. Indeed, the Bible suggests that the divine plan for the conquest of Canaan had begun at the very moment of his birth back in Egypt, where a slave baby under a decree of death by drowning in the Nile was miraculously spared and set on the path that carried him through the wilderness to the very border of the Promised Land.

Chapter Eleven

"MOSES IS DEAD"

A very old man walks silently past the tents, feeling his way with a stick to make sure he doesn't trip on the tent ropes. He walks on. His people are moving to a greener country. Moses has an appointment with the jackals and vultures.

—BRUCE CHATWIN, *THE SONGLINES*

One final privilege was accorded to Moses—a farewell address to the Israelites as they camped in the plains of Moab—and then the death sentence that Yahweh had pronounced upon him back at Kadesh was to be executed at last. Moses, who once claimed to be slow of speech, had proved himself an accomplished rhetorician, and now he delivered one last burst of oratory, a series of three speeches so lengthy and so ornate that the text takes up the entirety of the Book of Deuteronomy. The valedictory of Moses is at once a bittersweet memoir, a last will and testament, an ideological manifesto, an apocalyptic vision of both earthly paradise and earthly hell, and a prophecy in which the Israelites are both damned and redeemed.

"I call heaven and earth to witness against you this day, that I have set before thee life and death, the blessing and the curse," thundered Moses in one of the lapidary pronouncements that decorate his long good-bye. "Therefore choose life." (Deut. 30:19)

On the day of his farewell address, which the Bible places "in the fortieth year, in the eleventh month, on the first day of the month" (Deut. 1:3), the Israelites were still encamped in the rugged wilderness of Moab, but they were no longer the ragged band of runaway slaves whom Moses had led out of Egypt so many years before. The slave generation was dead and gone, and their children had proved themselves to be a generation of warriors, tough and ruthless. As Moses spoke his last words to the nation of Israel, the disciplined ranks of battle-hardened soldiers gathered before him were ready for the command that would send them across the Jordan River at last.

" 'You have dwelt long enough in this mountain—turn you, and take your journey,' " Moses called out to the Israelites, quoting the antique words that Yahweh had spoken at the sacred mountain of Horeb so many years before. " 'Behold, I have set the land before you—go in and possess the land which the Lord swore unto your fathers, to Abraham, to Isaac, and to Jacob, to give unto them and to their seed after them.' " (Deut. 1:6–7, 8)[1]

His words rang out as a kind of battle cry, and here we can imagine old Moses as a general on the eve of a momentous clash of arms, rallying the troops and charging them up for the attack. Did the soldiers raise their swords and spears in affirmation? Did they raise their voices in a chorus of martial fervor? Surely they were ready at that moment to rise up and move out, to throw themselves upon the enemy in the opening battle of a holy war. But Moses did not end his address with a cry of havoc, nor did he let slip his dogs of war. What the Bible reports is that Moses, a man who seemed to be trying to postpone the inevitable moment of his own death, just kept on talking.

REVERIE

Moses was 120 years old on the day of his farewell address, still grieving the loss of his brother and sister, and perhaps still embittered at the fate Yahweh had decreed for him so capriciously. And so it is not surprising that his mind seemed to wander as he spoke—odd thoughts flashed in and out of his consciousness, random observations fell from his lips, and his powers of recollection functioned only fitfully. Suddenly, it seems, Moses found himself in a deep and sometimes bitter reverie.

"And I spoke to you at that time, saying, 'I am not able to bear you myself alone,' " he recalled in the scolding tone that must have been deeply familiar to his audience. "How can I myself alone bear the heavy burden you are to me, and put up with your complaints?" (Deut. 1:9, 12)[2] Then, as if suddenly remembering why he had brought up the subject in the first place, Moses reminded the Israelites of his decision to lighten his burden of office by appointing captains over the infantry and judges over the people, although he seemed to have quite forgotten that it was his father-in-law, Jethro, who came up with the whole idea. "And ye answered me," Moses mused aloud, "and said: 'The thing which thou hast spoken is good for us to do.' " (Deut. 1:14)

Abruptly, Moses began to reminisce about the long march they had just completed, the trek from Horeb to Kadesh through a "great and terrible wilderness." Yet some of the most memorable details of the last forty years seemed to escape him. Yahweh brought the Israelites out of Egypt "by trials, by signs, and by wonders, and by war, and by a mighty hand, and by an outstretched arm, and by great terrors," Moses recalled, but he uttered not a word about the Ten Plagues.[3] And then, just as abruptly, he returned to the subject at hand—the native-dwelling tribes and nations whom they would now face in the conquest of Canaan. "Dread nought, neither be afraid of them," Moses said of the adversaries on the far side of the Jordan. "Behold, the Lord thy God hath set the land before thee; go up, take possession as the Lord, the God of thy fathers, hath spoken unto thee." (Deut. 1:21, 28; 4:34)[4]

As Moses cast his memory back to the grand saga of the Exodus, his recollections differed from what we read in the other books of the Bible, sometimes slightly and sometimes substantially. In the Book of Numbers, for example, when Moses petitioned the king of Edom for permission to cross his land, the king flatly refused and the Israelites were forced to make a long detour around the border of his kingdom. But to hear Moses tell the same tale in the Book of Deuteronomy, the very opposite took place: "You are about to go through the territory of your kinsmen the descendants of Esau," Moses now recalled, referring to the Edomites by their ancient lineage. "You may purchase food from them for silver, and eat it, and you may buy water to drink." (Deut. 2:3–4)[5]

Even such signal events as the encounter with Yahweh at Sinai were twisted in the retelling. For example, the Israelites had been terrorized by the thunder and lightning atop Sinai and had begged Moses to act as their go-between: "Speak thou with us, and we will hear, but let not God speak with us, lest we die." (Exod. 20:16, 18) Now, however, Moses recalled the events quite differently. "And the Lord spoke unto you out of the midst of the fire," he told them. "Ye heard the voice of words, but ye saw no form, only a voice." Moments later, he offered yet a third version of the same event. "The Lord spoke with you face to face in the mount out of the midst of the fire," said Moses, and then he added: "I stood between the Lord and you at that time, to declare unto you the word of the Lord, for ye were afraid because of the fire and went not up unto the mount." (Deut. 5:4–5)[6]

Sacred objects and crucial encounters that figured so prominently in the Book of Exodus were simply left out of the farewell address. The rod of God and the tent of meeting, for example, are not mentioned at all in Deuteronomy,[7] nor are the miraculous provision of quail, the rebellion of Korah, or the bronze serpent that Moses had fashioned as a cure for snakebite.[8] Moses mentioned Miriam in passing, but he said nothing about any blood ties between them (Deut. 24:9), and he dismissed the momentous events at the Red Sea with a single oblique reference that did not mention the miraculous parting of the waters.[9] (Deut. 11:4) He boasted of the utter devastation of the Amorites under King Sihon—"We captured all his cities at that time and put to death everyone in the cities, men, women, and dependants, we left no survivor" (Deut. 2:34 NEB)—but the recent campaign against the Midianites, which resulted in similar carnage, somehow slipped his mind.

Other incidents of the Exodus were given an entirely new spin. Nothing is reported in the Book of Exodus about how Yahweh reacted to the prominent role that Aaron played in the making and worship of the golden calf, but now Moses revealed for the first time that Yahweh had been ready to strike down Aaron in anger. Only the intercession of Moses saved his older brother: "The Lord was greatly incensed with Aaron also and would have killed him, so I prayed for him as well at that same time." (Deut. 9:20 NEB) And Moses neglected to mention his punishment for striking a rock rather than speaking to it at Meribah-kadesh. He came up with a somewhat more self-serving explanation for the fact that he would not cross into the Promised Land: "The Lord was wroth with me for *your* sakes." (Deut. 3:26)[10]

As if to reassure the Israelites that they would not be left alone and leaderless when he died, Moses promised that Yahweh would be their champion during the invasion of Canaan:

> The Lord your God who goes at your head will fight for you and he will do again what you saw him do for you in Egypt and in the wilderness. You saw there how the Lord your God carried you all the way to this place, as a father carries his son. Be strong and of good courage, fear not, nor be affrighted, for the Lord thy God will not fail thee, nor forsake thee. (Deut 1:30–31, 31:6)[11]

Even as Moses was bucking up the Israelites, however, God was whispering words of warning into his ear. "This people will rise up and go astray after the foreign gods of the land, and will forsake Me, and break My covenant," said Yahweh. "Then My anger shall be kindled against them in that day, and I will forsake them, and I will hide My face from them, and they shall be devoured, and many evils and troubles shall come upon them, so that they will say in that day: 'Are these evils come upon us because our God is not among us?'" (Deut. 31:16–17)[12]

Moses promptly passed along the bad news to his audience. "The Lord will bring a nation against thee from far, from the end of the earth, as a vulture swoopeth down, a nation whose tongue thou shalt not understand, a nation of fierce countenance, and he shall besiege thee in all thy gates," Moses warned. "Then you will eat your own children, the flesh of your sons and daughters whom the Lord your God has given you, because of the dire straits to which you will be reduced when your enemy besieges you." (Deut. 28:49–51, 53, 56–57)[13]

The Israelites who listened to Moses must have been bewildered by the way he lurched between hope and despair, victory and defeat. At one moment, Moses was bracing and comforting, and the very next moment, scolding and punishing. As he rambled on, they came to understand that the soothing promise—"Yahweh will not fail thee, nor forsake thee"—came with a big "if." Good fortune was conditioned on good behavior. And before Moses was finished with his speechifying on the plains of Moab, his vision of the destiny of the Chosen People would turn from a shimmering utopia to a bitter apocalypse, and the Promised Land would turn from a place of peace and plenty to a wasteland in which mothers fight with their husbands to eat the afterbirth of their dead babies.

PIOUS FRAUD

The farewell address of Moses might strike us as the ramblings of an old man in his dotage, a man whose memory was failing and whose moods swung violently and unpredictably. But the author of Deuteronomy did not intend to depict Moses as spent and befuddled. Quite to the contrary, the Bible specifies that Moses was still vigorous in his advanced old age: "His eye was not dim, nor his natural force abated."* (Deut. 34:7) Rather, the schizophrenic quality of the biblical text can be explained by the scholarly supposition that the Book of Deuteronomy, like the other Five Books of Moses, is the work of more than one author, each one working at a different period of history. The earliest contributors to Deuteronomy held out the hope of a utopian future, and the later ones knew a bitter reality—and the final editors of the text harmonized the two points of view in a simple theological equation: The Chosen People will be rewarded if they are faithful to Yahweh, and punished if they are not.

The original text in the Book of Deuteronomy is conventionally attributed to an author who lived during the reign of Josiah, monarch of the southern kingdom of Judah, in the late seventh century B.C.E., an era of reformation and renewal during which a zealous king was purging the Temple at Jerusalem of the paganistic rituals and beliefs that had tainted the faith of ancient Israel. But the text of Deuteronomy was apparently revised more than once, during or after the Babylonian Exile that began in 586 B.C.E., when the last Davidic king had been driven from the throne and the Temple was in ruins. The source of the original text, known to scholars as "D^1," probably lived and worked at a time when it was still possible for a priestly author to cheerfully insist that the Temple would always stand and a descendant of David would always reign in Jerusalem. The source who edited and augmented the text, known as "D^2," witnessed or knew of the devastation that unfolded in the early sixth century—the Temple was in ruins, the throne of David was empty, and the last Davidic king had been forced to watch the murder of his children before being blinded and dragged off to Babylon to work as a slave in a mill (2 Kings 25:7).

Some scholars claim to detect yet more authors and editors at work in the Book of Deuteronomy, and so the scholarly literature includes references to "D^3," "D^4," and so on. What's more, the biblical sources known collectively as the Deuteronomist may have known and used documents and traditions that varied in some details from what was available to the Yahwist, the Elohist, and the other biblical authors and editors. So the apparent gaps in the memory of Moses as he reminisced in the Book of Deuteronomy, the sudden shifts from cheer to

---

*The literal translation ("neither had his freshness fled") suggests that Moses was still sexually potent. "He suffered none of the infirmities of age," as J. H. Hertz observes, "and the natural freshness of his body had not become dried up."

despair, and the contradictions between what Moses said in his fare-well address and what he was shown to do in earlier books of the Bible may be explained by the multiple authorship of the Book of Deuteronomy.

Yet Deuteronomy is not the kind of cut-and-paste job that we find elsewhere in the Five Books of Moses, and Bible scholarship still refers to its original author as *the* Deuteronomist (or "D"). The biblical sources whose fingerprints are found in such abundance in Genesis, Exodus, Leviticus, and Numbers—the Yahwist, the Elohist, the Priestly source, the Redactor—are mostly absent from Deuteronomy. While the authors and editors of the other books of the Bible often seem at odds with each other on fundamental questions of history and faith, the Book of Deuteronomy presents a theological party line that is straightforward and single-minded. Israel is the "special possession" of Yahweh, the Deuteronomist insisted, but the covenant between God and Israel is an iffy proposition at best. The Israelites will be blessed if they keep up their end of the bargain, cursed if they do not.

But politics as well as theology are at work in Deuteronomy. The single most important clue to the identity and motives of the Deutero-nomist is a curious law that does not appear elsewhere in the Five Books of Moses, a law that required the Israelites to offer sacrifices to Yah-weh only at a single central sanctuary. As it turned out, the Temple of Solomon in the royal city of Jerusalem would be established as the great national shrine of Israel, but only several hundred years *after* the sup-posed date of the farewell address of Moses as reported in Deuteronomy. Still, the Deuteronomist insisted that Moses had the idea in mind all along.

"Take heed to thyself that thou offer not thy burnt-offerings in every place that thou seest, but in the place which the Lord shall choose in one of thy tribes," Moses warned the Israelites in his farewell address. "But unto the place which the Lord your God shall choose out of all our tribes to put His name there, even unto His habitation shall ye seek, and thither thou shalt come; and thither ye shall bring your burnt offer-ings, and your sacrifices, and your tithes." (Deut. 12:5–6, 13)[14]

All other shrines and sanctuaries throughout the land of Israel—"upon the high mountains, and upon the hills, and under every leafy tree"—were to be "utterly destroyed." The purge decreed by Moses was directed at the places where pagan gods and goddesses were worshipped: "And ye shall break down their altars, and dash in pieces their pillars, and burn their Asherim* with fire; and ye shall hew down the graven images of their gods, and ye shall destroy their name out of that place." (Deut. 12:3) But the same decree applied to any site where worship was offered other than "the place which the Lord your God shall choose to cause His name to dwell there." (Deut. 12:11) By a tradition that came to be accepted long after Moses was dead and gone, the place that was to enjoy a divine monopoly on the offering of sacrifices and the rituals of worship was the Temple at Jerusalem.

The remarkable notion that Yahweh would accept sacrificial offerings from only a single sanctuary in all of Israel is not mentioned elsewhere in the Five Books of Moses and was unknown to even the most pious of the early Israelites. According to the Bible, the patriarchs and the early kings of Israel presided over rituals of sacrifice to Yahweh at altars and shrines throughout the land, and the Bible does not suggest that they erred in doing so. Only when the Book of Deuteronomy suddenly came to light in 622 B.C.E. during the reign of Josiah, the reformer-king of the southern kingdom of Judah, did the Israelites suddenly wake up to the fact that Yahweh found the other altars to be repugnant.

Conveniently, and rather suspiciously, a long-lost scroll containing the entirely new idea of a single place of worship turned up during the repair of the Temple at Jerusalem in the reign of Josiah: "I have found the book of the Law in the house of the Lord," reported the high priest Hilkiah to Josiah (2 Kings 22:8), and Bible scholarship suggests that the scroll was the Book of Deuteronomy, or at least a major portion of it, including the curious passages that established the centralization of worship in Jerusalem. The mysterious document was submitted to a prophetess named Huldah, and once she authenticated it, Josiah relied on the newly discovered laws of Yahweh in carrying out his policy of centralizing the spiritual authority of his kingdom in his royal capital at Jerusalem.

Josiah destroyed the rival shrines and sanctuaries (or "high places") that were scattered throughout the land and purged the Temple at Jeru-

---

*Asherim were carved wooden poles or living trees that were venerated as the symbol and embodiment of Asherah, a goddess of the Canaanite pantheon who was thought to be the consort of the supreme god, El, and thus the mother of all lesser gods and goddesses. See chapter eleven, "A Goddess of Israel," in *The Harlot by the Side of the Road.*

salem of the trappings and practices he found objectionable, including sacred harlotry and the worship of pagan gods and goddesses. But the purge did not stop with "sodomites" and idolaters; Josiah also destroyed the altars throughout his kingdom where priests of Yahweh made otherwise pious offerings to the God of Israel. Significantly, Josiah pulled down the altar at Bethel where Jeroboam had erected the golden calf so long before: "That altar and the high place he broke down, and burned the high place, and stamped it small to powder," goes the biblical report, which describes how Josiah destroyed the golden calf of Jeroboam in precisely the same manner that Moses destroyed the golden calf of Aaron (2 Kings 23:15).

Yet another clue to the identity and ulterior motive of the Deuteronomist can be found in the linkages between the incident of the golden calf at Sinai, as described in the Book of Exodus, and Josiah's role in stamping out the "sin of Jeroboam," as recounted in the Second Book of Kings. Scholars regard Deuteronomy as the keystone of a longer biblical narrative known as the Deuteronomistic History, which includes the books of Joshua, Judges, First and Second Samuel, and First and Second Kings. The authors and editors who collected and combined the dramatic narratives that we find in these six biblical books are collectively known as "the Deuteronomistic Historian," and they recast the entire history of ancient Israel in the same ideological mold used in the Book of Deuteronomy.

The Deuteronomistic Historian, for example, reported the "sin of Jeroboam" in setting up the golden calves in the sanctuaries at Dan and Bethel—and he paused in his telling of the tale to predict that King Josiah would come along three centuries later and tear them down! (1 Kings 13:2 ff.) It was the Deuteronomistic Historian who condemned Jeroboam for the offering of sacrifices at shrines outside of Jerusalem and praised Josiah for putting an end to the practice. For his courage and discernment, Josiah was singled out as a second Moses. "And like unto him was there no king before him that turned to the Lord with all his heart, and with all his soul, and with all his might, according to all the law of Moses," wrote the Deuteronomistic Historian of Josiah in the Second Book of Kings, echoing a passage in Deuteronomy that applies to Moses, "neither after him arose there any like him." (2 Kings 23:25)

All of these curious interconnections—and, above all, the fact that the newly discovered scroll seemed to anticipate and validate the reforms of Josiah—prompted a nineteenth century Bible scholar named

W.M.L. DeWette to proclaim the Book of Deuteronomy a "pious fraud," an elaborate and ingenious forgery that was concocted by Josiah and the priests who served him in order to give a scriptural basis for the Josianic reform and, especially, the policy of centralization of worship in ancient Israel.[15] For that reason, conventional wisdom among Bible scholars suggests that the Deuteronomist was a relative latecomer to Bible authorship when compared to the Yahwist and the Elohist. Indeed, some scholars suspect that the brief report of the death of Moses that we find in the Book of Deuteronomy (Deut. 34:5) was actually lifted from the Book of Numbers, where it may have originally appeared, in order to enhance the authenticity and credibility of the Deuteronomist's work. Thus Moses was assigned the role of "declarer" (maggid) and teacher (melammed) in Deuteronomy,[16] but the words he was made to speak in his farewell address flowed from the goose-quill pen of some nameless priest who lived and worked several centuries later.

Yet even if the Deuteronomist was a forger, he was responsible for nothing less than a revolution in the faith of ancient Israel. The paganistic rites and rituals that had attached themselves to the worship of Yahweh—the standing stones and wooden poles and graven images that decorated not only the "high places" but the Temple itself—were condemned and destroyed, and along with them went many of the relics and rituals that are so lovingly described in the earlier books of the Bible.

No longer was the Ark of the Covenant regarded as a throne on which Yahweh rode; rather, the Deuteronomist understood the Ark to be a humble wooden chest in which the words of the law were stored. The rod of God that Moses was thought to have wielded, the almond-studded rod of Aaron, the souvenir jar of manna, the healing figure of the Nehushtan, and the tent of meeting where God and Moses chatted "face to face" are discarded and forgotten in Deuteronomy.

Even the endearing but childlike notions of God that we find in the earlier books of the Bible are revised in Deuteronomy. There, instead of a deity who hunkered down in the mud of Creation and sculpted the first man out of clay, who dropped in unannounced at the tent of Abraham and Sarah for an impromptu meal of cutlets and curds, who paraded in front of Moses and allowed him a glimpse of the divine backside, Moses presented an abstract and aloof deity who remains in heaven and allows only his "name" to dwell on earth.[17]

Deuteronomy, then, is "a turning point in the evolution of the faith of Israel," in the words of modern Bible scholar Moshe Weinfeld.[18] And so the invention of ethical monotheism, with which Moses is traditionally credited, may belong to one or more anonymous priests of antiquity whom we know only as the Deuteronomist. The farewell address of Moses, so exalted and so enduring, so fundamental to what we regard as the authentic Judeo-Christian tradition, would have seemed bizarre and utterly baffling to Moses himself.

THE SECOND LAW

Much of the farewell address of Moses is devoted to a meticulous and sometimes tedious reprise of the vast body of sacred law, including some commandments that we have already encountered in the other books of the Bible and some that appear nowhere else in the Bible. That is why the book in which the farewell address is recorded came to be known as "Deuteronomy," a Greek word that means "Second Law."

> And now, Israel, what doth the Lord thy God require of thee, but to fear the Lord thy God, to walk in all His ways, and to love Him, and to serve the Lord thy God with all thy heart and with all thy soul, to keep for thy good the commandments of the Lord, and His statutes, which I command thee this day? (Deut. 10:12–13, 16)[19]

Much of Deuteronomy must have been familiar to the Israelites. Moses repeated the Ten Commandments—or, as he put it, "the ten words" (Deut. 4:13)—and the ancient principles of lex talionis, the law of retaliation: "Life for life, eye for eye, tooth for tooth." (Deut. 19:21) He reminded them of the strict dietary laws imposed on them by God, carefully cataloging the animals that were acceptable to eat because they are clean (or "kosher") and those that were forbidden because they were unclean, including the rock-badger, the hoopoe, and the bat (Deut. 14:2–18).

But Moses subtly revised the law of Sinai, leaving out some clauses that seemed so important in the earlier books of the Bible, adding new clauses that appear nowhere else in the Torah. The Second Law is more concerned with ethical conduct and social justice in day-to-day life than with the rituals of animal sacrifice that are so painstakingly detailed in Exodus, Leviticus, and Numbers. The hungry were to be fed, the rights of the powerless were to be respected, the stranger was to be not only respected and protected but cherished. "Love ye therefore the stranger," Moses commanded, "for ye were strangers in the land of Egypt." (Deut. 10:19) Even something so basic and so concrete as the ritual of circumcision was put to use by Moses as a metaphor for an even more intimate commandment. "Circumcise therefore the foreskin of your heart," thundered Moses, suggesting that God sought a heartfelt spiritual commitment and not merely a sign carved into the flesh (Deut. 10:16).

"Justice, justice, shalt thou follow," commanded Moses, summing up the ringing message of the Second Law, "that thou mayest live, and inherit the land which the Lord thy God giveth thee." (Deut. 16:20)

A certain pious grandeur suffuses all of the Second Law, and the elevated language of the Deuteronomist sets his work apart from the rest of the Five Books of Moses. Here we find the first utterance of the words that have become the fundamental confession of faith in Judaism: "Hear, O Israel: the Lord our God, the Lord is One."* (Deut. 6:4) Here, too, is the credo that encapsulates the sacred history and the solemn destiny of Israel in a few spare lines that were to be recited upon the offering of the first fruits of the harvest in the land of Israel, a credo that celebrates the nomadic ideal of freedom but pointedly denies a role for Moses in the momentous saga of liberation that is the Exodus.

> And thou shalt speak and say before thy God: "A wandering Aramean was my father, and he went down into Egypt, and sojourned there, few in number; and he became there a nation, great, mighty, and populous. And the Egyptians dealt ill with us, and afflicted us, and laid upon us hard bondage. And we cried unto the Lord, the God of our fathers, and the Lord heard our voice, and saw our affliction, and our toil, and our oppression. And the Lord brought us forth out of Egypt with a mighty hand, and with an outstretched arm, and with great terribleness, and with signs, and with wonders. And He hath brought us into this place, and hath given us this land, a land flowing with milk and honey." (Deut. 26:5–9)

---

*The literal translation of the Shema, as the declaration is known in Jewish usage, is less elegant and more provocative because it does not necessarily rule out the existence of other gods. "Hear O Israel! Yahweh our God is one Yahweh." (Deut. 6:4 NEB and Anchor Bible)

Other laws promulgated by Moses for the first time in the plains of Moab were considerably less exalted. Moses exempted from military service any man who was afraid to fight, and specified that Israelite soldiers were to carry wooden paddles along with their weapons of war so they would be able to dig holes and bury their excrement, although he offered a theological rationale for these rules of field hygiene. "For the Lord thy God walketh in the midst of thy camp to deliver thee," explained Moses, and he wanted to make sure that God would "see no unseemly thing in thee, and turn away from thee." (Deut. 20:8, 23:14) He prescribed a strange ritual of exculpation in the event a man was found dead but no killer was identified—the elders were obliged to break the neck of a heifer, wash their hands over the body of the dead bovine, and speak out loud: "Our hands have not shed this blood, nor have our eyes seen it." (Deut. 21:6–7)[20] And he paused to deliver a shrill condemnation of cross-dressing: "A woman shall not wear that which pertaineth unto a man, neither shall a man put on a woman's garment; for whosoever doeth these things is an abomination unto the Lord thy God." (Deut. 22:5)

Whether sacred or profane, glorious or mundane, every point of law in Deuteronomy is charged with a single idée fixe: the destiny of Israel will be determined by whether or not the Israelites live up to the bargain that God and Moses made on Sinai. The voice of Moses in Deuteronomy is "an ideological voice concerned above all with retributive justice and a covenant of law," as Bible scholar Robert Polzin writes, "rather than with mercy and a covenant of grace."[21] Obedience to the law of Moses would be richly rewarded: "Blessed shalt thou be in the city, and blessed shalt thou be in the field, blessed shall be the fruit of thy body, and the fruit of thy land." (Deut. 28:3–4)[22] Defiance would be cruelly punished: "Cursed shalt thou be in the city, and cursed shalt thou be in the field," warned Moses, who promised that Yahweh would smite transgressors "with hemorrhoids and with the scab, and with the itch, with madness, and with blindness, and with astonishment of heart." (Deut. 28:16–18) And these afflictions would be the least of their woes, because obedience to Yahweh was literally a matter of life or death.

"Behold, I set before you this day a blessing and a curse," said Moses, repeating the phrase that is the mantra of the Deuteronomist. "The blessing, if ye shall hearken unto the commandments of the Lord your God, which I command you this day; and the curse, if ye shall not hearken unto the commandments of the Lord your God." (Deut. 11:28)[23]

SLAVES BUT NO BUYERS

So Moses tantalized his audience with the blessings that Yahweh would bestow upon them if they obeyed the sacred law, starting with the conquest of the Promised Land and the death or expulsion of the native-dwelling people of Canaan.

> When the Lord thy God shall bring thee into the land, and shall cast out many nations before thee, the Hittite, and the Girgashite, and the Amorite, and the Canaanite, and the Perizzite, and the Hivite, and the Jebusite, seven nations greater and mightier than thou, and when the Lord thy God shall deliver them up before thee, and thou shalt smite them, then thou shalt utterly destroy them. (Deut. 7:1–2)[24]

The Israelites were to give no quarter to their adversaries: "Of the cities of these peoples, that the Lord thy God giveth thee for an inheritance, thou shalt save alive nothing that breatheth." (Deut. 20: 16–17)[25] And then Yahweh would allow the Israelites to take for themselves the wealth of conquered Canaan as the spoils of war. "Great and goodly cities, which thou didst not build," recited Moses, perhaps with a certain stinging irony, "and houses full of all good things, which thou didst not fill, and cisterns hewn out, which thou didst not hew, and vineyards and olive-trees, which thou didst not plant, and thou shalt eat and be satisfied." (Deut. 6:10–11)[26]

Moses was even more explicit when he described the curses that Yahweh would inflict upon the Israelites if they failed to obey the divine law, if they allowed themselves to be corrupted by gods and goddesses whose rites were so pleasurable and so seductive. Indeed, Moses conjured up a vision of Bosch-like horror in which the land of milk and honey would be turned into the landscape of suffering and death, a vision so shattering that the words of Moses still bring a lump to the throat.

Israel would be invaded and ravaged by its enemies, warned Moses. Famine and pestilence would afflict anyone unlucky enough to survive the conqueror's blade. Terror and chaos would turn town and country-side into a hell on earth. "And thou shalt grope at noonday, as the blind gropeth in the darkness," Moses railed. "Thou shalt betroth a wife, and another shall lie with her; thine ox shall be slain before thine eyes, and thou shalt not eat thereof; thy sons and daughters shall be given unto another people." (Deut. 28:29–30)[27] Hungry and homeless, even the most "delicate and tender" of the menfolk would fight with their own wives to eat the flesh of their children, and the womenfolk would be reduced to gnawing the afterbirth of their newborns. "The sights you see will drive you mad," said Moses (Deut. 28:34 NEB), and the days and nights would pass as if in a fever dream, an ordeal so grueling and so gruesome that the Israelites would pray only for an end to it all.

> And thy life shall hang in doubt before thee; and thou shalt fear night and day, and thou shalt have no assurances of thy life. In the morning you shall say: "Would it were evening!" and at evening thou shalt say: "Would it were morning!" (Deut. 28:67)[28]

The final curse, paradoxically enough, would be a sharp and sudden reversal of fate—the Promised Land would be forfeited, the Chosen People would be rejected, and the Israelites would find themselves right back where they started forty years before!

"The Lord will bring you sorrowing back to Egypt by that very road of which I said to you, 'You shall not see that road again,'" Moses warned, "and there you will offer yourselves to your enemies as slaves and slave-girls—but there will be no buyer." (Deut. 28:68 NEB)

THE DAY HAS COME WHEN YOU MUST DIE

Suddenly, Moses lashed out in anger at the "stiff-necked" Israelites, blaming them for his sorry fate—he had already forfeited the blessing of Yahweh, and he was doomed to a lonely death in exile while the Israelites marched on without him into the Promised Land. Now he paused in his discourse to recall the moment when the terrible decree had been pronounced upon him.

"And I besought the Lord at that time, saying: 'O Lord God, Thou hast begun to show Thy servant Thy greatness, and Thy strong hand;

for what god is there in heaven or on earth, that can do according to Thy mighty acts?' " Moses railed. " 'Let me go over, I pray Thee, and see the good land that is beyond the Jordan, that goodly hill-country and Lebanon.' But the Lord was wroth with me for *your* sakes, and hearkened not unto me; and the Lord said unto me: 'Let it suffice thee; speak no more unto Me of this matter.' " (Deut. 3:23–26)[29] Just as the law that Moses brought down from Sinai demanded the sacrifice of some blameless ram or bullock as a sin-offering for the wrongdoings of others, now Moses regarded himself as the scapegoat who would be made to suffer for the faithlessness and defiance of the people he had been called upon to lead out of Egypt.

"Now the Lord was angered with me for your sakes, and swore that I should not go over the Jordan, and that I should not go in unto that good land, which the Lord thy God giveth thee for an inheritance," Moses ranted on. "But I must die in this land, I must not go over the Jordan, but ye are to go over, and possess that good land." (Deut. 4:21–22)

At last, Moses seemed to run out of both laws and memories, and he fell silent. A few matters of protocol remained, however, and Moses postponed the imminent and inevitable moment of death by pausing to write down the words of his farewell address on a scroll. Then he handed the scroll to the priests who attended him with the command that it be placed for safekeeping next to the Ark of the Covenant. When the Israelites reached Canaan, Moses ordered, the words of the law were to be inscribed on plastered stones for all to see, and the book he had just written was to be taken out and read aloud to the assembled Israelites every seven years, "that they may learn, and fear the Lord your God, and observe to do all the words of this law." (Deut. 27:2, 31:12) Because, Moses pointedly reminded them, they surely could not be relied upon to remember and obey the Second Law on their own.

"For I know thy rebellion, and thy stiff neck," Moses sniped one last time. "Behold, while I am yet alive with you this day, ye have been rebellious against the Lord, and how much more after my death?" (Deut. 31:27)

Finally, a voice that Moses alone heard, a voice that Moses alone knew and recognized, spoke the words that he had long dreaded to hear.

"Behold, thy days approach that thou must die," Yahweh told

Moses. "Call Joshua, and present yourselves in the tent of meeting, that I may give him a charge." (Deut. 31:14)

Then, as the entire assembly watched and listened, Moses attended to the last few crucial matters. First came the formal designation of his successor. "I am a hundred and twenty years old this day" announced Moses. "I can no longer go out and come in, and the Lord hath said unto me: 'Thou shalt not go over this Jordan.' " (Deut. 31:1–2) So he summoned Joshua, a man they already knew as a war hero, an intrepid spy, and a faithful lieutenant of Moses, and confirmed him as the maximum leader of the Israelites. "Be strong and of good courage," Moses said, "for thou shalt go with this people into the land which the Lord hath sworn unto their fathers to give them, and thou shalt cause them to inherit it." (Deut 31:7)

Then, at the whispered instructions of Yahweh, Moses composed a song of praise, sang it aloud and taught it to the priests, so that when he was dead and gone, and the Israelites had "eaten their fill, and waxen fat, and turned unto other gods," the song would remind them of the day when they had been fairly warned of what would happen if they strayed. "Put it in their mouths," Yahweh said, "that this song may be a witness for Me against the children of Israel." And just as God intended, the Song of Moses was both awe-inspiring and bloodcurdling, praising Yahweh for sparing the Chosen People "in the waste, a howling wilderness," and warning of the terrible fate that would surely befall them when they forgot his largesse in days ahead (Deut. 32:10).

> See now that I, even I, am He,
> And there is no god with Me;
> I kill, and I make alive;
> I have wounded, and I heal;
> And there is none than can deliver out of My hand.
>
> . . . .
>
> If I whet My glittering sword,
> And My hand take hold on judgment;
> I will render vengeance to Mine adversaries,
> And will recompense them that hate Me.
> I will make Mine arrows drunk with blood,
> And My sword shall devour flesh.
>
> (Deut. 32:39, 41)

Then Moses bestowed a blessing of his own on the children of Israel, tribe by tribe, just as Jacob had done on his deathbed in Egypt so long ago. "Let Reuben live, and not die, in that his men become few," he said of the Reubenites. "Hear, Lord, the voice of Judah, and bring him in unto his people." And so Moses went, naming Levi, Benjamin, Joseph, Zebulun, Gad, Dan, Naphtali, and Asher. Curiously, Moses came up with blessings for only eleven tribes, although elsewhere the Bible numbers the tribes of Israel at twelve or thirteen.[30] "Happy art thou, O Israel, who is like unto thee?" concluded Moses in a sentiment so cheerful that it strikes us as bitterly ironic. "A people saved by the Lord." (Deut. 33:29)

TO SLEEP WITH THE FATHERS

At last Moses could delay the end no longer: "Moses made an end of speaking all these words to all Israel." (Deut. 32:44) Having listened to the self-serving explanation for his impending death that Moses had just offered to his people, Yahweh pointedly reminded him of the real reason for the decree: "Because ye trespassed against Me in the midst of the children of Israel at the waters of Meribah-kadesh, in the wilderness of Zin, because ye did not uphold my holiness among the Israelites," said Yahweh, "thou shalt not go thither into the land which I gave to the children of Israel." (Deut. 32:51–52)[31]

And then the death watch began in earnest. The last hours of Moses were spent in the company of Yahweh alone, the invisible deity who had been his master and his friend, his torturer and his comforter, for the last forty years; the deity who had once changed his mind about killing Moses but who was now ready to act on the same terrible resolve. Like a condemned man offered a last meal, Moses was permitted one tantalizing glimpse of the Promised Land on whose soil he would never set foot.

"Get thee up into the top of Pisgah, and lift up thine eyes westward, and northward, and southward, and eastward, and behold with thine eyes; for thou shalt not pass over this Jordan," Yahweh had said to Moses once before, and the very last words that he spoke to Moses carried the very same instruction, the same reproach, the same sentence of death: "Get thee up into this mountain, unto mount

Nebo,* and behold the land of Canaan, which I give unto the children of Israel for a possession, and die in the mount whither thou goest up, and be gathered unto thy people." (Deut. 3:27, 32:49–50)[32]

Whether Moses experienced the last grudging gesture of Yahweh as a taunt or a reward, the Bible does not say and we cannot know.

"I REFUSE TO DIE"

So trivial was the imagined offense of Moses at Meribah-kadesh, so arbitrary was the punishment imposed on him by Yahweh, and so distressing was the very notion of the death of Moses that both the Deuteronomist and the sages who came later struggled to explain away the capital sentence. The Book of Deuteronomy, as we have already noted, puts an entirely different spin on the matter: Moses was a wholly righteous man who was made to die in order to atone for the sins of the Israelites. The rabbis credited God with a more generous motive: God had already decided that Moses would be resurrected on the Day of Judgment along with the rest of the slave generation so that he could lead them into the Promised Land, and that is why he made Moses die along with them in the wilderness. The supposed sin of striking the rock at Meribah-kadesh, the rabbis reasoned, was "only a pretext God employed that He might not seem unjust."[33]

Even so, the sages were willing to entertain the notion that Moses, described as the meekest and mildest of men in the Bible, turned suddenly defiant in the face of death, and the rabbinical literature preserves a collection of remarkable tales in which Moses refuses to go gentle into that good night. Moses addresses fifteen hundred prayers to God to spare his life, goes one such tale, "so that heaven and earth and all forms of creation trembled." If God is determined that he should not set foot in the Promised Land, Moses suggests, why not at least turn him into a bird so that he can fly across the Jordan? Or if God is intent that he

---

*Nebo and Pisgah are two different places in the mountains overlooking Canaan. By now, we should not be surprised to find that the Bible conflates two place-names without explaining which one Moses actually ascended. To resolve the apparent ambiguity, scholarship and tradition suggest that Pisgah was the name of the higher of two peaks atop Nebo.

should die in the wilderness, Moses has an ingenious proposal. "Cut me in pieces," he implores, "throw me over the Jordan and revive me there." Like a cranky child, he draws a circle on the ground, stands within it, and vows not to move from the spot until God relents.

According to a tale from the Midrash, Moses engages in one last debate with the cranky and mercurial God he has known so well and for so long. Perhaps Moses will be able to change God's mind as he has done more than once before.

"I refuse to die," Moses is made to say to God, "for I want to live."

"Enough!" replies God. "Thus far shalt thou go and not farther."

"What sin have I committed," Moses retorts, "that I should die?"

"Thou must die, because death has been decreed upon the first man," answers God, neatly sidestepping the question by pointing out that, ever since Adam, the life of every human being must eventually come to an end.

"Lord of the Universe, let me enter the land of Israel and live there at least two or three years," says Moses, bargaining with God like a bazaar merchant. "Let me live so that I may be able to tell the future generations how Thou didst rain manna from Heaven and bring forth water from the rock."

"If thy life were to be spared," God replies, "the children of Israel will look upon thee as a god and worship thee."

And so it goes, back and forth, until God brings the unseemly haggling to a sudden end with a take-it-or-leave-it proposition that puts Moses to the ultimate test of faith.

"Moses, I swore two oaths, one that thou shouldst not enter the Promised Land, and the other that I will never destroy the children of Israel," God warns. "If it is thy wish that I should break the first oath, then I may also break the other."

"Lord of the Universe, may Moses die and a thousand others like him," says Moses, "but let not one soul of the children of Israel be destroyed."[34]

The final vow attributed to Moses is utterly in vain, of course. Moses would die just as Yahweh had decreed, and so would countless thousands and even millions of the children of Israel in the centuries and millennia that followed. Even in the fairy-tale world that is preserved in the Midrash, a sense of tragic futility taints the last moments in the life of Moses—God does not change his mind and commute the death sentence. And so the life of Moses can be understood as a tragedy, both in the classic and the existential sense of the word—he was cast adrift at birth in a hostile world, he spent a long and lonely life in constant pursuit of a goal that always eluded him, and he died a lonely death.

THE VIEW FROM MOUNT NEBO

The last sight that Moses saw with mortal eyes was a vista of the Promised Land in all of its length and breadth, one final miracle by the God who was even then preparing to kill him. From Mount Nebo, Moses glimpsed as far north as the city of Dan, as far south as the Negev, across the breadth of Canaan to the Great Sea. "This is the land which I swore unto Abraham, unto Isaac, and unto Jacob," Yahweh reminded him. "I have caused thee to see it with thine eyes, but thou shalt not go over." (Deut. 34:4)

Exactly how Moses died is not revealed in the Bible, which offers only a spare and emotionless report.

So Moses the servant of the Lord died there in the land of Moab, according to the word of the Lord. And he was buried in the valley in the land of Moab over against Beth-peor, and no man knoweth of his sepulchre unto this day. (Deut 34:5)

A much more elaborate and exalted scene was imagined by the sages. God descends from heaven in the company of three archangels to attend to the death of Moses and extracts the soul of Moses from his body amid comforts and splendors worthy of a king. The angel Gabriel arranges the couch upon which Moses reclines, Michael spreads a garment of royal purple, and Zagzagel places a woollen pillow for his weary head. Only then does God summon the soul of Moses from his body with tender words—and an intriguing change of gender.

"My daughter!" God was made to say to the female spirit in the body of Moses. "Do not hesitate, and I will take thee up to the highest Heaven where thou wilt dwell under the Throne of Glory, like the Seraphim, Ophanim and Cherubim."

When she demurs—"I prefer to remain in the body of Moses, the righteous man"—God bestows a single tender kiss upon the lips of Moses, gently drawing out his last breath of life and, along with it, the reluctant soul.[35]

One poignant tradition in the rabbinical literature insisted that Moses did not die at all. Like Enoch before him and Elijah after him, the sages imagined, Moses was spared the agonies of a mortal death—perhaps he simply "walked with God . . . and was not," as the Bible says of Enoch (Gen. 5:24), or maybe he "went up by a whirlwind into heaven," as the Bible says of Elijah (2 Kings 2:11–12). Miraculously removed from the world of ordinary men and women, Moses "is alive and serving on high."[36] The same Midrashic tradition is evoked in the New Testament when the transfiguration of Jesus is witnessed by Moses and Elijah (Matt. 17:3), two biblical figures who were thought to have been granted the privilege of direct passage to heaven.

The death scene as reported in the Bible was far simpler. Moses is "solitary as he has always been, more solitary than he has ever been before," writes Martin Buber, likening the great man at the moment of his death to "one of those noble animals which leave their herd in order to perish alone."[37] And yet Moses was *not* alone—he was attended by the deity he had served for so long, and it was that deity who killed him. The Hebrew phrase used by the biblical author to describe how Moses died "admits of the meaning 'by the mouth of YHVH,' " concedes Buber, which is what prompted the sages to imagine that God killed Moses with a divine kiss, an image of both exquisite tenderness and abject horror. The death of Moses, then, is an ironic reversal of Yahweh's gift of life to the first man: God once put his lips to the lifeless Adam "and breathed into his nostrils the breath of life" (Gen. 2:7), but now God put his lips to the living Moses, still vigorous at 120, and drew out the last breath of a long and tortured life.

FROM HENCE TO HEAVEN

So Moses passes "from hence to heaven," as Philo described the death scene, "leaving this mortal life to become immortal."[38] The ministering angels weep openly at the death of Moses, the rabbis imagined, and so do heaven and earth, the sun and moon and stars. The women and children of Israel beat their breasts in grief in an "excess of this sorrow and lamentation," according to Josephus, "nor did ever any grief so deeply affect the Hebrews as did this upon the death of Moses."[39] But they are denied any role in the burial of Moses. God himself was imagined to have carried off the body of Moses to some unknown place, where he dug a grave and laid the mortal remains to rest in a mountain crag overlooking the Promised Land. The body remains miraculously uncorrupted—"Although Moses' body lies dead in its grave," the rabbis wrote, "it is still as fresh as when he was alive"[40]—and the soul is exalted.

"O My son Moses, much honor has been stored up for thee in the future world, for thou wilt take part in all the delights of Paradise, where are prepared three hundred and ten worlds," God was made to say to Moses in one of the rabbinical tales. "Thy light will not fade, for My majesty will shine before thee, My glory will clothe thee, My splendor will shelter thee, My radiance will make thy face beam, My sweetness will delight thy palate, and one of My many sceptres upon which is engraved the Ineffable Name shall I give to thee."[41]

Not every praise-singer was quite so carried away. Philo, catering to a sophisticated readership in the Roman world, dispensed with the divine kiss of death, the weeping constellations, the delights of Paradise, and the other sentimental touches; instead, he insisted that Moses was summoned by "the Father, who now changed him . . . wholly and entirely into a most sun-like mind." Thus was "this man Moses," so fully mortal in the hard life that he lived, transformed from a human being into an idea, from a creature of flesh and blood into a construct of pure reason.

God, the biblical author, and the sages seemed to prefer Moses that way. All of them feared that Moses would come to be praised above God for the events of the Exodus or, even worse, regarded as a god in his own right. A thoroughly human impulse elevated kings and emperors to the rank of gods throughout the ancient world and encouraged the cults of personality that decorated their tombs with offerings and sacrifices. For that reason alone, the rabbis suggested, God buries Moses in a secret place so that "no man knoweth of his sepulchre unto this day"—if the location of the grave of Moses remained a mystery, then God would not be troubled by the sight of pilgrims who sought out his burial place in order to venerate Moses (Deut. 34:5). Yahweh, of course, had never concealed the fact that he was a jealous god, and the object of his jealousy at that moment was Moses himself.

"MOSES IS DEAD"

The Israelites mourned the passing of Moses for the prescribed period of thirty days, the Bible reports, and we might imagine that the encampment on the plains of Moab was afflicted with the sense of desolation and despair that accompanies the passing of any great leader in a time of crisis, the sense of being left suddenly orphaned in a threatening world. And yet the Bible falls suddenly and curiously silent on the subject of Moses, and he literally disappears from the biblical narrative once his death has been reported. Not unlike an out-of-favor commissar who is airbrushed out of a photograph of the Soviet leadership atop Lenin's tomb, Moses begins to fade before our very eyes.

Seldom is the name of Moses found in the biblical writings that follow the Five Books of Moses, and Moses is hardly mentioned at all in the Psalms and the prophetic books. Jeremiah, in a reference that damns with faint praise, seemed to regard Moses and Samuel as equals (Jer. 15:1), and both the Psalmist and the Prophets were far more adoring of David than of Moses.[42] Judaism is not "Mosaism," one commentator insisted; but another commentator was willing to allow that it might be called "Davidism."[43] The rabbis venerated Moses as a lawgiver and a teacher—Moshe Rabbenu, ("Moses, Our Master")—but they were always reluctant to overpraise him for fear that God would be denied his due for the "signs and wonders" of the Exodus; that's why, for example, Moses is pointedly absent from the traditional Haggadah, the text for the observance of Passover.[44] Christian tradition went still further: "Moses is dead," wrote Martin Luther, by which he signified that the Sinai covenant had been superseded by the New Testament, and Moses himself wholly eclipsed by Jesus of Nazareth.

Yet Moses is granted one fleeting moment of honor by the biblical author before he disappears from Holy Writ. The biblical account of his life comes to an end with a poignant epitaph that is mostly free of the bombastic words that Yahweh always seems to elicit from the biblical sources. An open-eyed reading of the Bible reveals that Moses was never depicted as divine or even heroic—he was meek and even cowardly at some moments, angry and even murderous at other moments, deeply flawed and sometimes even dysfunctional, and his very flaws make it all the more remarkable that he was chosen by Yahweh at all. But the final epitaph allows that Moses was unique even if flawed, and his relationship with God was uniquely intimate even if profoundly troubled.

"And there hath not arisen a prophet since in Israel like unto Moses, whom the Lord knew face to face," goes the final passage of Deuteronomy and the closing note of his life story, "in all the signs and the wonders, which the Lord sent him to do in the land of Egypt, to Pharaoh and to all his servants, and to all his land; and in all the mighty hand, and in all the great terror, which Moses wrought in the sight of all Israel." (Deut. 34:10–12)

A subtle and faintly subversive idea can be detected in the epitaph of Moses. Against all evidence in the biblical text—the words and deeds of Moses in the guise of king, magus, and generalissimo, so commanding and enduring in the destiny of humankind—pious tradition insists that Moses was only a servant and a messenger of God. The words he uttered, the miracles he worked, the laws he handed down were the handiwork of the unseen deity called Yahweh, we are asked to believe. Yet the last words of the biblical account of the life of Moses can be understood to suggest otherwise—God may have recruited him and sent him to do his bidding, but it was Moses, after all, who showed the "signs and wonders, the mighty hand and all the great terror," not only to "all of Israel" but to the whole world. And it was Moses who wrote them indelibly into human history.

Chapter Twelve

THE SEARCH FOR THE HISTORICAL MOSES

Noble Alexander, was your Ilion really situated in layer
VIIa? Are you so sure that Achilles ever lived? Perhaps
you show an honourable veneration for something that is
a figment of the imagination.
—JAN DE VRIES, *HEROIC SONG AND*
HEROIC LEGEND

On a stele of polished basalt in a gallery of the British Museum, the image of a kneeling man can be discerned among the dozens of other figures inscribed into the cold black stone. He is believed to be Jehu, an obscure monarch who sat on the throne of the northern kingdom of Israel in the late ninth century B.C.E., and he is shown in a gesture of obeisance to the Assyrian emperor who subjugated him, Shalmaneser III. "Silver, gold, a golden bowl, golden goblets, a golden beaker, pitchers of gold, lead, sceptres for the king and balsam-wood I received from him," goes the inscription on the so-called Black Obelisk, which offers the only contemporary image of an Israelite king ever recovered from the archaeological record.[1]

No such evidence confirms the existence of Moses. But the remnants and relics of biblical Israel are so sparse that the utter absence of Moses in any source except the Bible itself is neither surprising nor decisive. Nothing outside the Bible, after all, confirms the existence of Abraham, Isaac, or Jacob, Saul or David or Solomon. One day, perhaps, an archaeologist will retrieve some fragment of parchment or some shard of pottery bearing the name of Moses. But even then, we will not know with certainty whether the three Hebrew characters that make up the name Mosheh belonged to a purely mythical character in the legend and lore of ancient Israel or a flesh-and-blood human being who actually did the things that are described so memorably in the pages of the Bible.

Yet something deep in our nature urges us to keep looking for hard evidence that Moses actually lived and died. The same profound curiosity that drives the whole enterprise of Bible scholarship and biblical archaeology prompts us to wonder: Who was the *real* Moses, the flesh-and-blood man who stands behind the biblical figure? Many different and sometimes contradictory answers have been offered over the centuries and millennia, but the question is still being asked thirty-five hundred years or so after his supposed birth in Egypt and his death on the frontier of the land of Israel.

For that reason alone, Moses is still very much alive in our hearts and minds, and he still possesses the power to challenge and provoke us the same way that he goaded a generation of Israelites during the long march toward the Promised Land.

"UNTIL HE HIMSELF WILL TELL US"

For the true believer in any of the Bible-based faiths—Judaism, Christianity, and Islam—the question of the "historicity" of Moses is faintly blasphemous. The Bible is the Received Word of God as given to Moses atop Sinai, or so goes a catechism that is common to all three faiths. Everything we need to know about Moses and the events of the Exodus, everything we are *allowed* to know, is to be found within its pages. If Moses remains a veiled mystery, it is because God did not intend us to know more than what is revealed in the Bible—and Moses said so in his farewell address to the Israelites.

> The secret things belong unto the Lord our God; but the things that are revealed belong unto us and to our children for ever, that we may do all the words of the law. (Deut. 29:28)

If we discern ambiguities and contradictions in the Bible—if we ask, for example, how Moses could have written the passage that describes his own death—the true believer simply shrugs: "God moves in a mysterious way," in the words of William Cowper, "His wonders to perform."

That is why fundamentalist Bible commentator Paul Bork cheerfully acknowledges that he cannot figure out how Moses could have been the author of the Five Books of Moses—and then declares himself willing to wait until "he himself will tell us in the new earth."[2]

Such simple truths have always been regarded as sufficient by fundamentalists, and those who insisted on asking uncomfortable questions about the authorship or historical accuracy of the Bible have been made to suffer or die for their impertinence. When Spinoza persisted in pointing out the flaws and contradictions that he found in Holy Writ, for example, he was excommunicated and his books were burned. But the impulse to ask questions is perhaps the single most important characteristic of human intelligence, and it is the glory of human civilization that the rack and the auto-da-fé and the fatwa have never deterred even the most devout men and women from reading the Bible with open eyes, an open mind, and an open heart.

SPIN DOCTORS

All that we can say about the historical Moses is that someone like the man described in the Bible *might* have lived at some unknowable time and place in the far-distant past, and his exploits *might* have been the grain of sand around which the pearly accretions of legend and lore slowly built up over the centuries until he became the rich and provocative figure whom we find in the pages of the Bible.

We can say with a bit more assurance that the bards and chroniclers of ancient Israel were probably telling tales about Moses at an early stage in the long and gradual process by which the Bible was composed. As the oral traditions were collected and reduced to writing by scribes and court historians, starting around 1000 B.C.E. and continuing for the next six or seven hundred years, Moses came to be used as a narrative device to stitch together the major episodes in the sacred history of Israel—the Exodus from Egypt, the giving of the Law, the making of the covenant with Yahweh, the wandering in the wilderness, and the conquest of Canaan. Thus, for example, Martin Noth suggests that the earliest versions of the Exodus and the Sinai covenant may have been preserved by two separate groups of Israelites—"and Moses, of course, would have played a major role in neither of the two events."[3]

By the sixth century B.C.E., when the southern kingdom of Judah was conquered and the aristocratic and priestly elite marched into exile in Babylon, the scraps and fragments of sacred history and ritual law were collected and compiled into a work that resembled the core of the Hebrew Bible as we know it. But even then the biblical authors and editors probably continued to tweak and polish the text for a couple more centuries, putting a new theological spin on the primal history of Israel, adding quaint and colorful details to enliven the familiar narratives. So Moses became an even more complex and sometimes contradictory character as he was given new scenes and dialogue by the successive generations of priests and scribes, each one working according to his own agenda and his own aesthetic.

When the Bible chronicles the oppression of the Israelites in Egypt—"And they made their lives bitter with hard service, in mortar and in brick" (Exod. 1:13)—the biblical author may have been describing the landscape of Babylon in the sixth century B.C.E. rather than Egypt a thousand years or so before. By contrast, some of the particulars of the biblical account of Moses in Midian may have been inspired by the popular Egyptian tale of Sinuhe, a prince of the twentieth century B.C.E. who falls out of favor with Pharaoh, flees to the land of Canaan, and marries the eldest daughter of a local chieftain who sheltered him— "One might call it a 'best-seller,' the first in the world, and about Canaan, of all places," as one Bible historian puts it.[4] And the spectacular manifestations of God—"by day in a pillar of cloud . . . and by night in a pillar of fire"; the smoke that ascended from Sinai "as the smoke of a furnace"; and "the voice of the horn exceeding loud" (Exod. 13:21, 19:16, 18)—can be understood as metaphorical descriptions of the familiar rites of the Temple at Jerusalem: the fire where sacrifices were offered, the clouds of incense, the sound of the ram's horn or the silver trumpet.

The flourishes of the biblical authors were usually intended to make a theological point. The eerie account of Yahweh's night attack on Moses is so raw and primitive that some scholars see it as an authentic fragment of the earliest traditions of ancient Israel—and yet the passage may have been the result of intentional "archaizing" by a priest of the post-exilic era who wanted to impress on his readers the importance of circumcision, a rite that had fallen out of favor among the other cultures of the Near East.[5] By making the text *seem* old, one scholar proposes, the biblical author bestowed an "aura of antiquity" on the "new-fangled Priestly notion" of circumcision, thus enhancing the credibility of what may have been a relatively late addition to the biblical text.

The challenge, then, is "to cut through the secondary accretions," as George Coats puts it, "to recover the kernel of genuine tradition."[6] At the deepest of the many layers of biblical text, the argument goes, there must have been a real Moses, if only because a life story so rich in detail and dialogue, so complex and full of contradiction, could not have been made up out of whole cloth. Such reasoning essentially begs the question of the historicity of Moses, but it appears to be the best argument that can be made in favor of his mortal existence.

"Do we possess any historical testimony about Moses? We have none," concedes Elias Auerbach, who is not bothered at all by the lack of corroborating evidence. "There can be no doubt whatever about the historicity of Moses' personality, certainly no more than about the historicity of Buddha or Jesus." And he declares, mostly as a matter of faith, that Moses "is no doubt one of the greatest geniuses to whom the world has given birth, a man in his fullness, one in a thousand years."[7]

Yet if we insist on looking for the "kernel of genuine tradition" at the core of the Bible, if we follow the scholars as they probe and parse out the biblical text, what we find beneath the layers of myth and legend is not necessarily a solid core of historical fact but merely the oldest version of the mythic Moses. "There remained about him," acknowledges Auerbach, "the enigmatic, the demoniacal, the strange."[8]

MAN AND SYMBOL

Some of us, however, are able to hold two opposing thoughts about Moses in our minds at the same time. The mortal man may not much resemble the character who is described in the Bible, but even if Moses was mostly or only a legendary figure, what matters most is the use to which the figure of Moses has been put in the real world. The search for the historical Moses is less important—and ultimately less interesting—than the quest for the moral and spiritual values that we might extract from his biblical life story.

"Not a single one of all these stories, in which Moses is the central figure, was really written about Moses," insists Gerhard von Rad. "Great as was the veneration of the writers for this man to whom God has been pleased to reveal Himself, in all these stories it is not Moses himself, Moses the man, but God who is the central figure."[9]

Thus the question of whether there was a "real" Moses who resembled the biblical Moses, the question of whether or not Moses existed at all, is probably the wrong one to ask. "The Western mentality . . . always seeks to answer the historic questions: Is this real? Is this objectively true? Did this really happen?" muses Bishop John Shelby Spong in *Liberating the Gospels*. "With these questions to guide us, the Western mind has always had trouble embracing the truth found in myth, legend, intuition, or poetry."[10] Yet it is myth and legend, poetry and parable, that we find throughout the Bible, and especially in the Five Books of Moses.

Scientists may attempt to explain away the "signs and wonders" of the Exodus as natural phenomena, arguing, for example, that the burning bush on Horeb was "a variety of the gas-plant or Fraxinella" whose "oil is so volatile that it is constantly escaping and if approached with a naked light bursts into flames,"[11] or that the thunder and lightning and quaking of the theophany atop Mount Sinai were caused by a thunderstorm, an earthquake, or a volcanic eruption.[12] But even the showiest manifestations of God can best be understood as a metaphor for a spiritual experience that was much more subtle and understated.

"The literal truth was that God spoke to the heart of Moses," explains Brevard Childs. "[T]he poetic truth was that He spoke in thunder and lighting from the crest of Sinai."[13]

Once we read beyond the Five Books of Moses, "the poetic truth" is all that remains because "the man Moses," as he is sometimes called in the Bible, disappears from the biblical text and is rarely mentioned again. The Book of Joshua invokes his name now and then—"Every place that the sole of your foot shall tread upon," God told Joshua, "to you have I given it, as I spoke unto Moses" (Josh. 1:3)—and Joshua is shown to reenact some of the memorable events of the Exodus, sending spies into Canaan (Josh 2:1) and using the Ark of the Covenant as Moses once used the rod of God to stop the flow of the Jordan "while all Israel passed over on dry ground."* (Josh. 3:17)

---

*Revisionist Bible scholar John Van Seters proposes that elements of the Book of Joshua may have predated the biblical life story of Moses, and thus he suggests that J may have patterned his (or her) account of the miracle at the Red Sea in the Book of Exodus after the crossing of the Jordan.

But Moses was now only a talismanic name and a faint memory, not a living presence. He is used in the Book of Joshua to symbolize the divine sanction of Joshua's leadership in the conquest of Canaan: "This day will I begin to magnify thee in the sight of all Israel, that they may know that, as I was with Moses, so I will be with thee." (Josh. 3:7) The eclipse of Moses is nearly total in the prophetic books of the Hebrew Bible, and we find that Hosea could not bring himself to mention Moses by name when he recalled the events of the Exodus. (Hos. 12:14)

The New Testament regards Moses as the precursor of the Messiah, and obliquely invokes his example to authenticate Jesus of Nazareth as the promised one whose coming is predicted in the Hebrew Bible: "For had ye believed Moses," said Jesus, "ye would have believed me, for he wrote of me." (John 5:46) Thus the slaughter of the innocents by Herod is meant to remind us of the slaying of the firstborn by Pharaoh; the miracle of loaves and fishes recalls the feeding of the multitude on manna and quail; the forty days and forty nights that Jesus spent in the wilderness harks back to the sojourn of Moses on Sinai. Jesus was quick to quote the words of Moses: "It is written, that man shall not live by bread alone," said Jesus to the devil when challenged to turn a stone into bread (Luke 4:4 KJV).* But Moses is unmistakably diminished in the New Testament—when his ghostly figure appears at the transfiguration of Jesus, he is presented along with Elijah as no more than a bystander (Matt. 17:3)—and ultimately he is wholly discarded.

"Verily, verily, I say unto you, Moses gave you not that bread from heaven," taught Jesus, "but my Father giveth you the true bread from heaven." (John 6:32)

If we are to resurrect Moses, if we are to make him come alive again, then we must read the biblical life story of Moses "with religious imagination and empathy, as one would read a piece of poetry," in the words of Bernhard Anderson.[14] By these lights, the "historical" Moses recedes from sight and a transcendent Moses takes his place. "The story is more than simply an account of historical events, and the Law is more than merely a basis for social order and religious purity," writes Egyptologist

---

*"And He afflicted thee, and suffered thee to hunger, and fed thee with manna, which thou knewest not, neither did thy fathers know; that He might make thee know that man doth not live by bread only, but by everything that proceedeth out of the mouth of the Lord doth man live." (Deut. 8:3)

Jan Assmann. "Exodus is a symbolical story, the Law is a symbolical legislation, and Moses is a symbolical figure."[15] Exactly what Moses is meant to symbolize, however, has never been obvious or indisputable, and the hardest task of all is to find a meaning in the life of Moses that makes sense in our own tumultuous world.

THE IDEAL MOSES

The only "real" Moses, then, is the one whose example can be understood and applied in the here and now. Today, more than ever before, the Bible must stand or fall as a source of moral and spiritual instruction rather than as a work of history—otherwise, the Bible is really nothing more than a historical curiosity. By struggling to prove or disprove the historicity of Moses—or any biblical figure, for that matter—we may succeed in informing and amusing ourselves, we may even shed new light on the origins of the Bible as a work of literature, but we are in danger of missing the whole point of Holy Writ.

"I care not whether this man Moses really existed," wrote Ahad Ha'am, one of the pioneers of modern Zionism, at the turn of the century. "Even if you succeeded in demonstrating conclusively that the man Moses never existed, or that he was not such a man as we supposed, you would not thereby detract one jot from the historical reality of the ideal Moses, the Moses who has been our leader not only for forty years in the wilderness of Sinai, but for thousands of years in all the wildernesses in which we have wandered since the Exodus."[16]

Even so, "the ideal Moses" whom Ahad Ha'am invokes so confidently is hardly more distinct than the mutable and many-faced figure we find in the pages of the Bible. Of the various contradictory roles that Moses is made to play in the Bible, many of us prefer the Emancipator who "proclaim[ed] liberty throughout the land" and ordered that slaves should be set free en masse in the year of the jubilee (Lev. 25:10), the True Empath who called on the Israelites to "love ye the stranger" because they had once been "strangers in a strange land" (Deut. 10:19), the Lawgiver who instructed the Israelites to leave the corners of their fields unharvested so that the poor and the powerless might find something to eat because the Israelites had known poverty and powerlessness themselves (Lev. 19:19).

Thou shalt not pervert the justice due to the stranger, or to the fatherless; nor take the widow's raiment to pledge. But thou shalt remember that thou wast a bondman in Egypt, and the Lord thy God redeemed thee thence; therefore I command thee to do this thing. (Deut. 24:17–18)

But, as we have seen, Moses is also a punishing inquisitor who put his own people to the sword when they dared to dance around the golden calf, a bloodthirsty autocrat who called down plague and hellfire on any man or woman who asserted the right to speak directly to God, a ruthless man of war who looked on the captive women of Midian—the kinfolk of his own wife and his half-Midianite sons—and asked: "Have ye saved all the women alive?" (Num. 31:15)

The contrast between the kinder, gentler Moses and the cruel and coldhearted one is not merely a matter of academic interest. Today, some narrow-minded people rely on the Bible to condemn their fellow human beings for the most intimate aspects of their private lives: "Thou shalt not lie with mankind as with womankind; it is abomination" (Lev. 18:22) is the only verse in all of the Mosaic code that unambiguously condemns gay sexuality, but it is often cited nowadays by fundamentalists. Yet they are highly selective and self-serving in their reading of Scripture, and they apparently do not know or do not care that the Bible also commands us to stone to death a rebellious son (Deut. 21:18), for example, and forbids us to wear clothing that contains both linen and wool (Deut. 22:11).

Indeed, some zealots claim to find a warrant in biblical law for the maiming and murder of their fellow human beings. The assassination of Yitzhak Rabin by a Jewish law student who opposed his efforts at making peace with the Palestinian Arabs, for example, was defended as justifiable homicide by a few radical casuists who relied on a tortured interpretation of the Torah. And when one Orthodox rabbi in Israel, seeking to condemn intermarriage between Jews and non-Jews, invoked the example of the Israelite prince who was slain for sleeping with a Midianite woman (Num. 25:8), his remark was interpreted by some knowledgeable Bible-readers as a call for the murder of Jews in mixed marriages.

Moses has been used as a mouthpiece to promulgate a great many laws, and not even the self-proclaimed "Bible literalists" actually embrace the Mosaic code in its entirety. Some of the sacred laws of Sinai clearly applied only to the time and place in which they were first handed down; some have been construed in ways that bear little resemblance to their literal meaning; some have been interpreted out of existence. And since some of the laws of Moses are life-affirming and some are life-threatening, we are obliged to pick and choose among them. Moses himself understood and assumed that God had bestowed upon humankind the gift of free will, and he repeatedly called upon the Israelites to use it.

"THE MOSAIC DISTINCTION"

Of course, Moses is not an unsullied symbol of freedom. In fact, he must bear some measure of responsibility for introducing an innovation in the history of religion that cannot be easily harmonized with the ecumenical ideas about God and humankind that may be the only real hope for peace and harmony in our troubled world.

Until Moses came along, as we have seen, the ancients were open-minded about matters of faith: they freely borrowed each other's gods and goddesses; they sacrificed at each other's temples; and if they engaged in acts of terrible brutality toward one another in both war and peace, the carnage had nothing to do with fear or hatred of a rival faith. A kind of rough-and-ready utilitarianism was at work—if a strange new god or goddess seemed attractive or effective, then he or she would be embraced. Thus did the pantheon of ancient Egypt, for example, come to include the gods and goddesses of Canaan at a time when Moses had not yet revealed the First Commandment: "Thou shalt have no other gods before Me." (Exod. 20:3)

Moses introduced the notion that all gods but Yahweh are false— "no-gods," according to a curious phrase that appears in the Song of Moses (Deut. 32:21). Even more crucially, however, he insisted that the worship of false gods was not merely futile but utterly corrupt and perverse—an "abomination" that "roused Him to jealousy." (Deut. 32:16) Here is the cutting edge of the fundamental theology of the Hebrew Bible: God blesses us when we keep faith with him and comply with his sacred law—and curses us when we do not. "I will hide My face from them," warned God in phrases that still seem threatening. "I will see what their end shall be." (Deut. 32:20) It is a theology that suggests an unsettling answer to the question "Where was God at Auschwitz?"

And, long before the Holocaust and long after, the same harsh credo has been invoked with bloody results by crusaders and inquisitors, autocrats and theocrats, to punish anyone whose beliefs are different than their own.

"Let us call the distinction between true and false in religion the 'Mosaic distinction,' " explains Egyptologist Jan Assmann, "because tradition ascribes it to Moses."[17]

Yet at certain sublime moments, Moses can also be seen as a compassionate and forgiving man who deeply understood the thoroughly human frailties and foibles of his fellow creatures, a bold and courageous man who told God to his face that he ought not to exterminate them merely because they were insufficiently pious and obedient. "O Lord, why shouldst thou vent thy anger upon thy people?" Moses boldly challenged Yahweh when he threatened to "wipe them off the face of the earth." (Exod. 32:11–12)[18] "Where was Moses at Auschwitz?" we might wonder, since we know that he was willing to argue with God himself to preserve human life against the "devouring fire" of divine wrath.

And so, even though "the Mosaic distinction" is still wholeheartedly embraced by some Jews, Christians, and Muslims who insist on regarding each other as sinners and infidels, the rest of us may find a more compelling message in the life of Moses, one that pulses with empathy and social justice. The moral counterweight to the Moses who condemned the Midianites to death is the Moses who commands us to respect and protect the stranger among us, a commandment that suffuses the whole of what we reflexively and unthinkingly call the Judeo-Christian tradition.

> And if a stranger sojourn with thee in your land, ye shall not do him wrong. The stranger that sojourneth with you shall be unto you as the home-born among you, for ye were strangers in the land of Egypt: I am the Lord your God. (Lev. 19:34)

The same stirring credo has been embraced and repeated by good-hearted men and women down through the long and sometimes bloody history of humankind. A story is told about Hillel, a revered Jewish teacher of the first century C.E., who was challenged by a cynic to teach him the Torah while standing on one foot. "What is hateful to you, do not unto your neighbor," replied Hillel, thus summing up the essential wisdom of the Bible. "All the rest is commentary." Jesus of Nazareth was even more plainspoken: "Love your enemies, bless them that curse you, do good to them that hate you." (Matt. 5:44 KJV) The same simple credo remains the keystone of the Judeo-Christian tradition. "We have built every idea of moral civilization on it," as Cynthia Ozick puts it in *Metaphor & Memory*.

THE WORD IN YOUR HEART

Moses himself understood the urgency and immediacy of the moral challenge that he placed before the Israelites and, as if to anticipate their complaints, he insisted that the obligation to act righteously is something to be done in the here and now.

> For this commandment which I command you this day is not too hard for you, neither is it far off. It is not in heaven, that you should say, "Who will go up for us to heaven and bring it to us, that we may hear it and do it?" But the word is very near to you: it is in your mouth and in your heart, so that you can do it. (Deut. 30:11–14)[19]

Here we find the ultimate challenge presented by Moses to humankind, then and now. We are called upon to hear and heed what we find in our hearts, the "still small voice" by which God once manifested himself to the prophet Elijah (2 Kings 19:12). At the end of his troubled and tumultuous life, Moses seemed to understand a basic and self-evident truth: no miracle, no commandment, no promise of heavenly reward, no threat of divine punishment will ever be enough to compel a human being to act righteously.

Indeed, the life story of Moses can be read as one long song of disappointment and despair—the disappointment of God in the species that he created and the people upon whom he chose to bestow his blessing, the despair of Moses at their thoroughly human flaws and failings. One of the favorite debating points among theologians is why the Israelites were so defiant toward a deity who sought to free them from slavery, feed them on the food of angels, send them as conquerors into the land of milk and honey—and yet their stubborn refusal to submit themselves to the will of God is exactly what made them human in the first place.

Real men and women, as we all know from personal experience, find it terribly hard to behave in the way that God and Moses—as well as priests, rabbis, and ministers—have always encouraged them to behave. Like the Israelite men and women who tired of manna and yearned for the fleshpots of Egypt, we are sometimes governed by irrational appetites and restless imaginations. Like the prince of Israel who bedded his Midianite lady friend in the sight of his own family, we are sometimes enticed by pleasures of the flesh even when it is hurtful to those we love. Like the discouraged warriors who wanted to replace Moses with a more easygoing leader and head back into slavery, we are sometimes tempted to do what is easiest rather than what is best for us.

At the heart of the matter, though, Moses seemed to understand that human beings are blessed with free will and must decide for themselves. That is why he pleaded with God, not once but repeatedly, to spare the Israelites from divine genocide. God was willing to exterminate the Chosen People and start over with him, but Moses challenged God to keep the faith. And Moses was no less confrontational in his dealings with the Israelites. They were prone to act out of weakness rather than strength, to indulge their worst passions and thereby forsake the blessing of God, but he challenged them to listen to their hearts.

> I call heaven and earth to witness against you this day, that I have set before thee life and death, the blessing and the curse; therefore choose life, that thou mayest live, thou and thy seed. (Deut. 30:19)

So the farewell address that Moses delivered to the people of Israel within sight of the Promised Land echoes down through the centuries and millennia to us. He is still a goad and a gadfly, a stubborn truthteller who refuses to allow us to be too comfortable or too complacent. No matter how we conceive of Moses, no matter how we remember him, he insists on confronting us with tough choices—love or hate, hope or despair, compassion or cruelty—and he insists, too, that we must choose for ourselves. And so the last word on Moses, and our urgent prayer, ought to be: May we choose wisely and well.

As always, and above all, my first thought is for Ann Benjamin Kirsch, the love of my life since the age of fourteen, and our children, Jennifer and Adam, whose affection, constancy, verve, wry sense of humor, and vivid presence are the font and the foundation of my life and work.

Ann and Jenny patiently endured the experience of living in close quarters with a scribbler on overlapping deadlines, and they made room in their own busy and accomplished lives to trek with me to far-flung destinations. During one hectic period, the four of us found ourselves in the same place at the same time for only a few precious days in Boston and environs, where we celebrated Adam's graduation from college between signings and interviews, and then ricocheted off in different directions.

Adam, a poet, critic, and journalist of impressive achievement, was my principal research assistant on *Moses* as he was on *The Harlot by the Side of the Road*, working tirelessly and resourcefully in the collections of the Andover-Harvard Theological Library, the New York Public Library, the University Research Library at UCLA, and, most recently, the Lauinger Library at Georgetown University. On a few rare occasions when we found ourselves on the same coast, we prowled the bookstores together, the Gotham and the Strand in New York, the Book Den in Santa Barbara.

Among the many blessings in my life, one of the richest and most rewarding is the friendship and colleagueship of my law partner, Dennis Mitchell. It is literally true, and not merely a platitude, that *Moses* would not have been written at all without his generous support and encouragement. Dennis is not only a gifted attorney, but also a man of perfect integrity, deep compassion, lively good humor, and a stirring sense of right and wrong—a real *mensch*, as my late father (and his) would have said. More than that, he is confidant, counselor, and boon companion, and every day is a good day when I hear the wheels of the luggage cart on which he carries his paper-laden briefcase creaking down the hall as he arrives at the office each morning.

Moses: A Life was inspired by Laurie Fox of the Linda Chester Literary Agency, who wondered aloud what I might discover if I went in search of Moses along the same byways that I explored in *The Harlot by the Side of the Road*. And it was not our first life-changing conversation. Ever since I first met Laurie, who was then a promising young writer working behind the counter of Charlotte Gusay's George Sand Books in West Hollywood, I have admired her gifts as an actor, poet, and novelist, cherished her friendship, and relied on her superb skills as a literary agent.

I rely, too, on the counsel of Linda Chester, so radiant and wise, whose advice has always been both bracing and comforting, and whose gift for making dreams come true would seem magical if it were not so firmly rooted in her savvy and sophistication.

Once I went in search of the True Empath, I was further encouraged along the way by Virginia Faber, my editor at Ballantine, whose absences from the office in the last stages of editing were explained to me in a cheery shorthand phrase: "She's on a date with Moses." Ginny's elegance and style, her discernment and deft touch, her unfailing good sense and good taste, enhanced not only the book itself but the whole experience of writing it.

Ballantine is the home of a remarkable concentration of gifted, dedicated, and high-spirited book people, chief among them Linda Grey and Judith Curr, whose warmth, interest, and encouragement have been so heartening to me.

At Ballantine, I have been privileged to work with a great many other lovely and talented men and women, most often Rachel Tarlow Gul in New York and Marie Coolman, Heather Smith, Regina Su, and Vann Luu in the West Coast office, but my work has also benefitted from the kind and expert attentions of Ellen Archer, Mark Bloomfield, Amy Brown, Hillary Cohen, Stan Cohen, Cathy Colbert, Betsy Elias, Ruth Frenkel, Kathleen Fridella, Jim Geraghty, Kim Hovey, Alice Kesterson, Rachel Kind, Kristine Mills-Noble, Beverly Robinson, Honi Werner, Adrian Wood, and Jason Zuzga. And I am especially grateful to Janet Fletcher, who copy-edited the manuscript with a sharp eye and a sense of engagement.

Clare Ferraro, who believed in *Moses* from the beginning, and Liz Williams each played an important role in the early stages of the book before moving from Ballantine to new berths in publishing, and I cherish their friendship and their good wishes, so often and so affectionately expressed.

Van Morrison sings of the "guides and spirits along the way who will befriend you," and I am fortunate to have encountered many such souls at various crucial points in my life. With a full heart, I acknowledge and thank the mentors among them: Murray Bower, Jon Carroll, Henry Dersch, Herschel Lymon, Jack Miles, Harvey Mindess, Carolyn See, Ron Silverman, and Marshall Sylvan.

Along with Jack Miles and Carolyn See, several other authors of lofty achievement have been generous enough to encourage my own efforts, including Karen Armstrong and Harlan Ellison.

Booksellers across the country have been welcoming and encouraging, but I must make special and appreciative mention of Doug Dutton, Diane Leslie, Lise Friedman, Ed Conklin, and the other good folk at Dutton's in Brentwood; Stan Hynds and Linda Urban at Vroman's in Pasadena; and Stan Madson and Jeanne D'Arcy at the Bodhi Tree in West Hollywood.

For their many expressions and gestures of support and encouragement over the years, each one different but each one precious to me, I gratefully and affectionately acknowledge:

My mother and stepfather, Dvora and Elmer Heller;

Our cherished friends, Raye Birk and Candace Barrett Birk, who lent their superb voices to the audio edition of *The Harlot by the Side of the Road*;

Judy Woo, Angie Yoon, James Brown Orleans, Larry Zerner, Scott Baker, A. J. Trotter, and Gregg Homer, valued colleagues and dear friends who make the daily routine of office work so pleasurable and so rewarding;

The Solomon Family—Pat and Len and their daughters, Leah,

Rachel, and Sarah—with whom we have long shared first and second night seders and countless other warm and enriching moments;

Tony Cohan at Acrobat Books, publisher of my books on publishing law;

Steve Wasserman, Tom Curwen, Nick Owchar, Susan Salter Reynolds, Cara Mia DiMassa, Ethel Alexander, Larry Stammer, and Mary Rourke at the Los Angeles *Times*;

Larry Mantle, Rod Foster, Ilsa Setziol, Linda Othenin-Girard, and Jackie Oclaray at KPCC-FM in Pasadena;

Jan Nathan at the Publishers Marketing Association;

Gene Lichtenstein at the *Jewish Journal*;

Gary Jaffe, Joanna Pulcini, and Judith Ehrlich at the Linda Chester Literary Agency;

Linda Michaels, Teresa Cavanaugh, and Ann Tente at the Linda Michaels Ltd. International Literary Agency;

Judith Kendra and Sarah Ainslie at Rider Books in London;

John Hunt, Lisa Hunt, and Iris Murray at Audio Literature in San Bruno; and

Roxana Acosta, Hava Ben-Zvi, Kathy Bloomfield, Joyce Craig, Inge-Lise DeWolfe, Jacob Gabay, Georgia Jones-Davis, Jill Johnson Keeney, Rae Lewis, Rusty McLoughlin, Deborah Robbins, Marilyn Sanders, Leila Segal, and Mitch Shapiro.

Endnotes

CHAPTER ONE
THE MOSES NO ONE KNOWS

1. Gerhard von Rad, *Moses* (London: United Society for Christian Literature, Lutterworth Press, 1960), 10.

2. Louis Jacobs, "Rabbinic View," in "Moses," *Encyclopedia Judaica,* corrected ed. (Jerusalem: Keter Publishing House, n.d.), vol. 12, 394.

3. E. L. Allen, "Jesus and Moses in the New Testament," *Expository Times* (Edinburgh) 67 (October 1955–September 1956): 104.

4. David Winston, "In Hellenistic Literature," in "Moses," *EJ*, vol. 12, 390.

5. R. F. Johnson, "Moses," in *The Interpreter's Dictionary of the Bible* (Nashville: Abingdon Press, 1962), 448. Quoted in George W. Coats, *Moses: Heroic Man, Man of God* (Sheffield, England: JSOT Press, 1988), 41.

6. Winston, *EJ*, vol. 12, 390.

7. Ari Z. Zivotofsky, "The Leadership Qualities of Moses," *Judaism* (American Jewish Congress) 43(3), n. 171 (summer 1994): 259.

8. Artapanus is quoted by Eusebius in *Preparatio Evangelica* 9:27, and cited in Winston, *EJ*, vol. 12, 391.

9. Angelo S. Rappoport, *Ancient Israel* (London: Senate, 1995), vol. 2, 330, citing, inter alia, *Berachoth.*

10. David Weiss Halivni, *The Book and the Sword* (New York: Farrar, Straus & Giroux, 1996), 164.

11. Martin Buber, *Moses: The Revelation and the Covenant* (New York: Harper & Row, 1958), 123, citing Nowack, *Der erste Dekalog,* 1917, and Beer, *Moses und sein Werk,* 1912.

12. Abram Leon Sachar, *A History of the Jews*, rev. ed. (New York: Alfred A. Knopf, 1967), 16.

13. J. H. Hertz, ed., *The Pentateuch and Haftorahs*, 2d ed. (London: Soncino Press, 1981), 704, n. 11.

14. Martin Luther King Jr., "I See the Promised Land," in *A Testament of Hope: The Essential Writings of Martin Luther King, Jr.*, ed. James Melvin Washington (San Francisco: Harper & Row, 1986), 286.

15. Adapted from *The Holy Scriptures According to the Masoretic Text* (Philadelphia: Jewish Publication Society, 1961) (JPS). All quotes from the Bible are drawn from the JPS unless otherwise noted. I use the phrase "adapted from . . ." to indicate that I have omitted or rearranged portions of the original text or have combined text from more than one translation of the Bible. I have taken the liberty of making minor changes in punctuation, capitalization, and the like, or omitting words and phrases that do not alter the meaning of the quoted material, without indicating these changes in the text.

16. Voltaire, *Philosophical Dictionary*, quoted in Peter Gay, *Freud: A Life for Our Time* (New York: W. W. Norton, 1988), 608.

17. Spinoza quoted in Richard Elliot Friedman, *Who Wrote the Bible?* (Englewood Cliffs, N.J.: Prentice-Hall, 1987), 21.

18. Coats, 1988, 16.

19. Elias Auerbach, *Moses*, ed. and trans. Robert A. Barclay and Israel O. Lehman (Detroit: Wayne State University Press, 1975), 9.

20. von Rad, quoted in Coats, 1988, 30.

21. Brevard S. Childs, *Exodus: A Commentary* (London: SCM Press, 1974), 144.

22. Introduction by Shalom Spiegel in Louis Ginzberg, *Legends of the Bible* (Philadelphia: Jewish Publication Society of America, 1956), xi.

23. Childs, 1974, 33.

24. Sigmund Freud, *Moses and Monotheism*, trans. Katherine Jones (New York: Vintage Books, 1967), 32, n. 1.

25. Flavius Josephus, *The Life and Works of Flavius Josephus*, trans. William Whiston (Philadelphia: John C. Winston Company, n.d.), 75, (translator's note).

26. Philo of Alexandria, *The Essential Philo*, ed. Nahum N. Glatzer (New York: Schocken Books, 1971), 192.

27. Notes from Oliver Taplin, "Homer," in *The Oxford History of the Classical World*, ed. John Boardman, Jasper Griffin, and Oswyn Murray (Oxford: Oxford University Press, 1986), 50.

28. Coats, 1988, 21, citing the work of Brevard S. Childs. "A large consensus has emerged which agrees that more than simply a literary narrative is involved, but that the text reflects an ongoing religious institution of covenant renewal going back far into Israel's early pre-monarchial history."

29. Geo Widengren, "What Do We Know about Moses?" in *Proclamation and Presence*, ed. John I. Durham and J. R. Porter (Macon, Ga.: Mercer University Press, 1983), 21.

30. Freud, 38.

31. Auerbach, 7.

32. Paul F. Bork, *The World of Moses* (Nashville: Southern Publishing Association, 1978), 51, 54.

33. Coats, 1988, 11, citing John Bright.

34. Auerbach, 215.

35. Coats, 1988, 11.

36. Philo, *Hypothetica*, quoted in Winston, *EJ*, vol. 12, 391.

37. Josephus, *Apion* 1:32, 228, and Reinach quoted in Winston, *EJ*, vol. 12, 390.

38. Freud, 38.

39. Childs, 1974, 433.

40. Jacobs, *EJ*, vol. 12, 394.

41. Moshe Greenberg, "Critical Assessment," in "Moses," *EJ*, vol. 12, 389.

42. Moshe Greenberg, *Understanding Exodus* (New York: Behrman House for Melton Research Center of the Jewish Theological Seminary of America, 1969), 201–202, citing Greta Hort.

43. Buber, 80.

44. Robert Polzin, *Moses and the Deuteronomist* (New York: Seabury Press, 1980), part 1, 14. "The invalidity of the 'shorter is older' guideline used in historical critical study now seems fairly clear from modern studies. . . . It remains a puzzle why more recent works . . . still invoke the principle."

CHAPTER TWO
BORN AT THE RIGHT TIME

1. Ronald J. Leprohon, "Egypt, History of," "Middle Kingdom—2d Intermediate Period (Dyn 11–17)," in *The Anchor Bible Dictionary*, ed. David Noel Freedman, vol. 2, 347. See also Werner Keller, *The Bible as History*, 2d rev. ed. (New York: William Morrow, 1981), 98–99.

2. Louis Ginzberg, *The Legends of the Jews*, trans. Henrietta Szold (Philadelphia: Jewish Publication Society of America, 1909–1938), vol. 2, 245, citing, inter alia, *Midrash Bereshit Rabbah*.

3. Original translation by Brevard S. Childs in *Exodus: A Commentary* (London: SCM Press, 1974), 4.

4. Ginzberg, vol. 2, 260, citing, inter alia, *Midrash Ha-Gadol*.

5. Ginzberg, vol. 2, 248–249, citing, inter alia, *Midrash Shemot Rabbah*.

6. Angelo S. Rappoport, *Ancient Israel* (London: Senate, 1995), vol. 2, 200, citing, inter alia, *Yashar Shemot*.

7. Martin Noth, *Exodus: A Commentary*, trans. J. S. Borden (Philadelphia: Westminster Press, 1962), 21.

8. The words of Sally Sander are displayed along with the testimony of other Holocaust survivors at the Holocaust Memorial in Boston, Massachusetts, where I copied out the inscription on the back of an envelope during a visit in June 1997.

9. Philo of Alexandria, *The Essential Philo*, ed. Nahum N. Glatzer (New York: Schocken Books, 1971), 200.

10. Ginzberg, vol. 2, 249, citing, inter alia, *Midrash Shemot Rabbah*.

11. Childs, 1974, 16.

12. Ginzberg, vol. 2, 253, citing, inter alia, Talmud section *Sotah*.

13. Rappoport, vol. 2, 205, citing, inter alia, *Shemot Rabbah*.

14. Childs, 1974, 23.

15. Ilana Pardes, *Countertraditions in the Bible* (Cambridge: Harvard University Press, 1992), 82.

16. Pardes, 82.

17. Ginzberg, vol. 2, 257, citing, inter alia, *Shir*.

18. Rappoport, vol. 2, 211, citing inter alia, *Yashar Shemot*.

19. Israel H. Weisfeld, *This Man Moses* (New York: Bloch Publishing Company, 1966), 32.

20. Rappoport, vol. 2, 211–212, citing, inter alia, *Yashar Shemot*.

21. Moshe Greenberg, *Understanding Exodus* (New York: Behrman House for Melton Research Center of the Jewish Theological Seminary of America, 1969), 31.

22. Rappoport, vol. 2, 237, citing, inter alia, *Shemot Rabbah*.

23. Ginzberg, vol. 2, 257, n. 23, citing, inter alia, *Midrash Shir Ha-shirim Rabbah*.

24. Philo, 1971, 192.

25. Martin Buber, *Moses: The Revelation and the Covenant* (New York: Harper & Row, 1958), 28.

26. Elias Auerbach, *Moses* (Detroit: Wayne State University Press, 1975), 68.

27. Rappoport, vol. 2, 191, citing inter alia, *Yashar Shemot*.

28. Greenberg, 19.

29. Rappoport, vol. 2, 190, citing, inter alia, *Yashar Shemot*.

30. George W. Coats, *Moses: Heroic Man, Man of God* (Sheffield, England: JSOT Press, 1988), 183, quoting Walter Zimmerli.

31. Ginzberg, vol. 2, 265, citing, inter alia, Talmud section *Sotah*.

32. James S. Ackerman, "The Literary Context of the Moses Birth Story (Exodus 1–2)," in *Literary Interpretations of Biblical Narratives*, ed. Kenneth R. R. Gros Louis et al. (Nashville: Abingdon Press, 1974), 91.

33. Greenberg, 27.

34. Greenberg, 37.

35. Greenberg, 38, n. 1.

36. Ginzberg, vol. 2, 261, citing, inter alia, *Yashar Shemot*.

37. Ginzberg, vol. 2, 258, citing, inter alia, *Mekhilta de-Rav Shimon ben Yoachai*.

38. Greenberg, 38.

39. [Pseudo-Philo], *The Biblical Antiquities of Philo*, trans. M. R. James, (New York: Ktav Publishing House, 1971), 102.

40. Ginzberg, vol. 2, 262, citing, inter alia, Talmud section *Sotah*.

41. Noth, 1962, 25.

42. Ginzberg, vol. 2, 264, citing, inter alia, *Mekhilta de-Rav Shimon ben Yoachai*.

43. Ginzberg, vol. 2, 270, citing, inter alia, *Midrash Devarim Rabbah*.

44. Ginzberg, vol. 2, 263, citing Josephus, *Jewish Antiquities*.

45. Childs, 1974, 8, citing Hugo Gressmann.

46. Noth, 1962, 27.

47. J. Maxwell Miller and John H. Hays, *A History of Ancient Israel and Judah* (Philadelphia: Westminster Press, 1986), 60.

48. Buber, 35.

49. Coats, 1988, 46, citing James B. Pritchard, ed., *Ancient Near Eastern Texts* (Princeton: Princeton University Press, 1955), 119.

50. Childs, 1974, 9.

51. Childs, 1974, 10.

52. Childs, 1974, 11, 16.

53. Childs, 1974, 11.

54. Childs, 1974, 10.

55. Childs, 1974, 10.

56. Rappoport, vol. 2, 206, citing, inter alia, *Yashar Shemot*.

57. Ginzberg, vol. 2, 256, citing, inter alia, *Yashar Shemot*.

58. Rappoport, vol. 2, 209, citing, inter alia, *Yashar Shemot*.

59. Ginzberg, vol. 2, 269, citing, inter alia, Talmud section *Sotah*.

60. Rappoport, vol. 2, 220–221, citing, inter alia, *Shemot Rabbah*.

61. Ginzberg, vol. 2, 269, citing, inter alia, Talmud section *Sotah*.

62. Childs, 1974, 24.

63. Pardes, 83.

64. Pardes, 88.

65. Pardes, 89.

66. Rappoport, vol. 2, 219, citing, inter alia, Talmud section *Sotah*.

67. Ginzberg, vol. 2, 267, citing, inter alia, Talmud section *Sotah*.

68. Rappoport, vol. 2, 219–220, citing, inter alia, Philo, *De Vita Mosis*.

69. Ginzberg, vol. 2, 266–267, citing, inter alia, Talmud section *Sotah*.

70. Rappoport, vol. 2, 222, citing, inter alia, *Leviticus Rabbah*.

71. Philo, 1971, 193.

72. Childs, 1974, 12.

73. Rappoport, vol. 2, 217, citing, inter alia, Beer, *Das Leben Mosis*.

74. Childs, 1974, 25.

75. Rappoport, vol. 2, 217, citing, inter alia, Jellinek, *Beth Ha-Midrash*.

76. Ginzberg, vol. 2, 269–270, citing, inter alia, *Yashar Shemot*.

77. Roland de Vaux, *The Early History of Israel*, trans., David Smith (Philadelphia: Westminster Press, 1978), 329.

78. Pardes, 82–83. See also JPS, 67, n. b.

CHAPTER THREE
A PRINCE OF EGYPT

1. Angelo S. Rappoport, *Ancient Israel*, (London: Senate, 1995), vol. 2, 220, citing, inter alia, *Yashar Shemot*.

2. Louis Ginzberg, *The Legends of the Jews*, trans. Henrietta Szold (Philadelphia: Jewish Publication Society of America, 1909–1938), vol. 2, 267, citing, inter alia, Talmud section *Sotah*.

3. Brevard S. Childs, "The Birth of Moses," *Journal of Biblical Literature* 84, part 2 (June 1965), 112.

4. Ginzberg, vol. 2, 270, citing, inter alia, *Yashar Shemot*.

5. Flavius Josephus, *The Life and Works of Flavius Josephus*, trans. William Whiston (Philadelphia: John C. Winston Company, n. d.), 76.

6. Philo of Alexandria, *The Essential Philo*, ed. Nahum N. Glatzer (New York: Schocken Books, 1971), 191.

7. Josephus, 76–77.

8. Philo, 195. The supposed childlessness of Pharaoh's daughter prompted one Bible commentator to propose a woman named Hatshepsut, daughter of the pharaoh Thutmose I, as the adoptive mother of Moses. History confirms that Hatshepsut, after the death of her brother and consort, Thutmose II, ruled ancient Egypt as regent for her young stepson, but she was apparently childless herself. "Since only men could become pharaohs," writes fundamentalist Bible commentator Paul Bork, "she gave herself a male appearance by wearing a beard and insisting that the people address her as 'he' instead of 'she.'" Bork speculates that Hatshepsut favored Moses over her stepson as successor to the throne of Egypt, thereby alienating the courtiers and falling victim to a conspiracy that sought her death. Bork points out that Hatshepsut

disappeared suddenly and inexplicably from the chronicles of ancient Egypt—monuments and inscriptions bearing her name were defaced by her stepson, who eventually ascended to the throne as Thutmose III, and her mummy was never found. Bork's theory would place Moses several centuries earlier than the dating favored by conventional scholarship.

9. Rappoport, vol. 2, 222–23, citing, inter alia, *Yashar Shemot*.

10. Rappoport, vol. 2, 223, citing, inter alia, *Yashar Shemot*.

11. Rappoport, vol. 2, 223, citing, inter alia, *Yashar Shemot* and Josephus, *Antiquities*.

12. Rappoport, vol. 2, 223–224, citing, inter alia, *Yashar Shemot*.

13. Rappoport, vol. 2, 223, citing, inter alia, *Yashar Shemot*.

14. Rappoport, vol. 2, 225, citing, inter alia, *Yashar Shemot*.

15. Rappoport, vol. 2, 225, citing, inter alia, *Yashar Shemot*.

16. Adapted from Rappoport, vol. 2, 225, citing, inter alia, *Yashar Shemot*.

17. Adapted from Ginzberg, vol. 2, 275, citing Josephus, *Antiquities*.

18. Adapted from Rappoport, vol. 2, 225, citing Abulfaraj, *Histor. Dynast*.

19. Philo, 195.

20. Philo, 196.

21. Rappoport, vol. 2, 225, citing Abulfaraj, *Histor. Dynast*.

22. Rappoport, vol. 2, 232, citing, inter alia, *Yashar Shemot*.

23. Rappoport, vol. 2, 232–233, citing, inter alia, *Yashar Shemot*.

24. Philo, 197.

25. Philo, 197.

26. Rappoport, vol. 2, 232, citing, inter alia, *Yashar Shemot*.

27. Sigmund Freud, *Moses and Monotheism*, trans. Katherine Jones (New York: Vintage Books, 1967), 9.

28. Freud, 10.

29. Freud, 16.

30. Freud, 11.

31. Freud, 31–32.

32. Martin Buber, *Moses: The Revelation and the Covenant* (New York: Harper & Row, 1958), 7, n. 1.

33. Peter Gay, *Freud: A Life for Our Time* (New York: W. W. Norton, 1988), 204.

34. Jan Assmann, *Moses the Egyptian* (Cambridge: Harvard University Press, 1997), 20–21, 151–152.

35. Assmann, 35–36, citing *Historicae Philippicae*.

36. Assmann, 11.

37. Rappoport, vol. 2, 219, citing, inter alia, Jellinek, *Beth Ha-Midrash*, vol. 2.

38. Sir J. Gardner Wilkinson, *A Popular Account of the Ancient Egyptians*, (London: John Murray, 1854), vol. 1, 2.

39. T.G.H. James, *Pharaoh's People* (London: Bodley Head, 1984), 78.

40. Assmann, 11.

41. David Daiches, *Moses: Man in the Wilderness* (London: Weidenfeld & Nicolson, 1975), 219–220, quoting Gerhard von Rad.

42. Werner Keller, *The Bible as History*, 2d rev. ed. (New York: William Morrow, 1981), 104–105.

43. William F. Albright, "Moses Out of Egypt," *The Biblical Archaelogist* 36, no. 2 (February 1973), 55.

44. Wilkinson, vol. 1, 1–2.

45. James, 102.

46. T. Eric Peet, *Egypt and the Old Testament* (Liverpool: University Press of Liverpool; and London: Hodder & Stoughton, 1922), 21.

47. Keller, 92–93, 105–107.

48. James, 17.

49. Keller, 98–99.

50. James, 26.

51. Peet, 93.

52. Bernhard W. Anderson, *Understanding the Old Testament*, 2d ed. (Englewood Cliffs, N.J.: Prentice-Hall, 1966), 44–45.

53. Richard Elliot Friedman, *Who Wrote the Bible?* (Englewood Cliffs, N.J.: Prentice-Hall, 1987), 159.

54. Will Durant, *The Story of Civilization*: vol. 1, *Our Oriental Heritage*, (New York: Simon & Schuster, 1935, 1954), 277.

55. James, 105.

56. Rappoport, vol. 2, 236–237, citing, inter alia, *Shemot Rabbah*.

57. Rappoport, vol. 2, 233–235, citing, inter alia, *Yashar Shemot* and *Shemot Rabbah*.

58. Rappoport, vol. 2, 234, citing, inter alia, *Yashar Shemot* and *Shemot Rabbah*.

59. Rappoport, vol. 2, 233, citing, inter alia, *Yashar Shemot*.

60. Ari Z. Zivotofsky, "The Leadership Qualities of Moses," *Judaism* (American Jewish Congress) 43(3), no. 171 (summer 1994), 260.

61. Rappoport, vol. 2, 240, citing, inter alia, *Shemot Rabbah*.

62. Philo, 201.

63. Rappoport, vol. 2, 238, citing, inter alia, *Shemot Rabbah*.

64. Ginzberg, vol. 2, 279, citing, inter alia, *Shemot Rabbah*.

65. Rappoport, vol. 2, 238, citing, inter alia, *Shemot Rabbah*.

66. Ginzberg, vol. 2, 280, citing, inter alia, *Shemot Rabbah*.

67. Rappoport, vol. 2, 239, citing, inter alia, *Shemot Rabbah*.

68. Rappoport, vol. 2, 239, citing, inter alia, *Shemot Rabbah*.

69. Rappoport, vol. 2, 240, citing, inter alia, *Shemot Rabbah*.

70. Philo, 201.

71. Rappoport, vol. 2, 240, citing, inter alia, *Shemot Rabbah*.

72. George W. Coats, *Moses: Heroic Man, Man of God* (Sheffield, England: JSOT Press, 1988), 49.

73. Brevard S. Childs, *Exodus: A Commentary* (London: SCM Press, 1974), 30.

74. Zivotofsky, 259.

75. Adapted from JPS.

76. Childs, 1974, 30.

77. Ginzberg, vol. 2, 281, citing, inter alia, *Shemot Rabbah*.

78. Ginzberg, vol. 2, 281–282, citing, inter alia, *Shemot Rabbah*.

79. Rappoport, vol. 2, 243, citing, inter alia, *Yashar Shemot*.

80. Rappoport, vol. 2, 243, citing, inter alia, *Yashar Shemot*.

81. Childs, 1974, 31.

CHAPTER FOUR
THE FUGITIVE

1. Angelo S. Rappoport, *Ancient Israel* (London: Senate, 1995), vol. 2, 263, citing *Megillath Esther* in *Zeena Urena*.

2. Bruce Chatwin, *The Songlines* (New York: Penguin Books, 1988), 200.

3. Philo of Alexandria, *The Essential Philo*, ed. Nahum N. Glatzer (New York: Schocken Books, 1971), 202.

4. Louis L. Ginzberg, *The Legends of the Jews*, trans. Henrietta Szold (Philadelphia: Jewish Publication Society of America, 1909–1938), vol. 2, 283–284, citing, inter alia, *Yashar Shemot*.

5. Ginzberg, vol. 2, 285, citing, inter alia, *Yashar Shemot*.

6. Ginzberg, vol. 2, 286, citing, inter alia, *Yashar Shemot*.

7. Ginzberg, vol. 2, 286, citing, inter alia, *Yashar Shemot*.

8. Ginzberg, vol. 2, 287, citing, inter alia, *Yashar Shemot*.

9. Ginzberg, vol. 2, 287–288, citing, inter alia, *Yashar Shemot*.

10. Ginzberg, vol. 2, 287–288, citing, inter alia, *Yashar Shemot*.

11. Ginzberg, vol. 2, 288, citing, inter alia, *Yashar Shemot*.

12. Ginzberg, vol. 2, 288, citing, inter alia, *Yashar Shemot*.

13. Rappoport, vol. 2, 249, citing, inter alia, *Yashar Shemot*.

14. Flavius Josephus, *The Life and Works of Flavius Josephus*, trans. William Whiston (Philadelphia: John C. Winston Company, n.d.), 78.

15. Josephus, 79.

16. Ginzberg, vol. 2, p. 289, citing, inter alia, *Yashar Shemot*.

17. Murray Lee Newman Jr., *The People of the Covenant* (New York: Abingdon Press, 1962), 83.

18. Martin Buber, *Moses: The Revelation and the Covenant* (New York: Harper & Row, 1958), 99.

19. Martin Noth, *Exodus: A Commentary*, trans. J. S. Bowden (Philadelphia: Westminster Press, 1962), 31.

20. George E. Mendenhall, "Midian," in *Anchor Bible Dictionary*, ed. David Noel Freedman (New York: Doubleday, 1992), vol. 4, 817.

21. Philo, 203.

22. Robert Alter, *The Art of Biblical Narrative* (New York: Basic Books, 1981), 58.

23. Ginzberg, vol. 2, 291, citing *Zohar* II, 12b (see footnote 86).

24. Josephus, 79.

25. Philo, 203.

26. Adapted from Philo, 204.

27. Ginzberg, vol. 2, 291, citing, inter alia, *Shemot Rabbah*.

28. Ginzberg, vol. 2, 291, citing, inter alia, *Shemot Rabbah*.

29. Ari Z. Zivotofsky, "The Leadership Qualities of Moses," *Judaism* (American Jewish Congress) 43(3), no. 171 (summer 1994), 267, n. 9.

30. Ginzberg, vol. 2, 293, citing *Midrash Devarim Rabbah* (see footnote 92).

31. Ginzberg, vol. 2, 291, citing, inter alia, *Shemot Rabbah*.

32. Philo, 204.

33. Josephus, 89.

34. "In the Old Testament the *ger* designated originally a social class of the landless sojourner who lived without the protection of a clan. But the term had already been greatly expanded theologically when the people of Israel were described as a 'sojourner' in Egypt (Deut.23.8 f.)." Brevard S. Childs, *Exodus: A Commentary* (London: SCM Press, 1974), 35.

35. Mendenhall, *ABD*, vol. 4, 816.

36. Ginzberg, vol. 2, 289–290, citing, inter alia, *Shemot Rabbah*.

37. Ginzberg, vol. 2, 291, citing *Midrash Wa-Yosha* in Jellinek, *Beth Ha-Midrash*.

38. Ginzberg, vol. 2, 291–292, citing *Midrash Wa-Yosha* in Jellinek, *Beth Ha-Midrash*.

39. Rappoport, vol. 2, 255, citing, inter alia, *Pirkei de Rabbi Eliezer*.

40. Ginzberg, vol. 2, 293, citing, inter alia, *Midrash Wa-Yosha* in Jellinek, *Beth Ha-Midrash* (see footnote 96).

41. Ginzberg, vol. 2, 294, citing, inter alia, *Midrash Wa-Yosha* in Jellinek, *Beth Ha-Midrash*.

42. Ginzberg, vol. 2, 294, citing, inter alia, *Midrash Wa-Yosha* in Jellinek, *Beth Ha-Midrash*.

43. Ginzberg, vol. 2, 294, citing, inter alia, *Midrash Wa-Yosha* in Jellinek, *Beth Ha-Midrash*.

44. Moshe Greenberg, *Understanding Exodus* (New York: Behrman House for Melton Research Center of the Jewish Theological Seminary of America 1969), 67–68; 68, n. 1.

45. Philo, 204.

46. Philo, 205

47. Adapted from Ginzberg, vol. 2, 301, citing, inter alia, *Shemot Rabbah*.

48. Rappoport, vol. 2, 262–263, citing 1858 German translation by G. Rosen. See also op. cit., 244–245, Bin Gorion.

CHAPTER FIVE
THE MAN GOD BEFRIENDED, THE MAN GOD SOUGHT TO KILL

1. Louis Ginzberg, *The Legends of the Jews*, trans. Henrietta Szold (Philadelphia: Jewish Publication Society of America, 1909–1938, vol. 2, 296–298, citing, inter alia, *Yashar Shemot*.

2. Flavius Josephus, *The Life and Works of Flavius Josephus*, trans. William Whiston (Philadelphia: John C. Winston Company, n.d.), 79.

3. Adapted from JPS.

4. Adapted from NEB.

5. Adapted from JPS, which follows the practice of the King James Version by translating *Yahweh* as "The Lord." The NEB departs from traditional usage by translating *Yahweh* as "Jehovah," an old (and erroneous) phonetic rendering. Here, and in various other quotations from the JPS, I have taken the liberty of replacing "The Lord" with *Yahweh*, the word that actually appears in the original Hebrew text of the Bible.

6. "El Shaddai" was generally translated into Greek in the Septuagint as "Pantocrator," and from Greek into Latin in the Vulgate as *deus omnipotens*, and from Latin into English as "God Almighty."

7. Frank Moore Cross, *Canaanite Myth and Hebrew Epic* (Cambridge: Harvard University Press, 1973), 13 ff.

8. Josephus, 80.

9. Martin Noth, *Exodus: A Commentary*, trans. J. S. Bowden (Philadelphia: Westminster Press, 1962), 60.

10. Elias Auerbach, *Moses*, trans. and ed. Robert A. Barclay and Israel O. Lehman (Detroit: Wayne State University Press, 1975), 39.

11. Martin Buber, *Moses: The Revelation and the Covenant* (New York: Harper & Row, 1958) 52–53.

12. Brevard S. Childs, *Exodus: A Commentary* (London: SCM Press, 1974), 76.

13. Childs, 1974, 61.

14. Auerbach, 1975, 32–33, 37.

15. Auerbach, 1975, 30.

16. E. A. Speiser, trans., intro., and notes. *Genesis*. Anchor Bible. (Garden City, N.Y.: Doubleday, 1987.)

17. Childs, 1974, 69, citing the work of L. Koehler.

18. Moshe Greenberg, *Understanding Exodus* (New York: Behrman House for Melton Research Center of the Jewish Theological Seminary of America, 1969), 79, n. 1, citing Shemot Rabbah.

19. Adapted from JPS.

20. Adapted from JPS.

21. Adapted from JPS.

22. Adapted from JPS.

23. Adapted from JPS.

24. Adapted from JPS and NEB.

25. Adapted from JPS and NEB.

26. Childs, 1974, 79.

27. Adapted from JPS and NEB.

28. Adapted from JPS and NEB.

29. Greenberg, 70–71.

30. Keller, 137.

31. Noth, 1962, 39.

32. Philo of Alexandria, *The Essential Philo*, ed. Nahum N. Glatzer (New York: Schocken Books, 1971), 206.

33. Philo, 206.

34. Gerhard von Rad, *Moses* (London: United Society for Christian Literature, Lutterworth Press, 1960), 18, n. 1.

35. Angelo S. Rappoport, *Ancient Israel* (London, Senate, 1995), vol. 2, 270–271, citing *Shemot Rabbah*.

36. Rappoport, vol. 2, 271, citing *Shemot Rabbah*.

37. Ginzberg, vol. 2, 317, citing, inter alia, *Shemot Rabbah*.

38. Ginzberg, vol. 2, 325, citing, inter alia, *Shemot Rabbah*.

39. Ginzberg, vol. 2, 318, citing, inter alia, *Shemot Rabbah*.

40. Ginzberg, vol. 2, 317–318, citing, inter alia, *Shemot Rabbah*.

41. Ginzberg, vol. 2, 324, citing, inter alia, *Shemot Rabbah*.

42. Ginzberg, vol. 2, 322, citing, inter alia, *Mekhilta de Rabbi Shimon ben Yoachai*.

43. Ginzberg, vol. 2, 323, citing, inter alia, *Mekhilta de Rabbi Shimon ben Yoachai*.

44. Ginzberg, vol. 2, 326, citing, inter alia, *Midrash Lekah*.

45. Ginzberg, vol. 2, 321, citing, inter alia, *Shemot Rabbah*.

46. Ginzberg, vol. 2, 306, citing *Midrash Gedullah Mosheh* (see footnote 117).

47. Ginzberg, vol. 2, 307, citing *Midrash Gedullah Mosheh*.

48. Adapted from Ginzberg, vol. 2, 307, citing *Midrash Gedullah Mosheh*.

49. Ginzberg, vol. 2, 308, citing *Midrash Gedullah Mosheh*.

50. Ginzberg, vol. 2, 310–311, citing *Midrash Gedullah Mosheh*.

51. Ginzberg, vol. 2, 312, citing *Midrash Gedullah Mosheh*.

52. Ginzberg, vol. 2, 309, citing *Midrash Gedullah Mosheh*.

53. Noth, 1962, 32.

54. von Rad, quoted in George W. Coats, *Moses: Heroic Man, Man of God* (Sheffield, England: JSOT Press, 1988), 30.

55. Noth, 1962, 34.

56. Murray Lee Newman Jr., *The People of the Covenant* (New York: Abingdon Press, 1962), 51.

57. Rappoport, vol. 2, 274, citing *Shemot Rabbah*.

58. Rappoport, vol. 2, 275, citing *Pirke de Rabbi Eliezer*.

59. Marvin H. Pope, in *The Anchor Bible Dictionary*, ed. David Noel Freedman (Garden City, N.Y.: Doubleday, 1992), vol. 1, 721.

60. B. P. Robinson, "Zipporah to the Rescue," *Vetus Testamentum* 36, no. 4 (October 1986): 457.

61. G. Vermes, "Baptism and Jewish Exegesis," *New Testament Studies* (Cambridge University Press) 4 (1958), 309.

62. Robinson, 448.

63. Ginzberg, vol. 2, 328, citing *Midrash Aggada*.

64. Childs, 1974, 96.

65. Childs, 1974, 96.

66. Julian Morgenstern, "The 'Bloody Husband' (?) (Exod. 4:24–26) Once Again," *Hebrew Union College Annual* 34, (Union of Hebrew Congregations, 1963), 41.

67. Rappoport, vol. 2, 275, citing *Exodus Rabba*, Jellinek, *Beth Ha-Midrash*, *Nedarim*, and *Book of Jubilees*.

68. Auerbach, 1975, 50.

69. Rappoport, vol. 2, 302, citing, inter alia, *Exodus Rabba* and *Midrash Tanchuma*.

70. Greenberg, 203.

71. Greenberg, 72, n. 1.

72. Newman, 26.

73. Buber, 42.

74. Morgenstern, 1963, 43, n. 27, citing the work of A. J. Reinach and Hugo Gressmann.

75. Morgenstern, 1963, 43–44, n. 27, citing Gressman.

76. Hans Kosmala, "The Bloody Husband," *Vetus Testamentum* 12 (January 1962): 16–17.

77. Freud, 39, citing Eduard Meyer.

78. Ginzberg, vol. 2, 328, citing *Nedarim* 32a.

CHAPTER SIX
SIGNS AND WONDERS

1. George W. Coats, *Moses: Heroic Man, Man of God* (Sheffield, England: JSOT Press, 1988), 67.

2. Martin Noth, *Exodus: A Commentary*, trans. J. S. Bowdin (Philadelphia: Westminster Press, 1962), 51.

3. Louis Ginzberg, *The Legends of the Jews*, trans. Henrietta Szold (Philadelphia: Jewish Publication Society of America, 1909–1938), vol. 2, 328, citing, inter alia, *Mekhilta Yitro*.

4. Angelo S. Rappoport, *Ancient Israel* (London: Senate, 1995), vol. 2, 275–276, citing *Mekhilta Yitro*, *Midrash Agadah*, and *Shemot Rabbah* (where Jethro states the same objection to bringing Moses' family along with him to Egypt).

5. Ginzberg, vol. 2, 330, citing, inter alia, *Shemot Rabbah*.

6. Rappoport, vol. 2, 276, citing, inter alia, *Shemot Rabbah*.

7. Rappoport, vol. 2, 277, citing, inter alia, *Yalkut (Exodus)*.

8. Rappoport, vol. 2, 277, citing Jellinek, *Beth-Hamidrash*.

9. Rappoport, vol. 2, 278, citing, inter alia, *Shemot Rabbah*.

10. Adapted from JPS.

11. Cited in Brevard S. Childs, *Exodus: A Commentary* (London: SCM Press, 1974), 105.

12. Rappoport, vol. 2, 278–279, citing, inter alia, *Shemot Rabbah*.

13. Rappoport, vol. 2, 279, citing, inter alia, *Shemot Rabbah*.

14. Adapted from JPS and NEB.

15. Adapted from JPS and NEB.

16. Adapted from JPS and NEB.

17. Adapted from JPS and NEB.

18. Adapted from JPS and NEB.

19. Adapted from Ginzberg, vol. 2, 337, citing, inter alia, *Shemot Rabbah*.

20. Adapted from Rappoport, vol. 2, 281, citing *Shemot Rabbah*.

21. Ginzberg, vol. 2, 340, citing, inter alia, *Shemot Rabbah*.

22. Adapted from Rappoport, vol. 2, 282, citing *Sanhedrin*.

23. Rappoport, vol. 2, 282, citing *Shemot Rabbah*.

24. Adapted from JPS and NEB.

25. Childs, 1974, 152.

26. Rappoport, vol. 2, 280, citing, inter alia, *Shemot Rabbah*.

27. Rappoport, vol. 2, 281, citing Jellinek.

28. Adapted from Ginzberg, vol. 2, 347–348, citing, inter alia, *Shemot Rabbah*.

29. Adapted from JPS.

30. Childs, 1974, 154, citing *Sekel Tob*.

31. Adapted from JPS.

32. Adapted from NEB.

33. Adapted from NEB.

34. Adapted from NEB.

35. Adapted from JPS.

36. Adapted from NEB.

37. Adapted from JPS and NEB.

38. Lawrence Kaplan, " 'And the Lord Sought to Kill Him' (Exod. 4:24): Yet Once Again," *Hebrew Annual Review* 5 (1981): 67, citing J. Blau, "Hatan Damim," *Tarbiz* 26 (1956), 1–3.

39. Kaplan, 68.

40. Ginzberg, vol. 2, 366, citing, inter alia, *Sefer Ha-Eshkol*.

41. Ginzberg, vol. 2, 366, citing *Book of Jubilees*, 49.2.

42. Adapted from JPS.

43. Ginzberg, vol. 2, 365, citing, inter alia, *PK*.

44. Adapted from JPS and NEB.

45. Ginzberg, vol. 2, 358, n. 225, citing *Midrash Wa-Yosha* in Jellinek, *Beth-Hamidrash*.

46. Rappoport, vol. 2, 284–285, citing, inter alia, Jellinek, *Beth-Hamidrash*.

47. Rappoport, vol. 2, 285, citing Jellinek.

48. Rappoport, vol. 2, 285, citing, inter alia, *Midrash Tanchuma*.

49. Childs, 1974, 129, 156.

50. Roland de Vaux, *The Early History of Israel*, trans. David Smith (Philadelphia:

Westminster Press, 1978), 363. "Neither the vocabulary nor the plan of the story of the tenth plague, the death of the first-born, are the same of those of the first nine."

51. Martin Noth asserts that "there is no certain indication of the presence of E in the whole of the plague and Passover narrative." Noth, 1962, 111.

52. Murray Lee Newman Jr., *The People of the Covenant* (New York: Abingdon Press, 1962), 28. See also de Vaux, 362. "It is in fact probable that the oldest account told of one plague only," argued Elias Auerbach. "The first plague described in the oldest account, is . . . now the fifth, pestilence. . . . Thus the slaying of the firstborn is only a special consequence of the pestilence; and it leads immediately to the release of the Israelites."

53. Dennis J. McCarthy, "Dealing with Pharaoh," *Catholic Biblical Quarterly* 27 (1965): 344, n. 20.

54. Sigmund Freud, *Moses and Monotheism*, trans. Katherine Jones (New York: Vintage Books, 1967), 62–63.

55. Ginzberg, vol. 2, 343, citing, inter alia, *Siddur Eliahu Rabbah*.

56. Adapted from Ginzberg, vol. 2, 372, citing, inter alia, *Pirkei de Rabbi Eliezer*.

57. David M. Gunn, "The 'Hardening of Pharaoh's Heart,' " in *Art and Meaning*, ed. David J. A. Clines et al. (Sheffield, England: JSOT Press, 1982), 79.

58. Gunn, 85, quoting Ann Vater.

59. Thus Paul harkened back to the hardening of Pharaoh's heart in his teachings on divine election: "So it depends not on human will or exertion, but on God who shows mercy. For the scripture says to Pharaoh, 'I have raised you up for the very purpose of showing my power in you, so that my name may be proclaimed in all the earth.' " (Rom. 9:16–17 New RSV)

60. Gunn, 89.

61. Quoted at Gunn, 80, quoting Charles Isbell.

62. Adapted from JPS and NEB.

63. Philo of Alexandria, *The Essential Philo*, ed. Nahum N. Glatzer (New York: Schocken Books, 1971), 212.

64. de Vaux, 360.

65. Greta Hort, "The Plagues of Egypt," *Zeitschrift fur die Alttestamentliche Wissenschaft* (Berlin) 69 (1957) (neue Folge 28): 85.

66. Hort, 93.

67. Hort, 97.

68. So exhaustive are the instructions in Exodus 12 that the author specifies that two smaller families were allowed to share a single lamb, "taking into account both the number of persons and the amount each of them eats." (Exod. 12:4 NEB)

69. Adapted from JPS.

70. Adapted from JPS and NEB.

71. Noth, 1962, 89; Julian Morgenstern, "The Despoiling of the Egyptians," *Journal of Biblical Literature* 68 (1949): 22–24, n. 35.

72. Morgenstern, 1949, 22–24, n. 35.

73. Noth, 1962, 91–92; de Vaux, 367; Morgenstern, 1949, 22–24, n. 35.

74. Noth, 1962, 102.

75. de Vaux, 367.

76. de Vaux, 370.

77. "[T]he place which the Lord shall choose to cause His name to dwell," in the euphemism of the Deuteronomist (Deut. 16:2, 5). See chapter eleven.

78. Morgenstern, 1949, 24, n. 35.

79. Morgenstern, 1949, 22–24, n. 35.

80. Noth, 1962, 91–92.

81. Newman, 19.

82. George W. Coats, "Despoiling the Egyptians," *Vetus Testamentum* (Leiden) 18, n. 4 (October 1968): 453. "[T]he verb suggests borrowing, with the clear presupposition that objects so obtained would be returned."

83. Elias Auerbach, *Moses,* trans. and ed. Robert A. Barclay and Israel O. Lehman (Detroit: Wayne State University Press, 1975), 54.

84. Ginzberg, vol. 2, 372, citing, inter alia, Philo, *De Vita Mosis.*

85. Coats, 1968, 452. n. 2, citing David Daube.

86. Ginzberg, vol. 2, 371, citing *Mekhilta de Rabbi Shimon ben Yoachai.*

87. Coats, 1988, 97.

88. Morgenstern, 1949, 3.

89. Morgenstern, 1949, 18.

90. Noth, 1962, 101.

91. Morgenstern, 1949, 25.

92. Ginzberg, vol. 2, 373, citing, inter alia, *Tosefta Pesahim.*

CHAPTER SEVEN
EXODUS

1. The meaning of the Hebrew word conventionally translated as "went up armed" *(hamushim)* is "uncertain," according to the New JPS, 105, n. d; but the Vulgate, the Targums, and Rashi rendered it as "armed with weapons" (Brevard S. Childs, *Exodus: A Commentary* [London: SCM Press, 1974], 218). The Hebrew phrase that is literally translated as "with upraised hand" (New JPS) is understood to mean "confidently and fearlessly" (J. H. Hertz, ed., *The Pentateuch and Haftorahs,* 2d ed. [London: Soncino Press, 1981], 267, n. 8) or "defiantly" (NEB).

2. James Plastaras, *The God of Exodus* (Milwaukee: Bruce Publishing Company, 1966), 164.

3. Elias Auerbach, *Moses,* trans. and ed. Robert A. Barclay and Israel O. Lehman (Detroit: Wayne State University Press, 1975), 68.

4. Later, a formal census disclosed the male population of the Israelites over the age of twenty and "able to go forth to war" to be exactly 604,500 men (Lev. 1:46).

5. Auerbach, 68.

6. J. Maxwell Miller and John H. Hayes, *A History of Ancient Israel and Judah* (Philadelphia: Westminster Press, 1986), 60.

7. Noth, *Exodus: A Commentary,* trans. J. S. Bowden (Philadelphia: Westminster Press, 1962), 53 (translator's note).

8. Auerbach, 68.

9. Auerbach, 68–69.

10. Both George Coats and Sigmund Freud use the phrase "the Moses people" to refer to those who followed Moses himself during the events of the Exodus and those who recognized the primacy of Moses in the historical traditions of ancient Israel over

the centuries. See, e.g., George W. Coats, *Moses: Heroic Man, Man of God* (Sheffield, England: JSOT Press, 1988), 209; and Sigmund Freud, *Moses and Monotheism,* trans. Katherine Jones (New York: Vintage Books, 1967), 48.

11. Philo of Alexandria, *The Essential Philo,* ed. Nahum N. Glatzer (New York: Schocken Books, 1971), 212.

12. Adapted from JPS.

13. See chapter three.

14. In Miller and Hayes, 66.

15. T. Eric Peet, *Egypt and the Old Testament* (Liverpool: University Press of Liverpool, 1922), 124.

16. Peet, 75, citing H. R. Hall.

17. Martin Buber, *Moses: The Revelation and the Covenant* (New York: Harper & Row, 1958), 25

18. Niels Peter Lemche, "Habiru, Hapiru," in *Anchor Bible Dictionary,* vol. 3, 6–10.

19. Buber, 24–25.

20. Buber, 26.

21. John Keegan, *A History of Warfare* (New York: Vintage Books, 1994), p. 182.

22. Raphael Patai, *The Arab Mind* (New York: Charles Scribner's Sons, 1976), 74, 76.

23. J. A. Motyer, "Old Testament History," in *The Expositor's Bible Commentary,* ed. Frank E. Gaebelein (Grand Rapids: Zondervan, 1979), vol. 1, 261.

24. Peet, 126–127.

25. Philo, 216.

26. Flavius Josephus, *The Life and Works of Flavius Josephus,* trans. William Whiston (Philadelphia: John C. Winston Company, n.d.), 83.

27. Noth, 1962, 110.

28. Noth, 1962, 107–108.

29. Peet, 137: ". . . the translation 'Red Sea' [is] based purely on the fact that the Greek version uses this."

30. Peet, 144, n. 1. Peet points out that Numbers 21:4 also seems to equate the Red Sea with the Gulf of Aqaba.

31. Werner Keller, *The Bible as History,* 2d rev. ed. (New York: William Morrow, 1981), 126 (translator's note).

32. Noth, 1962, 108.

33. Buber, 75.

34. Peet, 144.

35. Peet, 138–139.

36. Noth, 1962, 109 (volcano); James Plastaras, *The God of Exodus* (Milwaukee: Bruce Publishing Company, 1966), 186 ("a meteorological phenomenon, possibly a whirlwind or a storm cloud").

37. Plastaras, 203.

38. Adapted from JPS and NEB.

39. Noth, 1962, 112.

40. Noth, 1962, 104, 111.

41. Philo, 217.

42. Josephus, 84.

43. Noth, 1962, 112.

44. Childs, 1974, 221.

45. Noth, 1962, 118. "[H]ere the Egyptians, flying headlong in the fear of God, rush right into the sea in their confusion and blindness. . . . J does not speak of a passage of Israel through the sea. Israel remained in their camp and according to v. 30 perhaps saw nothing at all of the actual flight and catastrophe of the Egyptians, but merely its consequences—the dead Egyptians which the sea threw up on its shores." See also Childs, 1970, 408.

46. Adapted from JPS and NEB.

47. Noth, 1962, 114.

48. Adapted from JPS.

49. Adapted from JPS and NEB.

50. Childs, 1974, 221.

51. Adapted from JPS and NEB.

52. Childs, 1974, 238.

53. Louis Ginzberg, *The Legends of the Jews*, tr. Henrietta Szold (Philadelphia: Jewish Publication Society of America, 1909–1938), vol. 3, 34, citing, inter alia, *Mekilta Shirah*.

54. Adapted from JPS.

55. Adapted from JPS and NEB.

56. Frank Moore Cross, "The Song of the Sea and Canaanite Myth," in *God and Christ*, ed. Herbert Brown et al. (New York: Harper & Row, 1968), 11. "In my view the hymn is not merely one of the oldest compositions preserved by biblical sources. It is a primary source for the central event in Israel's history, the Exodus-Conquest."

57. Noth, 1962, 121. "Of course we cannot establish any recognizable connection between [the Song of Miriam] and any of the known sources. Because it is in all probability of relatively great age it is most often assigned to the source J, but there is no conclusive argument in favor of this."

58. Philo, 219–220.

59. Noth, 1962, 121. "Its brevity suggests that it stems from a very early date." But Childs has criticized the assumption that "shorter is older": "On the one hand, Noth's position has relied too uncritically on the assumption that shortness in length reflects antiquity, but clearly the opposite situation is true at times." Childs, 1974, 247.

60. Brevard S. Childs, "A Traditio-Historical Study of the Reed Sea Tradition," *Vetus Testamentum* (Leiden) 20, no. 4 (October 1970): 411, n. 1. W. F. Albright dates the Song of Sea to the thirteenth century B.C.E., Frank M. Cross Jr. to the twelfth or eleventh century, Martin Buber to the reign of Solomon in the tenth century (Buber, 78), and Childs to the ninth century.

61. Auerbach, 65.

62. Auerbach, 62, 65. "This is . . . the whole song which is continually being repeated with the two voices alternating. Such a round dance and song, accompanied by continuous repetition of a one-line verse, can be found at Arab feasts today.

63. Adapted from JPS.

64. Hertz, 222, n. 1. *Hag* is "the common Semitic word for a pilgrimage to a sanctuary, where pilgrims took part in religious processions and ritual dances. Sacrifice was an essential part of such a festival."

65. Auerbach, 82.

66. Auerbach, 17.

67. Auerbach, 63, 64.

68. Auerbach, 93.

69. Auerbach, 64.

70. Auerbach, 214.

71. Auerbach, 64–65. See also Noth, 1962, 123.

72. Auerbach, 63.

73. Noth, 1962, 122–123. See, e.g., Exodus 4:11, 7:1, and Numbers 26:59, for passages in which Aaron and Miriam are linked to Moses as siblings.

74. David M. Gunn, "The 'Hardening of Pharaoh's Heart,' " in *Art and Meaning*, ed. David J.A. Clines et al. (Sheffield, England: JSOT Press, 1982), 86.

75. Coats, 1988, 114.

76. Noth, 1962, 104–105.

77. Noth, 1962, 121–122.

78. Martin Noth quoted in George W. Coats, *The Moses Tradition* (Sheffield, England: JSOT Press, 1993), 49. Coats accuses Noth of "nihilism" in his sometimes harsh appraisal of the historical reliability of the biblical text.

79. Childs, 1974, 242.

80. Childs, 1970, 413. "Particularly in the Old Testament poetic passages, often in the context of creation, there is reference to the slaying of the dragon, of crushing Leviathan or Rahab."

81. Childs, 1974, 190.

82. Childs, 1974, 190, discussing J. Pedersen.

83. Noth, 1962, 124.

84. Childs, 1970, 414.

85. Ginzberg, vol. 3, 24, citing, inter alia, *Midrash Wa-Yosha*.

86. Ginzberg, vol. 3, 18–19, citing, inter alia, *Midrash Wa-Yosha*.

87. Ginzberg, vol. 3, 20, citing, inter alia, *Mekilta Bashallah*.

88. Ginzberg, vol. 3, 22, citing, inter alia, *Targum Yerushalmi*.

89. Rappoport, vol. 2, 291, citing *Exodus Rabba*.

90. Rappoport, vol. 2, 291, citing, inter alia, *Pirke de Rabbi Eliezer*.

91. Ginzberg, vol. 3, 30, citing inter alia, *Mekilta Bashallah*.

92. Adapted from Rappoport, vol. 2, 294, citing, inter alia, *The Chronicles of Jerahmeel*. According to another story told by the rabbis, Pharaoh was made king over Nineveh and ruled five hundred years.

93. Cited in Will Durant, *The Story of Civilization*, vol. 1, *Our Oriental Heritage*, (New York: Simon & Schuster, 1935, 1954), 55.

94. Childs, 1974, 130. Childs is paraphrasing, not quoting, Artapanus, whose work is preserved only in the much later writings of the church father Eusebius.

95. Quoted in Childs, 1974, 230.

96. Quoted in Childs, 1974, 231.

97. Stanislav Segert, "Crossing the Waters: Moses and Hamilcar," *Journal of Near Eastern Studies*, Univ. of Chicago Press, vol. 53, no. 3, 1994, p. 195, 198.

98. Noth, 1962, 116.

99. Segert, 195, 198; Noth, 1962, 116.

100. Noth, 1962, 116.

101. Buber, 75.

102. L. S. Hay, "What Really Happened at the Sea of Reeds?" JBL 83 (1964), 399, quoted in Coats, 1993, 49.

103. Ginzberg, vol. 3, 8–9, citing, inter alia, *Yashar Shemot*.

104. Rappoport, vol. 2, 287–288, citing *Exodus Rabba*.

105. David Biale, *Power and Powerlessness in Jewish History* (New York: Schocken

Books, 1986), 72. "The Jews were not merely passive objects, at times protected by powerful rulers and at others slaughtered by the mob. In widely scattered times and places, they took up arms in self-defense and to pursue political objectives."

106. Menachem Begin, *The Revolt,* rev. ed. (Los Angeles: Nash Publishing, 1977), xxv.

107. Ginzberg, vol. 3, 15, citing *Yalkut.*

108. Ginzberg, vol. 3, 16, citing *Mekilta Beshallah.*

109. Ginzberg, vol. 3, 18, citing *Shemot Rabbah.*

110. F. M. Cross, "The Song of the Sea and Canaanite Myth," in *God and Christ,* (New York: Harper & Row, 1968), 17.

111. Childs, 1970, 412.

112. Noth, 1962, 122.

CHAPTER EIGHT
THE SORCERER AND THE SORCERER'S APPRENTICE

1. Angelo S. Rappoport, *Ancient Israel* (London: Senate, 1995), vol. 2, 29, citing, inter alia, *Exodus Rabba.*

2. Louis Ginzberg, *The Legends of the Jews,* trans. Henrietta Szold (Philadelphia: Jewish Publication Society of America, 1909–1938), vol. 3, 42, citing, inter alia, Philo.

3. Rappoport, vol. 2, 200.

4. Adapted from JPS.

5. Bernard S. Childs, *Exodus: A Commentary* (London: SCM Press, 1974), 266. "Verses 22b-25a stem from an earlier source, probably from J, even though there is some inner friction in v. 23 caused by the etiology."

6. Childs, 1974, 266, 269, citing Clericus.

7. Ginzberg, vol. 3, 39, citing, inter alia, *Mekilta Wa-Yassa.*

8. Childs, 1974, 266.

9. Ginzberg, vol. 3, 41, citing, inter alia, *Mekilta Wa-Yassa.*

10. Ginzberg, vol. 3, 42, citing, inter alia, *Mekilta Wa-Yassa.*

11. JPS, 84, n. a.

12. Adapted from JPS.

13. Martin Noth, *Exodus: A Commentary,* trans. J. S. Bowden (Philadelphia: Westminster Press, 1962), 135.

14. Ginzberg, vol. 3, 45, n. 94, citing, inter alia, *Abot.*

15. Ginzberg, vol. 3, 44, citing, inter alia, *Hagigah.*

16. Ginzberg, vol. 3, 44, citing, inter alia, *Tehillim.*

17. Ginzberg, vol. 3, 44, citing, inter alia, *Tan.B.*

18. Ginzberg, vol. 3, 46, citing, inter alia, *Mekilta Wa-Yassa.*

19. Ginzberg, vol. 3, 48, citing, inter alia, *Tan.B.*

20. Rappoport, vol. 2, 361, citing, inter alia, *Temurah.*

21. Elias Auerbach, *Moses,* tr. and ed. Robert A. Barclay and Israel O. Lehman (Detroit: Wayne State University Press, 1975), 85.

22. Noth, 1962, 132.

23. Childs, 1974, 283; Werner Keller, *The Bible as History,* 2d rev. ed. (New York: William Morrow, 1981), 128.

24. Childs, 1974, 282.

25. Keller, 129-130.

26. Ginzberg, vol. 3, 43, citing, inter alia, *Mekilta Wa-Yassa.*

27. James Plastaras, *The God of Exodus* (Milwaukee: Bruce Publishing Company, 1966), 190.

28. Rappoport, vol. 2, 299–300, citing *Yoma.*

29. Philo of Alexandria, *The Essential Philo,* ed. Nahum N. Glatzer (New York: Schocken Books, 1971), 213.

30. Adapted from NEB.

31. Gerhard von Rad, quoted in George W. Coats, *Moses: Heroic Man, Man of God* (Sheffield, England: JSOT Press, 1988), 30.

32. Childs, 1974, 256, citing and criticizing George Coats.

33. Coats, 1988, 109–110.

34. Sigmund Freud, *Moses and Monotheism,* trans. Katherine Jones (New York: Vintage Books, 1967), 113.

35. Freud, 42–43, citing the work of Ernest Sellin.

36. Freud, 42–43.

37. Peter Gay, *Freud: A Life for Our Time,* (New York: W. W. Norton, 1988), 647, citing Ernest Sellin.

38. Jay Y. Gonen, *A Psychohistory of Zionism,* New American Library, 1975, p. 10.

39. Freud, 49.

40. Freud, 49.

41. Martin Buber, *Moses: The Revelation and the Covenant* (New York: Harper & Row, 1958), 7, n. 1.

42. Quoted in Gay, 314–315.

43. Gay, 647.

44. Adapted from JPS and New JPS.

45. Auerbach, 78.

46. Noth, 140.

47. Ginzberg, vol. 3, 51, citing, inter alia, *Mekilta Wa-Yassa.*

48. Childs, 1974, 314.

49. Adapted from JPS.

50. Childs, 1974, 316.

51. Robert Graves, *Lawrence and the Arabs* (London: Jonathan Cape, 1927), 38.

52. Noth, 143.

53. Adapted from JPS and New JPS.

54. Buber, 90.

55. Noth, 141.

56. Ginzberg, vol. 3, 12, citing *Zohar.*

57. Ginzberg, vol. 3, 57, citing, inter alia, PK.

58. Ginzberg, vol. 3, 60, citing, inter alia, *Mekilta Amalek.*

59. Auerbach, 77.

60. Auerbach, 74.

61. Childs, 1974, 313.

62. Adapted from JPS.

63. Keller, 135.

64. Auerbach, 74.

65. JPS, 86, n. c.

66. Adapted from JPS.

67. Adapted from Ginzberg, vol. 3, 62, citing, inter alia, *Tan.B.*

68. Adapted from JPS.

69. Childs, 1974, 326.

70. Noth, 1962, 148–149; Auerbach, 87.

71. Exodus 18:4, JPS, 86, n. d.

72. Ginzberg, vol. 3, 256, citing, inter alia, Yelammedenu in *Yalkut I*.

73. Ginzberg, vol. 3, 134, citing, inter alia, *Berakot*.

74. Adapted from Ginzberg, vol. 2, 316, citing, inter alia, *Zohar III*.

75. Adapted from JPS.

76. Adapted from JPS and NEB.

77. Childs, 1974, 328.

78. Childs, 1974, 332.

79. Moshe Greenberg, *Understanding Exodus* (New York: Behrman House for Melton Research Center of the Jewish Theological Seminary of America, 1969), 48–49.

80. Ginzberg, vol. 3, 65, citing, inter alia, *Mekilta Yitro*.

81. Buber, 96.

82. John Van Seters, *The Life of Moses:* (Louisville, Ky: Westminster/John Knox Press, 1994), 211.

83. Greenberg, 48.

84. Noth, 1962, 148.

85. Murray Lee Newman Jr., *The People of the Covenant* (New York: Abingdon Press, 1962), 87, quoting Karl Budde (emphasis added).

86. Childs, 1974, 322. Childs calls the Kenite Theory "a brilliant cul-de-sac," and says that it "suffers from serious problems, and in its classic form, has few present-day defenders."

87. Auerbach, 89.

88. Auerbach, 90. Auerbach cautions against placing too much emphasis on the role of Jethro in the faith of Israel: "To say that this Midianite priest was . . . the true founder of the YHWH religion in Israel, is an entirely erroneous assertion. . . . [T]he real contents of both the religion and the law are an Israelite heritage, bearing as they do the stamp of the highly gifted personality of Moses."

89. Greenberg, 48, n. 1.

90. Ernest Axel Knauf, "Reuel," in *Anchor Bible Dictionary*, vol. 5, 693.

91. Flavius Josephus, *The Life and Works of Flavius Josephus*, trans. William Whiston (Philadelphia: John C. Winston Company, n.d.), 9. "Jethro . . . was one of the names of Raguel."

92. Julian Morgenstern, "The Ark, the Ephod and the 'Tent of the Meeting'" (Continued), *Hebrew Union College Annual* 18. (1943–1944), 38.

93. Rappoport, vol. 2, 301, citing *Midrash Tanchuma* and *Pesikta Rabbati*.

94. Ginzberg, vol. 3, 13, citing, inter alia, *Mekilta Bashallah*.

95. Ginzberg, vol. 3, 28, citing, inter alia, Abkir in *Yalkut I*.

96. William F. Albright, "Moses Out of Egypt," *Biblical Archaeologist*, 36, no 1. (February 1973): 72.

97. Gerhard von Rad, *Moses* (London: United Society for Christian Literature, Litterworth Press, 1960), 31.

98. Noth, 1962, 163.

99. Buber, 77.

100. Adapted from NEB and New JPS.

101. Childs, 1974, citing Gressmann and Beer.

102. Auerbach, 123.

103. Noth, 1962, 71–72.

104. Ginzberg, vol. 2, 352, citing, inter alia, *Mekilta de Rabbi Shimon ben Yoachai*.

105. Ginzberg, vol. 2, 352, citing, inter alia, *Shemot Rabbah*.

106. Buber, 123, citing Nowack.

107. Freud, 62–63.

108. Adapted from *The New Oxford Annotated Bible with the Apocryph*, New Revised Standard Version, ed. Bruce M. Metzger and Roland E. Murphy (New York: Oxford University Press, 1994).

109. Adapted from JPS.

110. Rappoport, vol. 2, 280, citing *Exodus Rabba*.

111. Adapted from JPS.

112. Childs, 1974, 333.

113. Adapted from JPS.

114. Buber, 95.

CHAPTER NINE
GOD OF THE MOUNTAIN, GOD OF THE WAY

1. Adapted from JPS and NEB. I have slightly altered the order of events as reported in Exodus 19:20–25 and Exodus 20:15–18. According to the chronology of the biblical text, the exchange between Moses and the Israelites—"let not God speak with us, lest we die"—comes *after* Moses has ascended Sinai and received the Ten Commandments from the mouth of Yahweh (Exod. 20:1–14). The order of events in the received text of the Bible, however, is probably distorted by the fact that the Redactor or some other biblical editor combined several sources, each one giving a slightly different version of what happened at Sinai.

2. Adapted from JPS and NEB.

3. Brevard S. Childs, *Exodus: A Commentary* (London: SCM Press, 1974), 435, citing *Exodus Rabbah*.

4. Elias Auerbach, *Moses*, trans. and ed. Robert A. Barclay and Israel O. Lehman (Detroit: Wayne State University Press, 1975), 172.

5. James Plastaras, *The God of Exodus* (Milwaukee: Bruce Publishing Company, 1966), 253.

6. Plastaras, 247; Martin Noth, *Exodus: A Commentary*, trans. J. S. Bowden, Old Testament Library (Philadelphia: Westminster Press, 1968), 155.

7. Noth, 1968, 161.

8. Childs, 1974, 388, n. 13.

9. Auerbach, 173.

10. Auerbach, 198.

11. Raymond F. Collins, "Ten Commandments," in *The Anchor Bible Dictionary*, vol. 6, 384.

12. Childs, 1974, 418.

13. Childs, 1974, 420–421.

14. Childs, 1974, 423, citing A. Alt.

15. Auerbach, 179.

16. Angelo S. Rappoport, *Ancient Israel* (London: Senate, 1995), vol. 2, 309, citing inter alia, *Exodus Rabba*.

17. Auerbach, 178.

18. Childs, 1974, 436.

19. Auerbach, 198.

20. Auerbach, 145.

21. Louis Ginzberg, *The Legends of the Jews*, trans. Henrietta Szold (Philadelphia: Jewish Publication Society of America, 1909–1938), vol. 3, 119, citing, inter alia, *Pirkei de Rabbi Eliezer*.

22. Childs, 348, citing and criticizing Mendenhall.

23. James Plastaras, *The God of Exodus* (Milwaukee: Bruce Publishing Company, 1966), 208.

24. Julian Morgenstern, "The Ark, the Ephod, and the 'Tent of the Meeting'" (Continued), *Hebrew Union College Annual* 18 (1943–1944): 2.

25. Morgenstern, 1943–1944, 3, 8–9, 11.

26. Morgenstern, 1943–1944, 13.

27. Richard Eliot Friedman, *Who Wrote the Bible?* (Englewood Cliffs, N.J.: Prentice-Hall, 1987), 43. The portable sanctuary that sheltered the Ark is first described as a simple tent fashioned of goats' hair and rams' skins that have been dyed red (Exod. 26:7, 14)—"the tent of meeting" (*ohel mo'ed*), as it is sometimes called—but P rather dreamily conflated the "tent" with the Tabernacle (*mishkan*), a much more elaborate structure consisting of an acacia-wood frame, long curtains hung from golden rings, and a series of interior partitions. The Tabernacle was the place where God sojourned during his visits to the Israelites—the Hebrew word (*mishkan*) means literally "dwelling-place." Notably, the Mosaic code specifies that all sacrifices to Yahweh (and various other ritual acts of high importance) must take place at the entrance to the Tabernacle, a commandment with profound implications in the politics of ancient Israel since it established Jerusalem, the presumed site of the Tabernacle, as the *only* place where Yahweh could properly be worshipped.

28. Murray Lee Newman Jr., *The People of the Covenant: A Study of Israel from Moses to the Monarchy* (New York and Nashville: Abingdon Press, 1962), p. 58.

29. Auerbach, 118.

30. Adapted from JPS and NEB.

31. Adapted from JPS.

32. Jack Miles, *God: A Biography* (New York: Alfred A. Knopf, 1995), 125. "According to the eminent linguist and Bible scholar Marvin H. Pope, *kabod* probably alludes to male genitalia at Job 29:20, where 'glory' is still the correct translation even though genitalia are to be understood."

33. Ginzberg, vol. 3, 137, citing, inter alia, *Berakot*.

34. Ginzberg, vol. III, 137–138, citing, inter alia, *Pirkei de Rabbi Eliezer*.

35. Buber, 117–118.

36. Plastaras, 243.

37. Adapted from JPS and NEB.

38. Ginzberg, vol. 3, 141, citing, inter alia, Nedarim.

39. Philo of Alexandria, *The Essential Philo*, ed. Nahum N. Glatzer (New York: Schocken Books, 1971), 272.

40. Rappoport, vol. 2, 303–304, citing, inter alia, *Midrash Shir-Hashirim*.

41. Ginzberg, vol. 3, 92, citing, inter alia, *Mekilta de Rabbi Shimon ben Yoachai*.

42. Adapted from JPS.

43. Friedman, 81.

44. Adapted from JPS and NEB.

45. Adapted from JPS.

46. Adapted from NEB.

47. Ginzberg, vol. 3, 172, citing, inter alia, *Shemot Rabbah*.

48. Adapted from JPS.

49. Adapted from JPS.

50. Ginzberg, vol. 3, 130, citing Yoma.

51. Moses Aberbach and Leivy Smolar, "Aaron, Jeroboam and the Golden Calves," *Journal of Biblical Literature* 86, (June 1967): 129.

52. Aberbach and Smolar, 132.

53. Aberbach and Smolar, 134–135.

54. Aberbach and Smolar, 134, n. 27, citing O. Eissfeldt.

55. George W. Coats, *Moses: Heroic Man, Man of God* (Sheffield, England: JSOT Press, 1988), 174.

56. Coats, 1988, 174.

57. Plastaras, 237. Plastaras attributes the view that Exodus 32 was a "fabrication" to "[o]lder critics of the Wellhausen persuasion" and insists that "[s]cholars are now inclined to accept the antiquity of the tradition behind the narrative of Exodus 32." Plastaras argues that Jeroboam's installation of golden calves at the shrines to Yahweh "must have represented a return to an older, though perhaps not fully respectable tradition."

58. Friedman, 48, 72.

59. Aberbach and Smolar, 137, 138–139.

60. H. H. Rowley, "Zadok and Nehushtan," *Journal of Biblical Literature* 58 (1939): 127.

61. Aberbach and Smolar, 138. "It is clear, as has indeed been pointed out, that the accounts of Exodus 32 and Numbers 12 originally included Aaron's punishment."

62. Adapted from JPS and NEB.

63. Adapted from JPS and NEB.

64. Adapted from JPS.

65. Ginzberg, vol. 3, 93, citing, inter alia, *Pesikta Rabbati*.

66. John Van Seters, *The Life of Moses* (Louisville, Ky: Westminster/John Knox Press, 1994), 358.

67. Ginzberg, vol. 3, 143, citing, inter alia, *Shemot Rabbah*.

68. Van Seters, 357–358, citing and criticizing the theories of W. Propp ("trivial" and "hardly convincing") and J. Sasson ("speculative" and "problematic").

69. Coats, 1988, 174.

70. Auerbach, 141.

71. Coats, 1988, 131.

72. Noth, 1968, 156.

73. Noth, 1968, 159.

74. Bruce Chatwin, *The Songlines* (New York: Penguin Books, 1988), 194.

75. Auerbach, 152.

76. Karen Armstrong, *A History of God* (New York: Alfred A. Knopf, 1993), 19.

77. Adapted from JPS.

78. Adapted from JPS.

CHAPTER TEN
MAN OF WAR

1. Louis Ginzberg, *The Legends of the Jews*, trans. Henrietta Szold (Philadelphia: Jewish Publication Society of America, 1909–1938), vol. 3, 237, citing, inter alia, *BaR*.

2. Adapted from JPS.

3. C. Leonard Woolley and T. E. Lawrence, *The Wilderness of Zin* (London: Jonathan Cape, 1936), 37, 57.

4. Martin Noth, *Numbers: A Commentary*, trans. James D. Martin (Philadelphia: Westminster Press, 1968), 78.

5. JPS, 174, n a.

6. Adapted from JPS.

7. Adapted from JPS.

8. JPS, 176, n. a.

9. Noth, 1968, 94.

10. Noth, 1968, 94.

11. Ginzberg, vol. 3, 256, citing, inter alia, ARN.

12. Adapted from JPS and NEB.

13. Adapted from JPS. (The original text has been shortened and rearranged.)

14. Adapted from JPS.

15. Adapted from JPS.

16. Noth, 1968, 154.

17. Adapted from JPS.

18. Adapted from JPS.

19. Adapted from JPS and NEB.

20. Adapted from NEB.

21. Adapted from JPS.

22. Philo of Alexandria, *The Essential Philo*, ed. Nahun N. Glatzer (New York, Schocken Books, 1971), 213.

23. Philo, 270.

24. Ginzberg, vol. 3, 292, citing, inter alia, Mo'ed Katan.

25. Ginzberg, *Ancient Israel* (London: Senate, 1995), vol. 3, 292, citing, inter alia, *BaR*.

26. Angelo S. Rappoport, *Ancient Israel*, (London: Senate, 1995), vol. 2, 232, citing, inter alia, *Yalkut*.

27. Bernhard W. Anderson, *Understanding the Old Testament*, (2d ed.), (Englewood Cliffs, N.J.: Prentice-Hall, 1966), 58, n.11a.

28. Rappoport, vol. 2, 324, citing, inter alia, *Pesikta Sutarta*.

29. Ginzberg, vol. 3, 307, citing, inter alia, *Seder 'Olam*, and Elias Auerbach, *Moses*, trans. and ed. Robert A. Barclay and Israel O. Lehman (Detroit: Wayne State University Press, 1975), 26.

30. Adapted from JPS.

31. JPS, 187, n. a.

32. Adapted from JPS.

33. Noth, 1968, 3.

34. Auerbach, 101. Auerbach suggests that "Barnea" means "gushing spring."

35. Noth, 1968, 106.

36. Auerbach, 67–68, 105.

37. Auerbach, 68.

38. Woolley and Lawrence, 75, 87.

39. Martin Buber, *Moses: The Revelation and the Covenant* (New York: Harper & Row, 1958), 172.

40. Auerbach, 27.

41. George W. Coats, *Moses: Heroic Man, Man of God* (Sheffield, England: JSOT Press, 1988), 25.

42. Murray Lee Newman Jr., *The People of the Covenant* (New York: Abingdon Press, 1962), 74.

43. Newman, 74.

44. Auerbach, 67.

45. Coats, 1988, 28, citing Gressmann.

46. Geo Widengren, "What Do We Know about Moses?" in *Proclamation and Presence,* ed. John I. Durham and J. R. Porter (Macon, Ga.: Mercer University Press, 1983), 44.

47. Auerbach, 67.

48. Auerbach, 82.

49. Auerbach, 98.

50. Auerbach, 213.

51. Widengren, 44.

52. Auerbach, 107–108.

53. Thomas Mann, *The Tables of the Law,* quoted in Israel H. Weisfeld, *This Man Moses* (New York: Bloch Publishing Company, 1966), xviii–xix.

54. Adapted from JPS.

55. Adapted from Rappoport, vol. 2, 340–341, citing, inter alia, Jellinek.

56. JPS, 188, n. a.

57. Adapted from JPS and NEB.

58. Adapted from Ginzberg, vol. 3, 336, citing, inter alia, *Rosh ha-Shanah.*

59. Adapted from JPS.

60. Ginzberg, vol. 3, 356, citing, inter alia, *Exodus Rabba.*

61. Noth, 1968, 193.

62. Ginzberg, vol. 3, 384–386, citing, inter alia, *Sanhendrin.* By tradition, Cozbi was thought to have been the daughter of Balak, the king of Moab who sent Balaam to curse the Israelites.

63. Adapted from JPS.

64. Adapted from JPS.

65. Adapted from JPS.

66. Adapted from JPS.

67. Adapted from JPS.

68. Adapted from JPS.

69. Adapted from JPS.

70. Adapted from JPS.

71. Adapted from JPS and NEB.

72. Noth, 1968, 199.

73. J. H. Hertz, *The Pentateuch and Haftorahs,* 2d ed. (London: Soncino Press, 1981), 704.

74. Ginzberg, vol. III, 413, citing, inter alia, *Shir.*

75. Adapted from NEB.

76. Adapted from JPS and NEB.

77. Adapted from JPS.

78. Adapted from JPS and NEB.

CHAPTER ELEVEN
"MOSES IS DEAD"

1. Adapted from JPS.

2. Adapted from JPS and NEB.

3. John Van Seters, *The Life of Moses* (Louisville, Ky: Westminster/John Knox Press, 1994), 81. "[T]he plagues were quite unknown to the writers of Deuteronomy and therefore a late and subsequent development. Deuteronomy speaks of the 'diseases of Egypt' that the Israelites experienced during the sojourn (Deut. 7:15; 28:60). These statements could hardly permit the possibility of the plague narrative of Exodus, which speaks of Yahweh afflicting the Egyptians with diseases but excluding the Israelites."

4. Adapted from JPS.

5. Adapted from NEB.

6. Adapted from JPS.

7. Van Seters, 215. See also Murray Lee Newman Jr., *The People of the Covenant* (New York: Abingdon Press, 1962), 63. The reference to the Tabernacle in Deuteronomy 31:14–15, which is "generally regarded as being non-Deuteronomic in origin," is to be distinguished from the tent of meeting. "It is striking, and undoubtedly significant, that Deuteronomy makes nothing of the tent."

8. Van Seters, 233, 383.

9. Van Seters, 141.

10. Adapted from JPS.

11. Adapted from NEB and JPS.

12. Adapted from JPS.

13. Adapted from JPS and NEB.

14. Adapted from JPS.

15. Richard Elliot Friedman, *Who Wrote the Bible?* (Englewood Cliffs, N.J.: Prentice-Hall, 1987), 101.

16. Robet Polzin, *Moses and the Deuteronomist* (New York: Seabury Press, 1980), part 1, 10.

17. Moshe Weinfeld, tr., intro., and comm., *Deuteronomy 1–11*, Anchor Bible (New York: Doubleday, 1991), 37–39.

18. Weinfeld, 37.

19. Adapted from JPS.

20. Adapted from JPS.

21. Polzin, part 1, 50.

22. Adapted from JPS.

23. Adapted from JPS.

24. Adapted from JPS.

25. Adapted from JPS.

26. Adapted from JPS.

27. Adapted from JPS.

28. Adapted from JPS.

29. Adapted from JPS.

30. Elias Auerbach, *Moses*, trans. and ed. by Robert A. Barclay and Israel O. Lehman (Detroit: Wayne State University Press, 1975), 181. "The confusion became still greater in the 'Blessing of Moses' (Deut. 33) for, even including Levi, only eleven tribes were enumerated; Simeon was omitted altogether. To add up to the number

twelve, Joseph was again divided into Ephraim and Manasseh in a late addition to the text (v. 17b)."

31. Adapted from JPS and NEB.

32. Adapted from JPS.

33. Adapted from Ginzberg, vol. 3, 313, citing, inter alia, BaR.

34. Rappoport, vol. 2, 343–349, citing, inter alia, *Deuteron Rabba*.

35. Rappoport, vol. 2, 358–359, citing, inter alia, Jellinek. See also Ginzberg, vol. 3, 472, citing, inter alia, Baba Batra.

36. James L. Kugel, *The Bible as It Was* (Cambridge: Harvard University Press, Belknap Press, 1997), 544, citing *Midrash ha-Gadol*.

37. Martin Buber, *Moses: The Revelation and the Covenant* (New York: Harper & Row, 1958), 201.

38. Philo of Alexandria, *The Essential Philo*, ed. Nahum N. Glatzer, (New York: Schocken Books, 1971), 269.

39. Flavius Josephus, *The Life and Works of Flavius Josephus*, trans. William Whiston (Philadelphia: John C. Winston Company, n.d.), 139–140.

40. Ginzberg, vol. 3, 473, citing, inter alia, Sifre D.

41. Ginzberg, vol. 3, 430–431, n. 894, citing, inter alia, Petirat Mosheh.

42. Geo Widengren, "What Do We Know about Moses?" in *Proclamation and Presence*, ed. John I. Durham and J. R. Porter (Macon, Ga.: Mercer University Press, 1983), 23–24, 28.

43. Martin Noth, *The Old Testament World*, trans. Victor I. Gruhn (Philadelphia: Fortress Press, 1966), 376–81.

44. Jan Assmann, *Moses the Egyptian* (Cambridge: Harvard University Press, 1997), 10.

CHAPTER TWELVE
THE SEARCH FOR THE HISTORICAL MOSES

1. Werner Keller, *The Bible as History*, 2d rev. ed. (New York: William Morrow, 1981), 237–238.

2. Paul F. Bork, *The World of Moses* (Nashville: Southern Publishing Association, 1978), 51, 54.

3. James Plastaras, *The God of Exodus* (Milwaukee: Bruce Publishing Company, 1966), 206, n. 5, citing the work of Martin Noth.

4. Keller, 77.

5. B. P. Robinson, "Zipporah to the Rescue," *Vetus Testamentum* 36, no. 4 (October 1986), 459.

6. George W. Coats, *The Moses Tradition* (Sheffield, JSOT Press, 1993), 47–48.

7. Elias Auerbach, *Moses*, trans. and ed. Robert A. Barclay and Israel O. Lehman (Detroit: Wayne State University Press, 1975), 216.

8. Auerbach, 171.

9. Gerhard von Rad, *Moses* (London: United Society for Christian Literature, Lutterworth Press, 1961), 8–9.

10. John Shelby Spong, *Liberating the Gospels* (San Francisco: HarperSanFrancisco, 1996), 18.

11. Keller, 137, citing Harold N. Moldenke.

12. Martin Noth, *Exodus: A Commentary*, trans. J. S. Bowden (Philadelphia: Westminster Press, 1962), 109 (volcano); Plastaras, 186 ("a meteorological phenomenon, possibly a whirlwind or a storm cloud").

13. Brevard S. Childs, *Exodus: A Commentary* (London: SCM Press, 1974), 382, quoting Driver.

14. Bernhard W. Anderson, *Understanding the Old Testament*, 2d ed. (Englewood Cliffs, N.J.: Prentice-Hall, 1966), 37.

15. Jan Assmann, *Moses the Egyptian* (Cambridge: Harvard University Press, 1997), 4.

16. Ahad Ha'am, *Selected Essays by Ahad Ha-'am*, trans. Leon Simon (Philadelphia: Jewish Publication Society of America, 1944), 308–309.

17. Assmann, 2.

18. Adapted from NEB.

19. Adapted from JPS.

Recommended Reading
and Bibliography

RECOMMENDED READING

The works listed in the bibliography below are all of the sources that I consulted in researching and writing *Moses: A Life*. Special mention must be made, however, of several books of unique achievement and distinction.

God: A Biography by Jack Miles, *A History of God* by Karen Armstrong, and *The Book of J* by Harold Bloom and David Rosenberg are modern masterpieces of biblical exegesis, and each of these important books has been deeply influential in my own reading and writing on biblical topics. *Who Wrote the Bible?* by Richard Elliott Friedman is a superb introduction to modern scholarship in the field of biblical authorship. And if a single book beckoned me back to the Bible and made it come fully alive as a work of literature, it was Joseph Heller's *God Knows*, a comic novel about King David. All of these authors—Heller, Miles, Armstrong, Friedman, Bloom, and Rosenberg—are worthy practitioners of *midrash*, a tradition of biblical commentary that invites us to read the Bible with open eyes, an open mind, and an open heart in order to extract fresh meanings out of ancient texts.

The Anchor Bible Dictionary is an accessible, comprehensive, and intriguing reference tool for any reader of the Bible and biblical scholarship, and the *Encyclopaedia Judaica* is a general reference work on Jewish topics that is especially helpful in understanding the intricacies of Bible history and commentary.

BIBLIOGRAPHY

Bibles

When quoting from various English translations of the Bible, I have used abbreviations in the text to identify the source of the quote. These abbreviations are given in the list below, along with the full title and bibliographical information for the various Bibles. Following the abbreviations lists, there is a list of other versions of the Bible that I have consulted. Where no specific source is listed in the text or the endnotes, the quotation is taken from the 1961 edition of the Jewish Publication Society's *The Holy Scriptures According to the Masoretic Text*.

JPS   *The Holy Scriptures According to the Masoretic Text*. Philadelphia: Jewish Publication Society, 1961.

KJV   *The Holy Bible Containing the Old and New Testaments in the King James Version*. Nashville: Thomas Nelson Publishers, 1985.

NEB   *The New English Bible with the Apocrypha*. 2d ed. New York: Oxford University Press, 1970.

New JPS   *Tanakh, The Holy Scriptures: The New JPS Translation According to the Traditional Hebrew Text*. Philadelphia: Jewish Publication Society, 1985.

RSV   *The New Oxford Annotated Bible with the Apocrypha*. Revised Standard Version, Containing the Second Edition of the New Testament. Edited by Herbert G. May and Bruce M. Metzger. New York: Oxford University Press, 1973.

Andersen, Francis I., and David Noel Freedman, tr., notes, and comm. *Hosea*. Anchor Bible. Garden City, N.Y.: Doubleday, 1980.

Boling, Robert G., tr., notes, and comm. *Joshua, Anchor Bible*. Garden City, N.Y.: Doubleday, 1982.

The Complete Parallel Bible: Containing the Old and New Testaments with the Apocryphal/Deuterocanonical Books. New York: Oxford University Press, 1993.

Hertz, J. H., ed. *The Pentateuch and Haftorahs*. 2d ed. London: Soncino Press, 1981.

Metzger, Bruce M., and Roland E. Murphy, eds. *The New Oxford Annotated Bible with the Apocrypha*. New York: Oxford University Press, 1994.

The New American Bible. Catholic Bible Association of America. Chicago: Catholic Press, 1971.

Speiser, E. A., tr., intro., and notes. *Genesis. Anchor Bible*. Garden City, N.Y.: Doubleday, 1987.

Weinfeld, Moshe, tr., intro., and comm. *Deuteronomy 1–11. Anchor Bible*. New York: Doubleday, 1991.

Reference Works

Barnavi, Eli, ed. *A Historical Atlas of the Jewish People: From the Time of the Patriarchs to the Present*. New York: Alfred A. Knopf, 1992.

Browning, W.R.F., ed. *A Dictionary of the Bible*. Oxford and New York: Oxford University Press, 1996.

Encyclopedia Judaica. 17 vols. corrected ed. Jerusalem: Keter Publishing House, n.d.

Freedman, David Noel, ed. *The Anchor Bible Dictionary*. 6 vols. New York: Doubleday, 1992.

Gilbert, Martin. *Atlas of Jewish History*. rev. ed. New York: Dorset Press, 1984.

The Interpreter's Dictionary of the Bible. New York: Abingdon Press, 1962.

May, Herbert G., ed. *Oxford Bible Atlas* (3d ed.) New York and Toronto: Oxford University Press, 1984.

Other Books

Ackerman, James S. "The Literary Context of the Moses Birth Story (Exodus 1–2)." In *Literary Interpretations of Biblical Narratives*, edited by Kenneth R. R. Gros Louis et al. Nashville: Abingdon Press, 1974.

Ahad Ha'am. *Selected Essays by Ahad Ha-'am*. Translated by Leon Simon. Philadelphia: Jewish Publication Society of America, 1944.

Albright, William Foxwell. *From the Stone Age to Christianity*. Baltimore: The Johns Hopkins Press, 1940.

Alter, Robert. *The Art of Biblical Narrative*. New York: Basic Books, 1981.

Altmann, Alexander, ed. *Biblical Motifs: Origins and Transformations*. Cambridge, Massachusetts: Harvard University Press, 1966.

Anderson, Bernhard W. *Understanding the Old Testament*. 2d ed. Englewood Cliffs, N.J.: Prentice-Hall, 1966.

Armstrong, Karen. *A History of God: The 4000-Year Quest of Judaism, Christianity, and Islam*. New York: Alfred A. Knopf, 1993.

Assmann, Jan. *Moses the Egyptian: The Memory of Egypt in Western Monotheism*. Cambridge: Harvard University Press, 1997.

Auerbach, Elias. *Moses*. Translated and edited by Robert A. Barclay and Israel O. Lehman. (orig. 1953). Detroit: Wayne State University Press, 1975.

Avery, Catherine B., ed. *The New Century Handbook of Classical Geography*. New York: Appleton-Century-Crofts, 1991.

Barzel, Hillel. "Moses: Tragedy and Sublimity." In *Literary Interpretations of Biblical Narratives*, edited by Kenneth R. R. Gros Louis, et al. Nashville: Abingdon Press, 1974.

Begin, Menachem. *The Revolt*. (orig. 1951). rev. ed. Los Angeles: Nash Publishing, 1977.

Biale, David. *Power and Powerlessness in Jewish History*. New York: Schocken Books, 1986.

Bloom, Harold, and David Rosenberg. *The Book of J*. New York: Grove Weidenfeld, 1990.

Boardman, John, Jasper Griffin, and Oswyn Murray, eds. *The Oxford History of the Classical World*. Oxford: Oxford University Press, 1986.

Bork, Paul F. *The World of Moses*. Nashville: Southern Publishing Association, 1978.

Buber, Martin. *Moses: The Revelation and the Covenant*. (orig. 1946). New York: Harper & Row, 1958.

Chatwin, Bruce. *The Songlines*. New York: Penguin Books, 1988.

Childs, Brevard S. *Exodus: A Commentary*. London: SCM Press, 1974.

Coats, George W. "Humility and Honor: A Moses Legend in Numbers 12" in Clines, David J. A., et al., eds. *Art and Meaning: Rhetoric in Biblical Literature*. Sheffield: Journal for the Study of the Old Testament, Supplement Series 19, 1982.

———. *Moses: Heroic Man, Man of God*. Journal for the Study of the Old Testament, supplement series 57. Sheffield, England: JSOT Press, 1988.

———. *The Moses Tradition*. Journal for the Study of the Old Testament, supplement series 161. Sheffield, England: JSOT Press, 1993.

Cross, Frank Moore. *Canaanite Myth and Hebrew Epic: Essays in the History of the Religion of Israel*. Cambridge: Harvard University Press, 1973.

———. "The Song of the Sea and Canaanite Myth." In *God and Christ: Existence and Providence*, edited by Herbert Brown et al. New York: Harper & Row, 1968.

Daiches, David. *Moses: Man in the Wilderness*. London: Weidenfeld & Nicolson, 1975.

Durant, Will. *The Story of Civilization*, vol. 1, *Our Oriental Heritage*. New York: Simon & Schuster, 1935.

Farah, Caesar E. *Islam: Beliefs and Observances*. Woodbury, N.Y.: Barron's Educational Series, 1970.

Freud, Sigmund. *Moses and Monotheism*. Translated by Katherine Jones. (orig. 1939). New York: Vintage Books, 1967.

Friedman, Richard Elliot. *Who Wrote the Bible?* Englewood Cliffs, N.J.: Prentice-Hall, 1987.

Gaebelein, Frank E., ed. *The Expositor's Bible Commentary*, vol. 1. Grand Rapids: Zondervan, 1979.

Gay, Peter. *Freud: A Life for Our Time*. New York: W. W. Norton, 1988.

Ginzberg, Louis. *Legends of the Bible*. Philadelphia: Jewish Publication Society of America, 1956. (A one-volume abridgement of Ginzberg's *The Legends of the Jews*, cited below.)

———. *The Legends of the Jews*. Translated by Henrietta Szold. 7 vols. Philadelphia: Jewish Publication Society of America, 1909–1938.

Gonen, Jay Y. *A Psychohistory of Zionism*. New York: New American Library, 1975.

Graves, Robert. *Lawrence and the Arabs*. London: Jonathan Cape, 1927.

Greenberg, Moshe. *Understanding Exodus*. Heritage of Biblical Israel, vol. 2, pt. 1. New York: Behrman House for Melton Research Center of the Jewish Theological Seminary of America, 1969.

Gunkel, Hermann. *The Folktale in the Old Testament*. Translated by Michael D. Rutter. Sheffield, England: The Almond Press, 1987.

Gunn, David M. "The 'Hardening of Pharaoh's Heart': Plot, Character and Theology in Exodus 1–14." In *Art and Meaning: Rhetoric in Biblical Literature*, edited by David J. A. Clines, David M. Gunn, and Alan J. Hauser. Journal for the Study of the Old Testament, supplement series 19. Sheffield, England: JSOT Press, 1982.

Halivni, David Weiss. *The Book and the Sword: A Life of Learning in the Shadow of Destruction. (Throes of the Holocaust.)* New York: Farrar, Straus & Giroux, 1996.

Harris, Roberta L. *The World of the Bible*. New York: Thames & Hudson, 1995.

Harris, Stephen L. *Understanding the Bible: A Reader's Introduction*. 2d ed. Palo Alto, Calif., and London: Mayfield Publishing Company, 1985.

James, T.G.H. *Pharaoh's People: Scenes from Life in Imperial Egypt*. London: Bodley Head, 1984.

Johnson, Alan F. "Jesus and Moses: Rabbinic Backgrounds and Exegetical Concerns in Matthew 5 as Crucial to the Theological Foundations of Christian Ethics." In *The*

Living and Active Word of God: Studies in Honor of Samuel J. Schultz, edited by Morris Inch and Ronald Youngblood. Winona Lake, Ind.: Eisenbrauns, 1983.

Johnson, Paul. *A History of the Jews*. New York: Harper & Row, 1987.

Josephus, Flavius. *The Jewish War*. Translated by G. A. Williamson. New York: Dorset Press, 1985.

———. *The Life and Works of Flavius Josephus*. Translated by William Whiston. Philadelphia: John C. Winston Company, n.d.

Keegan, John. *A History of Warfare*. New York: Vintage Books, 1994.

Keller, Werner. *The Bible as History*. 2d rev. ed. New York: William Morrow, 1981.

King, Martin Luther, Jr. "I See the Promised Land." In *A Testament of Hope: The Essential Writings of Martin Luther King, Jr.*, edited by James Melvin Washington. San Francisco: Harper & Row, 1986.

Kugel, James L. *The Bible as It Was*. Cambridge: Harvard University Press, Belknap Press, 1997.

Lederer, Zdenek. *Ghetto Theresienstadt*. New York: Howard Fertig, 1983.

Magnusson, Magnus. *Archaeology of the Bible*. New York: Simon & Schuster, 1977.

Miles, Jack. *God: A Biography*. New York: Alfred A. Knopf, 1995.

Miller, J. Maxwell and John H. Hayes. *A History of Ancient Israel and Judah*. Philadelphia: Westminster Press, 1986.

Moorhouse, Geoffrey. *The Terrible Void*. Philadelphia: Lippincott, 1974.

Newman, Murray Lee, Jr. *The People of the Covenant: A Study of Israel from Moses to the Monarchy*. New York: Abingdon Press, 1962.

Noth, Martin. *Exodus: A Commentary*. Translated by J. S. Bowden. Old Testament Library. Philadelphia: Westminster Press 1962.

———. *Numbers: A Commentary*. Translated by James D. Martin. Old Testament Library. Philadelphia: Westminster Press, 1968.

———. *The Old Testament World*. Translated by Victor I. Gruhn. Philadelphia: Fortress Press, 1966.

Pardes, Ilana. *Countertraditions in the Bible: A Feminist Approach*. Cambridge: Harvard University Press, 1992.

Patai, Raphael. *The Arab Mind*. New York: Charles Scribner's Sons, 1976.

Peet, T. Eric. *Egypt and the Old Testament*. Liverpool: University Press of Liverpool, 1922.

Philo of Alexandria. *The Essential Philo*. Edited by Nahum N. Glatzer. New York: Schocken Books, 1971.

Plastaras, James. *The God of Exodus: The Theology of the Exodus Narratives*. Milwaukee: Bruce Publishing Company, 1966.

Polzin, Robert. *Moses and the Deuteronomist: A Literary History of the Deuteronomic History*, part 1. New York: Seabury Press, 1980.

[Pseudo-Philo]. *The Biblical Antiquities of Philo*. Translated by M. R. James. New York: Ktav Publishing House, 1971.

Rappoport, Angelo S. *Ancient Israel*, vol. 2. London: Senate, 1995.

Sachar, Abram Leon. *A History of the Jews*. rev. ed. New York: Alfred A. Knopf, 1967.

Sachar, Howard M. *A History of Israel: From the Rise of Zionism to Our Time*. 2 vols. New York: Alfred A. Knopf, 1979.

Smend, Rudolf. *Yahweh War & Tribal Confederation: Reflections Upon Israel's Earliest History*. Max Gray Rogers, trans. Nashville and New York: Abingdon Press, 1970.

Spong, John Shelby. *Liberating the Gospels: Reading the Bible with Jewish Eyes*. San Francisco: HarperSanFrancisco, 1996.

Van Seters, John. *The Life of Moses: The Yahwist as Historian in Exodus-Numbers*. Louisville, Ky.: Westminster/John Knox Press, 1994.

de Vaux, Roland. *The Early History of Israel*. Translated by David Smith. Philadelphia: Westminster Press, 1978.

von Rad, Gerhard. *Moses*. World Christian Books no. 32, 2nd series. London: United Society for Christian Literature, Lutterworth Press, 1960.

———. *Old Testament Theology*, vol. 1, *The Theology of Israel's Historical Traditions*. Translated by D.M.G. Stalker. New York: Harper & Row, 1962.

———. *The Problem of the Hexateuch and Other Essays*. Translated by E. W. Trueman Dicken. New York: McGraw-Hill Book Company, 1966.

Weiser, Artur. *The Old Testament: Its Formation and Development*. New York: Association Press, 1961.

Weisfeld, Israel H. *This Man Moses*. New York: Bloch Publishing Company, 1966.

Widengren, Geo. "What Do We Know about Moses?" In *Proclamation and Presence: Old Testament Essays in Honour of Gwynne Henton Davies*, edited by John I. Durham and J. R. Porter. Macon, Ga.: Mercer University Press, 1983.

Wilkinson, Sir J. Gardner. *A Popular Account of the Ancient Egyptians*, vol. 1. London: John Murray, 1854.

Woolley, C. Leonard, and T. E. Lawrence. *The Wilderness of Zin*. (orig. 1915). London: Jonathan Cape, 1936

Yerushalmi, Yosef Hayim. *Freud's Moses: Judaism Terminable and Interminable*. New Haven and London: Yale University Press, 1991.

Scholarly Journals and Periodicals

Aberbach, Moses, and Leivy Smolar. "Aaron, Jeroboam and the Golden Calves." *Journal of Biblical Literature* 86, part 2 (June 1967): 129–140.

Albright, W. F. "Jethro, Hobab and Reuel in Early Hebrew Tradition." *Catholic Biblical Quarterly* 25 (1963): 1–11.

Albright, William F. "Moses Out of Egypt." *Biblical Archaeologist* 36, no. 1 (February 1973): 48–76.

Allen, E. L. "Jesus and Moses in the New Testament." *Expository Times* (Edinburgh) 67 (October 1955–September 1956): 104–106.

Childs, Brevard S. "The Birth of Moses." *Journal of Biblical Literature* 84, part 2 (June 1965): 109–122.

Childs, Brevard S. "A Traditio-Historical Study of the Reed Sea Tradition." *Vetus Testamentum* (Leiden) 20, no. 4 (October 1970): 406–418.

Coats, George W. "Despoiling the Egyptians." *Vetus Testamentum* (Leiden) 18, no. 4 (October 1968): 450–457.

———. "History and Theology in the Sea Tradition." *Studia Theologica* (Oslo) 29: (1975): 53–62.

———. "Moses in Midian." *Journal of Biblical Literature* 92, no. 1 (March 1973): 3–10.

———. "The Song of the Sea." *Catholic Biblical Quarterly* 31 (1969): 1–17.

———. "What Do We Know of Moses?" *Interpretation: A Journal of Bible and Theology* 27, no. 1 (January 1974): 91–94.

Cross, Frank Moore, Jr. "The Song of the Sea and Canaanite Myth." *Journal for Theology and the Church* 5 (1968): 1–25.

Hort, Greta. "The Plagues of Egypt." *Zeitschrift für die Alttestamentliche Wissenschaft* (Berlin) 69 (1957) (neue Folge 28), 84–103.

Joines, Karen Randolph. "The Bronze Serpent in the Israelite Cult." *Journal of Biblical Literature*, vol. 87, part 3, September 1968, 245–256.

Kaplan, Lawrence. " 'And the Lord Sought to Kill Him' (Exod. 4:24): Yet Once Again." *Hebrew Annual Review* 5 (1981): 65–74.

Kosmala, Hans. "The Bloody Husband." *Vetus Testamentum* 12 (January 1962): 14–28.

Mann, Thomas W. "Theological Reflections in the Denial of Moses." *Journal of Biblical Literature*, vol. 98, no. 4, December 1979, 481–494.

McCarthy, Dennis J. "Dealing with Pharaoh: Exod. 7, 8–10, 27." *Catholic Biblical Quarterly* 27 (1965): 336–347.

Morgenstern, Julian. "The Ark, the Ephod and the 'Tent of the Meeting.' " *Hebrew Union College Annual* 17 (1942–1943): 153–265.

———. "The Ark, the Ephod and the 'Tent of the Meeting' " (Continued). *Hebrew Union College Annual* 18 (1943–1944): 1–52.

———. "The 'Bloody Husband' (?) (Exod. 4:24–26) Once Again." *Hebrew Union College Annual* (Union of Hebrew Congregations) 34 (1963): 35–70.

———. "The Despoiling of the Egyptians." *Journal of Biblical Literature* 68 (1949): 1–28.

Regensteiner, Henry. "Moses in the Light of Schiller." *Judaism* (American Jewish Congress) 43(1), issue no. 169 (Winter 1994): 61–65.

Robinson, B. P. "Zipporah to the Rescue: A Contextual Study of Exodus iv 24–26." *Vetus Testamentum* 36, no. 4 (October 1986): 447–461.

Rowley, H. H. "Zadok and Nehushtan." *Journal of Biblical Literature* 58 (1939): 113–141.

Segert, Stanislav. "Crossing the Waters: Moses and Hamilcar." *Journal of Near Eastern Studies* (University of Chicago) 53, no. 3 (1994): 195–203.

Vermes, G. "Baptism and Jewish Exegesis: New Light from Ancient Sources," *New Testament Studies* (Cambridge University Press) 4 (1958): 309–319.

Zevit, Ziony. " 'Clio, I Presume,' Expanded Review of *In Search of History* by J. Van Seters." *Bulletin of the American Schools of Oriental Research*, no. 260 Fall/November 1985, 71–82.

Zivotofsky, Ari Z. "The Leadership Qualities of Moses." *Judaism* (American Jewish Congress) 43(3), no. 171 (summer 1994): 258–269.

Index

Moses

A Life

Jonathan Kirsch

A Reader's Companion

FEATURING A
BALLANTINE
READER'S
COMPANION

A Conversation with Jonathan Kirsch, author of
Moses: A Life

Q: How did you first get involved with this project?

JK: This story actually begins with my earlier book, *The Harlot by the Side of the Road*, which used a similar approach in exploring Bible texts that were suppressed or censored because of their troubling context. One of the texts I looked at was the shocking story of God's murderous night attack on Moses as he was setting out for Egypt to liberate the Israelites from slavery. That story was the first clue indicating there was a different side to Moses than what I had been taught to see. It set me on the path of uncovering the whole story of his life.

Q: We have been taught to think of Moses as a symbol of freedom and emancipation. Is this accurate?

JK: It might come as an uncomfortable surprise to many Bible readers, but Moses is not always depicted in the Bible as an advocate of freedom or emancipation. It is perfectly true that he is shown to emancipate the Israelites from slavery in Egypt, and that is indeed a sublime moment in his life. But Moses is also shown to carry out purges and inquisitions, to suppress challenges to his own authority through violence and repression, and to conduct wars against nations other than his own. The challenge for us is to understand where these less familiar stories of Moses come from and what they were intended to mean by their original authors.

Q: Did a flesh-and-blood human being called Moses really exist?

JK: I suspect this may be the most challenging and difficult aspect of my book for many people. A major theme of *The Harlot by the Side of the Road*, which troubled some readers, was that the Bible contains stories of sexual passion and graphic violence. A major theme of *Moses: A Life*, which will perhaps trouble readers even more, is the notion that a flesh-and-blood Moses may not have existed at all.

Q: Are there any tracings in the archaeological record that correspond to biographical details about Moses or the remarkable things he is described to have done in the Bible?

JK: No. Moses is entirely absent from the historical record. For example, the Egyptians were obsessive chroniclers of their own history. They preserved amazingly detailed records, ranging from lists of kings who reigned over Egypt for two thousand years, to the types of games children played, to inventories of produce, and every detail in between. And yet this exhaustive record makes no mention of any events from the Bible, including those of the Exodus, which directly impacted on Egyptian society: the enslavement of the Israelites, the ten plagues, the liberation of the Israelites, and the defeat of Pharaoh and his army at the Red Sea. None of these events can be corroborated by archaeology or by research into the surviving texts of any other culture or civilization. The one and only source of what we know about Moses is the Bible.

Q: **Why is it important to understand who wrote the Bible if we are to truly understand the life of Moses?**

JK: There are people in all three Bible-based religions, Judaism, Christianity, and Islam, who take it as an article of faith that the Bible is the received word of God. They're not interested in exploring the question of who wrote the Bible. I respect people who take that position out of faith, and I'm not trying to change their minds. However, if you read the Bible with open eyes and an open mind, you will discover, as many years of modern Bible scholarship have shown, that it was written in bits and pieces by many different authors at many different times and places over centuries and even millennia. Each of these sources gives us a different picture of Moses—who he was, what he did, what he stood for.

Q: **In what ways did the Bible's authors use Moses to make theological or political points?**

JK: Some of the biblical sources were concerned about the rivalry for power between the monarchy and the priesthood; some were concerned about preserving the integrity of the people of Israel from the forces of assimilation and intermarriage; others sought to promote peaceful coexistence between the Israelites and the people amongst whom they lived. Each of these points of view prompted the various Bible sources to depict Moses in drastically different ways.

Q: **Why did you chose a chronological structure for *Moses: A Life* as opposed to a thematic structure?**

JK: The Bible tells Moses' story as a biography from birth to death. I chose to follow that same structure and chronology because I felt it was the best way to make the many conflicts and contradictions in the life of Moses more intelligible.

Q: **Moses' story calls into question our definition of leadership. Should we place primary emphasis on how well our leaders model approved behavior? Or should we measure success in terms of how well they achieve our national ends?**

JK: One of the great revelations I have experienced in writing about the Bible, both in *Harlot* and in *Moses*, is that the biblical heroes were not always heroic. They are depicted in the Bible as real men and women with real flaws and failings. And that teaches us a lesson about what we should expect to find in our leaders. A leader is, above all, a human being. We should not expect them to be perfect, but we should expect them to embrace the values, goals, and priorities that we embrace.

Q: **At the same time that *Moses: A Life* was originally published, there also appeared a new animated film about him, a self-help book based on his life, and a *Time* magazine cover story. Why do we remain so fascinated by Moses?**

JK: From time to time Moses seems to reappear in movies, children's stories, and other cultural art forms. He has become a constant in our popular culture. But there's currently a deeper source of interest in Moses that is possibly due to the approaching new millennium. As the year 2000 draws nearer, people are reaching back to the oldest sources of wisdom to gain insight and perhaps calm their fears about the coming of a new age. After all, several millennia have passed since the lifetime of Moses, and he's still with us. I suspect that that's reassuring to anyone who might be anxious about Y2K.

Q: **Moses is the only man in the Hebrew Bible to encounter God "face to face." How would you describe the relationship between God and Moses?**

JK: I describe them as being like an old couple in a bad marriage: they bicker, they haggle, they threaten, they can't live with each other and they can't live without each other. And that's exactly why the relationship between God and Moses comes across as so intimate and so immediate. Someone recently asked me what Moses teaches us by example about the proper relationship between God and humankind. The answer is that Moses teaches us that it is not only acceptable but praiseworthy to tell God when we think he is wrong. The Bible reveals that Moses stood up to God and told him he was wrong on more than one occasion.

Q: **How does the Bible's portrayal of Moses differ from the sacred writing and court histories of other figures from distant antiquity?**

JK: Ancient history and sacred writings tend to depict heroes, prophets, and kings as one-dimensional characters, plaster saints, icons. The Bible, on the other hand, depicts Moses as a complex and troubled man who strikes us as so very real precisely because he is so contradictory. Real people are capable of showing both fear and courage, and so is Moses in the Bible. Real people are capable of showing both compassion and cruelty, and so is Moses in the Bible. Holy scripture, which contains not only moments of great tragedy but also moments of great comedy, reveals Moses to be much funnier, at times, than we've been led to believe. One of the main points I want to make with this book is that Moses is not only very different from what we think he is but also much more interesting. The essential impression of Moses—and the real genius of his depiction at the hands of the biblical authors—is that he was born like every other infant, grew to manhood with all the impulses and excesses of which real men and women are capable, lived a life marked with passions that are perfectly human, and came to a tragic end that is no less riddled with ambiguity and contradiction than any other human life.

Q: **When you imagine Moses' appearance, what do you see?**

JK: I certainly don't see him as a big blond hunk like Charlton Heston. I think he is much more likely to have resembled what we might think of as a man with leathery skin, probably dark-haired and dark-eyed, a man of the desert.

Q: **Why is there a forty-year gap in Exodus between Moses' killing of an Egyptian overseer and his vision of God at the burning bush only one chapter later? What happened to Moses during those forty years?**

JK: What happened to Moses during the forty-year gap is a mystery for which the Bible simply does not offer an explanation. The ancient rabbis proposed all kinds of extraordinary exploits to fill in the space, but the best explanation scholarship can offer is that the life story of Moses was patched together from different sources. When joined together, these separate stories created gaps and inconsistencies. My favorite example is that Moses' father-in-law is given three different names in the Bible: Jethro, Reuel and Hobab. The best explanation is that the Bible contains three different versions of Moses' story, each of which recorded his father-in-law by a different name.

Q: **What background—both religious and secular—do you bring to this work?**

JK: What I bring to my study of the Bible is a broad experience in world literature combined with a personal foundation in religion and spirituality. I was born and raised a Jew. I've had a formal Jewish education, celebrated my bar mitzvah when I was thirteen, and currently belong to a synagogue in Judaism's Conservative movement. My professional training and experience, on the other hand, is as a book critic. I've written and lectured about literature for more than twenty-six years. What I've tried to do in *Moses: A Life* is combine these two backgrounds in an approach that treats the Bible as both a work of literature and a sacred text.

Q: **What biblical and historical sources did you use for your research?**

JK: I started with the literal texts of the Bible, including the familiar King James version, other, more contemporary, English translations, and original texts in Hebrew. I also researched a great many other ancient sources that are roughly contemporaneous with the Bible, including Aramaic translations and the writing of ancient authors who retold the Bible's stories. That was my basic source material. I moved from there into Jewish legend and lore that has been collected in two important anthologies: the Talmud and the Midrash. These are parables, fairy tales, legends, and other forms of storytelling that were collected by rabbis from ancient times through the Middle Ages. I also worked with the biblical commentaries of early church fathers and medieval Christian theologians. I moved from there into modern Bible scholarship, which really begins in the late nineteenth century and continues to our own time. And finally, I drew upon the latest discoveries and theories of Bible scholars and theologians who have studied and interpreted Biblical texts in light of modern scientific and archeological findings.

Q: **What surprised you most as you began researching this project?**

JK: I was surprised at my discovery that serious Bible scholars, for more than a century, have openly wondered whether Moses really existed. Like everyone else, I deeply assumed that the Bible had a core or kernel of historical fact, even if much of what we find in it is legend and lore. When I realized that pious men and women were willing to entertain the notion that Moses was purely legend, I was taken aback, as I suspect many readers will be. I also think that readers will be surprised at the complexity of Moses' personality and personal history. The fact that he was capable of cowardice, cruelty, and violence will be challenging and difficult for some to accept.

Q: **Why do consider the end of Moses' life so tragic?**

JK: Here is a man who went on a mission he really didn't want: to liberate the Israelites from slavery and establish for them a home in the promised land, the land of milk and honey. Moses fought God, he wheedled and cajoled, he tried to get himself excused from the task, but God talked him into it. After much hesitation, Moses finally agreed to spend forty years doing precisely what God asked him to do. However, on the brink of fulfilling his mission, Moses is forbidden entry into the land of Israel by God himself and condemned to die in the wilderness without ever setting foot in the promised land. The Bible tells us he was denied that final reward because of what strikes us as very trivial act of disobedience. As a result, everything he did over forty years of struggle counted for nothing. That, to me, is a tragedy.

Q: **You've written several other nonfiction works as well as two novels. Do you find the kind of nonfiction writing you've done with *Moses: A Life* and *The Harlot by the Side of the Road* easier or harder than novel writing?**

JK: I wouldn't say one is easier than the other, because all writing takes hard work. However, I found my true voice as a writer, and my passion, with *Moses* and *Harlot*. In that sense they were easier books to write, because the material was so fascinating to me.

Q: **What lessons should we learn from the story of Moses?**

JK: Moses is shown at some places in the Bible to be an autocrat and someone who refuses to share power or allow personal freedom. Nevertheless, throughout the Bible Moses respects and recognizes that men and women enjoy free will and the right to choose between good and evil. That, to me, is the most important lesson of the life of Moses. In Deuteronomy 30:19 Moses says, "I have set before thee life and death, the blessing and the curse; therefore choose life, that thou mayest live." He is a goad, a gadfly, and he can be very annoying. Indeed, the Israelites are shown to be perfectly fed up with him time and again. They get sick and tired of his constant nudging. Even God is sick and tired of Moses at times. But Moses never stops challenging us to choose for ourselves how we want to live.

Q: **What do you want readers to get out of this book?**

JK: I hope readers will find, as I have, that the Bible is a much more exciting, entertaining, and challenging book than we are led to believe by our early experiences in Sunday School, in church, in the synagogue, and even—when it comes to Moses—in the movie theater. I also hope readers will discover that Moses is very much a man of our own time and that he has something to teach us in the late twentieth century as we try to cope with many of the same challenges and risks presented in biblical texts. Above all, these include questions of how people of different faiths, races, and nationalities can learn to live with one another.

Reading Group Questions and Topics for Discussion

1. How did your perceptions of Moses change after reading *Moses: A Life*? How does Kirsch's depiction of Moses differ from others you may have seen or read? How is it different from depictions of other biblical figures or characters from ancient literature?

2. Throughout the ages, popular culture has served up images of Moses as a shimmering icon—someone who is strong, sure, and heroic. Why do you think so much of what the Bible says about Moses is left out of both sacred and secular art? What reasons might there be for the devout tradition, in both Judaism and Christianity, of portraying Moses as unfailingly good and meek, dignified and devout, righteous and heroic?

3. Kirsch raises the possibility that Moses may not have existed at all. After all, no ancient stone or artifact proves that there actually lived a man who brought the Israelites out of Egypt to Mt. Sinai and then to the land of Canaan. Do you think Moses was a real person?

4. What lessons can we learn by confronting the idea that Moses was an intensely flawed human being, if he even existed?

5. Kirsch's previous book, *The Harlot by the Side of the Road*, and *Moses: A Life* each received critical acclaim and bestseller status. Do you think the popularity of such books suggests a stronger yearning for spirituality among the public at large? If not, what do you think it does mean?

6. What impact did the different political agendas of biblical authors have on the depiction of Moses? Can you describe possible agendas of the various biblical authors?

7. Kirsch presents the idea, advanced by some historians, that Moses' birth story is simply a cut-and-paste reworking of the life of Sargon, an ancient Mesopotamian ruler. What do you think of this suggestion?

8. Moses is the only man in the Hebrew Bible to encounter God "face to face." How would you describe the relationship between God and Moses?

9. There is much evidence to suggest that Moses did not write—and could not have written—the books that are traditionally attributed to him. Kirsch writes, "The Bible, for example, speaks of Moses in

the third person, an odd way for a man to write of himself. Moses is described as the most humble man who ever lived, which strikes us as something a truly humble man would hardly boast about. Moses is credited with knowledge of people and events that would have been unknown to anyone living at the time of the Exodus, and yet, at the same time, he appears to have made mistakes about people and events that he ought to have known and seen for himself." How do you account for these discrepancies? What do they suggest to you?

10. The original Hebrew text of Exodus 4:24–26—the passage that seems to be describing an attempt by God to kill Moses—is especially difficult to decipher, because only two of the players in the scene are identified by name. The Bible tells us that it is Zipporah and Yahweh who encounter each other by night at the lodging-place, but Moses is not named at all. Nor are we allowed to see with clarity who is doing what to whom—or why. Who do you think God's attack is aimed at?

11. Why would God seek to kill Moses so soon after befriending him, anointing him as a prophet, and sending him on the crucial mission to liberate the Israelites from Egyptian slavery?

12. Throughout his life, Moses is forced to depend on women to preserve his life or rescue him from deadly peril. As an infant he is spared from Pharaoh's death sentence on the firstborn of the Israelites by two courageous midwives who refuse to carry out Pharaoh's decree. Moses' mother fashions an ark out of bulrushes and sets him adrift in the river, thus saving her son's life while appearing to comply with Pharaoh's order. His sister watches over the ark from afar to make sure that he is rescued, and it is Pharaoh's daughter who draws him out of the river and raises him as her adopted son. In the story of God's attack by night on Moses, it is his wife who saves him. How does this revise our perceptions of Moses as a powerful and potent figure, a prophet who is privileged to encounter God "face to face" because he is so nearly godlike himself?

13. Why do you think the Hebrew Bible reveals nothing at all about the experiences of Moses as a child or an adolescent in the court of Pharaoh? What happened to Moses in the forty-year gap between his slaying of the Egyptian overseer and his discovery of the burning bush?

14. When Moses killed the overseer, he was rescuing a fellow Israelite from a beating or worse and inflicting a kind of rough justice on a nameless functionary who symbolized the worst excesses of the Egyptian monarchy. And yet the Bible makes clear that Moses acted with icy calculation before actually delivering a death blow to the taskmaster. Do you think this killing was justifiable and praiseworthy or a cold-blooded act of brutality? How did the ancient biblical scholars justify the killing?

15. The rabbis of late antiquity and the Middle Ages seemed to prefer a depiction of Moses as a mild-mannered shepherd rather than as a ruthless man of war. What does this reveal about the experience of the Jewish people in exile and the strategy for survival they embraced until very late in the history of the Diaspora?

16. No one can accuse Moses of being a yes-man to the Almighty. Like Abraham before him, and Job after him, Moses was willing to challenge God, debate with him, even hector him. Indeed, the Bible allows us to see Moses as the ultimate naysayer and faultfinder, a man who could see all the flaws in God's plan. What does this suggest to you about our own relationship with God?

17. Kirsch points out that some scholars suggest there's an "anti-Moses tradition" that runs just beneath the surface of the biblical text and sometimes erupts into open condemnation. Can you give any examples of this? Do you agree with this scholarly suggestion?

18. Kirsch writes, "As simple (perhaps even simplistic) as they may seem, the Ten Commandments probably meant something different to the ancient Israelites than what they mean to us today." How would you describe those differences?

19. How do you explain God's harsh decree that kept Moses from entering the Promised Land? Why does the long, arduous, and faithful ordeal of Moses seem to count for nothing at all?

20. Moses' story calls into question our definition of leadership. Do you think we should place primary emphasis on how well our leaders model approved behavior, or should we measure success in terms of how leaders achieve our national goals?

21. In Moses' farewell speech to the Israelites before he dies, he states: "I have set before thee life and death, the blessing and the curse; there-

fore choose life, that thou mayest live, thou and thy seed." Kirsch argues that Moses wants to be remembered as a prodding and pushing prophet who commanded the Jews to do something meaningful in their new land. Do you agree with Kirsch's interpretation?

Excerpts from reviews of Jonathan Kirsch's
Moses: A Life

"Popular biblical interpreter Jonathan Kirsch . . . goes to work on the Exodus story, by turns weaving and unraveling the narrative like an exegetical Penelope. . . . [Kirsch] reveals all the stresses and contradictions that compose the Moses story—service and rebellion, yearning and despair, deliverance and futility, ecstasy and punishment."

—The New Yorker

"Notable among the several new books on the life of Moses . . . Kirsch is moved to acrid eloquence."

—Time Magazine

"*Moses: A Life* by Jonathan Kirsch explores hundreds of legends and interpretations of the prophet and his legacy. Moses is as entrancing today as he was on the day Pharaoh's daughter plucked him from the bulrushes."

—Life Magazine

"A brightly written work that shows how much life remains in [the Bible] . . . Kirsch reads the text with a fine sensitivity."

—Washington Post

"What becomes clear from Kirsch's book, and what will delight devout Christians, Jews and skeptics alike, is that the story of Moses is complex, resonant and, finally, ambiguous."

—Houston Chronicle

"*Moses: A Life* is a brightly written piece of work that shows how much remains in these old books, even as the 21st century presses ever closer."

—Detroit News/Free Press

© Marilyn Sanders

ABOUT THE AUTHOR

JONATHAN KIRSCH is an author, a book columnist for the *Los Angeles Times*, and a literary correspondent and book critic for National Public Radio affiliate KPCC-FM. His book reviews appear in the Religion section of the *LA Times* on Saturdays and in the Sunday Book Review. His NPR reviews and author interviews are broadcast on Mondays as part of the program *Air Talk*.

An attorney in private practice who specializes in entertainment and intellectual property matters, Kirsch also contributes a publishing law column to the newsletter of the Publishers Marketing Association.

Before embarking on the practice of law, Kirsch was senior editor of *California Magazine* (formerly *New West Magazine*), where he specialized in coverage of law, government, and politics. Previously, he worked as West Coast correspondent for *Newsweek*, as editor for *West* and *Home* magazines at the *Los Angeles Times*, and as a reporter for the *Santa Cruz Sentinel*. As a freelance writer, Kirsch has also contributed to *California Lawyer*, *Los Angeles Lawyer*, *New West*, *Los Angeles Magazine*, *New Republic*, *Publishers Weekly*, *Performing Arts*, *Human Behavior*, *L.A. Architect*, and other publications.

Kirsch is a member of the National Book Critics Circle, PEN Center USA West, the Author's Guild, California Lawyers for the Arts, the Los Angeles Copyright Society, and the Intellectual Property Sections of the California State Bar and the Los Angeles County Bar Association.

A former member of the Board of Trustees of the Los Angeles Copyright Society, Kirsch also serves as legal counsel to the Publishers Marketing Association and the *Jewish Journal of Greater Los Angeles*. He is the recipient of the Publishers Marketing Association 1994 Benjamin Franklin Award for Special Achievement in Publishing.

Kirsch was born in Los Angeles, attended high school in Culver City, and completed a bachelor of arts degree with honors in Russian and Jewish history and Adlai E. Stevenson College honors at the Santa Cruz campus of the University of California. A member of the California State Bar since 1976, he earned a Juris Doctor degree *cum laude* at Loyola University School of Law. Kirsch is married to Ann Benjamin Kirsch, Psy.D., a psychotherapist in private practice in Beverly Hills. They have two adult children, and they live in Los Angeles.